Fourth
Edition

Infants & Toddlers

Curriculum and Teaching

Linda D. Watson
Michael A. Watson
LaVisa Cam Wilson

Based on the CDA Competency Standards

Delmar Publishers

an International Thomson Publishing company I(T)P®

Albany • Bonn • Boston • Cincinnati • Detroit • London • Madrid
Melbourne • Mexico City • New York • Pacific Grove • Paris • San Francisco
Singapore • Tokyo • Toronto • Washington

NOTICE TO THE READER

Cover Illustration by Alexander Piejko

Delmar Staff

Acquisitions Editor: Erin O'Connor Traylor

Production Coordinator: Barbara A. Bullock

Art and Design Coordinator: Timothy J. Conners

COPYRIGHT © 1999
By Delmar Publishers
a division of International Thomson Publishing company
ɪ(T)ᴘ The ITP logo is a trademark under license.
Printed in the United States of America

For more information, contact:

Delmar Publishers
3 Columbia Circle, Box 15015
Albany, New York 12212-5015

International Thomson Editores
Seneca 53
Colonia Polanco
11560 Mexico D. F. Mexico

International Thomson Publishing Europe
Berkshire House
168–173 High Holborn
London, WC1V7AA
United Kingdom

International Thomson Publishing GmbH
Königswinterer Strasse 418
53227 Bonn
Germany

Nelson ITP Australia
102 Dodds Street
South Melbourne,
Victoria, 3205 Australia

International Thomson Publishing Asia
60 Albert Street
#15–01 Albert Complex
Singapore 189969

Nelson Canada
1120 Birchmont Road
Scarborough, Ontario
M1K 5G4, Canada

International Thomson Publishing—Japan
Hirakawa-cho Kyowa Building, 3F
2-2-1 Hirakawa-cho, Chiyoda-ku,
Tokyo 102, Japan

International Thomson Publishing France
Tour Maine-Montparnasse
33 Avenue du Maine
75755 Paris Cedex 15, France

ITE Spain/Paraninfo
Calle Magallanes, 25
28015-Madrid, Espana

    3 4 5 6 7 8 9 10 XXX 03 02 01 00

Library of Congress Cataloging-in-Publication Data

Douville-Watson, Linda
    Infants & toddlers : curriculum and teaching / Linda D. Watson,
  Michael A. Watson, LaVisa Cam Wilson. -- 4th ed.
       p.   cm.
     On t.p. of previous ed., LaVisa Cam Wilson's name appears first.
     Includes bibliographical references and index.
     ISBN 0-8273-8418-1
     1. Child care--United States. 2. Infants--United States.
3. Toddlers--United States. 4. Child development--United States.
5. Day care centers--United States. 6. Family day care--United
States. I. Watson, Michael A. II. Wilson, LaVisa Cam.
III. Title.
HQ778.63.D68 1998   98-17079
362.71'071--dc21   CIP

Contents

Acknowledgments   vi

Preface   ix

The CDA Competency Standards for Infant/Toddler
    Child Development Specialists   xi

About the Authors   xiii

**PART I   INFANT AND TODDLER DEVELOPMENT AND
CAREGIVER PREPARATION   1**

**Chapter 1   History and Trends in Infant and Toddler Care
and Development   2**

Introduction   3

Historical Perspectives on Development and Care   3

Current Perspectives on Development and Care   7

Cultural Diversity Programs   15

Chapter 2   The Unlimited Child and You   19

Theory of the Unlimited Child   20

Children with Special Needs   20

Five Need Levels   23

Five Major Developmental Areas   25

Ideal Caregiving   28

Theoretical Contributions   29

Neuroscience Research Findings   35

Summary of Theoretical Contributions   39

Chapter 3   The 3A's of Child Care   44

Introduction   45

The 3A's: Attention, Approval, and Affection as Tools   46

The Attachment Debate and Diminished Father and
    Mother Roles   47

The 3A's Part I: The Outward Expression   50

Definition of Caregiver Self-Health   52

The 3A's Part II: The Inward Expression   53

Using the 3A's Successfully with Infants and Toddlers   56

Chapter 4   Characteristics of Caregiving and Teaching   61

Personal Characteristics of Competent Child Care Specialists:
    Relating to Self   62

Relating to Infants and Toddlers   65
Acquiring Knowledge   65
Conscious Caregiving   66
Mastery: The Outcome of Using the 3A's Through the
    Attention Process   69
Positive Perspective (Formally Known as
    Positive Propaganda)   71
Your Work   74
Practical Concepts: Child Care Specialists'
    Behaviors and Strategies   74
Community Resources   90
Professional Preparation of the Caregiver   93

Chapter 5   What is Development and Learning?   98
The Whole Child   99
Areas of Development and Learning   101
Early Intervention and Inclusion of Special Needs Children   127

**PART II   ESTABLISHING A POSITIVE
            LEARNING ENVIRONMENT   131**

Chapter 6   Communicating with Parents and Staff   132
Why Communicate with Parents and Staff?   133
Communicating Successfully with Parents, Staff,
    and Children   133
Communication Situations   135
Resources for Parents and Staff   149

Chapter 7   Settings for Child Care   153
Family-Based Care   154
Center-Based Care   157
Program Emphases   159
Program Funding   161
Support Groups   162

Chapter 8   The Indoor and Outdoor Environment   167
Room Arrangement   168
Play Yard Arrangement   174
Materials   176
Conditions Fostering Safety and Health   180

Chapter 9   Designing Curriculum   200
Infant-Toddler Curriculum   201
Influences on the Curriculum   204
Children with Special Needs   216
The Process of Curriculum Development   219
Implementing Curriculum   224

PART III   **MATCHING CAREGIVER STRATEGIES AND CHILD DEVELOPMENT**   **249**

Chapter 10   **The Child from Birth to Four Months of Age**   **252**
Materials and Activities   253
Caregiver Strategies to Enhance Development   255

Chapter 11   **The Child from Four to Eight Months of Age**   **279**
Materials and Activities   280
Caregiver Strategies to Enhance Development   282

Chapter 12   **The Child from Eight To Twelve Months of Age**   **301**
Materials and Activities   302
Caregiver Strategies to Enhance Development   304

Chapter 13   **The Child from Twelve to Eighteen Months of Age**   **322**
Materials and Activities   323
Caregiver Strategies to Enhance Development   326

Chapter 14   **The Child from Eighteen to Twenty-Four Months of Age**   **343**
Materials and Activities   344
Caregiver Strategies to Enhance Development   346

Chapter 15   **The Child from Twenty-Four to Thirty Months of Age**   **364**
Materials and Activities   365
Caregiver Strategies to Enhance Development   370

Chapter 16   **The Child from Thirty to Thirty-Six Months of Age**   **384**
Materials and Activities   385
Caregiver Strategies to Enhance Development   387
Authors' Closing Note   401

Appendix A   **Developmental Prescriptions**   **403**
Appendix B   **Developmental Profile and Instructions**   **425**
Appendix C   **CDA Competency Standards for Infant/Toddler Caregivers in Center-Based Programs**   **428**
Appendix D   **The Celebration of Life Calendar**   **447**
   Glossary   **455**
   Index   **457**

Acknowledgments

The authors wish to thank the following persons for their support:

Milinda, our daughter, and Marcus, our son, for all the quiet time we needed;

Jay Whitney, Administrative Editor, and Erin O'Connor Traylor, Acquisitions Editor, whose confidence and support were the Genesis of this work;

All the CDA Candidates whose lives have shaped our work;

Ramon Murphy, M.D., for his connections with experts in numerous areas;

Cecilia McCarton, M.D., for her counsel and generosity of sharing materials;

The International Preschool, The Creche Infant/Toddler Program, Nancy Brown, and her fine staff;

George Igles, M.D., and Jonathon Cohen, Ph.D., of the Social and Emotional Learning Program at Teachers College, Columbia University, for their wonderful input;

Dr. Phil and Debbie Nuernberger for their warmth, hospitality, and professionalism;

The American Institute of Physics Child Care Centers;

Linda Castellanos and her staff at Woodbury, Long Island, for her collaboration;

And a very special thanks to Terri Braun for her generosity and time for the Third and Fourth Editions.

We thank you all!
—Linda Douville-Watson and
   Dr. Mike Watson

Fourth Edition Reviewers

Davia M. Allen, PhD.
Western Carolina University
Cullowhee, North Carolina

Melita Baumann
Glendale Community College
Glendale, California

Katie Best Butler, Ed.D.
College of the Mainland
Texas City, Texas

Jeanne Goodwin
Central Lakes College (emerita)
Brainerd, Minnesota

Robin L. Leavitt, Ph.D.
Illinois Wesleyan University
Bloomington, Illinois

Preface

This book is intended to guide the reader through the skills necessary to provide high-quality care for infants and toddlers in any child care setting. Standards based on current research and knowledge for Infant/Toddler Caregivers are used throughout the book. Appropriate individual techniques and activities are provided for each child. The text is comprehensive so that professionals can use it to teach prospective child care developmental specialists all the essential skills necessary to function at nationally accepted standards of quality, and the language used along with easy-to-follow practical examples allow for self-study by caregivers in training. Child care specialists, administrators, and parents will find practical information that can be put to immediate use to promote the highest quality child care possible for all children.

TEXT ORGANIZATION

We have maintained the same basic structure that previous readers have found helpful of presenting material as it relates to current CDA Goals and Objectives. Shaded CDA symbols are listed to the left of the text to guide the reader according to national standards for caregiving. The book is divided into three parts:

Part I. Infant and Toddler Development and Caregiver Preparation presents an overview of the history, theories, and strategies in the fields of child development and care to prepare the reader for certification. *Chapter 1* provides both historical and current overviews of environmental, social, cultural, and governmental influences in child care. *Chapter 2* presents theories and definitions of development, learning, and teaching, and how these are applied to enhance the development and care of infants and toddlers. *Chapter 3* discusses caregiver self-health, definitions, and applications of the 3A's of child care, and how the "attachment debate" is related to diminished father and mother roles. *Chapter 4* presents a model of conscious caregiving combining practical principles and techniques from current theories and research in the field. *Chapter 5* delineates important aspects of development and learning, and establishes the structure for providing helpful activities and experiences to children.

Part II. Establishing a Positive Learning Environment provides the reader with definitions, knowledge, and skills necessary to competently care for infants and toddlers in the home, school, or child care setting. *Chapter 6* provides the skills necessary to effectively communicate with children, parents, and staff and gives examples of the skills necessary to work with teenage parents. *Chapter 7* gives skills and procedures for conducting care in a variety of child care settings. *Chapter 8* covers standards and principles necessary to ensure safe and effective indoor and outdoor settings for children, and presents common safety issues. *Chapter 9* presents practical techniques for designing curriculum and planning, structuring, and implementing a program of care including special needs children.

Part III. Matching Caregiver and Child Development (Chapters 10 through 16) presents seven developmental levels ranging from birth through thirty-six months of age, along with tasks, materials, and specific activities for each age. Developmental Profiles and Prescriptions are provided to establish a structure in which specific activities are accomplished so the caregiver is aware of goals and growth in the major areas of development. This section provides specific techniques, activities, and solutions to most of the problems confronted in the growth and development of infants and toddlers.

MAJOR REVISIONS IN THE FOURTH EDITION

We have included hundreds of new citations from the recent explosion of information in human learning and development. With the advent of the internet and availability of worldwide research and information, selecting the best information in child care, parenting, and child development was a major challenge in writing this edition. We have presented the most representative and practical information on topics with the goal of giving the reader functional information and techniques to use in actual care settings. Since writing the Third Edition, social policy, cultural diversity in child care and development, and parental assessment and education have become major areas of importance, New sections have been added to inform the reader on these important topics. Major content revisions in this Fourth Edition also include changes in environment, social policies, and governmental factors that impact child care (e.g., poverty, HIV, and health care) (Chapter 1); major developmental and learning theorists and their practical contributions (Chapter 2); definitions of caregiver self-health and powerful tools for positive interactions with children (Chapter 3); issues related to cultural diversity and specific strategies and activities for appreciating and celebrating cultural identities and differences, including The Celebration of Life Calendar to help children experience holidays from many cultures (Chapter 9 and Appendix D); and added sections to help caregivers provide care to infants and toddlers with special needs and definitions of the terms "curriculum" and "teaching", provided as guides to optimal care throughout the book.

INSTRUCTIONAL FEATURES

The following special features are included in this Edition:
- Chapter overviews, behavioral objectives, a specific chapter outline, and CDA Functional Areas are provided at the beginning of each chapter.
- References, student activities, and questions for review are provided at the end of each chapter.
- A Glossary of Terms is included at the end of the book. Important terms are presented in bold type within the chapters.
- Sample Developmental Prescriptions are provided for each age from birth to 36 months, along with behavioral descriptions explaining each.
- Numerous pictures and illustrations are included throughout to illustrate the concepts and materials presented.

The CDA Competency Standards for Infant/Toddler Child Development Specialists

Competency Standards for child development specialists who specialize in infant/toddler development and care have been established by Child Development Associates (CDA), an association which uses six behavioral Goals and thirteen Objectives to evaluate child development specialist performance. A nationally recognized CDA Credential is awarded child development specialists who successfully complete a rigorous assessment based on these standards.

Whether you as the reader are a child development specialist in education, an early childhood educator, parent, or class instructor, it is essential to familiarize yourself with the CDA Goals and Objectives listed on the following page, and with the complete CDA Standards in Appendix C before proceeding with the text.

This book guides the reader through the national standards for competent caregiving by listing specific goals and objectives in shaded oval symbols to the left of related text. For example, the text on theories of child development relates to CDA GOAL VI. (Commitment to Professionalism)–13 (Professionalism).

Once the reader is familiar with the CDA Goals and Objectives, the text will serve as a guide to learn and practice the skills necessary to function according to nationals standards as a competent child development specialist for infants and toddlers.

Instructors will also find the Goals and Objectives a useful instructional tool for formal child development specialist preparation. Specific text related to the goals and objectives can provide the instructor with a structure for discussion, organization, and assessment of the skills and information necessary for competent caregiving.

CDA COMPETENCY GOALS AND DEFINITIONS REFERENCE GUIDE

I To establish and maintain a safe, healthy learning environment
   1. **Safe:** Candidate provides a safe environment to prevent and reduce injuries.
   2. **Healthy:** Candidate promotes good health and nutrition and provides an environment that contributes to the prevention of illness.

3. **Learning Environment:** Candidate uses space, relationships, materials, and routines as resources for constructing an interesting, secure, and enjoyable environment that encourages play, exploration, and learning.

II. **To advance physical and intellectual competence.**

4. **Physical:** Candidate provides a variety of equipment, activities, and opportunities to promote the physical development of children.
5. **Cognitive:** Candidate provides activities and opportunities that encourage curiosity, exploration, and problem-solving appropriate to the developmental levels and learning styles of children.
6. **Communication:** Candidate actively communicates with children and provides opportunities and support for children to understand, acquire, and use verbal and nonverbal means of communicating thoughts and feelings.
7. **Creative:** Candidate provides opportunities that stimulate children to play with sound, rhythm, language, materials, space, and ideas in individual ways and to express their creative abilities.

III. **To support social and emotional development and provide positive guidance.**

8. **Self:** Candidate provides physical and emotional security for each child and helps each child to know, accept, and take pride in himself or herself and to develop a sense of independence.
9. **Social:** Candidate helps each child feel accepted in the group, helps children learn to communicate and get along with others, and encourages feelings of empathy and mutual respect among children and adults.
10. **Guidance:** Candidate provides a supportive environment in which children can begin to learn and practice appropriate and acceptable behaviors as individuals and as a group.

IV. **To establish positive and productive relationships with families.**

11. **Families:** Candidate maintains an open, friendly, and cooperative relationship with each child's family, encourages their involvement in the program, and supports the child's relationship with his or her family.

V. **To ensure a well-run, purposeful program responsive to particular needs.**

12. **Program Management:** Candidate is a manager who uses all available resources to ensure an effective operation. The Candidate is a competent organizer, planner, record keeper, communicator, and a cooperative coworker.

VI. **To maintain a commitment to professionalism.**

13. **Professionalism:** Candidate makes decisions based on knowledge of early childhood theories and practices. Candidate promotes quality in child care services. Candidate takes advantage of opportunities to improve competence, both for personal and professional growth for the benefit of children and families.

These competency goals form a foundation for a solid developmental curriculum. This book elaborates each functional area into a comprehensive curriculum for preparation as a child care professional.

About the Authors

Linda Douville-Watson, R.N., M.P.H., and a CDA Representative, has a training series on infant development; has co-authored F.A.R.E., a comprehensive parent training series; and has developed a training program entitled the 3A's of Caregiving. She is a principal in Workplace Child Care Consultants, Inc., which develops creative child care solutions for corporations, including planning, designing, and implementing in-house, corporate child care centers and programs.

Michael A. Watson is a Clinical Child Psychologist who has specialized in learning and development for thirty years. Dr. Watson taught and was a school psychologist in child care centers, preschools, district-wide special education programs, and elementary and high schools. He is past professor of Psychology at St. John's University and Hofstra University doctoral programs. He has published numerous research papers and articles on development and learning and is author of a nationally standardized test (The WALDO Developmental Learning Skills Tests—30 months to 8 years) and a comprehensive program to teach basic learning skills (the WALDO program—30 months to 8 years). Dr. Watson also co-authored a parent training and child rearing program entitled F.A.R.E. (Family Actualization through Research and Education). He is in private practice in New York and is a Child Development Associate Representative. His most recent work is The National Parenting Scales: A Comprehensive Measure of Parent Skills Using the CDA Standards.

LaVisa Cam Wilson taught in child care centers, kindergarten, and first grade. She was a professor of Early Childhood Education at Auburn University and served as a Child Development Training Project Director. Dr. Wilson served on the Board of the Day Care Council of America, and on the Board of Directors of the National Child Care Association for Childhood Education.

Part I

Infant and Toddler Development and Caregiver Preparation

Since publication of the Third Edition, an information explosion has occurred in child development and caregiving. As a result, caregivers-in-training need to learn more theories, principles, and skills to keep pace with the growing status of their profession.

The CDA Standards require that caregivers learn to take good care of themselves, as well as children, and to be aware of the needs of the child, the care setting, the family, the community, and society as a whole. This section provides the history and current trends in care, theories and principles of child development, and a structure and model of caregiving that helps prepare the caregiver for the challenging and rewarding modern profession of child care.

When you finish this section, you will have all the knowledge and principles necessary to effectively care for, and enhance the development of, each child in your care through your direct interactions with them. The following sections build on this base of knowledge to give you all the specific skills, techniques, and activities needed to confidently function as a professional caregiver.

1

History and Trends in Infant and Toddler Care and Development

OBJECTIVES

After completing this chapter, the child development specialist should be able to:

1. Define the terms mobile infant, young infant, toddler, preschooler, curriculum, teaching, and guide.
2. Describe theories of child development including the Ecological Systems Theory.
3. Describe Bronfenbrenner's theory as it relates to current child care trends.
4. State the use of mentors in current child care training.
5. Outline the major historical and current trends in child care.

CHAPTER OUTLINE

I. Introduction
II. Historical Perspectives on Development and Care
  A. Past Theories and Views
  B. Past Needs and Trends
III. Current Perspectives on Development and Care
  A. Current Theories and Views
  B. Current Needs and Trends
VI. Cultural Diversity Programs

CHILD DEVELOPMENT ASSOCIATE FUNCTIONAL AREAS

Learning Environment
Program Management
Professionalism

INTRODUCTION

We can understand the history and current trends in child care and development only after defining some of the basic terms used in the field. Definitions of the terms used in the title of this book give us a start in understanding child development and care:

Infants and Toddlers, in the scope of this book, is limited to the growth, development, and care of children from birth through thirty-six months of age. Three general age groups within this range are commonly used: birth to eight month olds are called **young infants**; nine through seventeen month olds are called **mobile infants**; and eighteen through thirty-six month olds are called **toddlers** (CDA Standards, Appendix C.).

Curricula, for purposes in this text, is defined as structured activities and experiences provided to infants and toddlers for the purposes of stimulating and enhancing growth and development. The standards for determining specific activities and experiences ranging from simple to more complex are the behaviors provided in the Developmental Prescriptions listed in Appendix A.

Teaching is used in the text to mean planned presentation of activities and experiences ranging from simple to complex with the goal of motivating infants and toddlers to learn and develop in five major Developmental Areas.

Guide means to direct toward some desirable end. This book is intended to direct the reader in learning skills and information necessary to effectively and efficiently care for infants and toddlers in ways that enhance the growth and development of each child in care.

Caregiver and Early Childhood Educator are used interchangeably throughout to refer to professionals who specialize in the direct care, development, and/or research with young children. Because the field is growing so rapidly at the beginning of the Twenty-first Century, other terms also used in the literature to describe professionals include "Early Childcare (or Childhood) Specialist," "CDAs (Child Development Associates)", "Childcare Workers", and "Child Development Specialist" (or "Researcher").

With these terms in mind, we now turn our attention to the history and current trends in infant and toddler care and development.

HISTORICAL PERSPECTIVES ON DEVELOPMENT AND CARE

Past Theories and Views

Prior to the Reformation in the Sixteenth Century, little importance was placed on children or child care. Children were considered to be little adults cared for by the females in the family. With the Reformation and the Puritan belief in **original sin** came harsh, restrictive child rearing practices, and the idea that the depraved child needed to be tamed (Shahar 1990).

The Seventeenth-Century Enlightenment brought new theories of human dignity and respect. Clear ideas regarding childhood were advanced which viewed young children much more humanely. For example, John Locke, a British philosopher, advanced the theory that infants and toddlers were a **tabula rasa**, or blank slate. According to this theory, children were not basically evil, but were completely molded and formed by their early experiences with the adults around them (Locke 1690/1892).

Another important philosopher of the Eighteenth Century, Jean-Jacques Rousseau, viewed young children as **noble savages** who are naturally born with a moral sense of right and wrong, and innate ability for orderly, healthy growth (1955). His theory was the first child-centered approach which advanced two important concepts still accepted today: the idea of **stages** of child development; and **maturation**, which means a naturally unfolding course of growth and development.

During the late 1800s Charles Darwin's theories of **natural selection** and **survival of the fittest** strongly influenced ideas regarding child development and care (1936). Darwin's research studying many animal species caused him to hypothesize that all animals were descendants of a few common ancestors. He believed that the development of children followed the same general plan as the evolution of the species. While this concept was later proven inaccurate, the careful observations of child behaviors resulted in the science of child study being born.

At the turn of the Twentieth Century, G. Stanley Hall was inspired by Darwin, and worked with one of his students, Arnold Gesell, to advance the **evolutionary theory** that child development is genetically determined and happens automatically. Hall and Gesell are considered to be founders of the child study movement because of their **normative approach** of observing large numbers of children to establish average or normal expectations (Berk, 1997). At the same time in France, Alfred Binet was establishing the first operational definition of intelligence by using the normative approach to standardize his intelligence test which is still sometimes used with young children (Siegler 1992).

It was not until Sigmund Freud postulated his **psychoanalytic theory** of personality development in the early 1900s that child development and care became a legitimate discipline (1938). For the first time, Freud explained how infants and toddlers are unique individuals whose earliest experiences and relationships form the foundation for self-concept, self-esteem, and personality, and why we experience life as adults the way that we do.

A proponent of Freud, Erik Erickson, expanded Freud's concepts into what became known as the **psychosocial theory** of child development. Erickson's theory, part of which is still used in child care today, predicted several stages of development including the development of trust, autonomy, identity, and intimacy. How these stages are dealt with by child development specialists determines individual capacity to contribute to society and experience a happy, successful life (1950). Erickson's stages are presented in Chapter 2.

While Freud and his disciples greatly influenced the fields of child development and care, a parallel approach was being studied called **behaviorism**. John Watson, who is considered the father of behaviorism, was influenced by a Russian physiologist named Ivan Pavlov and his scientific observations of animal **responses** to various environmental **stimuli** (Horowitz 1992). In a historic experiment, Watson taught an eleven month old named Albert to fear a neutral stimulus (a soft white rat) by presenting it several times accompanied by loud noises. Watson and his followers used experiments in **classical conditioning** to promote the idea that the environment is the primary factor which determines the growth and development of children.

B.F. Skinner expanded Watson's theories of classical conditioning to include his **operant conditioning theory** (1993). Skinner clearly demonstrated that child behaviors can be increased or decreased by applying **positive reinforcers** (rewards) such as food and praise, and **negative reinforcers** (punishment) such as criticism and withdrawal of attention.

During the 1950s, **social learning theories** became popular. These theories, led by Albert Bandura, accepted the principles of behaviorism and enlarged upon conditioning to include social influences such as **modeling**, **imitation**, and **observational learning** to explain how children develop (Grusec 1992).

The theorist who has influenced the modern fields of child development and care more than any other is Jean Piaget. Piaget's **cognitive-developmental theory** predicts that children construct knowledge and awareness through manipulation and exploration of the environment, and that cognitive development occurs through observable stages (Beilin 1992). Piaget's stages of cognitive development have stimulated more research on children than any other theory, and his influences have helped child development specialists view young children as active participants in their own growth and development. While recent research from **information processing theory** has brought some of Piaget's concepts into question, his contributions to child care and development have clear and practical applications in the Twenty-first Century. Piaget's stages are presented in Chapters 2 and 8.

Past Needs and Trends

While cultural and social expectations for child care roughly follow historical theories and views of child development, specific social and cultural influences such as religion, governmental policy, war, and economic demands have also affected the settings and approaches to child development and care.

Throughout history, the care and development of infants and toddlers has been the responsibility of the primary family unit and extended family which often included members of the local community as well as blood relatives (see Figure1–1). Even in cultures where governmental or religious needs required older children to be taken away from the family for training or education, infants and toddlers remained with the females of the home and community.

Figure 1–1 A grandparent can share in caring for an infant.

Prior to the Reformation, child care was primarily the responsibility of the females in the family unit. However, since social groups were small (for example, tribe, village, hamlet), children were often cared for by all the females within the community, and it was common practice for one family to take over care of the children of another family whose parents had died.

With increases in world population and the emphasis upon religious education brought about by the Reformation, the Church established orphanages and schools so that young children were cared for in institutional settings outside the family for the first time. In cultures where the population remained small and/or religious training was not a major influence, the family remained responsible for early child development and care.

Until the beginning of the Twentieth Century, the only exceptions to family care were extreme situations such as war, famine, or epidemics where infants and toddlers had to be cared for in groups because a large number of the females of the community had died.

The industrialization of the major world cultures created a conflict in the social belief that only mothers should provide total care for young children. In the early Twentieth Century in the United States, fewer mothers of infants and toddlers were in the workforce than there are today. Mothers who worked in areas in which they could not take their babies counted on older children, female relatives, or neighbors to care for their young. Professional child care settings as we know them today did not exist.

A factor at this time that affected the number of working mothers was the prevalence of stereotyped male and female roles. The social norm was that the husband was to provide for the family's financial needs, and the wife was to assume all domestic responsibilities including cooking, sewing, housework, and child care. Women who, from either financial need or desire, worked outside the home, were often considered "out of place."

Another influence on the number of working mothers with infants and toddlers was the prevailing belief that "only" the mother could provide proper care for young children. A sibling or relative was thought to be an acceptable substitute for the mother, but the belief generally was that another person could not meet the needs of infants or toddlers over a period of time. The mother-child attachment was thought to be crucial, and would be weakened if the infant was primarily cared for by someone else. The idea was that only the mother bonded well enough with her infant or toddler to meet the child's emotional needs. The advent of World Wars I and II brought more mothers into the workplace, and changed the stereotype view that only mothers could adequately care for young children.

Early research on child care was partly responsible for the social belief that only mothers could adequately care for young children. Institutionalized infants and toddlers provided the most easily accessible population for child study, so early research tended to concentrate on the effects of infant care by people other than the mother in hospitals and long-term care facilities. The results of this type of research generally found that the mother/child attachment was weakened in the type of situations studied (Bowlby 1951; Goldfarb 1943; Spitz 1945).

CURRENT PERSPECTIVES ON DEVELOPMENT AND CARE

Current Theories and Views

As we enter the Twenty-first Century, new theories, research, and effective approaches to enhance the growth and development of young children are being discovered. Among these exciting developments are information processing theories, ethnology, ecological systems theory, and sociocultural theory.

A recent approach, resulting from developments during the 1970s in human learning research and technology from computer design is called **information processing**. This approach involves the analysis of **sensory input**, the organization of information through **discrimination and association**, storage of information through memory, and the output of information through **verbal and motor responses** (Watson 1972). Information processing theories can be viewed as symbol manipulating systems through which information flows (Klahr 1992). Michael A. Watson's information processing theory is presented in detail in Chapter 2 as a basis of understanding the essential Developmental Learning Skills that young children use to perceive the world.

Another approach which is gaining more acceptance in child care is called **ethnology**. It was developed by two zoologists, Konrad Lorenz and Niko

Tinbergen (Dewsbury 1992). Ethnology refers to behavior patterns which promote survival, thereby following Darwin's theories. Two major concepts from ethnology that have been applied to early childhood are imprinting and critical periods of development. Through their studies of animal behavior, Lorenz and Tinbergen found that baby birds closely follow their mother (or mother substitute) and imitate her movements. Because this imprinting behavior occurs during a specific, limited period of time, the concept of "critical periods" of time for the development of skills and abilities has been applied to early childhood development with limited value.

A recent theory of child development is the **ecological systems theory** developed by Urie Bronfenbrenner, an American psychologist (1995). Brofenbrenner has expanded the view of influences on young children by hypothesizing four nested structures which influence development. At the innermost level is the **microsystem**, comprised of patterns of interactions within the immediate surroundings of the child. This system includes parents, child development specialists, direct influences interacting with the child, and the child's influences on the immediate environment. The **mesosystem** is the next level of influence, and includes school, day care, neighborhood, and local culture and community. The **exosystem** involves influences with which the child is not directly involved, but affects development and care such as parent education, parent workplace, and health and social services. The **macrosystem** consists of the values, laws, resources, and customs of the general culture in which a child is raised. This theory has wide applications in understanding and categorizing the factors which affect child care.

A final theory finding application as we move into the Twenty-first Century, and as the world is truly becoming a cross-cultural community, is the **sociocultural theory**. A Russian psychologist, Lev Semenovich Vygotsky, hypothesized that culture, meaning the values, beliefs, and customs of a social group, is passed on to the next generation through social interactions between children and their elders (1986). Cross-cultural research has supported this theory through findings that young children from various cultures develop unique skills and abilities that are not present in other cultures (Berk 1997).

It must be kept in mind that the United States is the world leader in the fields of child development and care, and we cannot assume that research findings on developmental skills and abilities from primarily caucasian American children directly apply to other cultures outside, or subcultures within, the United States. Only through taking a world view of child care based on universal aspects of development will we be able to determine the skills, abilities, and practices which optimally enhance the growth and development of infants and toddlers within the world community.

Current Needs and Trends

Current child care trends will be discussed within the framework of the Ecological System of Urie Bronfenbrenner: the microsystem, mesosystem, exosystem, and macrosystem (1995). In this system, human relationships are described as bidirectional and reciprocal. "Re-lat-ing" is the act of being with someone and sharing the same space and setting; expressing needs and accepting responsibility for interacting with each other.

Relating to children in a way that they feel equal is also expressed by other authorities in child development, such as Magda Gerber who feels that one of the most important aspects of relating to infants is a child development specialist's respect for the child as an individual. Linda Douville-Watson's theory also emphasizes a child development specialist's self-health, awareness of self, and consciousness of care which allows him or her to be mindful of good intentions toward the child, and which reflects clear thought and good planning resulting in positive outcomes for both. Examples of reciprocal and bidirectional relating are given throughout the text.

Trends in the microsystem involve effects that adults and children have on each other. For example, an adult who consciously uses attention, approval, and affection with children will elicit a positive response from children. An additional person (third party) present may also be affected. How this person is affected is determined by whether or not the reciprocal relationship is positive or negative. If the people interacting are supportive, the quality of the relationship is enhanced. An example of how a child development specialist can enhance an interaction as a third party is explained in detail later in the text under positive perspective (Douville-Watson 1992).

The microsystem is the closest system to the child. It contains the child, the immediate nuclear family, and specialists relating to the child. Today, there are more children in care in the United States with many vastly different backgrounds than ever before. Between 1988 and 1993, the number of children in child care increased nearly 1.5 million to a total of more than 10 million in the fall of 1993 (Casper 1996). These children represent widespread cultural differences in customs and parenting styles. Many come from families who are learning to define their own traditions. Some families depend on the early child care setting to introduce them to their own rich heritages. Respectful, mindful child care specialists and teachers are necessary in all child care settings to promote interest, acceptance, and pride with children and parents.

The mesosystem includes child care settings. In the past, it was thought that the immediate family (microsystem) reflected the greatest single impact on a child's life. However, with so many more people entering the workforce today, the need for child care is so great that this is no longer true. Many young children spend more waking hours with child development specialists than they do with their primary families, which is of great concern to many child care experts.

Gail Stewart Hand quoted Magda Gerber and Dr. Ron Lally in the *Knight Ridder/Tribune News Service* (6-28-94), when they both voiced the concern that ". . . rapid turnover in caregivers due to burnout, inconsistency, instability, including elementary schools, are not meeting children's individual needs as well as parental needs for support."

Magda Gerber is a national leader in infant care, and Dr. Ron Lally is a national expert in training. They further suggested that ". . . babies and young children need to be in the smallest groups possible." This is thought necessary because young children need consistency and a sense of permanence. Many people feel that the public school could do more to support its communities' young families. The following model is an example of a school program that demonstrates Urie Bronfenbrenner's second level of Ecological System Theory which states the mesosystem fosters children's development by encompassing connections between home, school, child care center, and neighborhood, including day care centers, neighborhood, home care, and schools.

Dr. Elliott Landon, Superintendent of Schools for Long Beach, New York, was responsible for establishing a model child care program within the public school system. Dr. Landon states, "We have a partnership between the community and parents." Dr. Landon's commitment demonstrates how the "parent-child and child development specialist-child relationships are likely to support development when there are links, in the form of and exchange of information, between home and day care settings" (see Figure 1–2) (Berk 1997).

Another current trend at the mesosystem level is the use of mentors. A mentor is described in Webster's Dictionary as an "experienced and prudent advisor." These advisors have been around informally for years, and are con-

Figure 1–2　School-based child care offers a familiar place to grow up.

sidered to be the best in their field. These kind-hearted coworkers who have been on the job for a long time, and are committed to their profession, help newcomers learn the ropes (see Figure 1–3). This was usually without any additional compensation or recognition. The time put into the job actually far exceeded the expected hours and the extra work performed on behalf of a coworker was excessive. In the child care field, it was also an expectation to work hard and extend yourself on behalf of your children. Such expert help, when available, was highly valued by coworkers.

In the 1980s, in response to the shortage of funds, isolated districts, and lack of trained personnel, the professional mentor became a creative answer for extending child care resources. Highly trained experienced teacher-consultants were officially introduced as professionals to facilitate child care specialists with in-service and hands-on training and support.

Mentors are the cream of the crop: experienced, well-trained, eager to share, teach, console, and broaden the horizons of newly appointed child development specialists. Mentors help with the frustration of adjusting to the integration of learned skills. They are different from supervisors in that they are normally not paid by the same source as teachers, and are not bound by the same responsibilities as a supervisor such as promoting, hiring, or firing. Mentors are revered for their successful outcomes. Their confidential assessments do not involve continued employment so they can help their proteges strive to reach their greatest potential as child development specialists, teachers, and decision-makers.

Figure 1–3 Mentors help newcomers learn the ropes.

The mentor helps establish mutual goals and expectations without involvement with the employer (this is acceptable as long as none of the practices jeopardize the well-being of children, which would obligate the teacher-trainer to report to the proper authorities). This relationship of trust is a support system that results in a win-win situation.

Mentor programs create a new step in the early childhood career progression by allowing staff members to advance professionally, while continuing to educate and teach children directly. By creating a step in the career path that acknowledges the specialized skill of teaching others to care for and educate young children, and by combining this step with financial reward, mentor programs challenge the perception of child care as unskilled work (Whitebook, Hnatiak, and Bellum 1996).

In 1996, mentor programs existed in over 40 communities across the country, according to the advisory committee on Head Start Quality and Expansion. Head Start and the United States Army Child Development Services established mentor programs for their preschool personnel. This progressive trend utilizes all the best child care resources available by the intelligent use of these experts in the field. It is a way to touch many with a few hands.

The mesosystem is clearly demonstrated by the productive, resourceful use of this model program, and by the development of professional mentor programs. The reader should note that the mesosystem operates best when there are supportive and consistent communication links between parent, child development specialist, and school directors.

The exosystem refers to social settings that do not contain the child, but still directly affect their development, such as community health services and other public agencies. This structure can best be demonstrated by grass roots groups who lobby and advocate for child care services.

In March 1997 on Long Island, New York, Ms. Gerry Linton, Director of Women's Services and Vice President in charge of Programming for the Long Island Coalition for Full Employment, co-chaired an open forum for child care advocates. Ms. Linton stated that "this forum centered on all interested in the welfare of children to advocate for quality, affordability and accessibility in child care."

Similar social activists worked in other states to insure quality child care. Margaret Crawley of the Michigan Coordinated Child Care Association, credits the increase in the number of the Child Development Associate (CDA) credentialed providers to strong legislative backing, training efforts, and collegiate support (1997).

Bibi Lobo Somyak, Deputy Director at the Corporate Fund for Children in Texas, states that several factors account for this training trend:

1. CDA is advocated by individuals and communities.
2. CDA candidates are recruited publicly.
3. CDA training is paid for in part by coalition funds (1997).

These and other local and regional organizations stress child care advocacy which sets higher standards of care, and impacts on each child in the community.

Other social policies also are impacted on the availability, affordability, and quality of care for very young children. The following current issues in development and care are discussed in depth in later chapters:

- Child Abuse and Neglect
- Homelessness
- Divorce and its Impact on the Family
- Needs for Special Children
- AIDS: Impact on the Community
- Adverse Environmental Factors
- Birth Problems
- Education of the Child Development Specialist

Now, we turn to trends within the macrosystem which is the most general of Bronfenbrenner's Ecological System's Theory. The child is ultimately affected by decisions made at this level because the macrosystem consists of the laws, customs, and general policies of the social system (government). This is where the availability of resources (money) are determined. The macrosystem structure of the United States went through a remarkable change in the late 1990s. This can be understood best by explaining the changes in Welfare Reform Legislature.

In the late 1980s and early 1990s child care needs significantly increased in the United States. In response to this need, providers expanded existing centers and opened new ones. This expansion increased the need for new curricula, materials, teachers, and directors while training programs centered their efforts on quality of services offered to families and children to continue to raise the standard of child care from a federally supported viewpoint. In 1996, that viewpoint was to change.

The Personal Responsibility and Work Opportunity Reconciliation Act was signed by President Clinton on August 22, 1996. The new law was designed to break the cycle of poverty by moving people from welfare into the workforce. This bill gave state governments the power to regulate funds and set parameters for child care training. It also allowed people to provide unpaid child care as a way to meet the work requirement. This provision set off an instant alarm to child care advocates everywhere.

"'To care for their children many mothers will rely on relatives and friends, some of whom will be loving and attentive and some of whom will not. . . . A recent study found that 40 percent of day care centers for infants and toddlers gave less than the minimal standard of care.'". . .

One out of every 10 children three years old and younger lives in extreme poverty at or below 50 percent of the federal poverty level. The 1994 report by the Carnegie Corporation, called Starting Points, identified "quiet crisis" in the lives of our youngest children. Ms. Hillary Clinton also spoke on the importance of a child's earliest years (Collins 97).

The new welfare law allows states to exempt new mothers from work requirements for a year. Some states, such as Wisconsin, require new mothers to start looking for work when their babies are twelve weeks old. In 1996, the budget for Early Head Start was $146 million, and Health and Human Services awarded grants to 143 sites. The money is used to provide a variety of services to poor families with children under the age of four and to poor pregnant women.

Vermont has a "Success by Six" Program, and North Carolina has instituted a flexible county program called "Smart Start" where teachers, parents, doctors and nurses, child care providers, ministers, and business people form partnerships to help young children and their families. "Several states are trying to help educate parents about parenting, home visits by social workers or nurses are among the most successful" (Collins 97).

Because of the emphasis on work, welfare reform created significant stress on the existing system of early childhood services, and created broad ramifications for quality, accessibility, and affordability of services for both poor and working families. M. Theresa Gnezda stated, "Early childhood advocates must remind state and local policy makers that true welfare reform requires making sure that child care is much more than custodial care" (1996).

The turn of the Twenty-first Century has brought growing concern for quality in child care, ability to meet teacher, director, and child development specialist needs for compensation, high-quality programs, and support in responding to the changing roles of the family that impact on child development specialist resources. This was described by Richard Clifford, President of the National Association for the Education of Young Children in 1996: "Will the new pressures brought on by Welfare Reform continue to keep us from addressing our basic concerns about the quality of services offered to the youngest citizens of our country? . . . Will reform force a reduction in the standards of care provided all children to accommodate larger numbers of children?" The Welfare Legislature statement rendering "unpaid child care" positions to be a viable alternative to employment did two things: first, it recognized that nonparents and substitutes, such as grandparents, family members, neighbors, and child care professionals, were primary caregivers; and second, it did not mandate that everyone caring for children at any level be educated.

As a result, most of the people who spent their professional lives working diligently to improve the standards of training for child care, aggressively approached their local governments to maintain not only training and care standards, but also to further raise them. This became necessary because many of the federally supported departments that funded and guaranteed these standards were no longer in existence. ". . . Good affordable day çare is not a luxury or fringe benefit for welfare mothers and working parents but essential brain food for the next generation."

CULTURAL DIVERSITY PROGRAMS

A current trend in child care is the development of programs emphasizing cultural diversity in child care settings. It is important for the child development specialist to accept the challenge to develop a cross-cultural curriculum which involves both parents and children, because many young families are just exploring their own cultural backgrounds.

Cross-cultural curriculum development fits into Vygotsky's theory as he viewed "cognitive development as a socially mediated process . . . as dependent on the support that adults and more mature peers provide as children try new tasks" (Berk 1997). This theory is also important because the vast amount of culturally rich material available in every culture help young families develop a concept of their own heritage.

It is important to recognize that another great challenge for child development specialists is to present a progressive cross-cultural curriculum representing diversity which involves parents and children alike. In a section called the "Celebration of Life" in Chapter 9, sampling of cross-cultural curriculum is discussed. Two excellent examples for center-based care are featured. The curricula of the International Preschool Child Care Facility associated with the United Nations, and the American Institute of Physics Child Care Centers, which is a highly recognized, award-winning center, is presented, along with suggested references and a reading list. Specific references for materials such as puppets, toys, stuffed animals, and simple age-appropriate objects that represent diversity also are explored. In addition, an intercultural calendar involving child development specialists, parents, and children is presented to honor significant dates for celebration. This is presented to emphasize the child development specialists' responsibility to acknowledge each child's uniqueness.

Urie Bronfenbrenner's ecological systems theory hypothesizes the interconnectedness of each person to others, and how one system affects another. It implies the importance of respecting each individual's uniqueness and considers carefully the decisions made at every level that affect us all.

A final emphasis in thought involves Transactional Theories, which view care from the perspective of how the child interacts with and affects the environment (Sameroff 1993). These theories help us understand that children are not passive recipients of whatever the environment provides, but that children are very involved in affecting the environment and aiding their own development. It is important for the child care specialist to understand that even newborns have a part in their growth and development, and their wants, needs, and desires must be respected.

To summarize, current trends in child care involve the bidirectional and reciprocal relationship between the child and his or her environment. More children with a wide diversity of backgrounds are in care which results in an increased need for provider education, parent education, including proper selection of care settings, innovative and flexible care programs, effective uses of resources, such as professional mentors, social and political advocacy for quality, affordable, and accessible care, and utilization of culturally diverse materials in child care curricula.

It is our individual responsibility to be consciously aware of the power of our actions, and the far-reaching future impact on children. Through understanding that the child development specialist also directly influences the family, community, and culture, one can truly understand the old African proverb which states " It takes a village to raise a child."

STUDENT ACTIVITIES

1. Describe Urie Bronfenbrenner's Ecological Systems Theory's four levels, and how each relates to current child care issues.
2. Write a short paragraph on how school districts can respond to the needs of preschool children using current trends in the field.
3. List three ways you can support the need for more education in child care.
4. Name three developmental theorists who have contributed to early development, and relate the contributions of each.

CHAPTER REVIEW

1. What is the historical setting for care of young children up to the Twentieth Century?
2. What theorist is considered to have contributed the most to child development and care?
3. What are four current trends in child care and development?
4. How is the microsystem different from the mesosystem?

REFERENCES

Advisory Committee on Head Start Quality and Expansion. 1993. *Creating a 21st Century Head Start, Final Report.* Washington, DC: Head Start Bureau, Administration Children, Youth, and Families.

Beilin, H. 1992. Piaget's enduring contribution to developmental psychology. *Developmental Psychology* 28, pp. 191–204.

Berk, L. E. 1997. *Child Development,* Fourth Edition. Massachusetts: Allyn and Bacon.

Bowlby, J. 1951. *Maternal Care and Mental Health.* Geneva: World Health Organization.

Bronfenbrenner, U. 1995. The bioecological model from a life course perspective: Reflections of a participant observer. In *Examining Lives in Context*, eds. P. Moen, G. H. Elder, Jr., and K. Luscher, pp. 599–618. Washington, DC: American Psychological Association.

Clifford, R. M. 1996. Partnerships with children. *Young Children* 52–1, p. 2.

Collins, J. 2-97. The Day-Care Crisis. *Time* Magazine Special Report.

Crawley, M. 1997. States' Efforts Lead to Increase in Number of CDAs: Michigan. *Washington, DC Council News & Views; CDA*, p. 5.

Darwin, C. 1936. *On the Origin of Species by Means of Natural Selection.* New York: Modern Library (Originally published 1859).

Dewsbury, D. A. 1992. Comparative psychology and ethology: A reassessment. *American Psychologist* 47, 208–15.

Douville-Watson, L. 1983. *Three A's of Infant Development: Lecture Series 2.* Bayville, New York: Instructional Press.

Douville-Watson, L. 1988. *Family Actualization Through Research and Education: FARE,* Third Edition. Bayville, New York: Instructional Press.

Erickson, E. H. 1950. *Childhood and Society.* New York: Norton.

Freud. S. 1973. *An Outline of Psychoanalysis.* London: Hogarth. (Original published 1938).

Gerber, M. 1989. *Educaring: Resources for Infant Educarers.* Los Angles: Resources for Infant Educarers.

Goldfarb, W. 1943. The effects of early institutional care on adolescent personality. *Journal of Experimental Education* 12:106–129.

Gnezda, M. T. 1996. Welfare reform: Personal responsibilities and opportunities for early childhood advocates. *Young Children 52–1*, pp. 55–58.

Grusec, J. E. 1992. Social learning theory and developmental psychology: The legacies of Robert Sears and Albert Bandura. *Developmental Psychology* 28, pp. 776–86.

Grolnich, W. S., and Slowiacvek, M. L. 1994. Parents involvement in children's schooling: A multi-dimensional conceptualization and motivational model. *Child Development* 65, pp. 237–52.

Hand, G. 1994. At risk stories for editors: Child and family studies. *Knight-Ridder/ Tribune New Service* 6-28-94.

Horowitz, F. D. 1992. John B. Watson's legacy: Learning and environment. *Developmental Psychology* 28, pp. 360–67.

Klahr, D. 1992. Information processing approaches to cognitive development. In *Developmental Psychology: An Advanced Textbook* (3rd. Ed.), eds. M. H. Bornstein and M. E. Lamb, pp. 273–335). Hillsdale, NJ: Erlbaum.

Lally, J. R., ed. 1992. *Language Development and Communication: A Guide, Infant/Toddler Caregiving Series.* San Fransico: Far West Lab.

Landon, E. 1997. *Open Forum for Childcare: A Panel Discussion.* Long Island Coalition for Full Employment. (Unpublished discussion).

Linton, G. 1997. *Open Forum for Childcare: A Panel Discussion.* Long Island Coalition for Full Employment. (Unpublished discussion).

Locke, J. 1892. Some thoughts concerning education. In *Locke on Education*, ed. R. J. Quick, pp.1–236. Cambridge: Cambridge University Press (Originally published 1690).

Nash, J. 1997. *Fertile Minds. Time* Magazine special report: How a child's brain develops and what it means for child care and welfare reform.

Rousseau, J. J. 1955. *Emile.* New York: Dutton. (Originally published 1762).

Sameroff, A. J., Seifer, R., Baldwin, A., and Baldwin, C. 1993. Stability of intelligence from preschool to adolescence: The influence of social and family risk factors. *Child Development* 64, 80–97.

Siegler, R. S. 1992. The other Alfred Binet. *Developmental Psychology* 28, pp. 179–90.

Skinner, E. A., and Belmont, M. J. 1993. Motivation in the classroom: Reciprocal effects of teacher behavior and student engagement across the school year. *Journal of Educational Psychology* 85, pp. 571–81.

Somyak, B. L. 1997. *States' Efforts Lead to Increase in Number of CDAs: Texas.* Washington DC: News & Views; CDA, pp. 5.

Spitz, T. 1945. Hospitalism: An inquiry into the genesis of psychiatric conditions in early childhood. *Psychoanalytic Study of the Child* 1:53–74.

Shahar, S. 1990. *Childhood in the Middle Ages.* London: Routledge & Kegan Paul.

Watson, M. A. 1972. *The Waldo Program of Developmental Learning Skills.* New York: Educational Activities.

Whitebook M., and Bellm, D. 1996. Mentoring for early childhood teachers and providers: Building upon and extending tradition. *Young Children 52–1*, pp. 59–64.

2
The Unlimited Child and You

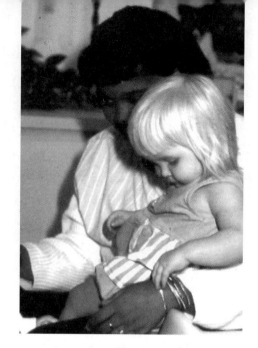

OBJECTIVES

After completing this chapter, the child development specialist should be able to:
1. Identify five need levels and define each.
2. Identify the five major developmental areas for assessment, and discuss how they differ from one another.
3. Understand how to view the child after having done an assessment of need levels and developmental areas.
4. Have a general understanding of the use of developmental profiles.
5. State theoretical contributions for each developmental area.

CHAPTER OUTLINE

I. Theory of the Unlimited Child
II. Children with Special Needs
III. Five Need Levels
IV. Five Major Developmental Areas
V. Ideal Caregiving
VI. Theoretical Contributions
   A. Physical Development
   B. New Neuroscience Research Findings
   C. Cognitive Development
   D. Emotional Development
   E. Social Development
VII. Neuroscience Research Findings
   A. Learning Skill Development
VIII. Summary of Theoretical Contributions

CHILD DEVELOPMENT ASSOCIATE FUNCTIONAL AREAS

    I. 1–3 Safe Healthy Learning Environment
    II. 2–7 Physical and Intellectual Competence
    III. 8–10 Social and Emotional Development and Positive Guidance
    IV. 12 Program Management
    V. 13 Professionalism

THEORY OF THE UNLIMITED CHILD

The scope of this book allows for discussion of only one child care philosophy and structure that the authors believe is most helpful in child care settings. The major contributions of early childhood theorists are presented within this structure. The structure and approach, which we call the Unlimited Child, states that every child has the capacity to develop all of the skills that any human being has ever developed. Unlike the tabula rasa theory of the past that claimed children could be molded to parental or societal specifications, current research indicates that we bring to life all of the potentials of our entire ancestry; all that it is possible for people to become is available in the potential of the newborn (Douville-Watson and Watson 1988).

Of course, there are environmental factors that limit our realizing our self-potential. A child born with physical handicaps such as brain damage will not realize as much potential in certain areas as a child born physically intact, and a child whose ancestry dictates adult height of under five feet will most likely not realize his or her potential to play professional basketball. However, within these limiting physical and environmental factors, every child has the potential for a fulfilling and productive life depending upon how well his or her needs and abilities are fulfilled and to what extent the skills necessary to become a happy and successful adult are taught by parents and caregivers.

CHILDREN WITH SPECIAL NEEDS

Early interventions for infants and toddlers who are at-risk are currently available ". . . in virtually every community in the United States, and in numerous other countries." (Guralnick and Bennett 1987). Children who are considered at-risk require specialized equipment, care, and curricula, and the child care specialist must learn how to care for children with special needs. Because it is impossible to cover all the special conditions and procedures necessary to care for at-risk children in one text, an overview of categories and characteristics is provided here. The child specialist should contact the associations and organizations necessary for specific information on how to care for individual children with special needs.

The following eight categories of infants and toddlers with special needs were taken from *The Effectiveness of Early Intervention for At-Risk and Handicapped Children*; (Guralnick and Bennett 1987).

1. Environmentally At-Risk Infants and Toddlers—children from socially and economically disadvantaged families, including homeless and poverty, are included in this category. Results from several studies reveal that the most effective interventions involve attending day care and families receiving parent training on an on-going basis. For more information, contact the local Health Department, Department of Social Services, and community charitable organizations such as the American Red Cross.

2. Biologically At-Risk Infants and Toddlers—children who experience central nervous system (CNS) damage; for example, CNS infections, trauma, ingestion of toxins, and sustained hypoxia (lack of oxygen). Research results on interventions ranging from special nursery settings and free nursing and medical care to infant stimulation by parents yield mixed results, with very short-term positive effects. Interventions for this population appear to be more effective with parents than with children. For more information, contact the American Medical Association, County Health Department, American Association of Pediatrics, and local pediatricians caring for individual children.

3. Children with Cognitive and General Developmental Disorders—infants and toddlers who exhibit delays in every facet of cognition; for example, information processing, problem-solving, and ability to apply information to new situations. Global delays in motor, language, and socioemotional areas are common with these children, and they tend to reach milestones in a similar manner as normal development, but at a much slower rate with lower final levels of development such as mental retardation, Down syndrome, and fetal alcohol syndrome. Research strongly indicates that early intervention programs prevent decline in intellectual functioning found in mildly retarded children without intervention. Programs with moderately and profoundly retarded children are more effective with active parental participation and training, but overall, appear to be less effective than with mildly retarded infants and toddlers. For more information, contact the American Association on Mental Deficiency, the local Special Education Administration, and specific associations such as the Down Syndrome Association.

4. Children with Motor Handicaps—infants and toddlers with motor handicaps exhibit delayed motor development, retention of primitive reflexes, and abnormal muscle tone as the result of CNS damage or malformation. The three major disabilities that are accompanied by motor handicaps are cerebral palsy, myelomeningocele, and Down syndrome. Infants and toddlers with motor handicaps usually exhibit delays in other developmental areas as well because learning occurs through ac-

tive exploration of the world. Research on interventions involving systematic exercise, and/or sensory stimulation and integration, indicate that early intervention can improve motor and sensory development and encourage parent support and acceptance. For more information, contact the American Medical Association, American Academy of Pediatrics, and local chapters of specific organizations such as the United Cerebral Palsy Foundation.

5. Children with Language and Communication Disorders—infants and toddlers who exhibit problems with the mechanics of speech (phonation, moving air from the lungs through the mouth, and articulation, formation of sounds) have speech disorders, and children with problems using the rules of language (labeling or forming sentences) have language disorders. Results of studies on various kinds of interventions suggest that the course and impact on communication disorders are modified through early intervention. For more information, contact the American Association for Speech and Language, Association for Speech and Hearing, and local chapters of associations for speech and language disorders.

6. Children with Autism—infants and toddlers with autism exhibit disturbance in developmental rates and sequences, responses to sensory stimuli, communication, and capacity to relate appropriately to people, events, and objects. The incidence of autism in the general population is very low: 4 to 5 in every 10,000 births, and frequently occurs along with other handicapping conditions such as mental retardation. Research on structured early intervention programs, which include parents, have yielded highly encouraging results. For more information, contact the National Society for Children and Adults with Autism, the American Psychological Association, or your local psychological association.

7. Children with Visual Impairments—infants and toddlers with severe visual impairments are found in approximately 1 out of 3,000 births with a wide variety of severity and etiology. The most important consideration is visual efficiency, which includes acuity, visual fields, ocular motility, binocular vision, adaptations to light and dark, color vision, and accommodation. Research findings indicate that early intervention helps visually impaired infants and toddlers perform closer-to-normal developmental expectations, and interventions using a team approach including parents, childcare specialists, and other professionals is more effective than individual treatment approaches. For more information, contact the National Society for the Prevention of Blindness, National Council for Exceptional Children, and local Health Department and agencies for the visually impaired.

8. Hearing Impaired Children—hearing impairments are classified by type (sensorineural, conductive, or mixed), time of onset (at birth or after), severity (mild to profound), and etiology. Research indicates that early

intervention programs should include parent counseling, staff with training in audiology, staff with speech and language training, inclusion of sign language as a normal program component, flexibility to help each family, and the inclusion of other deaf adults as resources to work with children. For more information, contact the Council for Exceptional Children, local Health Department, and the Association for the Deaf and Hearing Impaired.

It is essential that child care specialists not work with special needs children in isolation. When any of the conditions described here are suspected, the child care specialist must consult specialized professionals who are trained to evaluate, prescribe, and treat these children. In fact, every child care program should have medical and psychological services as a regular part of the evaluation and care of children. It is also important for each child care specialist to network with other child development professionals within the local area such as psychologists, pediatricians, and speech and language therapists. The research from interventions with all types of special needs children strongly indicates that a team approach, including parents, child care staff, and specialized professionals, is necessary to effectively keep special needs children as unlimited as possible.

Given that a team approach is necessary, several new curricula have been established for special needs infants and toddlers. The states of California, North Carolina, and Florida are among the nation's leaders in programs for infants and toddlers with special needs. For example, The Carolina Curriculum for Infants and Toddlers with Special Needs is in the Second Edition (1991), and provides strategies, activities, and techniques for most categories of special needs children which covers all developmental areas. The child care specialist should contact the State Department of Education in these states to obtain specific information on the care of special needs children.

FIVE NEED LEVELS

The responsibility for helping the unlimited child reach his or her potential is a joint effort between the caregiver, the family, the community, and society. How do you know where to start or even what to attend to? Maslow's hierarchy of needs is a good structure to use in beginning to view the infant and toddler.

Maslow defined a hierarchy of human needs which must be met in order for a person to be happy and fulfilled (Maslow 1954). At the most basic level are Physical Needs: food, air, water, elimination, shelter, and so on (see Table 2–1). As a general principle, the more immediately and completely the needs of infants and toddlers are fulfilled, the more secure and happy will be their development. One frustrating experience every caregiver of infants has, is not being able to determine which need is not being met, because infants cannot articulate need deprivation other than by crying. To help lessen their frustration, caregivers should systematically check out all needs at each of Maslow's levels.

TABLE 2–1   MASLOW'S HIERARCHY OF NEEDS

Level V	Self-Actualization Needs	Helping others, being creative, growing spiritually, etc.
Level IV	Ego Needs	Importance, being considered special, etc.
Level III	Social Needs	"3A's," friendship, companionship, bonding, etc.
Level II	Safety Needs	Protection from harm, security, consistency, etc.
Level I	Physical Needs	Food, air, water, shelter, etc.

Once a minimum of the needs at the Physical Level are fulfilled, the child can operate at Level II, Safety Needs: security, consistency, and the like. The more secure and consistent we can make the physical and psychological environment, the better. This is accomplished through routines, familiarity of people and surroundings, and so forth. The key to fulfilling safety needs is to reduce sudden and traumatic change as much as possible and for caregivers to remain calm during change.

When needs are minimally fulfilled at Level II, children are free to operate at Level III, Social Needs. Most people in our society spend the most energy trying to fulfill needs at this level. Even adults require the "3A's" of child rearing: attention, approval, and affection (Douville-Watson 1988). Human beings are social animals, so physical bonding, hugging, companionship, and friendship are essential to our well being. The research in development has clearly shown that infants and toddlers who receive large amounts of attention, approval, and affection develop faster and are healthier than children who are deprived of these resources (Furman 1992; Waters, E., Vaugh, B. E., Posada, G., and Kondo-Ikemura, K. (eds.) 1995).

Once basic needs are minimally fulfilled at Level III, children are free to fulfill Ego Needs at Level IV. Early theories hypothesized that newborns did not possess an "ego" (a sense of self as separate from the environment). Current research indicates that even though infants are symbiotically tied to others—that is, they experience a sense of dependence upon their primary caregivers—even newborns are capable of experiencing separateness or independence from others and the environment (Brazelton and Cramer 1990). As a result, infants and toddlers need to feel special and their individual dependence and independence needs to be respected. Despite the fact that they are very dependent upon us most of the time, when their lower-level needs are fulfilled, infants can play by themselves and experience competence on their own.

Level V, Self-Actualization Needs, are at the highest level, and most of us, unfortunately, don't function at this level often. These needs are to help other people, express creativity, and function on a spiritual level and they are only pursued when needs at lower levels are minimally fulfilled. It is a wonderful experience indeed to see infants or toddlers so fulfilled and happy that they seem to be in touch with the beauty of nature and are able to unselfishly give to others and explore their world creatively. Even though this level of fulfillment is difficult to achieve, it is certainly a worthwhile goal for all of us. In fact, it's impossible to give children what we do not possess ourselves, so as the caregiver, you must strive to fulfill lower-level needs to be free to operate at this Self-Actualization Level (see Figure 2–1).

The way to determine which need is deprived in an infant or nonverbal toddler is to start with Level I, Physical Needs, and check each need. Does the child need food, water, elimination, or relief from physical discomfort? Once physical needs are ruled out, move to the next level, Safety, and check out needs at that level. Continue checking needs at each level until you find the one that the child needs filled and then do whatever is necessary to fill the need. Keep in mind that this is a structure in which the whole child is cared for and there will be times when the child's deprived need cannot be determined.

FIVE MAJOR DEVELOPMENTAL AREAS

Now that we have an outline to define and assess need levels, let's look at the skill areas that are important in keeping children unlimited. These skill areas can then be put together in a graphic form developed by Watson and called a Developmental Profile (Watson 1977). As previously stated, a Development Profile is a graphic picture of a child's development compared to age expectancies in the five major developmental areas. Table 2–2 lists the five major skill areas important in human development. Assessment of each

Figure 2–1 Children are happy when needs at all five levels are filled.

TABLE 2–2   MAJOR DEVELOPMENTAL SKILL AREAS

Area I	**Physical:** height, weight, general motor coordination, visual and auditory acuity, etc.
Area II	**Cognitive:** reasoning, problem solving, concept formation, abstraction, imagination, creativity, etc.
Area III	**Emotional:** feelings, self-perception, perception of others related to self, confidence, security, etc.
Area IV	**Social:** interactions with peers, elders, and youngers, interactions one to one and in a group
Area V	**Developmental Learning:** Skills: visual, auditory, verbal, and motor skills necessary to accurately input, remember, and express information

child in care compared to age norms or expectations is necessary to help the child remain as unlimited as possible (Watson 1995).

Use the Developmental Prescription in Appendix A or another developmental hierarchy to evaluate what behaviors and skills the child can perform successfully and the point in the hierarchy where the child can't perform the behaviors (refer to Appendix B for Profile Construction). The last point where the child performs with success is translated into an estimate of month's development in that skill or area. For example, in evaluating a 12-month-old in Area I, Physical, the Developmental Prescription in Appendix A, 8–12 months, lists six behaviors under Muscular Control, Trunk and Leg. If the child being observed can successfully perform the first three behaviors, his development is estimated to be 10 months (half of the age range between 8 and 12 months). Evaluate each child in all the skill behaviors of the age range in order to establish an average age level for each of the five developmental areas on the profile. Remember that these are average estimates of ages and not specific tests.

Figure 2–2 graphically illustrates the estimates of a 12-month-old as compared to age norms on a Developmental Profile. The heavy line at 12 months indicates Juan's chronological age (C.A.) and each point indicates his development in each of the five areas. Specific skills under each area from the Developmental Prescription in Appendix A were evaluated to make up the points on the profile. By comparing relative strengths and weaknesses, programming can be done to enhance his development (refer to Appendix B for instructions on Developmental Profile Construction and Appendix A for specific age expectations). In the example, Juan is "above" age in responding to adult attention and "below" age expectancy in interacting in a group. From this profile we can see that activities should be done with Juan to help him feel more secure in a group setting and to help him function more independent of one to one interactions. Since his language skills are good, talking to him and having him respond in a group might help.

A word of caution is in order here. While needs and skills must be measured to provide a structure for keeping the child unlimited, estimates of skilled development are used only to determine goals and not to label chil-

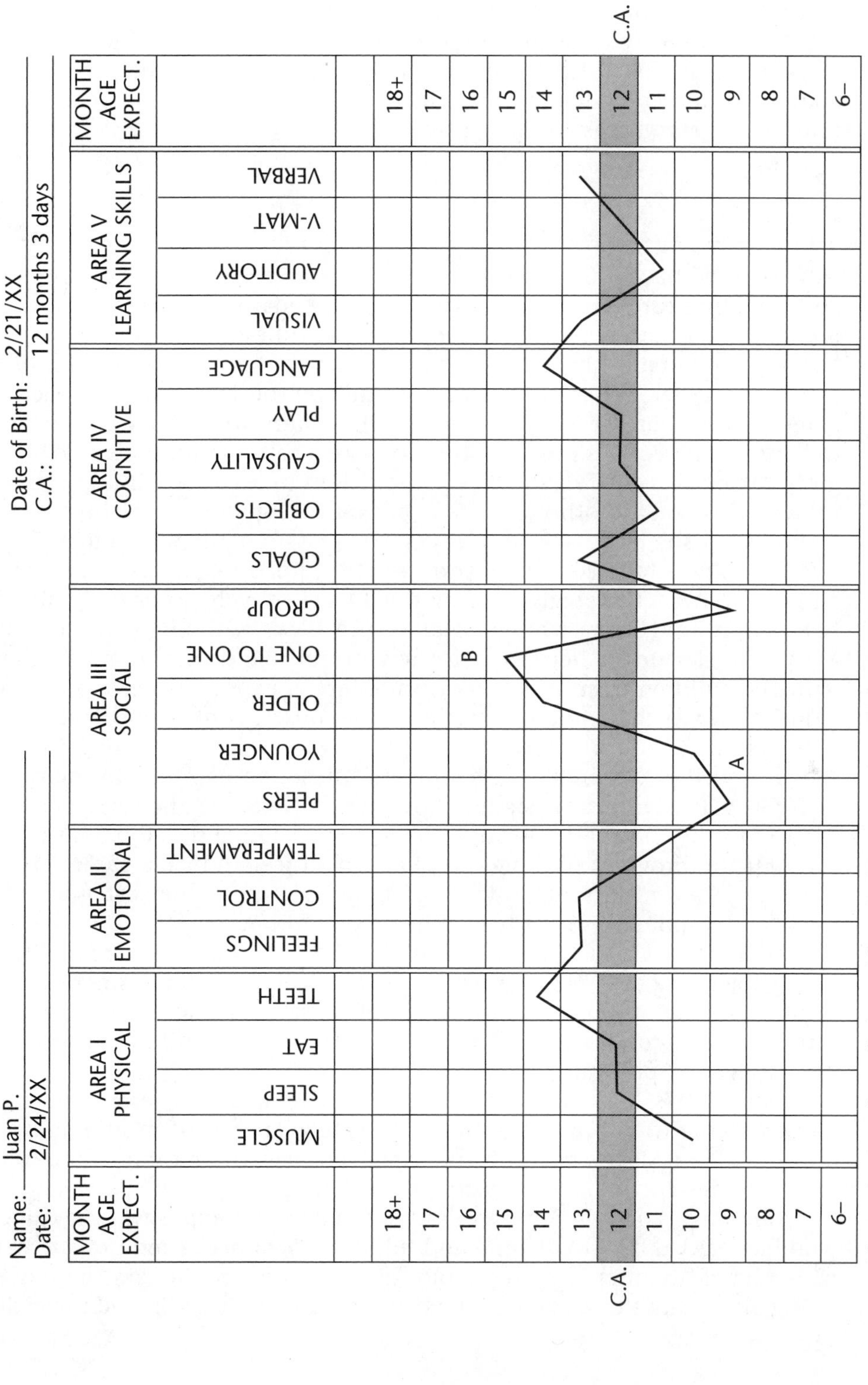

Name: Juan P.
Date: 2/24/XX
Date of Birth: 2/21/XX
C.A.: 12 months 3 days

MONTH AGE EXPECT.	AREA I PHYSICAL				AREA II EMOTIONAL			AREA III SOCIAL					AREA IV COGNITIVE					AREA V LEARNING SKILLS				MONTH AGE EXPECT.
	MUSCLE	SLEEP	EAT	TEETH	FEELINGS	CONTROL	TEMPERAMENT	PEERS	YOUNGER	OLDER	ONE TO ONE	GROUP	GOALS	OBJECTS	CAUSALITY	PLAY	LANGUAGE	VISUAL	AUDITORY	V-MAT	VERBAL	
18+											B											18+
17																						17
16																						16
15																						15
14																						14
13																						13
12 (C.A.)																						12 (C.A.)
11								A														11
10																						10
9																						9
8																						8
7																						7
6–																						6–

Notes: A = Juan has a little problem dealing with a group—sometimes is overwhelmed.
B = He responds very well to one to one adult attention.

Figure 2–2 Sample Developmental Profile

dren as "better" or "worse," or "ahead" or "behind." Variations in development are extremely wide and fluctuate, especially for infants and toddlers, so assess needs and skill levels on an ongoing basis and be timely in changing your goals to keep up with the rapidly changing child. Development is a continuing process wherein people grow in the same direction at different rates.

IDEAL CAREGIVING

Now that we have a framework in which to view the child, let's apply it to an ideal child care environment in which the goal is to keep a child unlimited; that is, always striving to reach his or her fullest potential.

Mary, age 30 months, enters the child care center at 7 A.M. each morning with her mother. She is greeted with a smile by the same caregiver each day. A few minutes are spent talking over what Mary's mother feels she needs today and she receives positive attention from both her mother and the caregiver. When Mary shows she is ready for Mom to leave by willingly going to her caregiver or the other children, her mother gives Mary a hug and kiss and tells her she'll be back, and leaves. She plays happily with a little boy for a few minutes, but as soon as another child joins her, Mary stops smiling and withdraws. The caregiver, using the 3A's effectively, joins them and puts her arm around Mary while she talks and plays with the other children. Mary snuggles under her arm for a few minutes and then resumes playing with the children. During the morning Mary is exposed to group and individual activities that enhance large and fine muscle control and motor development. She is also involved in games for awareness and labeling of feeling states, as well as vocabulary development. Although nap time in the room is at 10:30 A.M., Mary shows signs of tiredness at 9:45 and the caregiver allows her to take her nap early. At lunch, Mary's perceptual development is aided through the provider playing a see-hear-smell-feel-and-taste game with her food. Whenever Mary exhibits deprivation of a need, her caregiver sensitively and responsibly helps her fill her need right away.

Mary is helped to feel happy and fulfilled because the caregiver provides her with stimulating activities in each of the five Developmental Areas each day, focusing her attention on the positives in herself and the environment. The caregiver also provides her with a lot of the "3A's" of child care: Attention, Affection, and Approval.

When Mary's mother picks her up at 5:30 P.M., she is rested and happy and greets her with a hug and smile. The caregiver and the mother talk a few minutes about Mary's day and the caregiver gives the mother some follow-up activities to do with Mary during the evening.

While this scenario is ideal and can't always be accomplished, the caregiver who has learned how to identify and fulfill her own needs and provide herself with a lot of Attention, Approval, and Affection can give the same kind of nurturing and positive caregiving as she helps children be as unlimited as possible.

THEORETICAL CONTRIBUTIONS

Using the framework of the five developmental areas, we can now examine how the brain works, as well as some major contributions from theorists discussed in Chapter 1 toward keeping children unlimited.

Physical Development

Systematic observations of behavior by Darwin, Hall and Gesell, Watson, and Skinner, et. al., have resulted in an approach called **task analysis** which, when applied to physical development, yields a developmental hierarchy from simple to complex patterns of physical movements. For example, careful observation of the physical movements required in order to stand erect results in a hierarchy of behaviors starting with the simplest bending arm and leg joints and building through a series of natural steps such as rolling over and crawling to the final goal of standing erect. Contributions from behavioral pioneers have shown that any behavior can be task analyzed and broken down into a hierarchy of steps from the simplest to the most complex behavior necessary to perform the goal.

The Developmental Prescriptions presented in Appendix A are examples of general task analyses for infants and toddlers in the five major developmental areas. By carefully observing a child's behavior, the caregiver can determine the highest step the child can perform on the list, and then task analyze the specific steps necessary to help the child move to the next level in the hierarchy. Chapter 3 provides specific tools to help children remain unlimited by mastering physical skills and behaviors using task analyses. When the caregiver uses operant conditioning through reinforcing children's successes with the 3A's, children grow in physical and behavioral areas.

New Neuroscience Research Findings

Many scientists believe that there are a number of critical (sensitive) periods or "windows" in the first few years of childhood, when the brain demands certain types of input in order to create or stabilize certain long-lasting structures. In the first few months, the brain's higher centers explode with the aid of new synapses. By the age of two, a child's brain contains twice as many synapses and consumes twice as much energy as the brain of a normal adult.

University of Chicago pediatric neurologist, Dr. Peter Huttenlocher, indicates that the number of synapses in one layer of the visual cortex rises from around 2,500 per neuron at birth to as many as 18,000 about six months later. Other regions of the cortex score similarly spectacular increases, but on slightly different schedules. Fibers continue to form throughout life, and they reach their highest average densities (15,000 synapses per neuron) at around the age of two and remain at that level until the age of 10 or 11 (Nash 1997).

Cognitive Development

As mentioned in Chapter 1, the most widely used theories of higher cognition are Piaget's Cognitive-Developmental Theory (Beilin 1992), and recently receiving more study, Vygotsky's Sociocultural Theory (Rogoff and Chavajoy 1995). Chapter 8 details several applications of Piaget's theory in child care settings, but some major principles from his theory bear discussion here.

According to Piaget, children develop higher cognitive skills through four stages: 1) sensorimotor, 2) preoperational, 3) concrete operational, and 4) formal operational. Children use **schemes** or patterns of actions to learn at each of these stages through the intellectual functions of **adaptation** and **organization**.

Adaptation involves using schemes that have direct interactions with the environment; for example, grasping and dropping an object over and over. **Accommodation** involves changing schemes which do not work well. When children are in a familiar routine and are not required to learn new schemes, they function by means of **assimilation** which involves refining structures to more closely fit their schemes and cognitive structures. Piaget called this internal state of assimilation **cognitive equilibrium** which implies a consistent and comfortable condition. When children are placed into new and/or unfamiliar situations, they experience **cognitive disequilibrium** and perform more accommodation than assimilation.

The second cognitive function through which schemes are changed is called **organization**, which takes place internally without involvement in the environment. Organization is a process of rearranging new schemes and linking them with other schemes to form a cognitive system. For example, a baby will eventually relate schemes for sucking, dropping, and throwing with new, more complex schemes of near and far.

While many of the hypotheses of Piaget's theory have come into question by recent research demonstrating that infants and toddlers have many more cognitive skills than Piaget theorized (Rast and Meltzoff 1995), the principles and stages defined by Piaget have functional value for the caregiver in helping children remain unlimited in their cognitive development. Some additional contributions include discovery learning, awareness of readiness for learning, and acceptance of individual differences in learning rates.

Different from Piaget, Vygotsky viewed cognitive development as an interaction between children and their social environment. Vygotsky believed that, once language is developed, children engage in **private speech**; in other words, they talk to themselves as a means of self-guidance and direction (1934/1986). Recent research supports this view with findings that children who use more private speech show more improvement on difficult tasks than children who do not use much private speech (Berk and Spuke 1995). In addition, children use more private speech as tasks become more difficult (Berk 1994), and children with learning problems use more private speech than children with normal learning skills (Diaz and Berk 1995).

Vygotsky hypothesized that higher cognitive processes develop from verbal and nonverbal social interactions. This is accomplished when more mature individuals instruct less mature individuals within the **zone of proximal development**. This term refers to a range of tasks that a child is ready to learn with the help of more skilled peers or adults. Learning takes place through making the language and actions of dialogues and demonstrations with adults part of the child's private speech, and organizing their own actions in the same way as the instructor. At least two aspects of this process have found research support: **intersubjectivity** and **scaffolding**.

Intersubjectivity refers to how children and adults come to understand each other by adjusting their views and perspectives to fit the other person. Scaffolding involves changing the support given a learner over the course of teaching a skill or concept. The instructor uses much praise and instruction in the early stages of teaching a skill, and task-analyzes the steps necessary to achieve the goal skill. As the learner starts mastering steps, the instructor withdraws instruction and praise in direct response to the learner's ability to perform successfully. Caregivers who effectively learn to use intersubjectivity and scaffolding help children remain unlimited, because children learn to use positive private speech and succeed more easily (Behrend, Rosengren, and Perlmutter 1992).

A final aspect of Vygotsky's theory involves the use of **make-believe play** in higher cognitive development. Vygotsky believed that children who engage in make-believe play use imagination to act out internal ideas about how the world operates, and to set rules by which play is conducted, which helps them learn to think before they act. Recent research on preschoolers supports this concept since children who engage in make-believe and pretend play are found to be more flexible and advanced in their problem-solving and thought processes (Lillard 1993).

New brain research indicates that "the electrical activity of brain cells changes the physical structure of the brain and this begins well before birth. A brain is not just a computer because the same processes that wire the brain before birth also drive the explosion of learning after birth. During the first year of life, the baby's brain produces trillions more connections than it can possibly use. Then, through competition the brain eliminates synapses that are seldom used starting around the age of 10 and leaves behind a pattern of emotion and thought" (Nash 1997).

Emotional Development

Contributions by Freud (1973/1938) and followers like Erickson (1950) have provided an understanding of the development and motivation for emotions. Freud theorized three distinct parts of the personality called the id which is present at birth, and is the source of our wants, needs, and desires. The ego emerges during early infancy, and is the "self," including self-concept and self-esteem. The superego is our conscience, or our value system of right and wrong. A person's emotional states are determined by how needs, wants, and desires are fulfilled using a value system of right and wrong. Freud theorized five psychosexual stages a developing child experiences that forms the foundation for personality: 1) the oral stage (birth to one year) involves sucking, eating, and exploring things with the mouth; 2) the anal stage (one to three years) when toilet training and interest in elimination becomes important; and 3) the phallic stage (three to six years) involves formation of sexual identity as male or female, and includes the Oedipus (male)/ Electra (female) conflict when we try to win the parent of the opposite sex away from the parent of the same sex. How this conflict is handled by parents and caregivers determines the amount of confidence and security we have in our male or female identity as adults. The last two stages occur during middle childhood and adolescence and include: 4) the latency stage, in which we form social values from adults and peers outside the home; and 5) the genital stage, during early adolescence. when we become sexually mature. The functional value of Freud's theory for caregivers is the understanding that young children need sensitive help to fill their emotional needs at each stage using a value system which teaches them that it is not necessary to hurt themselves or anyone else to be fulfilled and happy. When children's emotional needs are not filled, frustration and anger result, and the caregiver should help children express their negative feelings in healthy ways.

Erickson's Psychosocial Theory further adds to our understanding of emotional development and the qualities children need to become happy and successful adults. He defined eight psychosocial stages that humans experience throughout life. The first three are extremely important in the development of infants and toddlers:

1. *Basic trust versus mistrust*—children learn to trust or mistrust themselves and the world during infancy depending on the warmth and sensitivity with which they are given. When infants are required to wait too long for comfort, or they are handled harshly and insensitively, they develop basic mistrust of themselves and others.
2. *Autonomy versus shame and doubt*—once infants become mobile, a process of separation and individuation begins which eventually results in autonomy. Children need to choose and decide things for themselves, and when caregivers permit reasonable free choices and do not force or shame children, autonomy and self-confidence is fostered.
3. *Initiative versus guilt*—when caregivers support a child's sense of purpose and direction, initiative in the form of ambition and responsibility is developed. When caregivers demand too much self-control or responsibilities which are age-inappropriate, children respond by feeling over-controlled and/or guilty.
4. *Industry versus inferiority*—learning to work cooperatively with others promotes industry and a sense of competence. On the other hand, care-

givers who do everything for children or compete with children promote a sense of inferiority and incompetence.

5. *Identity versus identity diffusion*—self-chosen values and goals lead to security in a child's identity compared to adults controlling and making all decisions for the child, which lead to confusion regarding the meaning of their identity.

6. *Intimacy versus isolation*—using the 3A's results in a warm and affectionate bond between caregiver and child, and establishes the basis for later healthy intimate relationships. Withholding physical and emotional warmth results in children feeling isolated and rejected.

7. *Generativity versus stagnation*—giving to, and caring for, others along with productive work foster a sense of competence in the world and in life, compared to being selfish and ungiving which result in feeling stagnated and having no meaning of life,

8. *Ego integrity versus despair*—a very sad experience is to see a small child in despair. Even young children can reflect on what kind of person they feel they are and how they feel about their life. When their assessment is "I did good and the world is good," ego integrity is the result. When their assessment is "I'm bad and the world is bad," despair is the result.

Erickson's stages are important to help children develop the qualities that result in a happy, meaningful life. Activities based on the first three stages should be a part of the daily curriculum, and the caregiver should help promote confidence, security, and trust in each child.

Recent research regarding emotional development suggests that, while all emotions are present at birth, our emotional reactions are learned through "stages." The development of affective reactions and self-regulation of emotions appears to be the direct result of caregiving styles.

"What wires a child's brain, or rewires it after physical trauma, is repeated experience. When the brain does not receive the right information, the result can be devastating. Emotional deprivation early in life has a similar effect" (Nash 1997). For a more complete understanding of the development of emotions, the reader should refer to "Emotional Development: The Organization of Emotional Life in the Early Years; Cambridge Studies in Social and Educational Development" (Sroufe 1996).

Feelings are inborn, but emotional reactions are learned. It is important to teach young children to accurately identify their feeling states, and express them in healthy ways. It is often easy to determine the emotions of even young infants. For example, young babies often "beam" when happy, have a "tantrum" when frustrated or angry, and "coo and smile" when happy and at ease. Caregivers should label feeling states for nonverbal infants, and as young children develop language, they should be taught to accurately label and express their emotions. One effective tool for helping young children pay attention to and identify feelings is to use a Feeling Chart such as the one shown in Figure 2–3. This chart illustrates five primary emotions: At

Ease, Happy, Sad, Angry, and Afraid, and can be used to help children accurately label their internal feelings. All human emotions are normal and are therefore healthy; no feeling state is bad or no good. The main goal for affective education is to help children be consciously aware of their feelings, and to express them in ways that are helpful to the child and hot harmful to others. Chapters 4 and 8 provide specific tools for healthy awareness and expression of emotions.

Social Development

Contributions from numerous social learning theorists help us to understand how infants and toddlers develop relationships. The first relationships we have in the world with our parents and caregivers result in the formation of the self which, in turn, forms the basis for all future relationships.

Freud theorized that newborn infants are psychologically connected to their mother; there is not awareness of the baby being different or separate from the mother. This **symbiosis** is gradually replaced through the process of **separation and individuation** until the child develops a separate sense of self (1935).

William James (1890–1963) first identified two distinct aspects of the self: the I or **existential self** which is separate from the environment and other people, and maintains continuous existence over time; and the **reflective self** or the "me-not me" that perceives the physical, material, and relationship qualities of experience.

The emergence of **self-recognition** has been demonstrated in infants as young as nine months, and appears to be present in the majority of fifteen month olds (Bullock and Lutkenhaus 1990). Many theorists hypothesize that

Happy

At Ease

Sad

Angry

Afraid

Figure 2–3   Feelings Chart

the development of self lies in a **sense of agency**; for example, awareness that our actions cause other objects and people to react in predictable ways (Pipp, Easterbrooks, and Brown 1993). By two years of age, a sense of self is well established and toddlers respond to possessiveness of objects with "me" and "mine" (Levine 1983).

The opposite side of the coin from separation-individuation is presented in the widely accepted view of infant emotional ties to the caregiver in Bolwby's Ethological Theory of Attachment (Bowlby 1969). According to this theory, the infant's relationship to the parent starts as a set of innate signals which keeps the caregiver close to the baby and proceeds through four phases:

1. *The preattachment phase* (birth to six weeks) where the baby grasps, cries, smiles, and gazes to keep the caregiver engaged.
2. *The "attachment-in-the-making" phase* (six weeks to eight months) when the baby responds differently to familiar caregivers than to strangers. Face-to-face interactions relieve distress, and the baby has expectations that the caregiver will respond when signaled,
3. *The clear-cut attachment phase* (eight months to two years) when "separation anxiety" is exhibited, the baby protests caregiver departure, and acts deliberately to maintain caregiver attention.
4. *Formation of a reciprocal relationship phase* (18 months onward) where children negotiate with the caregiver, and are willing to give and take in relationships.

According to Bolwby (1980), young children internalize a warm and affectionate caregiver-child bond that becomes a vital part of personality. This image, which Freud called the internalized good mother, becomes the model for all future close relationships (Bretherton 1992).

NEUROSCIENCE RESEARCH FINDINGS

Caregivers often spend more waking time with children than parents. What holds true for parents in the new brain research is significant for child care specialists. "Indeed, parents are the brains first and most important teachers. They help babies learn by adapting the rhythmic, high pitched speaking style known as "Parentese" where mothers and fathers change their speech patterns in the same peculiar way. Parentese appears to hasten the process of connecting words to the objects they denote" (Nash 1997).

Caregivers should be very aware of factors that effect attachment security in young children. Sensitive caregiving that responds quickly to the child's signals and needs is the most important factor in keeping children unlimited. The findings from many studies clearly reveal that securely attached infants have primary caregivers who respond quickly to signals, express positive feelings, and handle their babies with tenderness and sensitivity. On the other hand, insecure babies have caregivers who dislike physical contact and behave insensitively to the child's needs (Isabella 1993). The best principle for infant and toddler social development is probably that young children cannot be given too much attention, approval, and affection; they can't be spoiled. Your sensitive caring sets the basis for all future relationships that young children will have throughout their lives.

Learning Skill Development

The most recent contributions to early childhood development are information processing theories. The most widely known computer-like model is the **store model** (Atkinson and Shiffrin 1968). In this model, information in the form of visual, auditory, and kinesthetic images are **inputted** into a **sensory register**, but quickly degrade unless they are stored in **short-term memory**. Short-term memory is the place where conscious operation on information occurs and where we apply strategies to make information meaningful. The longer and/or more times we hold information in short-term memory determines how likely the information will be stored in **long-term memory**. Long-term memory is the place which is largely unconscious and holds all the meaningful experiences of our life. The final part of this model involves the **response generator** in which we can decide to respond to stimuli at any point in the process.

A **levels of processing** model assumes that retention depends upon the depth to which information is processed. In this model, we can process information on a superficial **perceptual level**, such as lower or upper case letters in a word; on deeper **phonemic features**, such as the sounds associated with each letter symbol; or the deepest **semantic features**, such as the definition of the word (Craik and Lockhart 1972).

Watson (1978), from his work and extensive research with over 4,000 children, used many of the principles from the store and levels of processing models to develop an information processing model of the essential **Developmental Learning Skills** necessary to accurately process information in pre-academic skills such as letter and word recognition, spelling, and simple number combinations. The Developmental Learning Skills Model presented in Figure 2–4 has, at the base of learning, the mechanical physical and neurological acuity and capacity to coordinate the sensory systems necessary for learning **(Sensory Coordination: Level I.)**. The model illustrates the three major **sensory modalities** used to input most information; Visual (seeing), Auditory (hearing), and Kinesthetic (touching) input. We respond with either Motor or Verbal output. Children must possess the visual, auditory, and motor acuity and coordination necessary to accurately input stimuli, and they must develop sufficient fine motor coordination and verbal skills to output or respond accurately. It is essential when working with young children that accurate visual and auditory acuity and speech and language evaluations be performed regularly to insure that these mechanical bases for learning are functioning normally. For example, even minor ear infections, if left untreated over time, can drastically effect a young child's development of auditory and verbal learning skills.

Figure 2–4 lists **Level II.—Attentional Skills** as the next process, and includes **focal attention**, **prefocal attention**, and **perceptual screening** to ex-

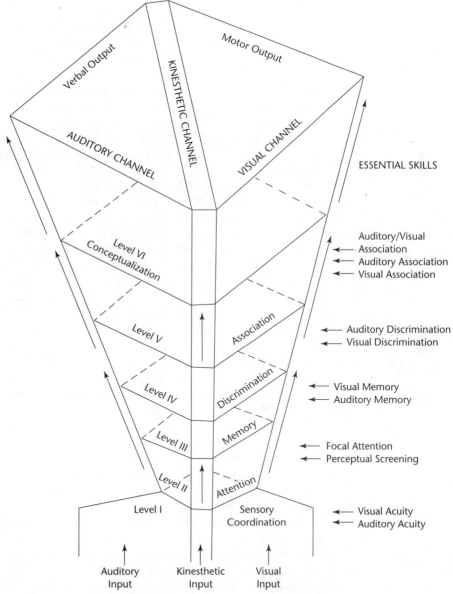

Figure 2–4   Watson's Developmental Learning Skills Model

plain how we input information from the environment into our brain. When we scan the environment without paying special attention to any details, or when we are so familiar with our surroundings that we don't notice specific details, we are using prefocal attention (similar to the sensory register in the store model). When we attend to specific visual, auditory, kinesthetic, olfactory, and/or taste stimuli, we are using focal attention. In order to focally attend successfully to an individual stimulus, it is necessary to block out all other distracting stimuli occurring at the same time. This process of screening out or eliminating irrelevant stimuli is called perceptual screening. For example, in order for a young child to hear your voice, he or she must focus auditory attention on the particular sounds of your voice while screening out all the other distracting visual, auditory, and other sensory stimuli occurring at the same time. Many of the problems exhibited by young children labeled as learning disabled, attention deficit, hyperactive, or distractable are really deficits in focal attention and perceptual screening skills. Further, the term "skills" is used here because auditory and visual focal attention and perceptual screening skills can be easily taught to young children (King 1979).

Once sensory coordination and focal attention occur successfully, specific stimuli can be recorded in **Memory—Level III**. In Watson's model, information is made more meaningful and is, therefore, held longer in conscious memory when stimuli are well discriminated, associated, and categorized into a concept. Therefore, memory is aided by the use of higher cognitive skills, as well as simple repeated presentations of stimuli. Caregivers should be aware that learning improves when age-appropriate material is made more meaningful to children by helping them discriminate differences, associate similarities, and fit specific stimuli into categories.

The process of separating the important (salient) elements of a stimulus from similar stimuli surrounding it is called **Discrimination—Level IV**. In Gestalt psychology, discrimination is viewed in terms of figure-ground where an object being focally attended to becomes the figure taking the forefront in our perception, and similar irrelevant stimuli become the ground and fades in our perception. For example, a common error in beginning discrimination is called reversal; for example, lower case letters "b" and "d" are confused with each other because the child is not focally attending to the important characteristic of the different direction of the letters.

Once stimuli are accurately discriminated and stored in short-term memory, they can be **Associated—Level V.**, which involves the process of connecting one stimulus with another on the basis of repeated presentation or similarities. For example, young children more often associate a picture of a chair with a picture of a table than with other choices such as a lamp or bike because table-chair are paired together much more often in experience. Much learning in the first three years of life is done at the association level, and early childhood experts should be aware of the associations they repeatedly present to children.

The highest level of information processing goes beyond simple perceptual skills and is called **Conceptualization—Level VI.** Conceptualization or concept formation is the process of placing specific stimuli into an abstract category. The term abstract in this sense means an idea not existing within the real world. For example, apples, oranges, and bananas exist in the real world because we can touch, see, taste, and smell them, but fruit is an abstract concept because it is a category name that does not exist within the world. Conceptualization is the process of placing individual stimuli within abstract categories and is the highest cognitive function necessary to perform simple academic skills such as letter and word recognition, spelling, and simple numerical operations.

A final important functional aspect of this model involves the **sensory modalities** used to process information required in learning tasks. Most adults are unaware of the information processing requirements of the tasks they require young children to perform. For example, the simple verbal request to "draw a picture of a person" requires that the child input auditory information, associate and conceptualize (what a person is), associate the auditory name with a visual image (what a person looks like), and then perform complex visual/motor skills to output the visual image. A good rule of thumb for caregivers, in order to keep the information processing requirements as simple as possible, is to stay within the same sensory modalities for task requirements. For example, if you want a child to learn names of different fruit, require auditory input and *verbal* output by discussing what each fruit looks, smells, and tastes like, how the shapes are different, and similarities between them. If you choose to use visual input (pictures), keep verbal discussion at a minimum and require visual/motor output (pointing to pictures or drawing). By keeping tasks within the same sensory input/output modality, you reduce the complexity of the task requirements as much as possible.

Watson (1979) determined eight Developmental Learning Skills to be essential prerequisites to learning pre-academic skills. These eight skills are presented in Figure 2–4 and in Chapter 8, and caregivers should systematically teach children over two years of age these eight skills as part of the daily curriculum to keep children unlimited in their learning skills.

SUMMARY OF THEORETICAL CONTRIBUTIONS

1. *Physical Development:* Major contributions from behavioral psychology starting with Darwin and continuing through current research provide us with task analysis of physical movements and behavioral skills. Breaking down goal behaviors into the natural steps starting with the behaviors the child can presently perform and proceeding to the goal behavior provides the caregiver with a powerful tool to keep children unlimited. When operant conditioning reinforcing children with a lot

of positive attention, approval, and affection is added, the caregiver can enhance the physical development of all children in care.

2. *Cognitive Development:* Piaget has provided more understanding and functional principles for higher cognitive development than any other theorist. The caregiver needs to be aware of the schemes that infants and toddlers use to interact with the environment through adaptation and cognitive organization (accommodation). Piaget's four stages of higher cognitive skills provide practical principles to use in keeping infants and toddlers unlimited in their higher cognitive development.

   Vygotsky provided caregivers with powerful principles of private speech, the zone of proximal development including how adults and children come to understand each other through intersubjectivity and scaffolding, and the important role of make-believe play. Use of these principles helps the caregiver keep children unlimited in their abilities to learn.

3. *Emotional Development:* Freud's psychosexual stages and the structure of personality including the id, ego, and superego provide caregivers with an understanding of the bases for feeling states. Caregivers can keep children unlimited when they help develop a healthy ego (self-concept and self-esteem) by teaching children how to identify and express their feelings, and fill their needs using a respectful value system that does not hurt the child or others.

   Erickson's Psychosocial Theory provides caregivers with stages for the development of essential personality characteristics such as trust, autonomy, and initiative. Caregivers can plan activities on a daily basis using Erickson's stages to help children remain unlimited in their happiness and personality development.

   Teaching young children to accurately identify and express feelings in ways that help them fill their needs and not hurt others is a goal every caregiver should have to help children remain unlimited.

4. *Social Development:* In order to apply principles for relationships and interactions, the caregiver must first understand the development of the self. William James first defined the existential (authentic) self and the reflective self (me-not me). Bolwby's Ethological Theory helps the caregiver understand how infants and toddlers participate in relationships through his four stages of attachment. Research findings from many studies demonstrate that warm and sensitive conscious caregiver-to-child interactions are essential to set the basis for keeping children unlimited in all their future relationships.

5. *Learning Skill Development:* Information processing theories help us to understand how children perceive the world and provide the caregiver with powerful tools to help children remain unlimited in their joy to learn. The store and levels-of-processing models provide understanding of how perception and memory occurs. Watson's Developmental Learning Skills model provides six levels of perceptual organization,

and how the input and output of stimuli through sensory modalities help children remain unlimited by using the essential perceptual skills necessary to process information in pre-academic tasks.

A final comment regarding the narrowness of the information presented in this discussion is in order. There are entire bodies of research and knowledge on each of the five Developmental Areas, so the reader should understand that the scope of this text allows for only an overview of each area, and that numerous theories and research findings could not be presented in this brief review.

STUDENT ACTIVITIES

1. Copy the Developmental Profile Form in Appendix B and assess one infant and one toddler by establishing a complete profile for each using the Developmental Prescriptions in Appendix A.
2. Observe two children and take notes on which Need Levels they appear to exhibit during the period of one hour.
3. Using the Developmental Prescriptions in Appendix A, task-analyze (write up the small steps) what you would do to help move a child's behavior from one developmental level to the next. For example, determine how you can help an infant move from "moves arms randomly" to "reaches" with arms.
4. Using the Developmental Prescriptions in Appendix A, work with one child to move him or her from one developmental level to the next one for a particular behavior.

CHAPTER REVIEW

1. List differences between the Unlimited Child theory and the Tabula Rasa theories of development.
2. Describe why needs at one level must be filled before a person can move to the next higher level.
3. Write down one experience during which you were able to function at the Self-Actualization need level.
4. Compare the behavior of two children of the same age in the Social Learning Skill Area.

REFERENCES

Atkinson, R. C., and Shiffrin, R. M. 1968. Human memory: A proposed system and its control processes. In *Advances in the Psychology of Learning and Motivation,* eds. K. W. Spence and J. T. Spence, Vol. 2, pp. 90–195. New York: Academic Press.

Behrend, D. A., Rosengran, K. S., and Perlmutter, M. 1992. The relation between private speech and parental interactive style. In *Private Speech: From Social Interaction to Self-regulation,* eds. R. M. Diaz and L. E. Berk, pp. 85–100. Hillsdale, NJ: Erlbaum.

Beilin, H. 1992. Piaget's enduring contribution to developmental psychology. *Developmental Psychology* 28, 191-204.

Berk, L. E. 1994. Why children talk to themselves. *Scientific American* 271(5), 78–83.

Berk, L. E., and Spuhl, S. T. 1995. Maternal interaction, private speech, and task performance in preschool children. *Early Childhood Research Quarterly* 10, 145–69.

Bowlby, J. 1969. Attachment and loss: Vol. 1. *Attachment.* New York: Basic Books.

Brazelton, T. B., and Cramer, Bertrand. 1990. *The Earliest Relationships: Parents, Infants & Drama of Early Attachments.* New York: Delacorte Press, pp. 25–26.

Bretherton, I. 1992. The origins of attachment theory: John Bowlby and Mary Ainsworth. *Developmental Psychology* 29, 759–75.

Bullock, M., and Lutkenhaus, P. 1990. Who am I? The development of self-understanding in toddlers. *Merrill-Palmer Quarterly* 36, 217–38.

Craik, F. I. M., and Tulving, E. 1975. Depth of processing and the retention of words in episodic memory. *Journal of Experimental Psychology: General* 104, 268–94.

Diaz, R. M., and Berk, L. E. 1995. A Vygotskian critique of self-instructional training. *Development and Psychopathology* 7,369–92.

Douville-Watson, L. 1988. *The 3A's of Child Care: Attention, Approval and Affection.* Oyster Bay, New York: Lifeskills Institute.

Douville-Watson, L. 1988. *Family Actualization through Research and Education; F.A.R.E.,* Third Edition. New York: Actualization, Inc.

Erickson, E. H. 1950. *Childhood and Society.* New York: Norton.

Freud, S. *An Outline of Psychoanalysis.* London: Hogarth. (Original work published 1938).

Furman, E. 1992. *Toddlers and Their Mothers: A Study in Early Personality Development.* Madison, CT: International Press.

Guralnick, M. J., and Bennett, F. C., Eds. 1987. *The Effectiveness of Early Intervention for At-Risk and Handicapped Children.* San Diego, CA: Academic Press, Inc.

Isabella, R. A. 1993. Origins of attachment: Maternal interactive behavior across the first year. *Child Development* 64, 605–21

James, W. 1963. *Psychology.* New York: Fawcett. (Original work published 1890).

Johnson, N. M., Jens, K. G., Attermeier, S. M., and Hacker, B. J. 1991. *The Carolina Curriculum for Infants and Toddlers with Special Needs,* Second Edition. Baltimore, MD: Paul H. Brookes Publishing Co.

King, C. E. 1979. Focal attention training in kindergarten through third grade attention deficit children. Unpublished Doctoral Dissertation, Hofstra University: Hempstead, New York

Levine, L. E. 1983. Mine: Self-definition in 2-year-old boys. *Developmental Psychology* 19, 544–49.

Lillard, A. S. 1993. Pretend play skills and the child's theory of mind. *Child Development* 64, 348–71.

Maslow, Abraham H. 1954. *Motivation and Personality.* New York: Harper and Row.

Nash, J. 1997. *Fertile Minds.* How a child's brain develops and what it means for child care and welfare reform. *Time* Magazine.

Pipp. S., Easterbrooks, M. A., and Brown, S. R. 1993. Attachment status and complexity of infants' self-and other-knowledge when tested with mother and father. *Social Development* 2, 1–14.

Rast, M., and Meltzoff, A. N. 1995. Memory and representation in young children with Down syndrome: Exploring deferred imitation and object permanence. *Development and Psychopathology* 7, 393–407.

Rogoff, B., and Chavajay, P. 1995. What's become of research on the cultural basis of cognitive development? *American Psychologist* 50, 859–77.

Sroufe, L. Alan. 1996. T*he Organization of Emotional Life in the Early Years.* Cambridge Studies in Social and Educational Development. New York: Cambridge University Press.

Vygotsky, L. S. 1986. *Thought and Language* (A. Kozulin, Trans.), Cambridge, MA: MIT Press. (Original work published 1934).

Waters, E., Vaughn, B. E., Posada, G., and Kondo-Ikemura, K. (Eds.) 1995. Caregiving, cultural, and cognitive perspectives on secure-base behavior and working models: New growing points of attachment theory and research. *Monographs of the Society for Research in Child Development* 60(2–3, Serial No. 244).

Watson, M. A. 1977. *Tests of Group Learning Skills.* Freeport, New York: Activity Records.

Watson, M. A. 1995. *WALDO Developmental Learning Program.* Glen Cove, New York: Instructional Press.

3
The 3A's of Child Care

OBJECTIVES

After completing this chapter, the child development specialist should be able to:
1. Use the 3A's of child care daily.
2. Compare the concepts of the 3A's with your own experience.
3. Clearly define differences between the 3A's of child care and the 3A's of self-health.
4. Incorporate the 3A's of child care and 3A's of self-health in your own life for one day as an experiment.
5. Observe and record the process of using the 3A's with a child.

CHAPTER OUTLINE

   I. Introduction
  II. The 3A's; Attention, Approval, and Affection As Tools
 III. The Attachment Debate and Diminished Father and Mother Roles
 IV. The 3A's Part I: The Outward Expression
     A. Attention
     B Approval
     C. Affection
  V. Definition of Caregiver Self-Health
 VI. The 3A's Part II: The Inward Expression
     A. Attention
     B. Approval
     C. Affection
VII. Using the 3A's Successfully with Infants and Toddlers
     A. Attention
     B. Approval
     C. Affection

CHILD DEVELOPMENT ASSOCIATE FUNCTIONAL AREAS

I. Learning Environment
II. Communication/Feelings
III. Independence/Self
IV. Mutual Respect
V. Guidance
VI. Professionalism

INTRODUCTION

The abilities to understand and academically fulfill requirements and to master specific skills such as bathing and feeding babies are necessary to your work, and may even extend into your personal life. These immensely important aspects of child care, however, are not enough.

Students studying child care need to integrate their self into their work. No other professional field is in need of self-integration more than this most humanistic endeavor. Taking charge of tomorrow's leaders on a daily basis demands human investment since it perpetuates all future human connections. Just how important are these future connections? Let's look at what other experts have to say.

"The child's self is constructed in the interpersonal relationships that bind her to others, she is known in the experience of connection and is defined by the responsiveness of human engagement" (Gilligan 1988).

"It is the context of relationships that the needs and wishes of very young children are met, or not. . . . It is in the context of relationships that infants and toddlers continue to develop expectations about how the world is, how the adults in that world behave, and their own place in the social world" (Pawl 1990).

"When there is a sudden breakdown in the relationship between caregiver and child, whether that is natural or due to conflict, the results can profoundly effect momentarily or cumulatively the meanings children give to themselves now and in later experience" (Douville-Watson 1995).

Jane Healy, in her book *Your Child's Growing Mind*, discusses the importance of warm, loving, verbal interactions between parent or caregiver and child, particularly in the first two years. She indicates that praise, prompt attention, and immediate feedback about objects in the environment develop better vocabulary and higher scores on later intelligence tests (Healy 1989).

How important are these human connections? ". . . every experience lives on in further experiences" (Dewey 1938, p. 28). Repeated emotional experiences are integrated into children's understandings about themselves, others, and the world they share (Denzin 1984). In this way, "the experiences and feelings of childhood endure" (Bowman 1989, p. 450); "they become part of children's biographies, providing the emotional foundation for future interactions and relationships" (Hatch 1995).

How important are these connections on long term life experiences? How do early life connections impact later years? Here is one study with remarkable conclusions. Jon Kabet-Zinn, Ph.D., in his book *Full Catastrophe Living Using the Wisdom of Your Body and Mind to Face Stress, Pain and Illness* (1991), discusses a 40-year longitudinal health study recording illnesses and subsequent deaths. The study, done by Dr. Caroline Bell Thomas on incoming medical students at Johns Hopkins Medical School, tracked life experiences through the disease process. The study found that "the importance of emotional experiences early in life may play a strong role in shaping our health later in life."

Phillip S. Riback, M.D. F.A.A.P., an assistant professor of neurology and pediatrics at Albany Medical College in Albany, New York, stated: "Since babies are so highly dependent on their caregivers for everything, it makes some sense that their emotional state, and eventually their own emotional responses, are affected by the emotions of those who care for them."

How important are human connections? Who is responsible for these outcomes? Hatch (1995) further writes, "When mother's importance is shared with others, such as fathers, preschool teachers, and day care providers, someone is still responsible for a variety of positive and negative outcomes." If we acknowledge our responsibility as caregivers, we can readily accept that "infants become partners in the give and take of human relationships" (Saarni 1989; Snow 1989).

Why do we call people who integrate their "self" every day in their work simply caregivers, providers, teachers, or specialists? Why don't we address them respectfully in terms of the possible outcomes of their personal investment? They should really be referred to as "Most Powerful Maker of the Highly Intelligent, Serenely Compassionate, Healthy, Adaptive, Future Human Race." Although wordy, it is an accurate description of the impact your daily commitment can have on children and their future outcomes.

So, Most Powerful Outcome Maker, what can you learn for your "self" that will allow you to be available, fresh, interested, involved, and ready to take on this awesome task? Indeed, caregivers must learn to plan to take good care of themselves, to not neglect their "self" in a day of routines, and to learn to identify and to use self-health techniques.

THE 3A'S: ATTENTION, APPROVAL, AND AFFECTION AS TOOLS

The 3A's of child care are tools which can be used to promote a positive environment and maintain a positive emotional connection between the young child and caregiver. The 3A's of child care—Attention, Approval, and Affection—are extremely powerful tools available to any person in just about any situation. They are not only valuable tools; their use is *essential* in the care of children.

All the examples about Attention, Approval, and Affection are meant to empower the caregiver and help facilitate an attitude change toward oneself by emphasizing that caregiver feelings have a profound effect on children. When these skills are applied to children, they represent tools that can be successfully used to motivate. When the caregiver uses these skills for personal development, he or she can enjoy the same benefit. These concepts are widely used in areas of psychology and medicine, and include techniques from the scientific study of bioenergetics and relaxation therapy. These techniques can effectively revitalize the caregiver and help him or her stay on center. They will provide that badly needed second to think and are most useful in fighting that inevitable outcome of caring for children all day called exhaustion.

THE ATTACHMENT DEBATE AND DIMINISHED FATHER AND MOTHER ROLES

An ongoing debate in the research literature concerns whether infants exhibit less secure attachment when day care versus home-reared. This debate cannot be discussed without considering the changing roles of mothers and fathers in the care of infants. As we saw in Chapter 1, one historical view was that *only* the mother could bond with the infant sufficiently to ensure healthy development. With the advent of a great number of infants and toddlers spending the majority of their day in child care, the question of how much attachment to one consistent person an infant requires in order to develop security and trust is being studied more intensely.

Researchers have identified a secure pattern of attachment and three insecure patterns (Ainsworth 1978; Main and Solomon 1990):

1. Secure attachment—when the infant uses a parent as a secure base, strongly prefers the parent over a stranger, actively seeks contact with the parent, and is easily comforted by the parent after being absent.
2. Avoidant attachment—when the infant is usually not distressed by parental separation, and may avoid parent or prefer a stranger when parent returns.
3. Resistant attachment—when the infant seeks closeness to the parent and resists exploring the environment, usually displays angry behavior after the parent returns, and is difficult to comfort.
4. Disoriented attachment—when the infant shows inconsistent attachment and reacts to the parent returning with confused/contradictory behavior (looking away when held or dazed facial expression).

A related characteristic to attachment is separation anxiety which appears to be a normal developmental experience since children from every culture exhibit it. Infants from various cultures all over the world have been found to exhibit separation anxiety starting around six months and increasing in intensity until approximately 15 months (Kagan et al. 1978). Separation anxiety is exhibited in securely attached infants, as well as different types of insecurely attached infants.

A summary of the research to date on infant attachment suggest that infants are actively involved in the attachment bond. Drastic changes in family circumstances detrimentally affect infant attachment such as divorce, death, or job loss, and babies are normally capable of attaching securely to more than one adult or parent. Caregiving that is supportive and sensitive to the child's needs using the 3A's promotes secure attachment, and insensitive or inconsistent care results in insecure attachment. Finally, secure infant attachment and continuity of caregiving is related to later cognitive, emotional, and social competence.

Several important implications for caregiving, parenting, and recent changes in father and mother roles result from these findings. The trend toward working mothers places more importance on fathers, other family members, and child care specialists to provide secure and consistent attachment and bonding with infants. Research on attachment security of infants with full-time working mothers suggests that most infants of employed mothers are securely attached, and while some studies report a difference between day care and home-reared children, not all studies report a difference (Roggman, et al. 1994). Since family circumstances have been shown to affect infant attachment, the stress level of the mother may partly explain differences (Owen and Cox 1988).

The question of whether fathers are capable of bonding and establishing secure attachment with infants has been positively answered by research. In 1978, Allison Clark Stewart published a landmark study which observed children at fifteen, twenty, and thirty months of age alone with their fathers, alone with their mothers, and with both parents present. Both unstructured or natural observations as well as structured or limited-choice situations were arranged. The major findings showed that children were equally attached to both parents, responded more to play initiated by their fathers in structured situations, and to their mothers under natural conditions. A major outcome of this study was the understanding that fathers affect their children directly and indirectly through the children's mother.

In 1992, Parke and Tinsley reported that social class made no difference in the fathers' response to their newborns, nor did attending childbirth classes. All the fathers studied looked at, touched, talked to, and kissed their newborns as much as their mother.

In 1992, Cox reported that, as with caregiving mothers, the more contact fathers have with their children, the more positively the relationship is affected.

Also in 1992, Laura Berk reported that, among the Aka hunters and gatherers of Central Africa, fathers devote more time to infant care than in any other known society. Husbands and wives are extremely close as they share hunting, food preparation, and social activities. The more they are together, the more the father bonds and forms attachment with the children.

In 1997, Laura Berk stated, "Fathers' affectional bonds with their babies are just as emotionally intense as mothers'." When interacting with infants, mothers devote more time to physical care and expression of affection and fathers devote more time to stimulating playful interactions.

It appears that, as the economic situation has brought mothers out of the home, the need for father's to be more involved in direct care has increased, and that fathers are capable of providing the kind of bonding and secure attachment that young children require to develop normally.

However, there are fewer fathers in American families today than there ever has been, including during World Wars I and II. Alarming statistics regarding the shrinking presence of fathers in families are presented by David Blankenhorn in *Fatherless America* who states; "Tonight, about 40 percent of American children will go to sleep in homes in which their fathers do not live." According to Blankenhorn, the importance of the father role in child care and development has been diminished to the point where even public and political figures have no difficulty openly admitting lack of responsibility for offspring. While Blankenhorn offers twelve proposals to reverse the trend of absent fathers, nowhere in the research presented or in solutions offered is the idea that fathers must take a more direct nurturing, bonding, or hands-on approach to parenting. In fact, in the definition of "The Good Family Man" which was derived from in-depth interviews with over 200 fathers, there is no direct mention of the need for fathers to nurture or directly participate in the daily hands-on care of young children.

One major outcome of the changing roles of mothers and fathers is that the primary care of infants and toddlers is becoming more the responsibility of child care specialists than parents, and yet the research clearly shows that infants need a strong and consistent bond with their parents in order to develop healthy self-concepts, and the trust and security necessary to form loving relationships as adults.

The child care program with the child care specialist, then, is the only place in society in a position to help parents and young children form and maintain healthy attachments. This can best be accomplished through child care programs ensuring that each infant and toddler have as few caregivers as possible who provide consistency and predictability over time. The second half of this awesome responsibility is to provide parent and family support and training to help parents form and maintain secure attachments with their children. Parent education should include the importance of fathers and other family members providing direct nurturing and caring of the children so that mothers can work and still have loving and healthy relationships with their children.

Caregiver behaviors which ensure consistent and secure bonding and attachment with infants and toddlers are the 3A's of child care. Child care specialists who fully understand the 3A's, use them effectively with children, and systematically model and teach parents to use them with their children, do more than any other present force in society to ensure emotional security for infants and toddlers.

THE 3A'S PART I: THE OUTWARD EXPRESSION

Attention

"Smile and the whole world smiles with you." We've often been put at ease when greeted by a stranger's smile or felt instant rapport with someone when he or she has returned our smile. So much is communicated without words; often the unspoken message reflects the exact meaning of how a person is feeling. When we realize that 70 percent of our total communication is nonverbal, it is easily understood why a smile says so much.

A smile is a way to attend to yourself and to someone else. When you bring attention to a behavior in another person, the behavior increases in frequency simply because you are paying attention to it. Whatever behaviors are attended to, whether good or bad, desired or undesired, increase in frequency. When you tell children they have done a good job, they seem to try harder the next time. The same is true of negative behaviors. When you label a child as bad, you will likely observe more bad behaviors in that child. The power of attention is remarkable.

Specific techniques for increasing positive behavior are discussed in a later chapter.

Approval

Approval from others teaches us to approve of ourselves. The best type of attention is approval. Approval of another person is a clear message to that person that you have positive regard for him or her. To children, approval says they have done something right and it helps them feel worthwhile. Approval builds trust and self-confidence, which in turn encourages children to try new things without fear. The most important concept a caregiver must learn is to always approve of the child, even when you disapprove of his or her behavior. For example, it must be made clear to the child that I like who you are, but not what you are doing right now.

Appropriate and consistent approval develops trust in the child. Once a sense of trust is developed, children can readily approve of themselves. According to Erickson's eight stages of man, the general state of trust suggests that one has learned to "rely on the sameness and continuity of the other providers, but also that one may trust oneself. . . ." (Erickson 1963).

Trust depends not only on the quantity (how many times you do a task), but also on the quality of the caregiver's relationship with the child. The caregiver's positive approval creates a sense of trust as a result of the sensitive way in which the caregiver takes time to care for the child's individual needs. Adults must convey to the child an honest concern for the child's welfare, and a deep conviction that there is meaning in what they are doing. Trust based on consistent positive caring allows the child to grow up with a sense of meaningful belonging and trust.

Affection

It is hard to describe a smile and the feeling that an approving smile generates without also recognizing that affection is generally felt by the people involved. Whether they are the sender or receiver of the smile, an approving smile communicates warmth and affection (see Figure 3–1). Gentle touching, kind words, compliments, and accepting eye contact are all ways in which people express affection.

When a caregiver masters the skill of giving attention to appropriate behaviors and communicating unconditional approval of the child, affection will be a natural outcome. There is no greater outward expression you can use than a combination of all 3A's when the child is trying to do what you expect. No clearer physical or emotional message can be given. To smile, hug, and verbally approve in a sincere way is the greatest motivator of positive behavior available to you.

In addition to creating a positive learning environment by increasing appropriate behavior in children, all 3A's used together can effectively promote self-health in the caregiver. The following discussion is taken from a lecture series entitled *Caregiver Self-Health* (Douville-Watson 1988).

Figure 3–1 Smiles communicate the 3A's.

DEFINITION OF CAREGIVER SELF-HEALTH

We define self-health as having the inner resources necessary for sustained energy. This sustained energy, as well as other skills you will learn in the chapter, will give you the tools necessary to continue to provide the high quality of child care you desire throughout the day.

The direction of attention in self-health does not go outside of you—it stays within you. You "attend" to yourself. The way to do this is simple, and you already do it even though you have not been aware of it. It is necessary to learn to be still, to be without motion, to indulge in quiet within yourself, and to create for yourself a place of peace. This special place is available to you whenever you "need a second to think," want to "get yourself together," or are trying to "be on center."

The following exercise will help you organize your inner self. With practice, you can provide all the self-nourishment needed to support your daily routine without the plague of "exhaustion." Practice this exercise at home after you have had a relaxing bath or shower:

1. Choose a quiet place where you can arrange to have no interruptions for at least a half hour.
2. Get comfortable. Many people sit on a pillow on the floor or in a chair, with their feet flat on the floor in front of them.
3. Close your eyes.
4. Breathe deeply through your nose (if possible) and try to consciously pull the air up from your lower abdomen without moving your shoulders. Take long, slow breaths that have a wave-like rhythm to them.
5. Stay in this posture. Try to avoid thinking about anything. Tell your mind to help keep your body quiet. Make your stomach into a "balloon" as you inhale.
6. Try to imagine a quiet, peaceful place that you know, perhaps a place where you've vacationed or felt safe when you were a child. Try to recreate this place in your mind. Visualize (with your eyes closed) what it looks like. Smell the special odors associated with this place. Feel the air move around you. Hear the noises as they gently pass your ears. Listen for the familiar sounds. Be with your "self." Be with yourself in your special place. Enjoy you!

This exercise is called attending. When you attend to yourself, you visit your inner self. You can learn to do this inward attending in a very short time. You can use this technique during a hectic work day to refuel yourself. When you have practiced using this tool at work during lunch time or on your short breaks, add this self-affirming inventory before returning to work: (1) I am ready to help; (2) I have the best interests of the child in mind; and (3) I am willing to be involved with their concerns now. This will help you redirect your energy back to the children.

Child care is hard work. It is also extremely rewarding, but as in any occupation, it can sometimes be stressful. The stress you encounter, however, can largely be avoided. In fact, low stress is healthy and high stress does not add anything useful to any situation.

Dr. Phil Neurnberger is one of the top corporate trainers in the country. For years he has been a model of a person who applies self-health techniques. In his latest book, *The Quest for Personal Power: Transforming Stress into Strength* (1996), he states, "We are the source of our own stress. Stress never happens to us; stress is our reaction to the things that happen to us. . . . No stress is necessary . . . when the mind is disturbed, that disturbance is reflected in our environment, in our social relationships, and in our bodies. A balanced, healthy mind, in charge of its power and resources, creates a healthy body and a healthy environment. On the other hand, an unbalanced, disturbed mind creates disturbances at all levels. To create a healthy body, a healthy environment, and a healthy culture, we must become masters of the subtle thoughts and emotions of our own minds." We are also responsible for our own state of ease.

The 3A's deal with the caregiver's self-care and self-health. Once the caregiver understands and practices these techniques, the experience generalizes into the care of the children. Only after caregivers take responsibility to care for themselves are they ready to deal with the needs of children. The fact is, you cannot give what you do not have. This is a basic premise of this book. The personal resources of the caregiver are monumentally important for successful outcomes with children.

Another basic premise of this book is that caregiving is a partnership between the adult and child. No one wants a partnership that is exhausting, draining, and without rewards. No healthy person can make a real commitment to such a relationship. That is why these techniques are essential for the caregiver. Take care of yourself so you have the resources to have your day centered on the child.

The outward expression of the 3A's uses Attention, Approval, and Affection as actual humanistic tools to help each child experience the commitment to your partnership. The most essential aspect of successful caregiving is the commitment to yourself in the care of children. By integrating yourself into your daily activities, you are able to begin to make the child in your care the primary focus of your work.

THE 3A'S PART II: THE INWARD EXPRESSION

Attention

The direction of attention in self-health does not go outside of you: it stays within you. You "attend" to yourself. An accepted and proven way to bring attention to yourself is to develop the skill of meditation. Meditation can either be a quiet exercise that you do by yourself in a quiet environment, or it can be an active, awake exercise that you incorporate into your daily activity as a way of focusing your positive intention on what you are doing at the time. Both forms of meditation are extremely helpful rejuvenators. Both are examples of inward expression of Attention and Self-Health.

Other wellness experts agree on the benefits of meditation. Jon Kabat-Zinn states the following: "In meditation, the breath functions as an anchor for our attention. Tuning in to it anywhere, we feel it in the body. It allows us to drop below the surface agitations of the mind into relaxation, calmness and stability . . . when we shift our attention to the breath for a moment."

"In meditation, the active mind is withdrawn to its source; just as this changing universe had to have a source beyond change, your mind, with all its restless activity, arises from a state of awareness beyond thought, sensation, emotion, desire and memory . . . in place of change or loss . . . there is a steadiness and you have a feeling of fullness" (Deepak Chopra 1993).

Bernie Seigel, world renowned wellness expert, writes about meditation in *Love Medicine and Miracles*; "I know of no other single activity that by itself can produce such great improvements in the quality of life."

The following is another exercise that will help you to organize your inner self. With practice you can provide all the self-nourishment needed to support your daily routine. Conscious caregiving requires you to take the opportunity to rest, breath, and relax. A simple and restorative tool to accomplish this is to use a Vivona Relaxation Technique (Vivona 1997). All you need is three minutes to focus your mind, your thoughts, and clear your mind:

1. Place yourself in a quiet area and focus your thoughts on yourself.
2. Clear your mind of problems.
3. Breathe deeply.
4. Use hypoallergenic hand cream and gently massage each finger, palm, and hand.
5. Continue focusing your thoughts on what you're doing, and how it feels for three minutes.
6. Stay in this posture. Try to avoid thinking about anything. Tell your mind to help keep your body quiet. If your thoughts begin again, recenter yourself by concentrating on your breathing.

Approval

The inward self-expression of approval is a second tool to use for improving self-health. When you listen to yourself quietly, you sometimes hear things you do not want to hear, and phrases that make you feel bad or unworthy, such as "You should have done this or that better." These useless phrases that you hear when you are quiet rob you of power to further your best interests. These outdated expressions accumulate in your brain over a lifetime. Although many people do not talk about it, the same thing happens to every adult human being. What we experience is simply an accumulation of old phrases that other people used, with good intentions, to control or to protect us in the past.

These outdated messages are there for us to master. "You talk" must be replaced by language that helps you identify what you need. Self-approval begins with an honest relationship with yourself. Self-health begins with understanding what you are feeling, the relevance of your feelings, and the conscious direction of your energy. Stopping the "you talk" begins with learning to witness what your mind is chattering about. You learn to observe this chatter by visualizing it as if you are at the movies. Let it go. Don't be involved with it. Say the words "cancel" or "stop." Then consciously let go of it. When you watch this process, you become aware of how much your mind wants to hang on to old messages. You simply say these phrases, "Go away. I don't need you now that I am an adult."

The next step is to change your inside talk to "I messages." "I messages" begin with statements like, "I want," "I feel," "I need." These are more relevant to your present needs, and are useful in your work of self-care. When you take responsibility for your own needs, you gain self-acceptance and approval. The way to gain self approval is to install new, conscious "You messages" that completely support and agree with the "I messages". For example, if you use the I message, "I want to succeed", self-approval will result when that I message is immediately followed by a conscious supportive you statement such as "You will succeed; You have the right to do well and can do well."

With a little daily practice at making I statements and conscious supportive you statements, you will begin to feel the confidence and security that comes from self-approval. When you can replace old you statements with I messages and supportive you statements, you will in turn be able to help children interpret their environment from this perspective, teaching them to say "I need," "I want," "I feel," when it is purposefully relevant to do so. Your voice then becomes part of the inside talk of young children; positive inside talk. They will use this to build their own foundation of the "self," as we see in this quote: "The crying child who is comforted begins to realize that she is not alone with her private experiences. She begins to realize that they are expressed to others and can be shared with them. Here is the cornerstone of the social structuring of experience that we call the self'" (Cahill 1990, p. 2).

These exercises will help you approve of yourself more openly. It is okay to recognize and state your worthwhileness out loud and congratulate yourself for a job well done. When you are able to praise yourself, you will more easily be able to praise others. "At the same time children create, differentiate, and individuate themselves, they come to understand themselves in the mirror of what others have constructed as a world" (Wartofsky 1983).

Affection

Affection is the natural outcome of positive attention and approval. Self-affection comes from the belief that we have the right to take care of ourselves and have our needs filled. Affection for yourself is a good example of self-health. It is a result of acknowledged self-attention and self-approval. It is the positive energy that comes from being able to affectionately relate to yourself and others, to have a sense of being worthy to give and receive, and to nurture and accept being nurtured by others.

The 3A's of child care—Attention, Approval, and Affection—are powerful tools. The outward and inward approach to expression will help you become actively aware and you will be motivated by your positive intentions to use them first with yourself and then teach them to your children.

USING THE 3A'S SUCCESSFULLY WITH INFANTS AND TODDLERS

The 3A's of child care are progressive work; a process in action. In all likelihood, you use the 3A's already without much thought about it. The 3A's are powerful and rejuvenating. They elicit responses in children that will sustain you in your vocation. When you learn to use self-health techniques with inward expression and understand your outward expression, you shape positive behaviors in children.

Observe your initial approach to an unknown infant. You get down to their level (floor, blanket, or chair), are calm, move slowly, make eye contact, enter their space, get even closer to them physically, smile, and gently begin some soft speech to engage them. If you believe you have permission from them to stay close, you keep eye contact and begin slowly to inquire as to what they are doing such as playing or eating. When they gesture, you follow the gesture with a similar response, this time making a sound that seems to identify their movement and keep pace with them. This usually elicits a smile, or giggle. Once again you smile and make noise. You may try gently touching a shoulder or finger, and before long, you are accepted as an approving addition to the child's space. This slow progression of rapport-building is also the slow progression of the use of the 3A's. First you give Attention, then Approval, and then Affection. Done consciously, both child and caregiver reap the benefits. All involved feel worthy of Attention, Approval, and Affection.

One of the most positive assurances of worthiness a caregiver can receive on a daily basis is that almighty hug given unconditionally as a gift from the gleeful toddler who sweeps down upon you when you are playing on the floor. This hug, which is often accompanied by a loud and joyful sound, enters your space with such focused positive energy that each of you feels the impact. The result of this positive energy is felt by the two of you, and brings out smiles on the faces of all who observe it.

Young children benefit from these important techniques. These tools help to shape the child's development as it relates to mastery. Mastery is related to a child's sense of well-being, self-achievement, and eventual self-esteem. Being aware of the tools available through the use of the 3A's helps encourage children to master their environment. Your outward expression of the 3A's helps build the child's inward development of what is called the self. Your patient, consistent use of these tools on a daily basis is what forms the child's inner self and places those inner voices there for their protection.

The language that is successful for you, the "I messages" and "You messages", and your use of inner approval is what will be an outward expression of your work with (and love of) children. Your interactions on a daily basis will become part of the inner voices each child hears. Therefore you must pay careful attention to the messages you send. Your help in interpreting the environment in a positive way, your encouragement and approval, and your affection and use of the "I message" becomes part of the child. The more you are able to be yourself, bring yourself to the child care setting, and integrate yourself with your work, the more able children will develop positive self-concepts.

Your ability to create a positive learning environment allows children to feel safe, to gather information, and eventually to trust their senses for information about their world. All young children register their experiences through their senses. Their physical sense of hot-cold-touch-smell-hearing-and-sight is easily seen. Erickson, in writing about autonomy, discusses the infant's ability to emotionally evaluate his worth as "a series of alternate basic attitudes such as trust vs. mistrust in terms of sense of' as sense of health' or sense of being unwell.'" Young children rely on their senses.

Think of yourself as a recharging station—a physically and emotionally rewarding place where children feel a sense of security. The field of bioenergetics refers to these senses as part of our Human Energy Field, and states that we give off energy and in turn "sense" each other's energy. Using the exercises already discussed allows you to keep your energy centered and positive, so you can bring that positive energy to the children in your care.

Barbara Brennan, in her book *Hands of Light*, speaks of energy as measurable and existing in all of us as the Human Energy Field. She states that "the Universal Energy Field is like a Cornucopia always continuing to create more energy" (Brennan 1989)(see Figure 3–2).

Delores Krieger talks about PRANA, the ancient name of the Universal Energy Source, when she teaches professionals at New York University to use energy to promote healing in hospital patients. In her book *The Therapeutic Touch*, she states: "Conceive of the healer as an individual whose health gives him access to an over-abundance of PRANA and whose strong sense of commitment and intention to help ill people gives him or her certain control over the projection of this vital energy" (Delores Krieger 1992).

The ability to help people by using this Human Energy Field is scientifically supported. So, as a child care specialist you can utilize these modern concepts to develop a strong sense of commitment and intention to help yourself and your children in child care settings. You can use the 3A's to create a positive learning environment and use the inward-focused skills to express appreciation of yourself and the vital impact you have on the children in your care.

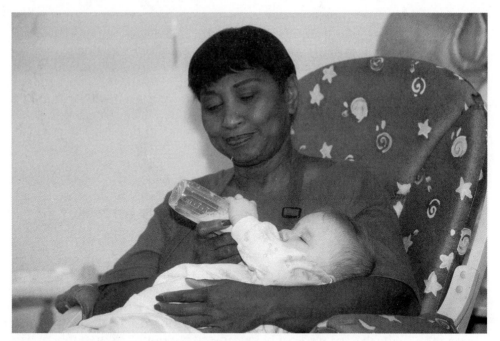

Figure 3–2 Children gravitate toward the caregiver's "Circle of Energy" to rest.

In summary, the healthiest relationships result in the experience of security and happiness most of the time. The best possible connection between caregiver and infant comes from each person being actively involved in the relationship, expressing and receiving a positive exchange.

When the 3A's are focused on children, they promote appropriate behaviors and enhance a positive learning environment for children. The caregiver structures a safe place in which the young child explores and masters all of his or her growing abilities by solving problems that naturally occur within the environment. A stable, positive environment promotes trust and confidence and allows the growing infant to express all of his or her needs.

When the 3A's are focused on self, they promote self-health, personal growth, and development of the caregiver. These skills help you to be more aware of your impact on children, and revitalize you so that you can sustain a high quality of care throughout the day. The knowledge you have learned promotes trust and ultimately teaches children, by your example, to be self-confident and have trust in themselves. The challenge presented to caregivers centers on their ability to maintain their own sense of well-being while caring for children (Gilligan 1982; Hochschild 1983).

Using the 3A's allows the children to experience the environment as a safe place to express needs, and to believe that expressing all emotion is healthy. This ability to express emotion without fear promotes a healthy, happy, well-balanced individual who feels competent to handle life's challenges.

STUDENT ACTIVITIES

1. Practice attending exercises for self-health two times this week, and take notes about your reactions.
2. Two times during the day, allow yourself five minutes to perform revitalizing exercises.
3. Apply all 3A's to two separate children, and write down their reactions.
4. List why the 3A's of self-health might affect your personal life in general.
5. Write a scenario using examples of the ways in which the 3A's might calm children and promote a positive learning environment.

CHAPTER REVIEW

1. List the 3A's of child care.
2. What is the difference between giving attention to children and attending to your inner self?
3. How do you go about approving of yourself?
4. Why is using all of the 3A's together a powerful tool for motivating children?
5. Why would learning skills to revitalize yourself help you fight off exhaustion during your day?
6. Define meditation, relaxation, self-health, and self-care.
7. What is the most important aspect of this chapter for you?

REFERENCES

Ainsworth, M. D. S., Blehar, M., Waters, E., and Wall, S. 1978. *Patterns of Attachment.* Hillsdale, NJ: Erlbaum.

Blankenhorn, D. G. 1995. *Fatherless America.* New York: HarperCollins Publishers.

Bowman, B. 1989. *Self-Reflection as an Element of Professionalism.* Teachers College Records, 90 (3), 444–51.

Brennan, B. A. 1989. *Hands of Light: A Guide to Healing Through the Human Energy Field.* New York: Bantam Books.

Chopra, D., M.D. 1993. *Ageless Body, Timeless Mind Harmony.* New York: Bantam Books.

Clarke-Stewart, K. A. 1978 Recasting the lone stranger. In *The Development of Social Understanding*, eds. J. Glick and K. A. Clarke-Stewart, pp. 109–76). New York: Gardner Press.

Cox, M. J., Owen, M. T., Henderson, V. K., and Margand, N. A. 1992. Prediction of infant-father and infant-mother attachments. *Developmental Psychology* 28:474–83.

Denzin, N. K. 1984. *On Understanding Emotion.* San Francisco: Jossey Bass.

Dewey, J. 1938. *Experience and Education.* New York: Macmillan.

Douville-Watson, L. 1988. Child care lecture series, *Caregiver Self-Health*. Oyster Bay, New York: Lifeskills Institute.

Douville-Watson, L. 1988. Child care lecture series, *The 3A's of Child Care: Attention, Approval and Affection*. Oyster Bay, New York: Lifeskills Institute.

Douville-Watson, L. 1995. Child care lecture series, *Concerned Conscious Care: The 3A's in Action*. Instructional Press, 21 Oakshore Dr., Bayville, NY 11709

Douville-Watson, L., and Watson, M. 1988. *Family Actualization Through Research & Education: F.A.R.E.*, Third Edition. New York: Actualization, Inc.

Erickson, E. H. 1963. The eight stages of man. In *Childhood & Society*. New York: W. W. Norton.

Gilligan, C. 1988. Remapping the moral domain: New images of self in relationship. In *Mapping the Moral Domain*, eds. C. Gilligan, J. Ward, J. Taylor, and B. B. Pardige, pp. 3–19. Cambridge, MA: Harvard University Press.

Hatch, J. A. 1995. *Qualitative Research in Early Childhood Settings*. Stamford, CT: Praeger Publishers.

Healy, J. 1988. *Your Child's Growing Mind*. New York: Doubleday.

Kabat-Zinn, J., Ph.D. 1991. *Full Catastrophe Living: Using the Wisdom of Your Body and Mind to Face Stress, Pain and Illness*. New York: Bantam Doubleday.

Kagan, J., Kearsley, R. B., and Zelazo, P. R. 1978. *Infancy: Its Place in Human Development*. Cambridge, MA: Harvard University Press.

Kreiger, D. 1992. *The Therapeutic Touch: How to Use Your Hands to Help or to Heal*. New York: Prentice-Hall.

Owen, M. T., and Cox, M. J. 1988. Maternal employment and the transition to parenthood. In *Maternal Employment and Children's Development: Longitudinal Research*, eds. A. E. Gottfried and A. W. Gottfried, p. 850119. New York: Plenum.

Main, M., and Soloman, J. 1990. Procedures for identifying infants as disorganized/disoriented during the Ainsworth Strange Situation. In *Attachment in the Preschool Years: Theory, Research, and Intervention*, eds. M. Greenberg, D. Cicchetti, and M. Cummings, pp. 121–60.

Neurnberger, P. 1996. *The Quest for Personal Power Transforming Stress Into Strength*. New York: G. P. Putnam Brothers.

Pawl, J. 1990. Infants in day care: Reflections on experience, expectation and relationships. *Zero to Three* 10 (3):1–6.

Riback, P. 7–97. *Health Kids K–111* New York: Magazine Corp.

Roggman, L. A., Langlois, J. H., Hubbs-Tait, L., and Rieser-Danner, L. A. 1994. Infant day-care, attachment, and the "file drawer problem." *Child Development* 65, pp. 1429–43.

Saarni, C. 1989. Children's understanding and strategic control of emotional expression in social transactions. In *Children's Understanding of Emotion*, eds. C. Saarni and P. L. Harris, pp. 181–208. New York: Cambridge University.

Siegel, B. 1988. *Love, Medicine and Miracles*. New York: Bantam Press.

Snow, C. 1989. *Infant Development*. Englewood Cliffs, NJ: Prentice-Hall.

Vivona, L. A. 1997. *Stress and the Art of Living: A Three Minute Relaxation and Focusing Exercise*. Bayville, NY: Vivona Trainings.

4

Characteristics of Caregiving and Teaching

OBJECTIVES

After completing this chapter, the child development specialist should be able to:

1. Understand what is meant by conscious care of children.
2. Understand the terms Changing of the Guard, Shadowing, Ruing, Mastery, the Outcome of Using the 3A's, Positive Perspective, and Your Work.
3. Understand organizational skills such as child specialist strategies, observing and recording, assessing the child specialist, assessing children, behavior, advocacy, and community resources.
4. Understand personal goals for caregiving.
5. Understand responsibilities of the child specialist's role
6. Understand responsibilities for continued growth and the commitment to competence.

CHAPTER OUTLINE

 I. Personal Characteristics of Competent Child Care Specialists: Relating to Self
    A. Child Specialist Health and Awareness
 II. Relating to Infants and Toddlers
III. Acquiring Knowledge
    A. About Yourself
    B. About Children
    C. About Parents
    D. About Child Care Specialists' Roles
    E. About Program Implementation
    F. About Caregiving Duties
    G. About Materials
IV. Conscious Caregiving

A.   Children's Needs and Conscious Care
V.   Mastery: The Outcome of Using the 3A's Through the Attention Process
   A.   The Approval Process
VI.   Positive Perspective
VII. Your Work
VIII. Practical Concepts: Child Care Specialists' Behaviors and Strategies
   A.   Affective Education
   B.   Expression of Feelings in Healthy Ways
   C.   Observing and Recording
   D.   Record Keeping
   E.   Assessing
   F.   Organizing
   G.   Managing
IX.   Community Resources
X.   Professional Preparation of the Caregiver

CHILD DEVELOPMENT ASSOCIATE FUNCTIONAL AREAS

I.   1 Safe
I.   2 Healthy
II. 4 Physical
II. 5 Cognitive
II. 6 Communication
II. 7 Creative
III. 8 Self
III. 9 Social
III. 10 Guidance
IV. 11 Families
V.   12 Program Management
VI. 13 Professionals

PERSONAL CHARACTERISTICS OF COMPETENT CHILD CARE SPECIALISTS: RELATING TO SELF

Child Specialist Health and Awareness

Physical health is necessary to provide the high energy level needed in caregiving. Good health is also necessary to resist the variety of illnesses to which you are exposed. The importance of a healthy staff is reflected in the American Academy of Pediatric's recommendations (1996) that the health record for each employee contains:

1. Evidence of freedom from active tuberculosis and an annual report of tuberculosis negative mantoux test;
2. Evidence of pre-employment examination or statement from the personal physician indicating a health status permitting the employee to function in his or her assigned role;

3. Evidence of recovery after specified communicable diseases;
4. Reports of periodic evaluations.

In addition, Hepatitis B vaccine injections are recommended, but not mandated, for employees in most states. You also need to discern whether your body is at ease. The body registers small concerns which tell you it has specific needs, and can be used to help you stay in balance. Listening to the physical feelings and signals that your body gives is called body awareness.

Child Care Specialists are Mentally Healthy. In your daily relationships, you must provide physical closeness and nurture for an extended time, give emotionally more than you receive, be patient to resolve conflicts caused by someone else, and calm one child right after you have been frustrated with another. Emotionally stable child specialists have learned how to handle a variety of emotional demands in their daily experiences and encourage greater mental health in others (see Figure 4–1).

Child Care Specialists have a Positive Self-Image. Your feelings of self-confidence and positive self-worth show that you believe in yourself. This gives you the strength to take risks, consider alternatives, and make decisions in situations where there may be no obvious correct answer.

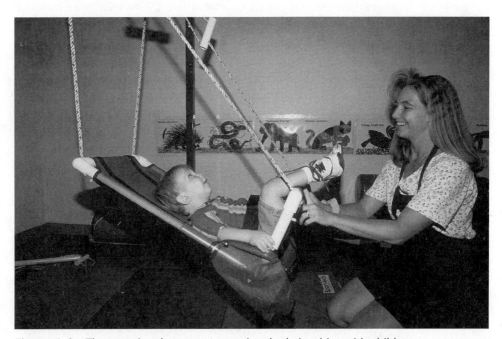

Figure 4–1 The caregiver has warm, emotional relationships with children.

Child Care Specialists have a Commitment to Excellence. Striving to do your best is essential for high-quality caregiving. Read, study, visit, observe, and talk with other child specialists. Your motivation and knowledge improves excellence.

Child Care Specialists are Caring. There is pleasure, enjoyment, and satisfaction in providing effective, high-quality care. Although some tasks may be difficult, unpleasant, or repetitious, overall caregiving should produce satisfaction every day (see Figure 4–2). The child specialist reflects caring feelings to the children, parents, and to other staff members. Positive feelings help build good team rapport.

Child Care Specialists are Professionals. Caregiving is a respected and essential profession. You provide a very important service to children, parents, and the community. The care you provide directly affects children at critical times in their lives. You have great influence and importance in the child's life and are rational and objective in your decisions and actions.

Child Care Specialists are Open-Minded. Your perceptions, common sense, and opinions are sources of information you can use in evaluating situations and making decisions. Awareness of your expectations and those of children help you remain open. Openly listening, thinking, and learning from the ideas and opinions of others helps to increase continued growth.

Child Care Specialists Enjoy Learning. It is not possible to finish learning everything you need to know to be an effective child care specialist. New information and experiences lead to new insights, understanding, and skills.

Figure 4–2 The caregiver develops skill in working with children and gains satisfaction from interacting with them.

Openness to learning helps you seek new ideas and take advantage of new opportunities to expand your knowledge and skills.

RELATING TO INFANTS AND TODDLERS

Child Care Specialists Care About and Enjoy Infants and Toddlers. You share joy in the child's attempts and accomplishments. You show concern for the child's well-being by planning, playing, listening, comforting, and providing physical and emotional closeness.

Child Care Specialists Respect Children. Each child is worthy of your respect. Your accepting behavior and considerate treatment shows that you consider each child to be an individual who is an important person.

Child Care Specialists Make Adjustments. Good interpersonal relationships call for give and take. Close daily contact requires an attitude of giving, adjusting, and receiving.

ACQUIRING KNOWLEDGE

About Yourself

Why do you want to be a child care specialist? What are your strengths? What are your weaknesses? What is your temperament? What are your interests? What are your values? What are your expectations of yourself and others? Are you willing to put forth effort to satisfy yourself and others? How much time and effort do you think is appropriate to put into caregiving? What plans do you have to learn about yourself, others, and your program?

About Children

Child development research continues to provide new information about children. The information helps identify each child's individual characteristics and levels of development. Knowledge of patterns of physical, emotional, social, and cognitive development influence how you plan for and act with children.

About Parents

Each family situation is unique and affects your caregiving. You should continually seek information from and maintain communication with parents. Parents have special needs, desires, and expectations of themselves, their children, and you.

About Child Care Specialists' Roles

The term caregiving encompasses emotional interaction, instructional planning, and various types of teaching and learning techniques involving children, parents, the community, and other staff. You need to balance many roles to provide high-quality care. Understanding the responsibilities of each role will help determine your strengths and how to increase knowledge and personal growth. Utilizing all aspects of self-health ensures stamina and the ability to provide consistent high-quality care.

About Program Implementation

There are many successful ways to nurture, provide care, and teach. Knowledge of these can help you adjust and individualize caregiving procedures to meet the specific needs of the environment and the children you serve.

About Caregiving Duties

Basic knowledge about children, parents, staff, and programs are foundations for good caregiving. High-quality caregiving occurs when you have clearly defined goals and tasks. Written goals, plans, and tasks keep your duties clear.

About Materials

Child care specialists must identify which materials are appropriate for various developmental levels of children. Collect materials and information from staff and resources in the community to add value to your program.

CONSCIOUS CAREGIVING

In Chapter 3, you learned about the importance of your ability to use all aspects of the 3A's. Being consciously aware of what you do with children is essential to reaping the emotional benefits of caring and not becoming exhausted. Your experiences vary and how you manage children of different ages also varies.

You are a child's first line of defense within the environment. You must be clear-headed and use all your senses to communicate with very young children. They depend on you for their survival, are unable to care for themselves, and try to communicate their needs. You must learn about how each child in your care is unique. You must learn to be a detective in order to solve the question, "What does this child need now?"

You may be familiar with the following concepts of Changing of the Guard, The Circle of Safety, Shadowing, or Ruing, although you may have called them by other names. The reason examples are given below is to associate these names with children for whom you care. They are concepts to help keep children safe, and to recognize your own important role as a child care specialist. Mastery, the Outcome of Using the 3A's, applies to children of all ages. These examples will take on greater meaning as you become more experienced. The example of "Your Work" will have continued meaning as you gradually attain and develop a conscious skill base, and progress through your career.

Children's Needs and Conscious Care

An important premise of this text is that all children function from a need base, and there should be no judgment placed on needs. There is often a difference between what a child needs and how he or she behaves. Children behave in certain ways because their needs were met when they behaved that way in the past. Therefore, children simply behave in the way their limited experience has taught them. Needs are conveyed as information, so children give you information to help them. If children seem demanding, cry loudly, or are easily upset, their experience may have been that their needs were not fulfilled quickly, and they fear not having their needs met at all.

It is not good for anyone to feel needy. When environmental conditions remain constant, children continue to behave as they have in the past to get their needs met. You, as a child care specialist, are important because you have the power to positively affect this child's environment by providing a deliberate, kind, and purposeful response as soon as you can identify what the child needs. This promotes the child's sense of security and trust in the environment.

Child care specialists must become aware of what they do. Love of your profession is realized as you become more conscious of what you want to achieve each day with each child in care. Purposeful intent of your actions is the goal. When you purposely take action, you become consciously involved in that action. Slow movement to gain rapport, a low hum, the vibration you provide, and your help to relax a child to sleep are all part of conscious care. Increased awareness of your nonverbal communication improves the connection between you and the children in care.

The following are techniques that you may already use with children. The purpose of mentioning them here is for you to become more aware of them in your daily routine.

The Changing of the Guard.   Imagine you are a palace guard in charge of the Crown Jewels. You have been highly trained not to be distracted from your job and the specific duties you must perform. When it is time to leave your post, you cannot give this vital position to just anyone. The person taking your place must be recognized by you as having the same authority as yourself. You and the new guard verbally and formally exchange places. This is necessary so the Crown Jewels are always being watched with the same level of care and commitment.

The child care specialist is the child's first environmental defense against harm. No matter where children are, no matter what they are doing, a designated adult must be responsible to keep them safe. If two specialists have five children, each child is designated by name to a specific specialist. When, for any reason, one specialist must leave, even for a short time, responsibility for that child is turned over temporarily to another child specialist, who calls them by name and tells them that you, Ms. Jones, will be with them until Ms. Smith gets back. The children should know the replacement's name, and be told when the primary caregiver will be back. When Ms. Smith returns, she should verbalize to the children that they are once again under her supervision.

Circle of Safety—Safeguarding the Child.   Picture a circle surrounding an infant lying on his or her back. The circle should be wide enough not to impede the developing need for movement, and should be empty except for the child. The circle is a controlled environment, and you are in control of that circle. Once movement begins, the circle must move with the child, providing a continuous safe circle for him or her to exist within. The child should be able to move, stretch, and safely explore while you constantly monitor the circle.

Protecting children involves creating a circle of safety around them that exceeds their developmental ability. This ensures a secure place for them to be safe. The child in the middle should be watched to ensure he or she is all right. Do this frequently, asking yourself, "Is the child safe?" During bath time or changing, examine the child's body. Does the skin look pink and healthy? Are there bruises? What is the condition of the child's clothes? Are there hazardous materials? Are the child's clothes clean, soft, and adequate in size?

When lying a child on his or her back, check the surrounding area where the child will be placed. Is it clean, open, and roomy enough to move unimpeded? Are the borders of the circle strong enough to keep the child within the safety zone? Never underestimate their ability to reach for, or get to, an object of interest.

For toddlers, you must prepare an even larger space. Do this by pretending you are the child. Examine the environment from all angles on your hands and knees, eliminating all possible problems. Check under furniture and cushions, remove attractive articles that might break, and cover sharp edges of furniture. This expanded area is the learning environment where the child and specialist will work. Have you removed objects of danger to minimize the "no's"?

The objective in preparing the space for a growing child is to promote a positive learning environment full of choices, so a child specialist can out-think, rather than out-run, children. The specialist's energy should be used to consciously plan for the child's well-being, exploration, and mastery.

Shadowing.   Remember seeing your shadow as a child? Your shadow was with you no matter where you went. It never seemed to get in your way. It never clouded your vision, or kept you from moving ahead. Shadowing a very young child is similar. You are shadowing when you are just behind a newly mobile infant, ready to catch, but not interfering with choices or keeping him or her from exploring or mastering the environment. The child should be aware that you are there. If danger appears, or the "circle of safety" suddenly shifts, be prepared to protect the child from harm.

The words you use when shadowing children should be calm and approving to encourage mobility rather than to gain attention. Shadowing allows the child to be in control. You are there to back up the child. Your presence is known, your availability is counted on, and your permission to make choices is given. Decisions such as the direction to be taken, stops to be made, objects to be explored, and how fast or slow the pace, are made by the child. This is the best of all worlds for the child: to be safe, encouraged, supported, and in control.

Ruing.   To rue is to mourn. Ruing is calming the mournful cry sometimes heard from a young infant. Most child care specialists have heard it. It is a sorrowful cry, pitiful in nature. Often, the specialist simply does not know what to do to soothe this child.

Ruing is an active technique used to sooth an unhappy or discontented child. To rue is to hold an infant close to your heart, and vocalize a pitch that is below the sound the child is making. Make your voice somewhat louder than the child's, and bring the pitch up tonally to match the infant's tone. Continue humming while holding the child against your chest so the baby can feel the vocalization's vibration. Continue to hum, letting the infant lead your joint sound pattern. Often, the infant becomes relaxed and will rue with you. Sometimes, you can change ruing into a song.

MASTERY: THE OUTCOME OF USING THE 3A'S THROUGH THE ATTENTION PROCESS

The 3A's have been discussed in terms of their usefulness for child specialist self-health, and as a structured system to promote desirable behavior in children. The following discussion adds to structuring the 3A's to help children internalize a sense of mastery, and provide a foundation for self-approving, self-talk, for the child.

Mastery is a step-by-step process with specific outcomes that can be observed and recorded. Your keen attention is necessary to know when to assist the child through this process. Patience is necessary because the process must be at the child's pace. Several attempts may be necessary over time to finish a task. Meaningful interaction between child and specialist is as important as the outcome of mastering a task.

In order to work with children, you must first gain their attention, then maintain it throughout the process. Using positive intention helps you stay with the children and is usually felt by the child.

The Approval Process

The approval process is self-rejuvenating when done with honest intention. When you express honest and approving intention, the positive energy that you give children is received as a motivating force. It is often called encouragement or coaxing, or in behavior modification terms, reinforcement. It works. Your approval comes from positive intention and it motivates. Your smile, eye contact, funny faces, winks, nods, verbalizations, and vocalizations are all approving behaviors and part of the approval process.

A single approving act may engage a child. Combining your attention and approval with affection has an exciting effect on the child. Learning to gauge children's responses to progressive use of the 3A's should be an important part of goal-setting for the child.

You should encourage, praise, and approve of children's actions as they progress toward set goals. This does not have to be loud or disruptive to others, and is meant to build your relationship as the children move toward goals through this developmental process. For example, when a child indicates the desire to hold an object and together you have tried several times and finally succeed, the work is validated in a sense of achievement by your attention, approval, and affection. This builds a feeling of confidence and a willingness to try the next time when the child reaches for the same object. The child may attempt the task on his or her own, or he may look for your encouragement or help, but eventually the child will feel confident enough to succeed without your help.

Verbal praise and appropriate words of encouragement help children of all ages. Timing of when to give approval depends on the needs of the child. The child may start out wanting something, but becomes too tired to finish. If the child is too tired, the primary need must be cared for first (holding the child until he or she goes to sleep). After the primary needs have been met, children will once again bring their attention to other activities.

By observing children, a child specialist can set goals using a Developmental Prescription. This information helps to set appropriate goals. It is important for children to succeed and gain a sense of achievement and mastery. When child specialists use knowledge, approval, and affection, they help children internalize a sense of self-worth. It is important to accept and respect at what level the developing child is functioning. Respecting children for where they are developmentally is part of the approval process.

Child care specialists can also help build strong self-images for the toddlers in their care. As good role models, and by using reinforcing positive self-talk, they can build language for the child to adopt. Positive self-talk is the internalization of messages children hear about themselves from others. These messages represent how they feel about themselves, and what they are capable of over time. If the messages are positive and encouraging, the child will become confident, but if they are negative, the child feels limited in the ability to succeed. These messages become the belief system of the child and the foundation for self-concept and future success or failure.

Scaffolding is a tool for promoting positive self-talk. By building sets of ideas and demonstrating how to use them, you can promote a foundation for positive self-talk. The chart below illustrates how scaffolding works when approval sustains the infant's attention. This approval validates children's mastery of their environment. Children internalize the validation they hear and make it their own as you reduce feedback.

CHILD BEHAVIOR	SPECIALIST RESPONSE	OUTCOME
1. Eyes object	Observes child	Specialist attention
2. Reaches for object	Encourages using words like "You can do it."	Approval for mastery attempt; increased child motivation
3. Looks at Specialist; tries to grasp objects again	Continues to encourage softly saying "Try again; you can do it!" Models success	Approval for mastery attempt; increased child motivation
4. Successfully grasps object	Praise, eye contact, gentle hug	Approval and affection for mastery of task
5. Smiles and shows excitement—brings object to mouth	Says "Nice job! I knew you could do it!"	Validation of mastery

Older children can be encouraged to verbalize "I'm a good boy," and the child specialist can affirm this by saying, "Yes, you're a good boy," thereby supporting positive self-talk.

POSITIVE PERSPECTIVE (Formally Known as Positive Propaganda)

As discussed in Chapter 1, Uric Bronfenbrenner's third party example uses Positive Perspective. "Positive Propaganda can be used in any child care situation to benefit the child's sense of well-being, and help formulate a foundation for self-esteem and future self-referencing for the child" (Douville-Watson 1995).

Successful relationships and social acceptance depend on developing internal controls. Children must learn to act without harming themselves, others, or the environment because they are not born with the experience for these internal controls. They need to be taught the tools to have successful, positive relationships. For the child care specialist, this includes the use of Positive Perspective. Understanding the relationship between the child care specialist and child and how you react to the child's behavior is crucial to quality child care.

One way of helping children act appropriately is to bring attention to the positive and cooperative things they do. By announcing positive behavior out loud, the child receives praise and validation from the people nearby, and will continue to do good things. When you verbalize positives about a person around another person instead of verbalizing negatives, you are promoting Positive Perspective. By combining the 3A's with Positive Perspective, the teacher strongly influences a child's behavior.

Think of Positive Perspective as another tool available to promote a positive relationship. When you use Positive Perspective, you tell the positive story to others around the child. You help give a different view of a situation than might be perceived by the children involved. For instance, you are a teacher (or provider) in a licensed group family child care center. You wait for 3-year-old Eroj to get off the bus. You have walked his 2½-year-old sister Inara to the bus stop with you. You greet Eroj with a smile and a hug. His sister is happy to see him. He has his art projects in both hands, and when he goes to hug you he drops the papers. His sister grabs them and, in the excitement of the moment she crumples one of them. Eroj becomes angry and begins to yell at his sister. She starts to cry. As you help him gather up his work, you place Inara on your hip and place your hand firmly on Eroj's shoulder. You say to him, "I'm so sorry you dropped your papers, you worked so hard on them and they are so well done (looking at papers he is showing you while walking). You should be proud of them. When we get back you can show everyone your work and then put them up on the wall if you like."

You would use Positive Perspective and continue by saying in Inara's presence, "You know, Eroj, Inara did not mean to crumple your papers. I know she would not do anything to hurt you. I know she misses you when you go to school because several times during the day she will stand by the door and say your name. I know she loves you and wants to be with you. She is just too little to act as grown up as you right now. It's just what 2½-year-olds do sometimes."

This Positive Perspective has a very specific "theme." The teacher brought Eroj information he would not have had and she deals with him in a very careful way. She greeted Eroj warmly, validated his feelings of anger and worthwhileness, soothed his sister by picking her up, and discussed the situation in front of Inara. She expressed positive observations about his relationship with his sister, telling him information he would not have unless she told him. In addition, the teacher was acting as Inara's advocate.

When the teacher told Eroj how his sister acted when he wasn't there she was using Positive Perspective. The theme or message the teacher promoted in the mind of Eroj was a positive one. The message said to him: "I am important to my sister and even when I am not with her I am missed. I am secure in my position with her because she thinks of me even though I am not there. I am loved by her." The message helps to promote a positive bond between them.

The same theme can be used as a tool with very young children. Caregivers can offer similar comfort to younger children by using statements like "Oh, I know Michael didn't mean to knock down your block pile Dori; he just lost his balance." The key to successful use of this tool is to know your child, know the facts in the situation, and frame a positive picture of the intentions and actions of the people involved.

The difference between Positive Perspective and the 3A's is that Positive Perspective influences the learning environment by telling a true story in a positive way about someone to a third party. The 3A's are used by the caregiver directly with a specific child.

The conscious use of Attention, Approval, Affection and Positive Perspective will help foster relationships with children. The relationships with your children are the core of your care. This prosocial relationship is the springboard from which children experience other relationships. The significance of many meaningful hours spent together cannot be overstated.

One of Judy Leipzig's main principles for fostering prosocial behavior is "First, develop a relationship with the child—the more loving and nurturing the better" (Leipzig 1986). Another extremely helpful reference for promoting Positive Perspective and other tools by creating prosocial environments is Alice Honig's group games (Honig 1988).

Miss Tara, a family child care provider, sits in a rocking chair in her den holding 5-month-old Marcus. Nearby, 27-month-old Clay, 15-month-old Kiera, 36-month-old Milinda, and 30-month-old Burton are playing. Miss Tara plays with Marcus, clapping his hands and laughing; Marcus looks at her and laughs. She lays him on his back on her lap, swings his arms, puts his hand in his mouth, and makes sounds. He reaches and puts his hands on Miss Tara's face, laughing and kicking his feet when she repeats his sounds. At the same time Miss Tara is also involved with the other children. She smiles at Clay, who is watching the other children; she smiles at Marcus. She points to Pooh Bear in response to Kiera's whimpers of "Bear" and she watches Shaun and Sarah sitting on the floor, with the lock blocks pail between them, as they construct objects.

Miss Audrey has her feet stretched out in front of her in the toddler room in a corporate child care center. Ryan is sitting on her lap and three other toddlers who are sitting around her are touching her with their hands or legs or leaning on her. Miss Audrey is holding a picture book, telling the story line by pointing to the pictures rather than by reading the words. She stops and asks Ryan to point to a tree. He puts his finger on a tree and Miss Audrey gives him a hug, turns him so he can see her smile, and says, "That's right, that is a tree."

Audrey's ability to "attend" to more than one child at a time is an excellent example of how the toddlers use her as a "re-charging station" as discussed in Chapter 3.

Miss Tara and Miss Audrey are consciously aware of the power of using the 3A's of Child Care effectively. They are emotionally involved with the children, providing a warm, stable, supporting, confirming relationship which helps infants and toddlers develop a healthy foundation for life. In addition to emotional needs, caregivers anticipate physical needs and respond to the children. They select enough toys to offer the children options in their choice of playthings. They prepare the room. They interact with other staff and with parents. And they plan to actively promote the children physically, emotionally, socially, and cognitively.

The caregiver is the most influential factor in determining the quality of care children receive. As a caregiver your personal characteristics and the professional responsibilities you assume powerfully affect your care of children and your relationships with parents and staff. Caregiving is a very complex task. Becoming a competent caregiver involves acquiring knowledge and developing skills in a variety of areas.

YOUR WORK

Your work with children is different from custodial care. Custodial care is simply the physical maintenance of children. Your work means applying meaning to what you do. Meaning involves consciously being emotionally present with children. It is an end toward which you direct your attention and gives form to your activity.

Your work is that for which you strive (see Figure 4–3). It is why you aspire to learn. You should not work independently with children until you are ready. This comes after the classes, the instruction, the theories, the papers, and the supervised training you receive. It comes with your growing desire to help, and it comes after you have changed your positive intention into a firm educational base of understanding. It continues because of the care you give yourself and your appreciation of even the smallest successes, because, as you work with children, you see children grow and change, and how you make a difference in their world. Your work is important because it is your way of making the world a better place, one child at a time. Your work is love of your profession.

PRACTICAL CONCEPTS: CHILD CARE SPECIALISTS' BEHAVIORS AND STRATEGIES

Eric, a four-and-a-half month old, is lying on the floor when he starts to cry. His child care specialist, Audrey, picks him up. She "eats" his tummy and he laughs. She holds him up in the air and he smiles. She gets his bottle, sits in a chair, and feeds him. Eric gazes at Audrey and smiles between sips.

Figure 4–3   The caregivers observe when the infant is able to stand with help.

Grasping her finger, he looks around the room. Audrey stands him in her lap, holds his hands to pull him to and fro, and kisses him. He laughs. She holds him while he dances and laughs. He watches Audrey's mouth and responds as she talks to him. He leans on her shoulder and burps as he fingers the afghan on the back of the chair.

The many child care specialist responsibilities are accomplished through interactions with the people and environment in the child care setting. Several educational tools are discussed below to help develop the knowledge and strategies needed to become a good observer, recorder, assessor, organizer, manager, and facilitator to support warm, emotional relationships.

Affective Education

Affective education is a process of identifying, labeling, and learning ways to express emotion. All emotions are normal and are, therefore, healthy. Expression of emotions is healthy as long as it does not hurt the person experiencing the emotion, anyone else, or property. The thoughts, feelings, and behaviors of healthy people are intergrated, and they experience all their emotions. Human beings have the right to feel good. This feeling is described as feeling at ease, whole, on center, or intact. This is the natural state of the body, which in medical terms, is homeostasis. This is a state of balance which the body strives to attain, and attempts to return to after illness or trauma. When people are conscious of this state, they are physically and emotionally aware of being on center or at ease with themselves. This is the feeling we want to promote in children.

A primary function of the child care specialist is to help children learn how to identify, give form to, label, and express their emotions. In Chapter 3, you learned how to experience your own emotions, and to be able to help children accomplish this themselves.

An important aspect of being a competent child specialist is becoming conscious of what you are doing with children. Being aware of your own body and how you feel is important. This text teaches that actions should be conscious, with ease, and not automatic. Automatic behavior demonstrates a lack of conscious effort. Awareness, on the other hand, refers to a full understanding of what you are doing when you are doing it. Self-awareness is necessary to conduct affective education with children.

Affective education for the very young requires the child care specialist to be an observer and a listener. It is imperative that children be in your sight and in their circle of safety. You must observe with your eyes and listen with your body to the sensitive cues young children give.

Your role of child care specialist helps you decipher the coded messages children's bodies give you. This is particularly important for nonmobile infants. "Teaching children about their own senses, what their bodies are telling them, and helping them express this state is an extremely important function of a conscious child-care specialist" (Douville-Watson 1997).

Affective education includes sharp detective work. You have the opportunity to shape a child's future by decoding their needs and rendering a meaningful response by helping them understand and label their feelings. You make the difference by helping them learn to trust their own feelings.

The affective education process starts with bringing attention to the child's internal state and labeling the child's feeling. Often the physical meter for children's feeling states is their whole body as it responds to different situations, especially their tummy area. The trained observer can easily identify children who are upset by their body language. "The prefrontal cortex receives a strong impulse from the great visceral nerve coming from the stomach area" (MacLean 1990). This feeling in the gut is the physical link between body intelligence and affect associated with social behavior. Before they are able to discuss or label feelings, children must learn to recognize their at ease state (see the Feelings Chart in Chapter 2). This is most recognizable while having fun and feeling happy.

Helping children to be aware of good feelings when they are in a state of ease is done after the child specialist has observed the children several times, and knows when the child is at ease. Ask children how their bodies feel when at ease or while playing and having fun. Often, children will simply smile. State the feeling you sense with nonverbal children and infants. Ask them if their tummies feel good. Then show them five faces (At Ease, Happy, Sad, Angry, and Afraid). Identify Happy, and point to their stomach area saying; "Your tummy feels happy! You're not sad, you're happy." If the child indicates that they agree, say "Yes, that's right; you feel happy."

Show the children a picture of a happy face and say, "You look like this picture." Children begin to associate this state with the happy face picture over time. Children will then be able to point to the picture and identify this state for themselves.

Give children feedback when they appear to be in a feeling state. Tell them that they look At Ease, Happy, Sad, Angry or Afraid. Show them the pictures and ask how their tummies feel. If the child says, "I feel bad," quickly respond with "You are good. Tell me how your tummy feels" and show them the pictures. You can also say, "Your body looks like your tummy feels, like this," and point to the appropriate picture that fits your interpretation of their body language. Then ask, "Is that right?"

As children learn to identify their own body responses, discuss when they started to feel unhappy or afraid. After listening, specific information about the children's conflicts can be addressed by the child care specialist. It is important to understand that there are no judgments placed on emotional reactions because all emotions are normal. When adults do not judge or blame feeling states, children learn to identify and express emotion and develop the potential to be healthy adults.

Expression of Feelings in Healthy Ways

The 3A's of childcare are the greatest behavior-shaping tools available to promote appropriate behavior, validate mastery, and build self-esteem. Using them in conscious affective education provides you with the most reliable way of promoting positive feelings and helping a child feel secure. Feeling secure is essential for children to be able to express negative emotion. View the actions of a child as simply coming from a need to express themselves. It is important to facilitate the expression and release of all emotions; especially anger and frustration.

To facilitate expression of emotions in a positive way, accept all emotions and the need to express them as normal. Toddlers are filled with energy. They are extremely curious and are very busy exploring their world. This often leads to frustration and all the unbridled emotions that go with learning how to handle new experiences. Conflicts arise from not getting what they want immediately. That is why having effective behavior-shaping techniques available and giving children an area to express feelings is essential.

Good caregiving is child-centered, meaning that children's needs are valid and important, and they need to express their feelings in positive ways.

A child care specialist who knows a child can observe how that child feels in certain situations and is emotionally available to pick up signals of frustration and alleviate a potential problem by distracting the child, involving him or her in a special project, or giving the child special attention. When you see that children need to release frustration, you can use an affective corner to help them express frustration; for example, involving them in hammering pegs or pounding pillows. When children have temper tantrums, make sure all furniture and harmful objects are out of the way. Remove undue attention from them until they are through, ask them privately to tell you what they felt if they can verbalize, and then welcome them into the group again. This is the most appropriate way to deal with tantrum behavior.

Toddler space needs to include a designated quiet and active area where the child can be observed unnoticed. You should be available to help the child release frustration. Planning a space for the release of frustration starts by understanding the developmental abilities of the specific children in care.

Ruing should be used with infants who express fear while being held. When an infant continues to cry for no apparent reason and all the measures listed in this text have been tried, the specialist is wise to allow another to help put the child at ease. Frustrations in child specialists are real feelings too and they need to be acknowledged. Often, primary child specialists with children who consistently cry, such as colicky babies, need to use rejuvenating techniques during breaks.

On occasion, children who bite or who are extremely aggressive cannot be directed and must be kept from hurting themselves and others. An area away from other children is useful for this purpose. No time limit is ever placed on a child, and a child may stay in the area for as long as necessary. The child is asked to stay in the area until he or she can follow the rules and rejoin the group. Biting, in particular, needs to be dealt with immediately. The child who bites needs to understand he or she has hurt someone else, and the caregiver may want to raise the tone of voice slightly to indicate disapproval. The child must apologize to the bitten child when appropriate. The child who was bitten must be comforted and reassured. It is the responsibility of the child care specialist to keep the children separate for a reasonable time to avoid continued conflict. Use the behavior limiting steps in Chapter 5 when children cannot follow the rules for remaining in the group setting.

Observing and Recording

Observer

Why Observe?   Observations provide important information needed for decision-making. Your observations contribute details about the child, the specialist, the curriculum, the materials and facilities, and the program and policies. Observation must precede teaching. It is an ongoing process.

Who to Observe?   Each child in the child care home or center needs to be observed. All program plans and implementation start with what the specialist knows about each child.

Each specialist contributes unique ideas and behaviors to the child care setting which others can identify by observing.

Each parent participates to varying degrees in the child care program. Observing how parents interact with children and adults helps specialists.

What to Observe? Children's behavior helps us learn about the child. Infants and toddlers often cannot use words to tell about themselves. Each child is unique. Child care specialists must identify the characteristics and needs of each child, because the child is the focal point of decisions and plans regarding time, space, and curriculum. Each child is continually changing. This growth and development sometimes produces expected, and sometimes unexpected changes. Living with someone every day, you may not notice some important emerging developments. Therefore, it is important to make periodic informal and formal observations on Developmental Prescriptions and Profiles and to record them so that the changes in the child can be noted and shared. This information will affect your planning for and interactions with the child.

Child care specialist behavior provides needed information. Ms. Sheila knew that she needed to improve her organization and planning. Every day she would forget some supplies she needed for snack time. She started making a checklist of snack items so she could make sure she had prepared everything. After snack time she noted whether she had all the supplies or whether she should add something else. Other specialists provided feedback also. By focusing and recording in this way, Ms. Sheila was able to improve herself. Each specialist is learning and continually developing skills. One caregiver may observe another caregiver in order to learn new strategies or to reinforce those the specialist already uses. Other people's observations can let caregivers know whether their actual practice matches the behavior intended. Continuing evaluation and planning along with feedback can help caregivers increase their effectiveness.

Ms. Josephine wanted to involve Monroe more when she shared a book with him. She selected a book she thought he would like and wrote down three questions to ask Monroe which would focus his thinking and questioning on objects from the book. She set up a small cassette tape recorder where she and Monroe would be sitting and she called Monroe over to share the book with him. Later, when Ms. Josephine listened to the tape recording of her time with Monroe, she discovered that she had talked all the time and told everything to Monroe rather than allowing him to talk, share, and question. Observations of interactions provide information about the kind of responses each person has to the other person or material. Observations help you learn how you have stimulated or inhibited the desired interaction (see Figure 4–4).

The child care setting including children, equipment, materials, and arrangement of space should be examined to determine safe and unsafe conditions. The use, misuse, and place of use of equipment and materials, traffic

Figure 4–4 Talking, listening, and playing with a child is an important child care specialist behavior.

patterns, much-used or little-used space, space where much disruptive behavior occurs, and the separation or overrunning of quiet and active space is evaluated. Make the necessary adjustments after you have evaluated how the setting works in relation to the children's needs.

How to Observe and Record   Observations may be informal or formal. You may glance across the room and see Sammy roll over. You know that is the first time you have seen that happen. On the parent message board you write, "Sammy rolled from front to back this morning." Sometimes a staff member will arrange to spend a few minutes specifically observing a child, a specialist, materials, or space. These observations can provide valuable information. Writing what you observe gives you and other people access to that information later on.

Descriptions may consist of one word or be very detailed and extensive. Write down the exact behavior or situation in narrative form, using as few judgmental and evaluative words as possible.

An ethnographic report describes a total situation: the time, place, people, and how they behave. Description of the total situation lets the specialist know about things which may not be evident in one part of a specific incident. Start with a general question such as "What is going on here?" Spradley identified nine major dimensions of every social situation:

1. Space: the physical place of places
2. Actor: the people involved
3. Activity: a set of related acts people do
4. Object: the physical things that are present
5. Act: single actions that people do
6. Event: a set of related activities that people carry out
7. Time: the sequencing that takes place over time
8. Goal: the things people are trying to accomplish
9. Feeling: the emotions felt and expressed (1980)

Adults unfamiliar with infants and toddlers think that the young child does not do anything. An early education student observed the following during outdoor play in a family child care home one summer afternoon. She was to focus on one child and write down everything she saw and heard that child do and say. The purpose of this assignment was to identify and categorize the various experiences initiated by a 13-month-old child. The observer was not to interject her own interpretations into the narrative.

The play yard contained Lynn, the specialist, and six children ranging from 7 months to 6 years of age. A portion of the report on Leslie, a 13-month-old girl, follows:

2:20   Lynn puts mat out and stands Leslie up in yard.
       Leslie looks around (slowly rocking to keep balance).
       Reaches hand to Lynn and baby talks.
       Looks at me and reaches for me.
       Takes 2 steps, trips on mat, so remains sitting on it.
       Turns around to face me.
       Cries a little.
       Reaches for Lynn, then to me (wants to be picked up).
       Tries to stand up.
       Looks around and watches Jason.
       Reaches hand toward Lynn.
       Watches Jason and sucks middle 2 fingers on right hand.
       Looks around.
       Tries to stand periodically, then seems to change mind.
       Swings right arm.
2:45   Takes Lynn's fingers and stands.
       Walks 2 steps onto grass.
       Swings right arm and brushes lips with hand to make sound—baby talk.
       Turns toward Lynn and babbles.
       Lane arrives. Leslie watches and rubs left eye with left hand.
       "Do you remember Leslie?" Lynn asks Lane.
       Leslie reaches out arms to Lynn and walks to her. Hugs her.

Listens and watches Lynn. Holds onto her for support.
Turns around and steps on pine straw and lifts foot to see what it is.
Watches Lynn tie Jason's shoe.
Lynn lifts her in air, then sets her on her knee.
She lies back in her lap and laughs.

Analysis of these descriptive statements shows that Leslie initiates a variety of interactions with people and materials. She is physically, emotionally, socially, and cognitively involving herself in her world. Specialist planning and facilitating can stimulate and build on Leslie's self-initiated behaviors.

Record Keeping

Record keeping has several purposes:

1. Sharing information with parents;
2. Planning curriculum, strategies, and program; and
3. Assessing children, child care specialists, and program.

Message Board   Some records are temporary, as is the daily message board for parents. During the time the parent is away, the infant is busily going about the business of growing up. Each new achievement, each practiced skill is an important part of the child's day. These achievements should be shared with parents. Parents want the specialist's general evaluation: How was Carlyle's day today? And they also want specific information: Phyllis drank from her cup by herself. Provide details rather than simply saying "He was good" or "She was better than yesterday."

Some records are permanent and are kept on file, for example, admission and health records, anecdotal or narrative records, and developmental pro-

MESSAGE BOARD
(wall chart)

CHILD'S NAME:		HOME SCHEDULE: (stays on board)	DATE: (Messages wiped off at end of every day)
E:	(Eating)		
S:	(Sleeping)		
T:	(Toilet)		
O:	(Other)		
EXAMPLE:			
DAN			FEB. 16
E:	8 oz.–3 hrs.		8:30—6 oz.; 12:00—7 oz.; 3:00—8 oz.
S:	3 naps; fights sleep		8:45–11:00; 12:30–3:00
T:	doesn't like soiled diapers		BM 11:00; 3:00
O:	Upset when sleep is interrupted		

files (see Appendix A for samples of permanent records). You and other staff will learn from experience what kinds of records are most helpful to your setting. If you never use some items of information, it is a waste of time to record them.

Taking the time to write something down seems to be the biggest obstacle to record keeping. Therefore, use records which can be written quickly and easily.

All specialist should use the same format for recording incidents. Many places use index cards and notebook entries. You can write and file the entries quickly, and find and use them very easily later. Computers permit another means of storing information.

Reporting Sheets   Reporting sheets provide information in a form which can be filed or taken home. The Infant Welfare Society of Evanston, Inc., says this about the "Care Sheets" used by caregivers in its Baby Toddler Center:*

1. Care Sheets: An important source of information, both to parents and to staff. For parents they serve to answer questions and provide feedback in a reliable, concrete manner. For us, they form a detailed, day-to-day record which reflects development, health, and program.

    Each child has a file for his or her care sheets, which passes with the child from group to group. Files are kept in a specific place which is known and accessible to staff. In order to protect the confidentiality of information, staff should give the files to parents, rather than have parents seek them out themselves. Therefore, it is important for "late" staff and substitutes to know the location of files.

    Copies shall be provided to parents, upon request, at the end of the week. Care sheets shall be shown to parents at conferences.

2. Content of Care Sheets:

    a. Routines: As a minimum, some information about each of the "care routines" must be included: a) Naps: times of going to sleep and waking; b) Eating: quality of appetite; c) Elimination: number of bowel movements. In addition, it is important to make note of atypical responses; e.g., restless sleep or nightmares in a child who normally sleeps peacefully or loose stools in a child who normally has firm ones. Relative to children with specific conditions of concern, more data is required. For example, for a child with a milk intolerance, notation should be made of milk products withheld or given. For a child who has a tendency to have intestinal problems, more information should be given regarding stools. For babies, notes about food served are necessary, in order to be alert to allergies.

    b. Activities: Care sheets shall indicate the major activities of each day, as well as whether and how long the child participated. This enables the care sheets, over time, to reflect preferences and abilities of the child.

Care Sheets reprinted by permission of the Infant Welfare Society of Evanston, Inc.

c. Special Information: Other pertinent information which shall be recorded includes, but is not limited to, the following: a) injuries which occur at the Nursery, regardless of source; b) injuries which occur outside the Nursery, and the explanation provided by the parent; c) times the child is sent home or not accepted and the reason, including unsuccessful attempts to send a child home; d) developmental milestones reached by the child, e.g., taking a first step or saying a new word. Special instructions from parents should also be noted.

3. Style of Care Sheets: Information must be given clearly (although grammar is unimportant). Therefore, statements must be objective, rather than judgmental. For example, say "Tommy cried off and on all morning" or "Joey fought with other children over toys 8 or 10 times today" rather than "John had a terrible day." Say "Jane SEEMED restless (or tired or unhappy) today" rather than "Judy WAS sad." This is important because evaluative or judgmental statements are "emotionally loaded" and often lead to misunderstanding, whereas factual, objective statements cannot be disputed.

In order to be effective, care sheets need to be written daily. In this way information is more easily remembered, and, more importantly, is available to parents and other staff, both late in the day and early the next day.

Care sheets shall be shown to parents at parent-staff conferences.

Caregivers may use a similar care sheet or devise one which very specifically fits their program.

Assessing

Assessing the Caregiver

Caregivers can assess their own behavior, using the Child Development Associate Competency Standards as criteria. As a part of the Child Development Associate training and assessment program, observations and records are made regularly. The caregiver's behavior is assessed in each of the functional areas (see Appendix C).

Honig and Lally developed checklists to assess caregivers who work with infants and toddlers. The list below shows categories of behaviors for professional child care providers of infants under 18 months:*

I. LANGUAGE FACILITATION
1. Elicits vocalization
2. Converses with child
3. Praises, encourages verbally

---

*Reprinted by permission from Alice S. Honig and J. Ronald Lally, "How good is your infant program? Use an observational method to find out." *Child Care Quarterly* 4(3):137–39.

4. Offers help or solicitous remarks
5. Inquired of child or makes requests
6. Gives information or culture rules
7. Provides and labels sensory experience
8. Reads or shows pictures to child
9. Sings to or plays music for child

II. SOCIAL-EMOTIONAL: POSITIVE
   1. Smiles at child
   2. Uses raised, loving, or reassuring tones
   3. Provides physical, loving contact
   4. Plays social games with child
   5. Eye contact to draw child's attention

III. SOCIAL-EMOTIONAL: NEGATIVE
   1. Criticizes verbally; scolds; threatens
   2. Forbids; negative commands
   3. Frowns; restrains physically
   4. Punishes physically
   5. Isolates child physically—behavior modification
   6. Ignores child when child shows need for attention

IV. PIAGETIAN TASKS
   1. Object permanence
   2. Means and ends
   3. Imitation
   4. Causality
   5. Prehension: small-muscle skills
   6. Space
   7. New schemas

V. CARE-GIVING: CHILD
   1. Feeds
   2. Diapers or toilets
   3. Dresses or undresses
   4. Washes or cleans child
   5. Prepares child for sleep
   6. Physical shepherding
   7. Eye checks on child's well-being

VI. CARE-GIVING: ENVIRONMENT
   1. Prepares food
   2. Tidies up room
   3. Helps other caregiver(s)

VII. PHYSICAL DEVELOPMENT
   1. Provides kinesthetic stimulation
   2. Provides large-muscle play

VIII. DOES NOTHING
(1975, 196–97)

Caregivers who work with toddlers from 18 to 36 months are assessed in the categories of behaviors shown below.

I. FACILITATES LANGUAGE DEVELOPMENT
1. Converses
2. Models language
3. Expands language
4. Praises, encourages
5. Offers help, solicitous remarks, or makes verbal promises
6. Inquires of child or makes request
7. Gives information
8. Gives culture rules
9. Labels sensory experiences
10. Reads or identifies pictures
11. Sings or plays music with child
12. Role-plays with child

II. FACILITATES DEVELOPMENT OF SKILLS
SOCIAL: PERSONAL
1. Promotes child-child play (cognitive and sensorimotor)
2. Gets social games going
3. Promotes self-help and social responsibility
4. Helps child recognize his own needs
5. Helps child delay gratification
6. Promotes persistence, attention span
SOCIAL: PHYSICAL
1. Small muscle, perceptual motor
2. Large muscle, kinesthesis

III. FACILITATES CONCEPT DEVELOPMENT
1. Arranges learning of space and time
2. Arranges learning of seriation, categorization, and polar concepts
3. Arranges learning of number
4. Arranges learning of physical causality

IV. SOCIAL-EMOTIONAL: POSITIVE
1. Smiles at child
2. Uses raised, loving, or reassuring tones
3. Provides physical loving contact
4. Uses eye contact to draw child's attention

V. SOCIAL-EMOTIONAL: NEGATIVE
1. Criticizes verbally, scolds; threatens
2. Forbids, negative commands
3. Frowns; restrains physically
4. Isolates child physically—behavior modification
5. Ignores child when child shows need for attention
6. Punishes physically
7. Gives attention to negative behavior which should be ignored

VI. CARE-GIVING: BABY
1. Diapers, toilets, dresses, washes, cleans
2. Gives physical help, helps to sleep, shepherds
3. Eye checks of child's well-being
4. Carries child

VII. CARE-GIVING: ENVIRONMENT
1. Prepares/serves food
2. Tidies up room
3. Helps other caregiver
4. Prepares activities, arranges environment to stimulate child

VIII. QUALITATIVE CATEGORIES
1. Encourages creative expression
2. Matches "tempo" and/or developmental level of child
3. Actively engages child's interest in activity or activity choice
4. Follows through on requests, promises, directions, discipline

IX. DOES NOTHING
(1975, 200–201)

Assessing Children

In her paper "Infant Assessment: Early Intervention," presented at the 1997 Annual Conference of the National Association for the Education of the Young Child, Linda Castellanos stated, "Much controversy has emerged about the assessment of young infants. As trained observers, we (caregivers) often suspect, but are not certain of what difficulties our youngest citizens have progressing through the developmental process. Assessment pinpoints developmental difficulties and allows the caregiver to confidently plan a program of treatment. Developmental Profiles and Developmental Prescriptions successfully diagnose current developmental lags and remediate them when possible. One can only speculate the far-reaching impact that this early intervention can have concerning the future endeavors of ones so young."

Caregivers must understand infant and toddler developmental milestones. They must know each child in their care. Caregivers must utilize the 3A's of child care. They must be able to evaluate the emotional, social, physical, and cognitive aspects of the child. They must know about materials and equipment and how to arrange and manage space. They must know how to assess each child and use the Prescriptions and Developmental Profile accurately.

Caregivers should act as assessor very prudently in this age of testing and making judgments about children. They should determine before making the assessments why the assessments are necessary, which ones are appropriate, and how they will be used.

Developmental assessment is used to determine the child's level of development. It may focus on one area, such as cognition, or the whole child, for example, physical, emotional, social, and cognitive. Since children are continually developing in all areas, periodic assessment is useful.

Developmental profiles or checklists can be developed by analyzing past descriptions and selecting categories of behavior or content. You can also develop checklists by listing objectives and competencies for children or caregivers. Checklists, however, only provide information about single incidents, and the information is isolated from the situation in which it occurred.

Developmental profiles or checklists of children's behaviors can be used most effectively by noting a behavior the first time you observe it. One day you may record one new behavior for Jeff, three new behaviors for Deborah, and nothing for Sandra.

We see infants perform many tasks. However, infants cannot tell us in words what they have learned. When you assess infants or toddlers on performance by planning to observe one instance of that activity, you should take care about interpreting the results, for a child may choose not to perform. A child may have learned something but not wish to perform on that occasion.

Few caregivers have received the specialized training required to use standardized assessment techniques and tests. If your program wants to carry out specialized assessment, seek out the necessary training first.

Organizing

Care Plans or Prescriptions

The caregiver organizes plans. Daily, weekly, and long-term planning are important guides to awareness and continuity of development. The child's developmental profile provides information about the child's strengths and about areas in which development may occur next. Planning specific experiences in advance for each child helps make sure you are considering the needs and development of the whole child, rather than focusing on one or two areas and forgetting other areas.

Schedule

The caregiver organizes the schedule. You decide how to use the major blocks of time and how much flexibility you need in that schedule to meet the child's needs. Consistent patterns of events help children learn order in their lives. This develops in them feelings of security and trust because they know that some parts of their world are predictable.

Materials

The caregiver organizes materials. Good infant programs need a variety of learning materials every day. The caregiver will want to select some materials to set out in the room and store away the rest. The caregiver decides when to change the materials and how to arrange them for the children to get to them.

Environment

The caregiver organizes the environment—the room and the play yard—to meet the developmental needs of the children. Caregivers rely on their knowledge of the individual children in their care as well as on their background in child development. Each caregiver decides how and when to change the environment.

Managing

Careful management of time, space, materials, and people is needed to provide meaningful daily experiences for children.

Time

The caregiver manages and coordinates time within the guidelines of the daily schedule and plans. You give Suzy a five-minute notice before outdoor play time since Suzy takes a long time to put her toys away and start getting ready to go outside. You feed lunch to Jack at 11:00 A.M., because he falls asleep at 11:30. You allow Vanessa to get up after her half-hour sleep, because she usually takes very short naps. You encourage Joshua to stay on his cot, knowing that he usually sleeps two hours. You continue to respect the needs of each individual child (see Figure 4–5).

Space

The caregiver manages space. Before the children arrive, you plan and organize the space in your caregiving environment. When the children are actively using that space, you will make suggestions, decisions, and adjustments to help each child have positive experiences. Orrin is piling up blocks near the shelf. Shiwanda is trying to reach a block. For Shiwanda to get the block she wants, she will probably bump into Orrin's pile of blocks. You can walk with Shiwanda around to the other side of Orrin where she can reach the block without getting into Orrin's space.

Materials

The caregiver manages materials. With very young children you make decisions about how many kinds of materials are needed, where they can be stored and where they can be used, what is safe or not safe, and how the materials can or cannot be used. Lois asks for a toy and begins pulling toys out of the toy box. She pulls out blocks, dolls, cars, puzzle pieces, fabric scraps,

Figure 4–5 The caregiver provides nurturing attention to the waking child.

and assorted other toys. She looks back and forth between the inside of the box and the clutter of toys on the floor. She finally walks away to another part of the room, leaving all the toys behind. Too many materials can be confusing, but too few can bore a child.

People
The caregiver manages and coordinates people. When two caregivers work with a group of children, they should coordinate their plans and their actions. While the director can provide guidance, the moment-by-moment actions require dialogue and give and take between the caregivers.

Caregivers coordinate the children's use of time, space, and materials. Willard, a 15-month-old, flings toys. One of the caregivers needs to help him move to a part of the room where he can fling toys safely.

COMMUNITY RESOURCES

Every community offers a variety of resources. The caregiver may need help in compiling and maintaining a list of resources.

Community resources serve several purposes. Some can be used in the daily program; some are good to use with children; and some are services which you refer parents to.

There are several sources of information relating to nutrition. The U.S. Department of Agriculture, through its Food and Nutrition Services (Washington, DC 20250), has numerous bulletins and books that present valuable ideas for lay people. Each state has a Cooperative Extension Service office in every county and a main office usually at the state's land grant university. Pediatricians, public health departments, and home economics nutrition specialists may provide flyers and bulletins. Printed materials are available on such topics as balanced diets, iron-fortified food, child obesity, and nutritious snacks.

Many communities have resources regarding good health. A child's pediatrician is a primary source of information concerning the child's health and how to maintain it. A crucial aspect in infant and toddler care is the flow of information among pediatrician, parent, and caregiver. The pediatrician needs the observations of the parent and caregiver in order to provide accurate recommendations and diagnoses.

The publication, *Blueprint for Action under the Healthy Child Care America Campaign*, sponsored by the U.S. Department of Health and Human Services, Child Care Bureau, Administration on Children and Young Families and the Maternal and Child Health Bureau, and distributed by the American Academy of Pediatrics, was written to provide communities with steps they can take to "either expand existing public and private services and resources, or to create new services and resources that link families with health and child care." This publication and others are available to the professional child care specialist at the American Academy of Pediatrics, 141 Northwest Point Boulevard, Elk Grove Village, IL 60007-1098, telephone (847) 981-7084, or fax (847) 228-5097. E-mail kids-docs@aap.org. Many excellent publications including *Caring for Our Children National Health and Safety Performance Standards: Guidelines for Out-Of-Home Child Care Programs* are available.

A pediatrician may serve as a health care consultant to a child care program, providing expertise to the staff, parents, and children. Pediatricians can contribute in a number of ways:

1. They may speak up as informed advocates on the quality of child care services in their community.
2. They may comment on child care educational materials, concepts, and programs.
3. They may provide care to children who are enrolled in child care.
4. They may be regular members of a health committee or board for one or more child care centers.
5. They may be employed full or part time by a large center or several centers as members of the health team. Their responsibilities would include "direct" services as well as health consultation to all staff from director to janitor.
6. They may act in an advisory capacity to state and local health, welfare, or education departments, and others who set standards for health in child care centers (American Academy of Pediatrics 1980, 50–51).

Public health nurses may be on the staff of local or county health departments. They serve several functions which affect families and child care programs. They are involved in health education programs which provide information through meetings, literature, and the media. They assist in communicable disease prevention through immunization programs. The Academy of Pediatrics has a wealth of information. For current publications or more information, readers can contact AAP Division of Public Relations at (847) 981-7084, 7131, 7945, or 7877. Address correspondence to:

The American Academy of Pediatrics
P.O. Box 927
Elk Grove Village, IL 60009-0927.
The AAP web page can be accessed at http://www.aap.org and on
Compuserve's SCI News/Med-Newslibrary of the Journalism Forum
(GO:JFORUM).

They provide information and guidance in setting up and maintaining a healthy and safe environment. Public health nurses may be available for on-site visits to provide information, in-service training, or to help caregivers analyze specific health problems.

In 1995, the U.S. Census Bureau reported that one in seven children had no health insurance, the highest number ever reported. This startling fact makes the need for child care settings of all kinds to access whatever free services are available in the community to ensure proper immunizations of young children, as well as to provide proper health guidance.

Well-child clinics provide services to children and families to foster and maintain health. Developmental examinations, immunizations, and health education information enable the physician and parent to regularly assess the child's development and to determine whether specific changes or assistance are needed to facilitate the child's health. Well-child clinics are provided by a number of facilities: hospitals, pediatric groups, health departments, churches, and nonprofit agencies. Determine whether well-child clinics are needed or available to children in your care.

Child abuse and neglect identification is increasing. According to the 1997 report for the Children's Defense Fund, "Every ten seconds, a child is reported abused or neglected." In 1995, 996,000 children—more than 2,700 a day—were abused or neglected, according to the National Committee to Stop Child Abuse. Attention to child abuse and neglect is long overdue. In the last few years governmental and professional organizations have become increasingly active in research and public information programs. Caregivers and parents need this information to assess their own situations to ensure that their behavior is neither abusive nor neglectful.

A public information campaign is helping to lessen the public stigma and to enable the adult to seek needed help. "The caregiver can help improve conditions for the child and the parent by recognizing a family in need and tactfully recommending the appropriate resources available to them" (Nassau County Coalition 1993). County departments of health, mental health, social services, or child care services can provide information and referrals for those who need it. Some communities have a crisis center or a telephone hotline to call for urgent assistance. Nationally, help is also available.

By law, many states require screening of child care providers, which may include fingerprinting. The purpose of this screening is to ensure that no person having contact with children is the subject of a report of child abuse or maltreatment. Child care providers are responsible for prohibiting abuse or maltreatment of children in their care and must not tolerate or in any manner condone an act of abuse or maltreatment. Incidents of child abuse or suspected child abuse, maltreatment, or neglect must be reported. In some states this is mandated by law.

Each state has its own definition of what constitutes abuse. It is the caregivers' responsibility to make sure that their agency has the applicable definitions and receives training on indicators and reporting mechanisms of child abuse and maltreatment. Generally it is the individual caregiver's responsibility to report suspected cases of abuse and to make a written report with dates and times and specific observations. It is the director's responsibility to make the report to the appropriate authorities.

Emergency care is sometimes needed. Several organizations have printed posters which provide information on simple first aid procedures you might use with a child. One is the chart prepared by the Committee on Accident Prevention and the Subcommittee on Accidental Poisoning, American Academy of Pediatrics. First aid given at the child care home or center may be all that is needed for Molly's skinned knee. However, more severe cuts, head bumps, or ingestion of harmful substances require immediate referral to other help. At the time a child enrolls in child care, fill out an information card supplying the names of the child's physician and the hospital the parents choose to use if an emergency room visit is necessary. This card should stay beside the telephone for immediate access in an emergency. The rescue squad or ambulance service number should also be posted near the phone. Telephone numbers for the local hospital poison information center and the state Poison Control Center should be posted by the telephone. The Poison Control Center has a flyer which presents needed information for Poisoning Emergency Action. Refer to Chapter 6 for a listing of agencies which may have information and services to assist you and your child care program.

PROFESSIONAL PREPARATION OF THE CAREGIVER

Both informal and formal educational opportunities are available to caregivers.

Informal experiences may be spontaneous or planned. An article in a magazine may stimulate your thinking by providing new information and raising questions. You may take time to do further thinking and discuss your ideas with other staff, or you may think of the ideas periodically and begin changing your caregiving techniques to incorporate what you have learned.

Formal educational opportunities are those that are planned to meet specific needs. You choose experiences to help you gain desired knowledge and skill. The following types of experiences contribute to your learning either by using your experiences with children, independent study, or a combination of both.

- A mentor or a more-experienced caregiver, which gives you opportunities to observe, participate, and discuss techniques. It is organized, supervised, and evaluated; isolated work does not count.
- Workshops, seminars: These may be sponsored by adult schools, colleges, universities, and professional organizations. They usually focus on a single topic or skill.
- Speakers: Libraries, colleges, and hospitals may sponsor speakers.
- Short courses provided by local or state groups or agencies.
- Continuing education courses sponsored by local schools and colleges.
- Technical school courses and programs in child care.
- Junior and senior college courses and programs in child care.
- Child Development Associate Certificate: "The Child Development Associate, or CDA, is a person who is able to meet the specific needs of children and who, with parents and other adults, works to nurture children's physical, social, emotional, and intellectual growth in a child development framework. The CDA conducts herself or himself in an ethical manner" (CDA, 1992).

The Council has designed both training and assessment systems for persons interested in the CDA Credential. For more information, contact:

Council for Early Childhood Professional Recognition
1341 G Street, NW, Suite 400
Washington, DC 20005
Telephone: (202) 265-9090 or 1-800-424-4310
Fax: (202) 265-9161

The CDA Competency Standards and assessment system for infant/toddler child specialists in center-based programs have been developed to support quality care for our youngest children by providing standards for training, evaluation, and recognition of child specialists based on their ability to meet the unique needs of these age groups.

The American Academy of Pediatrics publication, *Healthy Kids*, July 1997, published an article entitled "Building Brainpower" (Priller) which summed up the importance of child specialist preparation: "Even the earliest feelings experienced by a child can affect the brain and lay the groundwork for later emotions such as reacting to stress, trusting others, self-esteem, and understanding one's place in the world. Since babies are so highly dependent on their child specialists for everything, it makes some sense that their emotional states, and eventually their own emotional responses, are affected by the emotions of those who care for them. Healthy, happy babies come from a loving and nurturing environment established during the early years of life." Dr. Phillip S. Reback from Albany Medical College says; "A lot of warm, physical contact—hugging, skin to skin, body to body contact—is extraordinarily important for an infant's sense of security and well being."

The special developmental needs of very young children require that their care in a group setting be different from that of older children for several good reasons:

- The younger child is more dependent on the child specialist, more vulnerable to adversity, and is less able to cope with discomfort of stress from without or within;

- Physical, social, emotional, and cognitive development are more interrelated for infants than for older children, and more dependent upon a consistent relationship with an adult child care specialist; and

- The more involved and emotionally connected to the child the child specialist can be, the more secure the child feels when judged by the ease of their movements (Douville-Watson 1997).

STUDENT ACTIVITIES

1. Identify your strengths and weaknesses in the caregiver roles. Write a growth plan for yourself.

2. Observe one infant and one toddler for ten minutes each. Use narrative description to record what you see and hear. Categorize the behaviors of each.

3. Using the record of Leslie in the play yard, list her behaviors using the following categories:
   a. physical
   b. emotional
   c. social
   d. cognitive
   e. language

4. Define what conscious caregiving means to you.

5. Define affective education.

6. Observe two caregivers, each for ten minutes. Tally a mark in the appropriate category each time you observe the caregiver assume that role.

7. List four available community resources and explain how each can serve your child care program.

	CAREGIVER 1	CAREGIVER 2
Observer		
Caregiver		
Self		
Recorder		
Message Board		
Sheets, Notes		
Assessor		
Caregiver		
Child		
Organizer		
Plans		
Schedules		
Materials		
Environment		
Manager		
Time		
Space		
Materials		
People		
Behavior		
Facilitator		
Provider		
Nurturance		
Assistance		
Information		
Questioner		
Interpreter		

CHAPTER REVIEW

1. Review Chapter 2, The 3A's of Child Care.
2. Review mastery.
3. List four personal characteristics which you can use as a caregiver. Explain why each is important.
4. How can you generalize what you have learned in this chapter into your personal life?
5. How can you use observation in a child care program?
6. How can you become a more conscious caregiver?

	CAREGIVER ROLE	EXAMPLE
1		
2		
3		

REFERENCES

American Academy of Pediatrics. 1996. *Recommendations for Day Care Centers for Infants and Children*. Evanston, Il.

Castellanos, L., and Douville-Watson. 1997. *Assessing Infants*. National Association for the Education of Young Children Conference, Anneheim, CA.

Child Development Associate National Credentialing Program. 1992. *Child Development Associate Assessment System and Competency Standards Infant/Toddler Caregivers in Center-Based Programs*. Washington, DC: Author.

Council for Early Childhood Professional Recognition. 1992. *Council Model for CDA Assessment and Training*. Washington, DC: Author.

Coopersmith, S. 1967. *The Antecedents of Self-Esteem*. San Francisco: W. H. Freeman.

Douville-Watson, L. 1997. *Conscious Caregiving*. New York: Instructional Press, 21 Oak Shore Drive, Bayville, NY 11709

Douville-Watson, L. 1993. Lecture series II, *3A's of Infant Development*. New York: Instructional Press.

Honig, Alice Sterling. 1988. Baby moves: Relation to learning. International Early Childhood Conferences. Washington DC.

Honig, A. S., and Lally, J. R. 1975. How good is your infant program? Use an observation method to find out. *Child Care Quarterly* 4(3), Fall.

Infant Welfare Society of Evanston (Illinois) Inc. Care Sheets. Not dated.

MacLean, Paul D. 1990 *The Triune Brain in Evolution, Role in Paleacerebral Functions*. New York: Plenum Press.

Nassau County Coalition on Child Abuse and Neglect. 1993. Hempstead, New York.

Spradley, J. P. 1980. *Participant Observation*. New York: Holt, Rinehart & Winston.

5
What is Development and Learning?

OBJECTIVES

After completing this chapter, the child development specialist should be able to:
1. Identify areas of the young child's development and learning.
2. Identify patterns of the child's physical, emotional, social, and cognitive development.
3. Explain the relationship of sequence and rate of development to the child's individuality.
4. Support the importance of the caregiver's knowledge of the developing and learning child.

CHAPTER OUTLINE

I. The Whole Child
   A. Interrelatedness of the Child's Behaviors
   B. Interrelatedness of Interactions with Others
II. Areas of Development and Learning
   A. Physical Development
   B. Emotional Development
   C. Security and Trust
   D. Discipline
   E. Biting Behavior
   F. Social Development
   G. Cognitive Development
   H. Learning Skills Development
III. Early Intervention and Inclusion of Special Needs Children

CHILD DEVELOPMENT ASSOCIATE FUNCTIONAL AREAS

II. 4 Physical
II. 5 Cognitive

III. 8 Self
III. 9 Social
III. 10 Guidance
 IV. 11 Families
  V. 12 Program Management
 VI. 13 Professionalism

THE WHOLE CHILD

It is crucial for the caregiver to know about and understand the developing child. You will apply this knowledge and understanding as you plan appropriate experiences for each child and develop caregiver strategies.

This chapter elaborates and extends the concepts, theories, and principles presented in Chapters 1–4 of using practical applications with children. One problem in studying development and learning is that the topics must be taken apart and presented in detail before they can be integrated into a meaningful whole. This chapter integrates the specific knowledge presented this far into functioning with the whole child, and considers inclusion of special needs children in a program of normally developing infants and toddlers.

Interrelatedness of the Child's Behaviors

The child is a whole person—a physical, emotional, social, and cognitive being. Sometimes we speak of children as though they are just a collection of little parts: Joey's feet are always moving; Takisha is still drooling; Becky pinches everything. To understand the whole child it is sometimes helpful to look at separate characteristics or areas of development. A part of the learning process is to understand the related effects of experiences on the whole child.

When Kevin falls down and skins his knee, it does more than just break the skin on his knee. His nerves send impulses to his brain that he interprets as pain (physical and emotional). He hears himself cry (auditory input) and sees (visual input) the scrape and blood. His brain decides whether the pain is great or small (physical, emotional, and social). What he has learned about himself and his world influences his response to the pain after the initial surprise; he may scream, cry, whimper, or not say anything (temperament, verbal expression, and social). Kevin decides whether he will stay down to wait for someone's attention or whether he will pick himself up and ask for help for his bleeding knee, or whether he will start playing again (social and temperament).

Interrelatedness of Interactions with Others

Jeffrey, 4½ months old, just had his diaper changed and is lying on the floor on his back looking around. Miss Vivian, the caregiver, rolls him over, and he sees 14½-month-old Neola sitting close by. He reaches out and touches her and stares at her hand. He kicks his feet. He touches her arm and kisses her hand. He watches her wriggle her fingers and keeps grabbing her arm. Neola watches him and sucks on her fingers. Jeffrey watches her hands. Neola leaves and Jeffrey looks around the room, kicking his feet, flapping his hands, giggling, and babbling. He sucks on his fingers and kicks his feet. When another child comes over and cuddles him, he smiles. Miss Vivian picks him up and rocks him, rubbing his back and talking quietly to him. He kicks his legs and flaps his arms as he babbles. He quiets down and falls to sleep. Jeffrey, Neola, and Miss Vivian are actively involved with each other, each initiating, responding, and enjoying one another. Looking stimulated touching and talking, touching stimulated kissing and kicking. They shared their enjoyment of each other by looking and touching, giggling, babbling, and talking.

From the moment of birth the child and the people around the child affect each other. This dynamic interaction is sometimes deliberate and controlled and sometimes unconscious behavior. Caregivers working with infants and toddlers plan many experiences for children. Simultaneous with these planned experiences are the literally thousands of actions which are spontaneous, which stimulate new actions and reactions and challenge both the child and the caregiver (see Figure 5–1).

Figure 5–1   Children interact spontaneously with one another.

Magda Gerber (1989) has established an approach and structure for child care that emphasizes the interaction between child and caregiver. This approach is illustrated through her "ten principles of caregiving":

1. Involve children in activities and things that concern them.
2. Invest in quality time with each child.
3. Learn the unique ways each child communicates with you and teach them the way you communicate.
4. Invest in the time and energy necessary with each child to build a total person.
5. Respect infants and toddlers as worthy people.
6. Model specific behaviors before you teach them.
7. Always be honest with children about your feelings.
8. View problems as learning opportunities and allow children to solve their own problems where possible.
9. Build security with children by teaching trust.
10. Be concerned about the quality of development each child has at each stage.

These ten principles fit well with the goals and objectives of the CDA certification program. A caregiver who follows all ten of these principles will also fulfill some major requirements for CDA certification.

AREAS OF DEVELOPMENT AND LEARNING

Infants are born developing and learning. They are actively involved with themselves and the world. Development is more general and global; learning is specific. The child is constantly interacting with the world, making adjustments in his actions as he organizes and structures behaviors through schemes and information processed.

Children's levels of physical, emotional, social, and cognitive development affect their "zone of proximal development." Understanding the interrelationships among development, learning, and experiences is the basis for providing high-quality care.

Physical Development

Mary Lynn, 3 months old, sits in Ms. Annette's lap cooing and waving her arms. She smiles, grabs at Ms. Annette's nose, and listens to her talking. Ms. Annette lays Mary Lynn on the floor on her back and goes to another part of the room. Mary Lynn balls up a fist and sucks on it. She takes her fist out of her mouth and wrinkles up her face. Ms. Annette returns and plays with Mary Lynn, jiggling her leg and talking. Mary Lynn smiles, her tongue moving in and out of her mouth.

April, 19 months old, is riding her Big Wheel on the outdoor riding strip. She stands up, turns the bike around, gets on, and rides again. She runs into a trike, stands up, and moves the trike. She rides until she hits an object, and then stands up and turns the bike in different directions. She does not seem to be able to turn corners.

Mary Lynn and April are at different levels of physical development. Nevertheless, there are some similarities in their behaviors. Each is using her senses, muscular coordination, strength, and balance; each is actively moving in her world.

Newborns use all their senses: hearing, seeing, tasting, smelling, touching. During the first year their senses become physically developed; for example, their vision becomes similar to that of adults. Infants and toddlers then become involved in coordinating and controlling the use of their senses with their moving and thinking. Several perceptual and Developmental Learning Skills are involved in the use of senses.

Movement develops in a predetermined order. The direction of the infant's physical development is from head to foot and from mid-body out to the limbs, the fingers, and the toes. This directional development is readily observable in infants as they gain control of their necks, then backs and legs to turn over, then lower backs and legs to crawl, and finally necks, shoulders, backs, legs, feet, and toes to walk.

Infants develop control of their arm movements from erratic waving to accurate reaching. Their hand control develops from bumping and hitting to touching. Their fingers develop from reflexive pinching, grasping, and reflexive releasing to controlled opening and closing to pick up small and large objects.

Movement is essential. Children must move to gain control over some of their movements. Three areas of movement for infants are (1) sitting and standing upright (stability); (2) crawling and walking (locomotion); and (3) reaching, grasping, and releasing (manipulation). The movements and steps involved in skills can be task analyzed into their natural hierarchy of development.

Basic manipulative, nonlocomotor, and locomotor movements provide the basis for skilled movements:

During the first year of life infants grow more rapidly physically than they will for the rest of their lives. At birth the infant's head represents 20 to 25 percent of total body length compared to an adult's head, which represents about 10 percent of total body length (Lamb and Campos 1982, 29). In the first year the average infant triples birth weight. In the first two years the brain triples in bulk, "attaining 80 percent of its adult size" (Lamb and Campos 1982, 6). At birth the baby will have about twenty teeth growing inside the jaws. By 2½ all the baby teeth probably will have emerged (National Institute of Dental Research and the National Association of Community Health Centers, Inc. 1979). These phenomenal physical changes directly influence the curriculum for each child.

The chapters in Part III identify the task-analyzed sequence of physical development. Each child's Developmental Prescription (see Appendix A) will show similarities in sequence and variances in the rate of physical development.

Emotional Development

Young children develop reactions to many feelings and emotions in the first years of life. They experience fear and anxiety, anger and hostility, jealousy, shame, affection and love, pleasure, joy, trust and security, and pride.

Newborns seem sometimes to have an unfocused excitement. In the next few years, through their active involvement in their environment, they have pleasurable and nonpleasurable experiences. They tend to repeat pleasurable experiences as their parents and caregivers provide a base of trust and security for them. Children move through emotions rapidly; one minute they may scream, "I hate you," and the next minute jump into your arms, give you a big hug, and say, "I love you."

Security and Trust

Consistent and appropriate behavior from the caregiver is necessary to provide security for the child. Consistent but inappropriate behavior or inconsistent but appropriate behavior has been shown to be detrimental to development of security and trust.

The way to ensure consistent and appropriate caregiver behavior with children is to establish consistent routines and supply generous amounts of the 3A's of child care: Attention, Approval, and Affection. A major principle to use in shaping behavior is to reward behavior that approximates (comes closest to) the behavior you want with the 3A's, and to withdraw reward for behavior that you don't want. For example, when you ask Rose, who knows how to wash her hands, to wash up and she tries hard and does well for her level of skill development, you heap on the 3A's. If Rose doesn't try and just swishes under the water, you do not give her positive attention, approval, or affection. You don't let Rose move to the next activity until she chooses to do the task. Consistent application of this principle will help develop security and trust in the child; reward desired behavior with the 3A's and withdraw rewards when there is undesirable behavior. Security develops largely from consistent responses to specific behaviors and trust develops largely from acceptance and appreciation of the child (Greenspan and Pollock 1989).

Children need reasonable expectations. To have these reasonable expectations you need to know (1) normal patterns of development and (2) each child's individual pattern of development. Because the sequence of development is similar among children, you have some guidelines for your expectations. Because there is a range in the timing of development, you need to know where each child fits within that range (see Figure 5–2). If you expect children to accomplish things which are below or above them developmentally you produce undue stress. For example, you can expect 30-month-old Mark to be able to hold a spoon in his hand, fill it with food, and usually get it up to his mouth. You should not expect 9-month-old Naomi to have that level of muscular coordination. Use of Diagnostic Prescriptions and Profiles

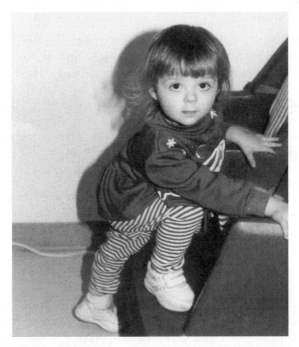

Figure 5–2 Knowing the child's level of development helps the caregiver feel comfortable when allowing the child to climb the stairs alone.

are important. Consistent updating of developmental steps helps children establish security and trust because they meet with success, mastery, and the 3A's rather than stress, frustration, and rejection.

Infants and toddlers depend upon their caregivers for many things. Caregivers who provide comfort and assistance help children learn that the caregiver can provide a secure place and can be trusted. Children who live in a world where their needs are ignored or only occasionally met will have difficulty building security and trust. One reason that caregivers have responsibility for fewer infants and toddlers than older children is so caregivers will be available to respond to the many needs of each dependent infant or toddler.

Young children's temperaments, feelings of self-esteem, and coping skills are important factors in their emotional development.

Temperament
Temperament has been defined as "the basic style which characterizes a person's behavior" (Chess, Thomas, and Birch 1965, 32). All children are born with particular temperaments. It will influence what they do, what they learn, what they feel about themselves and others, and what kinds of interactions they have with people and objects.

Chess, Thomas, and Birch worked with 231 children and their parents to investigate how babies differ in their styles of behavior and their temperament. How does individual temperament develop? What role does it play in personality development? What part does the environment play in shaping of personality? Is the mother's approach to the baby fixed, or does the baby's temperament affect the mother's handling? What were the specific circumstances in which the child's behavior occurred? (1965).

Their analysis of hundreds of observations and interviews revealed nine patterns of behavior. Within each pattern they found a range of behaviors. The following examples show each end of the ranges. The behavior of most people falls somewhere in between these extremes. Table 5–1 lists the nine categories and extremes of behaviors observed in each category.

The following descriptions further illustrate the extremes of these patterns.

Activity Level   Ryan runs into the room, yells "Hi," and goes to the blocks. He stacks them quickly, they fall down, and he stacks again and leaves them as they tumble down. He walks over to stand by Melba , the caregiver, who is reading a picture book to another child. Ryan listens a few minutes and then moves on to another activity. Ryan has a high activity level. He has always been very active. He kicked and waved and rolled a lot when he was a baby.

TABLE 5-1   BEHAVIOR CATEGORIES OF TEMPERAMENT

	EXTREMES	
BEHAVIORAL CATEGORY	MORE	LESS
(1) Activity Level	Hyperactive— can't sit still	Lethargic—sedate, passive
(2) Regularity	Unpredictable and inconsistent patterns	Rigid and inflexible patterns
(3) Response to New Situations	Outgoing, aggressive, approaching	Withdrawing, timid, overly cautious
(4) Adaptability	Likes surprises, fights routine, dislikes structure	Dislikes change, likes routine, needs structure
(5) Sensory Threshold	Unaware of changes in light, sound, smell, feels optimistic	Overly sensitive to changes in light, sound, smell, feels pessimistic, unrealistically negative, denies positive
(7) Response Intensity	Overly loud and animated; high energy	Overly quiet and soft, low energy
(8) Distractibility	Insensitive to visual and auditory stimuli outside self	Unable to focus attention, overly sensitive to visual and auditory stimuli
(9) Persistence	Persists until task completed, rigid and inflexible	Gives up easily, doesn't try new things

His body needs to move. He becomes very distressed when he is physically confined with a seat belt in the car or must sit quietly.

Benjamin sits quietly on the floor playing with nesting cans. He stacks the cans and then fits them inside. He accomplishes his task with few movements: his legs remain outstretched; his body is leaning forward slightly but not rocking back and forth; he has the cans close to him so his arms and hands need limited movement. Benjamin has a low activity level. He was a quiet baby, not kicking his blankets off or twisting and turning often. He becomes distressed when he has to rush around to put away toys or quickly get ready to go somewhere.

Regularity   Valeria may act like she is hungry for her first bottle at 9:00 one morning, not until 10:00 the next day, and at 8:30 the third morning. Her bowel movements occur at no regular times. Valeria's body is having difficulty establishing its biological time clock for eating, sleeping, and eliminating. She has an unpredictable body schedule.

Sarina has a bowel movement every morning at about 9:00, takes a bottle at about 9:30, and then takes a 1½ hour nap. Sarina has a well-established body schedule.

Approach or Withdrawal as a Characteristic Response to a New Situation   Jamol hides behind his mother as he enters the room each morning. He hides behind the caregiver whenever someone strange walks in the door. He stands by the wall and watches others play with the new ball. He leaves food he does not recognize on his plate, refusing to take a bite. Jamol is slow to warm up. He needs time to get used to new situations. Jamol is distressed when he is pushed into new activities. Being told that a new ball will not hurt him or that the strange food is good for him does not convince him. When he feels comfortable, he will play with the new ball. He needs time and space for himself while he becomes familiar with a situation.

Carlos arrives in the morning with a big smile. He looks around the room and notices a new puzzle set out on the table. He rushes over to it, asking the caregiver about it and giggling at the picture. He takes the puzzle pieces out, puts some of the pieces back in and then seeks assistance from the caregiver. Carlos warms up quickly. He is excited about new situations and eager to try new experiences.

Adaptability to Change in Routine   Llema is used to snack time at the table. She knows how to get her hands washed, seat herself, enjoy her snack with her friends, and then wash her hands and go play. Today the caregiver has planned a surprise. She takes the children out into a corner of the play yard and serves a special snack. Llema is upset because this new place for snack is different from what she is used to. Llema fusses and will not eat her snack. Llema follows routines well and finds security in their consistency. She has difficulty making adjustments when a routine is changed.

Desiree is delighted with having a surprise snack outdoors. She also adjusts quickly when the books are changed to a different shelf and the home living center is moved to a different part of the room. Desiree adapts well to changes. She takes them in stride and focuses on the experiences rather than the changes in routine.

Level of Sensory Threshold Jose is bothered by light when he is trying to go to sleep or is sleeping, so the caregiver holds a blanket to shield his eyes as she rocks him to sleep. Jose awakens when a door is quietly closed. Jose is very sensitive to noise, light, and pain. He is easily bothered by what others believe are mild sounds and light.

Ming "sleeps through anything." He can sleep in the same room with children who are playing. He does not need the room darkened. When he falls and bumps himself, he often does not even whimper. Ming has a high tolerance for sound, light, and pain. Sometimes the caregiver has to check his injuries to see if he needs help, since he may not realize his needs.

Positive or Negative Mood Angela looks at the toy shelf and says she does not like toys. She plays with a toy dog and complains about his tail. Angela's negative mood characterizes the way she views familiar experiences.

Elvira looks at the toy shelf and sees many toys she likes. She plays with a cat which has lost one eye and is limp from children's pinching fingers. Elvira loves the cat; she croons to it and cuddles it. Elvira tends to look on life positively. She is positive until something happens to hurt or anger her.

Intensity of Response Arturo has just put a lock block together and, turning to the caregiver, he excitedly screams in her face, "Look! Look!" His response to his achievement shows up in his loud voice and his wriggling body. When Arturo cries, he cries loudly. When he talks, he talks loudly. Arturo uses a high level of energy to express himself. He puts himself fully into his response.

Carla has just put some people into her lock-blocks car and is pushing the car around. She has a smile on her face and is humming. She stops by the caregiver, points to the people, and excitedly says, "Daddy!" Carla uses a low level of energy in expressing her excitement. Her smiling, humming, and words show she is happy and excited, but her responses are quiet. She talks quietly and she cries quietly.

Distractibility Tamela is dropping blocks into a plastic jar. She sees Sheri go by, pushing a buggy. Tamela stops putting in blocks and walks over to push another buggy. She walks by the caregiver, who is reading a book to Li. Tamela stops to listen for a few minutes and then, noticing Carolyn sliding, she goes to the slide and slides. Tamela is very distractible. She plays with something or does something she is interested in until another activity catches her attention. Then she leaves her activity to move on to the activity that has attracted her attention.

Geraldine is building a block structure. Two other children are building their own block structures. Geraldine reaches for and places the blocks she wants, occasionally looking at the others playing with blocks or glancing around the room. She notices other activities, but she concentrates her attention on her own activity with blocks. Geraldine can maintain a high level of concentration. She can continue a task even when other activities are occurring around her.

Persistence and Attention Span   Jesse takes the three puzzle pieces out of the puzzle. He successfully puts in the banana. He picks up the apple piece and tries to fit it into a space. When it does not fit, he drops the piece and leaves the table. Jesse gives up when he is not immediately successful. He does not keep trying.

Clayton takes the three puzzle pieces out of the puzzle. He then turns and pushes and turns and pushes each piece until he has returned all three pieces to their proper places. Clayton persists with an activity even when it may be challenging or frustrating or takes a long time. When he completes his task, he expresses his pleasure with smiles and words.

All people have temperament traits. Temperament behaviors can be modified but not changed drastically. Very physically active people will never become very physically quiet. As they develop, they can make adjustments and modifications to reduce and control their outer actions, but internally they still have a high need for movement.

Caregivers must identify each child's temperament as well as their own. For example, Olaf is playing with blocks. The tall stack he built falls over, one block hitting hard on his hand. He yells loudly. Ray is playing nearby and also is hit by a falling block. He looks up in surprise but does not say anything. What will you do? What will you say? What is "loud" to you? What is acceptable to you? Why is a behavior acceptable or not acceptable to you? Do you think Ray is "better" than Olaf because he did not react loudly? What you do and what you say to Olaf reflects your acceptance or rejection of him as a person, reflects whether you are able to help him adapt to his environment, and reflects your ability to adapt to the child.

Caregivers can help infants and toddlers make small adjustments in their temperament behaviors. And caregivers should consciously make some adjustments for their own temperaments. For example, since Benjamin has a low activity level, you can advise him to begin putting toys away several minutes before you expect him to complete the task. You adjust a little by giving him extra time, and he adjusts a little by working slightly faster than he might have.

Self-Esteem

Self-esteem can be defined as "the evaluation which the individual makes and customarily maintains with regard to himself: it expresses an attitude of approval or disapproval, and indicates the extent to which the individual believes himself to be capable, significant, successful, and worthy. In short, self-esteem is a personal judgment of worthiness that is expressed in the attitudes the individual holds toward himself" (Coopersmith 1967, 4–5).

Summarizing his data on childhood experiences which contribute to the development of self-esteem, Coopersmith related, "The most general statement about the antecedent of self-esteem can be given in terms of three conditions: total or near total acceptance of the children by their parents; clearly defined and enforced limits; and the respect and latitude for individual actions that exist within the defined limits" (1967, 236). It is important that children think they are worthy people. Coopersmith's three conditions for fostering self-esteem—acceptance, limits, respect—provide guidelines for caregivers.

Acceptance   Each child needs to feel accepted for who he or she is right now. Children need to feel worthy and appreciated. For adults to focus on what children ought to be or what they may become can give children the impression that they are not all right. What children build on for the future is their sense of being all right now. Caregivers can encourage children to demonstrate acceptance of other children.

Limits   Adults set boundaries on behavior to help infants and toddlers learn to live safely and acceptably in their world. Society has rules. Some are physical: play in the yard, not in the street (to keep from physical harm). Some are interpersonal: you play with your doll and Greta will play with hers (possession, ownership—temporary in this case).

The boundaries set for children must fit their developmental level and be observed consistently. For example, both Yolanda and Theresa have difficulty sharing, so the caregiver does not force one to share her airplane with the other. All the children have been told, however, that when someone is playing with a toy, no one else is to take it. Therefore, when Yolanda grabs the airplane Theresa is playing with, the caregiver reaches in to hold the airplane still while she reminds Yolanda about taking a toy someone else is playing with.

Respect   Ralphino is playing with a tractor. He must play with it in the space away from children building with blocks. Miss Jana watches him push his tractor around in a circle, push it under a chair and bring it out the other side, lift it to climb the side and seat of the chair and down the other side. Miss Jana allows Ralphino to explore with his tractor. He is not hurting the tractor or the chair as he moves the tractor under and over the chair. Miss Jana does not force Ralphino to be realistic, that is, to recognize that tractors don't really drive over chairs. She allows him to use his fantasies and explorations, encourages "private talk," and uses "scaffolding" to help him learn about his world.

Stress

Many situations may distress the child in child care. Some of these are

- separation from the parent
- adjustment to another caregiver
- adjustment to different surroundings (room, children, materials)
- developmental changes, e.g., later nap time (such changes should change caregiver's behavior)

- adjustment to developmental changes, e.g., walking allows child to move into areas which may be dangerous
- conflicts and anxieties from home, e.g., illness, divorce, death, abuse
- over- or under-stimulation

Everyone encounters stress. Caregivers can plan ways to reduce stressful situations and to assist infants and toddlers and parents in coping with stress.

Alice Honig (1988), among others, has published tools and techniques for reducing stress in young children. Among these are baby cuddling, infant body holding, floor freedom for babies, caregiver body language, and early rhythmic and motor relaxation. The reader should also use the material in Chapters 2 and 3 to help reduce stress and establish a calm and positive learning environment.

Coping

Coping means learning how to make adjustments and adaptations and helping others to do so. Infants from birth make adjustments to their life situations. They adjust themselves to heat, cold, wetness, and hunger. They express their pleasure or displeasure by smiling, cooing, squirming, and crying. They learn that their behavior—cooing, crying—can affect their wetness and hunger. What started as unplanned reactions become planned and controlled actions to get assistance. The infant is adjusting to a situation—wetness—by tolerating wetness for longer periods of time and by calling attention to his or her displeasure at being wet.

Through her research with young children, Murphy identified the coping tasks of infancy. In infancy and the early years the following major tasks face the child:*

1. Managing the various basic bodily functions, breathing, feeding, eliminating, sleeping, etc., and the drives which evolve from them.
2. Persistent day-by-day dealing with the stimulation from the environment, especially that associated with newness, pain, and over-stimulation; as part of this, strong stimuli; developing ways of using the environment, dealing with the opportunities and frustrations it offers, and developing a capacity for deriving and contributing pleasure.
3. Coping with periodic challenges rising from "developmental crises" or "critical phases" at times of maturation of new functions, or major shifts in the relation of the child to the environmental (such as weaning) as he gets older.
4. Mastering special impacts, traumata, or threats to integration from illness, accidents, and the like.

---

*Reprinted by permission from Lois Barclay Murphy, *The Widening World of Childhood* (New York: Basic Books, 1962).

5. Learning to use all of his resources to move, both autonomously and with help, toward his goals and toward mutually gratifying exchanges with the environment.

6. Becoming a member of his culture who can deal with the deepest feelings and conflicts involved in relationships with the parent of each sex and with siblings and peers and can communicate and participate in play and work (1962, 293).

Discipline

Many experts on infant and toddler development avoid discussing discipline out of fear that their comments will be used inappropriately with children. While the current authors understand this, and the only discipline necessary with infants under the age of two years is to understand and fill their needs, it is essential that caregivers be able to set limits to help children learn to follow rules that keep themselves, other people, and property secure and safe. Therefore, discipline is an essential aspect of helping children develop. The following principles and procedures were taken, in part, from *Childcare Accountability Programs: CAPS* and *Establishing a Positive Learning Environment* (L. Douville-Watson and Watson, M. A. 1996).

The term *discipline* is used here to mean teaching appropriate behavior and setting limits on inappropriate behavior. It *does not* mean punishing children or controlling their behavior. In fact, the first principle of discipline is that adults should not control children's behavior. The most an adult can do for a child is to help the child fill their needs and administer consequences for children's behavior (Watson 1997). One of the most common errors caregivers in training make is to assume responsibility for controlling children's behavior. When you feel responsible for a child's behavior, you set up a "no win" situation wherein you must try to control the child which is impossible. It is essential to accept the fact that even young infants largely control their behavior, and that the caregiver is responsible to help fill needs and provide consequences. Once you accept the limits of reality regarding your control, you are in a position to help children become motivated, cooperative, and remain at ease most of the time.

The current trend in discipline is to use the concept of "time-in" rather than "time-out". Time-in involves keeping young children involved in enjoyable activities which are developmentally appropriate and fill their needs and the caregiver focusing attention and energy on appropriate rather than inappropriate behaviors.

We have already discussed using the 3A's to help children learn appropriate behavior. When caring for children under 30 months of age, the only discipline required is to assess the needs of the child and help fill them. It is *never* appropriate to completely remove attention, affection, or approval from infants, nor is shaking, hitting, or being physically or emotionally "rough" in any way acceptable. Problems usually arise when we have done everything we can think of, and the baby still screams and cries. This is the time to give responsibility to another adult, and take a break from the child to a quiet place where you can relax. Once you have regained your composure, re-enter the situation and assess all the baby's need levels again until you find what the baby requires to become at ease. Check out and observe physical needs such as teething, ear infections, stuffed sinuses, gas, and constipation. When discomfort continues for more than two hours, call the parent and consult your health professional.

Once children become mobile and enter toddlerhood, they must learn to accept "no" about certain behaviors. However, the number of behaviors they must accept "no" to is much smaller than many adults demand. The main principle to use in selecting which behaviors children must accept "no" is to start with only those behaviors that are directly harmful to themselves, other people, or property. For example, hitting another child with a toy is *directly* harmful, but calling another child "stupid" is not *directly* harmful. While we want to teach that name-calling is not polite or respectful behavior, we do not associate the word "no" with it.

The goal is to teach children to immediately "stop and wait" when the adult firmly, but not harshly, says "no." This is most effectively accomplished through *"classical conditioning"* of the word "no" with "stopping and waiting." Responses are most easily associated when immediate and consistent consequences occur, so "no" should be consistently paired with an immediate consequence such as removing the child. For example, it is common for toddlers to go beyond physical boundaries such as the yard, sidewalk, or street. To teach a child to stay within boundaries, the caregiver should choose a safe boundary and clearly explain and model the boundary, then stay close while the child plays, but not between the child and the boundary. When the child starts to cross the boundary, the caregiver firmly says "no," and holds the child from crossing the boundary. The caregiver then quickly diverts the child's attention to something interesting inside the boundary and heaps on the 3A's when the child moves back inside the boundary. When this procedure is *consistently* followed several times, the child will lean to "stop and wait" when you say "no," and just as important, will feel good for having displayed self-control. The caregiver must never trust that the child will honor a "no" or consistently follow directions. Instead, the caregiver should always watch to protect the child from harm.

Establishing "no" helps the young child with separation/individuation to move into another important developmental stage which is sometimes unfortunately called "the terrible twos." This important phase of personality development is mislabeled as "terrible" by controlling adults who have difficulty accepting children saying "no" to them. It is essential that children be allowed to say "no" to caregivers in order to develop a healthy sense of self and establish ego boundaries. Caregivers who do not accept "no" when it is not harmful to the child, others, or property do great harm to the child's sense of their right to make decisions and establish boundaries with other people. The three most effective forms of discipline with children who say "no" to practically everything are give choices, divert attention, and reverse psychology.

People learn to make wise choices by being able to choose. Caregivers who give children choices that they can handle for their age avoid many confrontations and teach children to choose wisely. Questions which can be answered by "yes" or "no" are often requests for problems as is a statement that commands the child. For example, "Do you want lunch?" is likely to result in "no" as well as the statement "You're going to eat your lunch now." A much more effective approach is to give the choice: "Do you want a grilled cheese or lunchmeat sandwich for lunch? You choose."

Diverting young children's attention to safe and acceptable activities often is a way to avoid confrontations. For example, if you take a young child into a setting with many breakable objects, diverting the child's attention to objects and activities in the setting that are not breakable can avoid problems. Your attention and interest most often evokes interest on the child's part, so rather than attending to all the breakable things, pay attention and draw the child into activities that are safe and appropriate.

Sometimes, using reverse psychology is helpful in avoiding confrontations. With an oppositional two year old who is stuck saying "no" to everything, asking the child to do the opposite of what you really want can help. For example, if the child refuses to eat vegetables, you can ask the child to eat everything else but do not eat the vegetables. Often, the child will do what is healthy for them and eat the vegetables just to demonstrate their autonomy. While this may seem somewhat manipulative, it can avert more damaging confrontations when used wisely.

With behaviors that are not directly harmful to the child, others, or property, a set of positively phrased rules and positive consequences for following rules is the single best form of discipline for children over two years of age. One of the most powerful principles of behavior shaping is "attention of *any* kind increases the frequency of a behavior" (Skinner and Belmont 1993). Therefore, when you establish rules for children which are phrased in what *not* to do, you are actually increasing attention to those behaviors which results in *more*, not less, of the behaviors you do not want. All rules should be phrased as the positive behavior you want to encourage. For example, the rule "talking with our inside (quiet) voice" is preferable to "no loud talking", and the positive counterpart to "No Hitting" is "Being Polite."

The number of rules should never exceed four or five and they should be general enough so the caregiver can define specific behaviors which fit under each rule. For example, a rule that states "walk quietly in the hall" is too specific because you will need other rules to cover class, lunch room, and playground walking. A better rule which fits all walking settings is "walk quietly." Table 5–2 lists a typical Rule Chart for three year olds. Notice that the rules are phrased as positive expectations, they are general to accommodate many behaviors, and are easily associated with positive consequences.

TABLE 5–2 SAMPLE RULE CHART AND DAILY POSITIVE CONSEQUENCES: THREE YEAR OLDS

RULE	SAMPLE BEHAVIORS	DAILY CONSEQUENCE
1.	Being Polite and Respectful *e.g., saying please, thank you, saying positive comments to others, etc.*	Extra 10 minutes play time
2.	Being Cooperative and Friendly *e.g., following directions, asking only once, smiling at others, etc.*	Extra 15 minutes free time
3.	Trying to do Activities *e.g., following game rules, picking up after yourself, etc.*	Star toward Friday Special Activity
4.	Taking Turns Listening and Talking *e.g., waiting your turn to speak, listening until the other person is finished, etc.*	Telling a story during story time

Once rules are defined, discussed, and modeled, a positive consequence is established for each rule which can be provided on a daily basis. Consequences which are as naturally associated to the rules as possible should be used. For example, Table 5–2 lists extra play time as the daily consequence for being polite and respectful, and extra free time is the consequence for being cooperative and friendly.

Finally, do not expect perfection. Both Vygotsky's scaffolding and the behavior shaping principle of successive approximation tell us to accept the child at the level where they can presently perform, and sensitively help them move toward the goal behavior. If a child is presently only capable of following a rule 20 percent of the time, provide the positive consequence at that level, and as he or she learns to perform the behavior more often or better, increase the level expected to earn the consequence, but do not expect the rule to be followed 100 percent of the time because none of us is perfect.

"Catching the child being good" and heaping on the 3A's are extremely powerful in helping children behave appropriately, but when a child is chronically anxious, angry, or depressed, they may not be able to follow the rules. When this occurs with children over 30 months, the caregiver must be prepared to deal with the situation by using a series of "behavior limiting steps" to help the child follow the rules. Since drawing attention to a behavior increases it, the first limiting step is to give a child who is being disruptive a *nonverbal signal* such as getting eye contact or touching the side of your nose. This signals the child that their behavior is not acceptable and gives them a cue to change the behavior without drawing undue attention to the child. When the child corrects their behavior at this step, the caregiver should heap on the 3A's.

When a nonverbal signal does not help the child change their behavior, withdrawing the positive consequence for not following the rule is the next step. This gives the caregiver an opportunity to discretely discuss what the child was feeling that caused the loss of the privilege.

Occasionally, nonverbal signals and losing positive consequences are not sufficient for a child to follow the rules. In this case, the next step is for the caregiver to remove the child from the group and choose a solitary activity until they are ready to follow the rules. When the child complies and is ready to return, they should verbalize (if possible) how they need to behave to re-enter normal group activity. It is *never* acceptable, and is illegal in most states, to allow a child to be unsupervised by an adult, so the quiet area should be in a place away from other children but where an adult can observe and supervise the child. The key to this working is that the 3A's are not available until the child is willing to follow the rules.

Biting Behavior

Biting, which occurs quickly and without warning, is an extremely difficult aggressive behavior to change in infants and young toddlers. Caregivers are encouraged to practice the 3A's, provide adequate child-to-adult ratio with plenty of floor space, and provide a variety of toys to help prevent the occurrence of biting. However, when biting does occur, stating a firm "no" with a disappointed look at the child is appropriate. The child care professional should ask the toddler to apologize, if appropriate, and then say "we don't hurt, we are nice" while the hurt child is being comforted. According to the American Academy of Pediatrics, examples of appropriate positive discipline "include brief, verbal expressions of disappointment" (1996).

In addition to these procedures, information should be collected regarding what precipitated the bite. Often, this impulsive aggression consistently occurs after a set of circumstances that the biter can not tolerate such as feeling rejected. Therefore, getting specific information can help the caregiver change patterns to stop subsequent biting.

When all of these procedures fail, the final behavior limiting step is to have the child removed from the setting by the parent or administrator, and provide professional help to the parent and child so the underlying reasons for the child not being able to follow the rules can be addressed and resolved.

Focusing your attention on catching the child being good, establishing positive rules and daily consequences, and being prepared with a set of behavior limiting steps supplies the caregiver with all the disciplinary tools necessary. You can then help children develop healthy self-concepts and personality traits, and actually feel good about following the rules that keep them safe and secure.

Social Development

Self and Not Self
Infants and toddlers are "egocentric." They understand the world only from their own perspective. They think that when they hurt a finger, everyone

feels the hurt the way they do. They think that when they say "Dink," everyone knows exactly what they mean. They do not understand that there are other points of view.

Infants are learning about themselves. In the process of learning about "self," they learn about "not self." During the first year one major development is that children construct knowledge about themselves.

Recognition of one's physical self develops gradually during the first eighteen months. For example, Brian is touching the face on the mirror. Mrs. Larsen points to the child in the mirror and says, "Who is that?" Brian smiles and says, "Brian." Brian was able to match his mental image of when he looked at himself in the mirror before with what he now sees in the mirror. In the first year infants relate to their mirror image as though it is someone else. By 18 months of age toddlers identify themselves in the mirror.

The continuing development of self-concept is evident in the child's language. The pronouns, I, me, my, mine represent one's own point of view. You refers to someone else. Young children must learn that when they use the words I, me, my, mine, each means that particular child, and you is someone else. When children hear someone saying, "I want you to sit down in your chair," they must learn that "I" is the person who spoke and "you" means that particular child. In other words, each child is "someone else" to the other person. As children construct the concept of self and others, they generalize these language usage rules even though they are not conscious of the rules. Their language reflects the level of understanding about themselves and others. Many two-year-olds have difficulty with personal pronouns.

Interactions with Others

The children in Lynn's child care home are playing on the floor of the den. Andy, 16 months old, walks up to Cameron, almost 4, who is lying on the floor. Andy smiles, pats Cameron's back, and lies on top of him, humming. Andy rolls off Cameron and holds his legs in the air. He pulls on Cameron's belt loops and rolls up beside Cameron. Cameron is giggling and gives Andy a big hug. Andy is showing affection for Cameron, and Cameron is showing affection for Andy. Each is constructing a value of himself by feeling the affection of the other person toward him. The young child's sense of self is related to his experiences with others (see Figure 5–3).

Attachment   Fourteen-month-old Louise is walking in the yard carrying a small truck in her hand. She sees Randy, the caregiver, and squeals and giggles. She walks rapidly to Randy with arms up and a big smile on her face. Attachment is the special, close relationship between the infant and an adult. Attachment provides security for infants as they encounter new experiences in their world.

A strong, positive attachment develops out of lots of looking into each other's eyes, touching, stroking, and cuddling; it comes from rapid and consistent response to the infant's cries, and by the infant picking up cues from

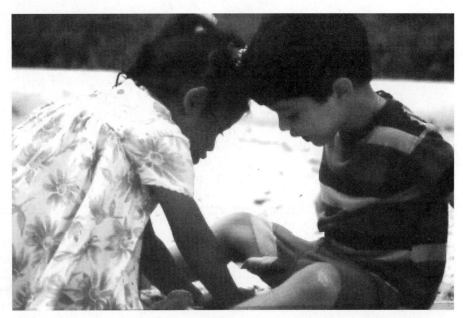

Figure 5–3 Young children value themselves when they know other children like them.

the adult that the infant has worth and is special. When the adult, whether parent or caregiver, responds quickly and appropriately to the infant's needs—for example, for food, for touching, for comforting—the infant builds trust in that adult.

Attachment to the parents and caregiver affects what the infant does later on. Strong attachment has a positive influence on the child's confidence in relating to the world for the rest of his or her life.

Most research regarding attachment has examined infants and their mothers. This research also applies to infant-caregiver relationships.

1. Each infant needs to establish an emotional attachment with a primary caregiver. This attachment develops through regular activities like feeding and changing diapers, as well as, cuddling, crooning, looking, and touching.

   The primary caregiver should provide physical contact, learn the infant's needs, schedule, likes and dislikes, temperament, and act in ways which comfort and stimulate the infant, and which respond to the infant's preferences.

   When more than one caregiver is responsible for a group of infants, care may be shared with other caregivers. The primary caregiver can share her knowledge about the infant's needs and preferences so other caregivers match their care to the infant. These caregivers should report observations of the infant's behavior to the primary caregiver.

The primary caregiver has two specific responsibilities: (a) establishing special attachment with the infant, and (b) gathering, coordinating, and sharing information with other caregivers and the infant's parents.

2. Each infant needs to have a caregiver respond quickly and consistently to cries or cues of distress. The infant then learns to trust the caregiver. When crying infants are left alone for several minutes before a caregiver checks to see what they need, or when the caregiver responds to their cries sometimes and leaves them alone sometimes, infants have difficulty establishing a strong attachment to the caregiver because it is difficult to develop a strong sense of trust. Responding to infants does not spoil them. The most important task an infant has is to develop trust in and attachment with the caregiver. For this to happen, the caregiver must respond quickly and consistently to the infant's needs.

3. The infant and the primary caregiver need special time together. This "getting to know you" and "let's enjoy each other" time is calm, playful time to relax, look, touch, smile, giggle, cuddle, stroke, talk, whisper, sing, make faces, and carry out other special activities. Sometimes this may be active time; for example, holding the infant up in the air at arm's length and talking and giggling and then bringing the infant almost face-to-face and talking or giggling. Other times it may be very quiet; for example, rocking the infant, cuddling, and softly stroking the infant's arms, legs, or back while not talking at all (see Figure 5–4).

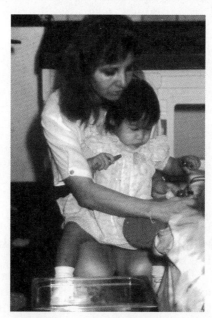

Figure 5–4 The caregiver spends special time with each child to look, touch, cuddle, and talk.

4. The caregiver must treat the infant as a special, important person. Infants pick up cues which show that you like or dislike them. Infants are not objects; they are individuals of worth with whom you establish an emotional relationship, as well as, provide for their physical, emotional, social, and intellectual needs.

Locus of Control

Our culture expects us to behave in appropriate ways. These expectations are passed on to infants by their families, caregivers, and peers. In order to live in a world with other people, young children must learn appropriate behaviors.

External Influences   Adults influence the infant's feeding. Infants give cues to indicate when they are hungry. At one time adults were advised to set feeding time in a rigid schedule. If infants were hungry before the schedule time, they were left to cry until the clock said it was time to eat. Now pediatricians recommend that adults follow the infant's internal clock for feeding time. When the infant gives adults hunger cues, adults supply food.

Each infant has individual sleep needs. In a child care home or child care center, sleep may be coordinated with the sleeping and awake times of other children. Caregivers should focus on providing sufficient space and time for some infants to sleep while others are awake. Blankets around cribs, dividers, and area lighting can help separate the sleepers. A misuse of control is to arbitrarily change the infant's sleeping time to fit into the caregiver's schedule. The 12-month-old has increasing hours of wakefulness but may still need a morning nap. Keeping one child awake all morning because no one else in the infant room takes a morning nap creates stress in that infant.

Early external influences also focus on the infant's movement. Restrictive clothing, cribs, playpens, and walkers keep children from moving where they want to. Some restrictions may be for the child's benefit (safety), and some may be for the benefit of the adult (to keep the child and toys in a playpen instead of scattered all over the floor). Adults may be tempted to use controls which benefit themselves, but sometimes these are too restrictive and harmful for the child. It may be handy for the adult to have four playpens, one for each infant and that child's toys. But infants need space in which to move for their muscular development and coordination, and they need stimulation from the novelty and variety made possible by moving around a room touching, pulling, tasting, and throwing different objects in different positions and locations.

Internal Controls   Two-year-old Sara asks for a glass of orange juice. When Ms. Price, the caregiver, says, "Yes, here's a glass of orange juice," and turns to the counter to get it, Sara starts screaming. Sara needs her desires met immediately—the instant she has stopped talking. Even though the caregiver's words say "Yes," it still takes her a few seconds to get the glass to where Sara can see it. Sara has not learned to "wait." After Sara has expressed her desire, she must control her feelings and actions. Instead of instant gratification, she now has to "hold" for those few seconds. Waiting or delaying gratification is a very frustrating process. In the early years the child slowly increases his "wait" time, but each desire is tested in each new situation.

During the first two years of life the infant gradually identifies causality; i.e., that one action causes something else to happen. As infants construct cause-and-effect relationships, they also learn to distinguish between what they cause and what others cause. When infants learn that they can cause reactions, they gain some power to control what they will do and when they will do it. They can use this newly developed power both positively and negatively to control themselves and their environment.

The struggle to be in control of one's behavior is a continuing process. Young children see a world full of objects they want and places they want to go. They think everyone should agree with their desires, and these desires direct much of their behavior.

Independence   After the first months of dependence infants become competent to do some tasks by themselves. The one- and two-year-old child also wants to do things independently. This assertion of independence is an important step.

Young children are happy accomplishing tasks by themselves. However, the desire for independence also causes frustration. Children sometimes want to do something that is unsafe or for which they are not physically able. Their judgment may not match the difficulty or danger of the task. Their internal desires and controls help them decide what they want to do and help them achieve their tasks. However, they also need assistance from others who exert external control for the children's safety and to help them achieve their intentions.

Control of one's own or others' behavior is an area requiring continuing adjustments. The dependent infant soon becomes a toddler vigorously asserting his or her independence. The caregiver must seek a balance of doing some things for the child, assisting the child to do other things, and in allowing the child to do yet other things all by him- or herself. The child's assertion of independence is healthy, but the child is not always knowledgeable and wise. The caregiver must therefore decide what is best to help the child accomplish tasks which reinforce the child's feelings of worth and competence.

Knowing that the infant will gain competence in walking by trying to walk, the caregiver can provide space and allow the infant to try to walk unassisted. The caregiver must give the infant opportunities to stand up, fall down, stand up, step, and fall down. The caregiver helps by providing space where the infant will not get hurt when falling and by encouraging and comforting the infant in his or her persistent efforts.

Caregivers must guard against allowing their own desires for neatness and order to unduly limit the child's experiences. For example, toddlers want to feed themselves. In the process of developing the necessary muscular control and concentration on the task of feeding, toddlers may drop much food on the floor, table, and themselves; they may spill their milk, juice, and other liquids many times; they may get food in their hair, in the caregiver's hair, and in anybody else's hair when they flip the food out of their spoons. You can help children feed themselves by helping them focus on their task, by providing food which is easily transportable in a spoon, and by providing a small yet adequate amount of food for them to eat so they can successfully accomplish their task. It delays development and limits toddlers' feelings of independence, worth, and competence if you do not allow them to feed themselves just so you will have no mess at mealtime.

Cognitive Development

Young children think differently from adults. Adults are logical thinkers; they consider facts, analyze relationships, and draw conclusions. Young children are pre-logical thinkers; their conclusions may be based on incomplete or inaccurate understandings of their experiences. For example, 2½-year-old Ivan has made a tilting stack of blocks. When he places a small car on top of the blocks, the stack tumbles down. Ivan tells Mrs. Young that the car broke the blocks. Ivan does not understand about gravity, about the need to stack blocks straight up rather than at a tilt, and about why the car's rolling wheels may have started the car's movement downhill. The object Ivan put on the stack just before it fell was the car, so as far as Ivan is concerned, the car broke the blocks.

Jean Piaget's research contributed significantly to the knowledge of cognitive development in young children. A brilliant young scientist, Piaget began his studies as a biologist. Later, listening to children respond to questions on an intelligence test, he became intrigued by their incorrect responses and the patterns of the children's verbal reasoning. Combining his scientific orientation, his knowledge of biology, and his experiences with the children's incorrect response patterns, Piaget began to study children's cognitive development. Piaget's clinical observation method included close observations of his own three young children as well as many other children in his extensive subsequent research. He observed what children did and wrote narrative descriptions, including the date, the participants, and the actions. Later, analyzing these detailed observations, he developed his theories of cognitive development.

Stages of Cognitive Development
Central to Piaget's theory is that there are stages of cognitive development. That is, four-month-olds are cognitively different from 24-month-olds.

Piaget contended that the sequence of development is the same for all children. However, the age and rate at which it occurs differs from child to child.

Piaget's first two stages of cognitive development involve children between birth and three years of age. These stages, the sensorimotor stage and the beginning of the preoperational stage, are those aspects of cognitive development relevant to an infant and toddler curriculum. Part III of this book includes detailed information about and suggested experiences to match the child's level of cognitive development.

Sensorimotor Stage   The sensorimotor stage of cognitive development occurs from birth to about age two. Piaget identified six substages.

Substage 1:   *Reflex*
                   Reflex actions become more organized.
                   Directed behavior emerges.
                   Birth to approximately 1 month.
Substage 2:   *Differentiation*
                   Repeats own actions.
                   Begins to coordinate actions, for example, hearing and looking.
                   Approximately 1–4 months.
Substage 3:   *Reproduction*
                   Intentionally repeats interesting actions.
                   Approximately 4–8 months.
Substage 4:   *Coordination*
                   Intentionally acts as a means to an end.
                   Develops concept of object permanence (an object exists even when the infant cannot see it).
                   Approximately 8–12 months.
Substage 5:   *Experimentation*
                   Experiments through trial and error.
                   Searches for new experiences.
                   Approximately 12–18 months.
Substage 6:   *Representation*
                   Carries out mental trial and error.
                   Develops symbols.
                   Approximately 18–24 months.

Preoperational Stage   The early part of the preoperational stage is called the preconceptual stage. The preconceptual substage occurs from about two to four years of age.

The child can now mentally sort events and objects. With the development of object permanence the child is moving toward representing objects and actions in his thinking without having to have actual sensorimotor experiences. The development and structuring of these mental representations are the tasks during the preoperational stage of cognitive development.

Preconceptual substage: Mentally sort objects and actions
                          Mental symbols partly detached from experience

Nonverbal classification
    graphic collections
        focus on figurative properties
        own interpretations
    no consistent classes of objects
    no hierarchy of classes
Seriation
    no consistent ordering of series of objects
Verbal preconcepts
    meanings of words fluctuate, are not always the same for child
    meanings of words are private, based on own experience
    word names and labels tied to one class
    focus on one attribute at a time—not class inclusion
Verbal reasoning
    transductive reasoning—from particular to particular
    if one action is in some way like another action, both actions are alike
        in all ways
    generalizes one situation to all situations
    reasoning sometimes backward—from effects to causes
    reasoning focuses on one dimension
Quantity
    How much?
    some, more, gone, big
Number
    How many?
    more, less
Space
    Where?
    use guess and visual comparison
    up, down, behind, under, over
Time
    remember sequence of life events
    now, soon, before, after (Cowen 1978).

Development and Learning

Piaget studied the interrelatedness of intelligence, development, and learning, and he made a distinction between development and learning.

Cognitive Functions   Piaget identified processes and functions in thinking. When you solve a problem, you have a feeling that "I understand it!" Piaget calls this equilibration, a cognitive balance. This cognitive balance may be only momentary. Soon you see, hear, touch, taste, smell, or mentally think of something which presents additional information which your mind seeks to process; this is called disequilibrium. If the additional information fits something you already know, you assimilate it into your concepts. If it does not quite fit, you must make accommodations. All people use these processes and functions.

For example, Shane is looking around and notices a ball on the floor. As he crawls to it, he bumps the ball so the ball rolls. He crawls to it again, picks up the ball, looks at it, licks it, and puts it down on the floor.

Shane started out in seeming equilibrium; that is, he seemed settled and quiet. Something caused disequilibrium; that is, something stimulated him. Shane responded to seeing the ball. What he saw may match in some way what he has seen before in previous play with a ball. He may have assimilated some idea about the ball. When he bumped the ball and it rolled, he was presented with additional information about the ball which did not fit into his present concept. Therefore, through accommodation, he makes adjustments in his concept of "ball" to now include the rolling movement. His disequilibrium is over, and he once again for an instant has attained equilibration, a sense of balance, of understanding his world. These processes or functions—assimilation, accommodation, and equilibration—occur continually through life.

Cognitive Structures   Shane's actions also show one of the structures of intelligence. Shane constructs concepts or schema as his mind organizes or structures its experiences. The schema or concept of ball is constructed as Shane see, touches, holds, and tastes a ball. When he sees the ball roll, that does not fit into his schema or structure of ball-ness. He continues to construct his knowledge of ball-ness by reorganizing his schema so that now rolling is included in ball-ness. Shane's schema of ball today is different from his schema yesterday, when he had never seen a rolling ball. Individual experiences and behavior bring about changes in schema.

Knowledge

Constructing Knowledge   Young children construct knowledge about themselves and their world. They cannot copy knowledge. They must act on their own and construct their own meaning. Each of their actions and interpretations is unique to them. They see an object and construct thoughts about that object. Young children's thinking organizes information about their experiences so they can construct their own understanding.

Types of Knowledge   Piaget identified three types of knowledge: physical knowledge, logico-mathematical knowledge, and social-arbitrary knowledge.

Physical knowledge is knowledge children discover in the world around them. Twenty-five-month-old Tommy kicks a piece of pinestraw as he walks in the play yard. He picks up the pinestraw, throws it, and picks it up again. He drops it in the water tray, picks it up, and pulls it through the water. Tommy has discovered something about pinestraw from the pinestraw itself. Tommy uses actions and observations of the effects of his actions on the pinestraw to construct his physical knowledge of pinestraw.

Kamii and Devries have identified two kinds of activities involving physical knowledge: movement of objects and changes in objects. Actions to move objects include "pulling, pushing, rolling, kicking, jumping, blowing, sucking, throwing, swinging, twirling, balancing, and dropping" (1978, 6). The child causes the object to move and observes it rolling, bouncing, cracking, and so on. The authors suggest four criteria for selecting activities to move objects:

1. The child must be able to produce the movement by his or her own action.
2. The child must be able to vary his or her action.
3. The reaction of the object must be observable.
4. The reaction of the object must be immediate (1978, 9).

A second kind of activity involves changes in objects. As compared to a ball which, when kicked, will move but still remain a ball, some objects change. When Kool-Aid® is put in water, it changes. Ann sees the dry Kool-Aid® and observes that something happens when it is added to water. She can no longer see anything that looks like the dry Kool-Aid®. She sees the water change color and can taste the difference between water without Kool-Aid® and water with Kool-Aid® in it. Her observation skills (seeing and tasting) are most important to provide her feedback of the changes that occur.

Logico-mathematical knowledge is invented by the child and involves relationships of objects.

Andrea is in the sandbox playing with two spoons, a teaspoon, and a serving spoon. She notices the spoons are "different." Although they fit into her schema of "spoon," she notices some difference in size. Thus, in relationship to size, they are different. At some time someone will label these differences for her as different or bigger or smaller than the other, but these words are not necessary for her to construct her concepts of sizes.

Social-arbitrary knowledge is knowledge a child cannot learn by him- or herself. It comes from "actions on or interactions with other people. Language, values, rules, morality, and symbol systems are examples of social-arbitrary knowledge" (Wadsworth 1978, 52) (see Figure 5–5).

Chad is eating a banana. He bites it, sucks on it, swallows it, looks at the remaining banana, and squeezes it. All of these are concrete actions which help him construct his physical knowledge of this object. Then someone tells him this object is a banana. The name, banana, is social-arbitrary knowledge. It could have been called "ningina" or "lalisa," but everyone using the English language uses "banana" to name that object.

In another example of social-arbitrary knowledge, Kurt follows Mrs. Wesley into the storage room. She sees him and says, "Kurt, go back into our room right now. You are not supposed to be in this room." Kurt did not make the decision that it is not permissible for him to be in the storage room; someone else decided and told him the rule.

Figure 5–5 The caregiver shares books which provide pictures, language, and stories.

Learning Skills Development

A final major area of development involves the skills necessary to accurately take in (input), put together (associate), remember (store in memory), and express (output) information. Children input stimuli from the environment through the five major senses: seeing (visual), hearing (auditory), feeling (kinesthetic), smelling (olfactory), and tasting (gustatory).

Several essential skills have been identified that children need in order to accurately perceive the stimuli in their world, and the caregiver should be aware of the information-processing requirements involved in tasks required of children (Watson 1995). When a child is asked to brush his or her teeth, for example, several visual, auditory, and kinesthetic skills are involved. The child must discriminate and remember the auditory directions, use visual discrimination, memory, and association to identify his or her toothbrush, use gross and fine motor coordination to actually brush, and associate auditory instructions with visual and motor skills.

It is extremely important that the caregiver become aware of the major information-processing skills and be sensitive to the perceptual requirements of the tasks they require children to perform. Table 5–3 lists the Developmental Learning Skills which have been demonstrated to be essential in tasks such as letter recognition, number concepts, and other pre-academic tasks.

TABLE 5–3 ESSENTIAL DEVELOPMENTAL LEARNING SKILLS

VISUAL CHANNEL	AUDITORY CHANNEL
Visual Attention	Auditory Attention
Visual Motor Control	Auditory Discrimination
Visual Discrimination	Auditory Memory
Visual Memory	Auditory Association
Visual Association	Auditory Association
Motor Output	Verbal Output

EARLY INTERVENTION AND INCLUSION OF SPECIAL NEEDS CHILDREN

The section in Chapter 2 on Children with Special Needs defined major categories of handicapping conditions, and general research findings and resources, for working with infants and toddlers. This chapter has spelled out functional principles for working with children exhibiting largely normal development.

Research from every category of special needs infants and toddlers strongly indicates that early intervention and inclusion in programs with normally developing children is helpful to the development of children with handicapping conditions. It is also important to understand that special needs children exhibit similar patterns and stages of development as normally developing infants and toddlers, but at a slower rate and with lower overall levels of development in certain areas.

The child care specialist should include special needs children in their program by ensuring that the following conditions are met:

1. Special needs infants and toddlers require more time and attention, so group size must be reduced.
2. Direct, active parent involvement in activities and procedures to assist development is necessary with special needs children, so parent education must be provided.
3. A team approach to including special needs children is essential. The child specialist, therefore, must work closely with specialized professionals such as psychologists, pediatricians, and speech therapists to design and implement appropriate interventions.
4. The child specialist must use specialized community resources and local and national associations to assist in the care and development of special needs infants and toddlers.

By assuring that these conditions are fulfilled, the child specialist can provide effective early intervention and include special needs children in the normal child care program.

STUDENT ACTIVITIES

1. During the children's alert play time observe two children of different ages between birth and 3 years, focusing on one area (physical, emotional, social, cognitive). Write down everything each child does and says for five minutes. Make a chart to compare the behaviors.

CHILD:	AGE:		CHILD:	AGE:
AREA:			**AREA:**	
Behaviors			Behaviors	

2. Observe one child between birth and 3 years interacting with one adult. List the behaviors each uses to get the other's attention.

	INITIATE	RESPONSE
Child		
Adult		
Child		
Adult		
Child		
Adult		

3. Use the developmental profile in Appendix A while observing one child between birth and 3 years for ten minutes. (If you do not have access to a child care center or child care home for observations, try the park, playground, laundromat, or supermarket.)

CHAPTER REVIEW

1. List four areas of development and learning.
2. What is the direction of the infant's physical development?
3. List four temperament patterns.
4. Define attachment as it relates to the child in a child care program.
5. List the stages of cognitive development of children from birth to 3 years of age.
6. Write one example of a child's behavior while constructing each of these kinds of knowledge:
   a. physical knowledge
   b. logico-mathematical knowledge
   c. social-arbitrary knowledge
7. Describe the learning model

REFERENCES

American Academy of Pediatrics, 1996. Caring for Our Children: National Health and Safety Performance Standards. American Health Association: Washington, DC.

Chess, S., Thomas, A., and Birch, H. G. 1965. *Your Child is a Person*. New York: Parallex.

Coopersmith, S. 1967. *The Antecedents of Self-Esteem*. San Francisco: W. H. Freeman.

Cowen, P. A. 1978. *Piaget with Feeling*. New York: Holt, Rinehart & Winston.

Douville-Watson, L., and Watson, M. A. 1996. *Child Care Accountability Programs. CAPS for Infants and Toddlers*. New York: Instructional Press, 21 Oak Shore Dr., Bayville, N.Y. 11707.

Fraiberg, S. H. 1959. *The Magic Years*. New York: Charles Scribner's Sons.

Gerber, M. 1989. *Educaring: Resources for Infant Educarers*. Los Angeles: Resources for Infant Educarers.

Greenspan, S., and Pollock, G. H., Eds. 1989. *The Course of Life*. Madison, CT: International University Press, Inc.

Honig, Alice Sterling. 1988. Baby moves: Relation to learning. International Early Childhood Conference, Washington, DC.

Kamii, C., and Devries, R. 1978. *Physical Knowledge in Preschool Education: Implications of Piaget's Theory*. Englewood Cliffs, NJ: Prentice-Hall.

Lamb, M. E., and Campos, J. J. 1982. *Development in Infancy*. New York: Random House.

Murphy, L. B. 1962. *The Widening World of Childhood*. New York: Basic Books.

National Institute of Dental Research and the National Association of Community Health Centers, Inc. 1979. *Good Teeth for You and Your Baby*. (NIH Publication No. 79-1255). Bethesda, MD: Authors.

Skinner, E. A., and Belmont, M. J. 1993. Motivation in the classroom: Reciprocal effects of teacher behavior and student engagement across the school year. *Journal of Educational Psychology* 85, pp. 571–81.

Wadsworth, B. J. 1978. *Piaget for the Classroom Teacher*. New York: Longman.

Watson, M. A. 1997. *Effective Tools for Disruptive Behaviors*. New York: Instructional Press, 21 Oak Shore Dr., Bayville, N.Y. 11707.

Watson, M. A. 1995. *Waldo Developmental Learning Skills Tests*. Freeport, New York: Instructional Press, 21 Oak Shore Dr., Bayville, N.Y. 11707.

Part II

Establishing a Positive Learning Environment

The four chapters in this section integrate the skills, principles, and theories learned in Part I into functional settings for care. Settings for care include communicating with, and using community resources for, families, understanding the variety of physical settings in which child care occurs, preparing positive indoor and outdoor environments, and designing and implementing curricula for infants and toddlers.

This section provides the caregiver with the tools necessary to assess individual children using Developmental Profiles, establish goals for growth using Developmental Prescriptions, and design and structure specific experiences and activities for each child and the group as a whole. In addition, the reader will be able to assess parent and family strengths and weaknesses so that communication with parents can optimally enhance the growth and development of children at home.

Infants and toddlers help to develop their own curriculum through engaging energetically in activities that contribute to their growth. By being sensitive to each child's unique needs, family strengths, cultural traditions, and community resources, a positive learning environment can be established and maintained for each child in care.

6

Communicating with Parents and Staff

OBJECTIVES

After completing this chapter, the child development specialist should be able to:
1. Develop procedures for informal and formal communications with parents.
2. Analyze the working relationships and responsibilities of the staff with whom the caregiver is working.
3. Analyze the caregiver's own performance in staff relationships.
4. Understand the active listening process.

CHAPTER OUTLINE

I. Why Communicate with Parents and Staff?
II. Communicating Successfully with Parents, Staff, and Children
  A. Active Listening: The "How" in Communication
  B. Mirroring
III. Communication Situations
  A. Parent Assessment and Education
  B. Teenage Parents
  C. Communicating with Staff
IV. Resources for Parents and Staff

CHILD DEVELOPMENT ASSOCIATE FUNCTIONAL AREAS

IV. 11 Families
V. 12 Program Management
VI. 13 Professionalism

Communication is essential to a child care program. For communication to be effective, the people involved must actively listen, think, and express their ideas and feelings in a meaningful way.

132

WHY COMMUNICATE WITH PARENTS AND STAFF?

Caregivers and parents seek a common goal: to provide high-quality experiences for children. In order to achieve this goal there must be communication between caregivers and parents and among the caregiving staff. Communication is a two-way process. It requires both active listening and effective expression.

The attitudes caregivers and parents have toward each other are reflected in the communication process. The nonverbal, emotional messages that are sent in the questions asked and the statements made will either help or hinder successful communication.

COMMUNICATING SUCCESSFULLY WITH PARENTS, STAFF, AND CHILDREN

In Chapter 2 we discussed the 3A's of child care and how they impact on the communication between caregiver and child.

The following are excerpts from F.A.R.E. (Family Actualization through Research and Education, Actualization, Inc. Douville-Watson and Watson 1988) on a communication technique called Active Listening.

The following communication diagram shows the general communication process. A "sender" (A) sends a message verbally and noverbally to a "receiver" (B) who interprets the message and gives the sender feedback as to what the message means to the receiver.

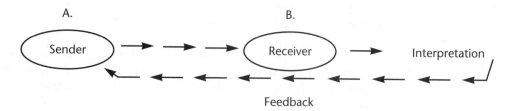

Active Listening: The "How" in Communication

Most of the common communication errors can be avoided by applying a technique called "Active Listening." This technique, which was developed primarily by psychologist Carl Rogers, has been put into very practical form for teachers and parents by the authors in the teaching program F.A.R.E. (Family Actualization through Research and Education, 1988). The most important skill in active listening is very simply to "feed back" the feeling message (not the words) of the sender in the words of the receiver. This simple definition of active listening requires further explanation because, although it may sound simple, it takes practice to learn to do it effectively.

Active listening differs from most common types of communication in the kind of feedback given to the sender. The type of feedback most commonly given is a "reaction" to what the words of the sender mean to the receiver. When we give this reactionary feedback, we most often close off the communication process because we become emotionally involved in the words of the message. Common reactionary feedback messages are: "You shouldn't say that!", "I don't agree with you!", "You're wrong!", and "I don't want to hear that kind of talk!"

Active listening, on the other hand, involves objectively listening, in a nondefensive way, for the deeper message of the sender and then giving "reiterating" rather than "reactionary" feedback. Rather than reacting to the words of the sender, the active listener interprets the entire message of the sender and gives it back to the sender.

The active listening communication process allows the sender to affirm, reject or, more commonly, clarify his message. By continuing to feed back the total message of the sender, the receiver can help the sender clarify the problem and, in most cases, arrive at his own solution.

An active listener also looks for nonverbal "body language" messages. The look on a person's face, the position of the body, and what the person does with his or her hands and arms can help you to understand the full message on the deepest level. Nonverbal behavior, as well as the words, feelings, and attitudes, combine to transmit the complete, deep message.

Although this technique may sound simple enough to learn, it requires active listening practice because most of us have learned to give reactionary feedback, particularly to children. With practice, however, caregivers will find the rewards of active listening worth the effort it takes to master the technique.

Here are some ways to test how well you are communicating with others:

1. Listen to the way you now respond to people. If you catch yourself reacting to the words of messages instead of the deeper meaning, you are "just talking." An active listener listens for the whole, deep message, including the words, feelings, attitudes, and behaviors.
2. An active listener never judges, criticizes, or blames another and listens for deeper feelings because feelings can never be wrong! Since the active listener looks for the deeper message, most feedback starts with words such as "It sounds like . . .", "You seem to feel . . .", "I hear you saying . . .", and other phrases which reflect the sender's feelings.
3. An active listener never responds to a message with advice or personal feelings. The idea of communication is to completely understand what the other person thinks and feels. This skill may be more difficult for caregivers to learn in their relationships with children in their charge because adults have so much more experience than children and it is hard to accept the fact that children can arrive at their own solutions to problems. Adults tend to want to teach and advise children before

they have completely understood the whole message that children are trying to communicate. One of the causes of the well-known "generation gap" is that children learn that adults don't understand them and don't "know where they're at." Even young children will furnish good solutions to problems if adults have the patience to "hear them out" and give back the meaning of the messages they hear and experience without teaching or advising.

4. An active listener only adds information to a message when the other person directly asks for it and after that person has completely expressed the entire message. You will know you have received the entire message when you hear real feelings and concern about what to do. At this point, feedback such as "Have you thought about what you can do?", or "How would you solve this?" will give the child a chance to ask for advice or begin problem solving on his or her own.

Mirroring

A simple but very effective technique for establishing rapport and making sure that the other person understands your messages, and that you understand theirs, is to use mirroring (Hendrix 1993). Mirroring simply means to repeat exactly what is said without adding or interpreting any of the speaker's words. When you communicate with staff, parents, or children, it can be very helpful to ask the person to repeat exactly what you say before they give their own response. When the other person mirrors you before responding, and you mirror them before responding, a sense of trust and understanding quickly develops that is very hard to obtain any other way. By mirroring each other, mutual respect and understanding is quickly developed. Mirroring is especially effective when communicating with others from cultural and/or language backgrounds different from your own.

Try mirroring with your family or friends first so you get the idea of how it works. The only words you are allowed to change in mirroring are personal pronouns, so if the other person says "I am happy", your mirroring response is "You are happy." One final rule in mirroring is that each speaker uses "I language" rather than "You language". "I language" starts with the word "I" and results in the speaker taking responsibility for their own thoughts, feelings, and behaviors. "You language", on the other hand, usually blames other people and stops the speaker from taking responsibility for themselves. By using "I language" when speaking and mirroring each other before you respond, most conflicts and misunderstanding can be cleared up without anger or hurt feelings.

COMMUNICATION SITUATIONS

Active Listening to Parents

Active listening helps caregivers understand parents as they express their concerns and raise questions about parenting. Parents are often isolated from other support systems and need the caregiver to listen to them and help them come up with solutions (see Figure 6–1). Active listening and mirroring helps overcome language and cultural barriers as well (Lally 1992).

Parents may want the caregiver to agree with them or reassure them, to confirm or reject ideas and pressures from family and friends. For example, Mabel rushed in one morning with her son and said, "I called my mother last night and told her I went back to work this week and she had a fit. She said it was too soon and that right now my place was at home." Listen to Mabel's words, her tone of voice; read her nonverbal cues, her facial expressions and degree of tenseness. She may be telling you that she is feeling frustrated and guilty, or she may be stating her mother's view while feeling fairly comfortable with her own choice of going back to work. You must listen to the whole story (words, tone, cues) to interpret accurately what Mabel is telling you.

Parents express their desires for their children. Phyllis said, "I want Velma to be happy. It bothers me to see her cry when I leave." Arlene stated, "I want Pearl to get used to babies because my baby is due next month." Listen to what the parent is saying not only about the child but also about the parent's own needs.

Actively listen to parents so that you will fully understand what care they expect you to provide. Some parents have very definite ideas and will tell you about them. Other parents do not say anything until they disagree with

Figure 6–1 Parents and caregivers need to communicate in order to ensure the best care for the child.

something, and then they may express frustration or be angry with you. Take in the parents' emotions as well as what they say to you.

Parents tell you much information about their children and themselves. Details about what the child does at home are needed by the caregiver each morning (see Figure 6–2). Listen carefully and record the information as soon as possible (see Chapter 9, Message Board).

Sharing with Parents

Information Parents need information about the daily experiences their child has in your care. The Message Board and Care Sheets (see Chapter 9) help you organize and record important things the child has done to share with the parent. Special experiences, like the child's excitement about a visiting rabbit, may go into the written record or the caregiver may tell the parent orally.

The child's rate and pattern of development can be shared with parents. Refer to the child's developmental profile (see Appendix A) to focus on recent developments and identify developmental tasks the child may soon be mastering.

Share ideas for stimulating the child's development (see Chapters 10–16), emphasizing the difference between facilitating and pushing the child. Parents are often very interested in written directions for and drawings of age appropriate activities and homemade toys (see Chapter 9–16).

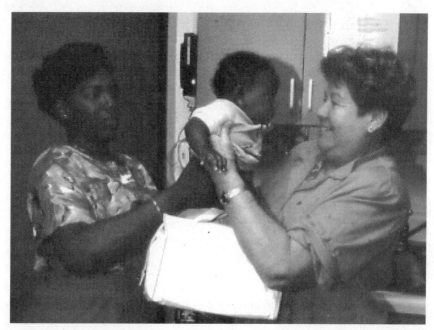

Figure 6–2 Parent and caregiver assist the child in making the transition between home and the child care program.

Share information relating to parents' concerns about their child. Mabel may be interested in information relating to the effect of day care on two-month-old children. Phyllis may be ready for information about separation anxiety. Arlene may need information which helps her understand that Pearl's sharing Mommy with the new baby involves much more than practice in getting used to babies. Changing sleeping and eating patterns and toilet-training are also areas that parents frequently raise questions about with caregivers.

Parents need information about the child care program. Before the child is admitted, the program director shares program goals, policies, and a description of the daily program and the practical use of the developmental prescription with parents. Many programs will include a developmental screening of the child as part of the initial evaluation of the incoming child. This will help guide caregivers as they make their decisions about program implementation. Many situations arise that parents need to clarify and discuss with caregivers. For example, Sal wants his 23-month-old daughter Gabriele to stop using her fingers when she eats. The caregivers can help Sal by sharing development information with him and assuring him that eating with fingers is perfectly normal at this age and use of utensils will come later when fine motor control is further developed.

Feelings　Caregiving involves feelings and emotions. Parents want to know that you are concerned about their child and about them. In a variety of ways let parents know that you like and respect their child. Parents look for caregivers who can and do accept and like their child and who provide emotional security.

Share the excitement of the child's new developments with the parent. The first time you see children pulling themselves up on the table leg, or teetering two steps, or holding utensils, or riding a tyke bike, or turning book pages, or hugging a friend, or asking to go to the toilet, or catching a ball, you are excited and pleased with their accomplishments. When you share these experiences with the parents, let them know how excited you are.

Express sympathy for the child or parent in situations where there is hurt. Express empathy with the parent in some of the trying, frustrating experiences which they encounter with children.

Expectations　Share your goals and expectations of the child care program with parents. Your casual statements may take on more meaning than written goal statements. Ms. Horsely describes a situation in which she encouraged a child's independence: "We want to help children become as independent as they can, so when Louella resisted my helping her take off her bib, I let her try to take it off by herself. She got stuck once, and I helped her lift one arm out, and then she could do the rest by herself. Her big smile and chatter showed me how pleased she was."

Parents are interested in what you expect of yourself as a caregiver. What kinds of things do you do? How committed are you? How friendly are you?

Do you think you are more important than parents? Do you extend and supplement parents or do you expect to supplant them? You communicate these expectations through your words, attitudes, mannerisms, and interactions with children and parents.

What do you expect of the children in your care? A child care program emphasizing the development of the whole child and individuality among children is supported by caregivers who facilitate that development. Assure parents that development does not follow a rigid schedule and is not identical among children. Parents often compare their child's development with another child's and gloat or fret at what they see. Caregivers who show that they believe children behave differently within a broad range of normal activity let parents know that adults can challenge children without putting harmful pressure on them.

Caregivers expect many things of parents. Some expectations you may express; others you should keep to yourself. You might expect parents to

- Love and like their child.
- Want to hear special occurrences in their child's day.
- Want to learn more about their developing child.
- Be observant of the child's health or illness.
- Be willing to share information about the child with the caregiver.
- Respect the caregiver.

Some parents will not meet your expectations. Because caregiving occurs in the family as well as in the child care program, you will need to resolve your differences with the child's parents.

You may need to change your expectations of parents. We speak of accepting children as they are. You need to take the same attitude toward parents. They come to the child care program because they need care for their child outside the home. They usually are not looking for situations that place additional demands and expectations on them as parents. So long as parents abide by the policies relating to health, attendance, and fee payment, they are doing their part to support the program. Information to help parents grow can be offered but not forced upon them. You may increase your awareness of the unique situation the parent faces by simply actively listening to them without judging them.

Involving Parents

In Decision-Making Some programs involve parents in decision-making. Many not-for-profit child care centers have policy boards which include parents. These boards may make recommendations and decisions about center policy. Sometimes parents even serve on boards that make administrative decisions about hiring and firing staff and selecting curricula. However, few family child care homes and for-profit child care centers involve parents in decision-making about policy, staff, or curricula.

Parents of infants and toddlers must be involved in some decisions relating to their child's care. The parent or pediatrician selects the infant's milk or formula; the caregiver does not make that decision. Parent and caregiver must share information about the child's changing eating and sleeping schedules. The length of time from afternoon pick-up to mealtime to bedtime varies among families. Since late afternoon naps or snacks may improve or disrupt evening family time, parents should discuss with you what schedule is best for the child and its family. Toilet-training must be coordinated between parent and caregiver. Both share information about the appropriateness of timing, the failures and successes of the child, and the decision to discontinue or continue toilet-training. If a parent insists that toilet-training be started or continued when you think the child is not ready, share with the parent information about the necessary development of the child before training can occur. Tell the parent about actions children take when they are showing an interest in or a readiness for toilet-training. Share with the parent the harmful effects on children of consistent failures and parental pressures. When the child is ready for toilet-training, the procedures at home and in child care must be the same so that the child does not become confused. Reassure the parent that you do not mind changing their child's diapers. Emphasize that this is another time for them to spend relating positively eye-to-eye.

With Children   Most parents of infants and toddlers in child care are employed. Therefore, parental involvement during the child care day is often limited to arrival and pick-up time. The parent can help the child take off a coat or unpack supplies when leaving the child in the morning, and can share with the caregiver information about the child's night, health, or special experiences. At pick-up time the caregiver initiates conversations about the child's experiences and projects during the day, while the parent helps the infant or toddler make the transition back to being part of the family by hugging the child or helping put on outdoor clothes.

Parent Assessment and Education

Within the past few years, there has been a growing need to quantify the skills and characteristics necessary to be a competent parent. Social and governmental interest in family values, increased laws regarding parent responsibilities, and the need for better parent education have necessitated identification, definition, and assessment of the skills which comprise competent parenting. In response to these needs, instruments to measure parent competence have been designed, most of which are checklists and survey tools with questionable theoretical and research foundation.

A new set of scales, The National Parenting Scales: N.P.S. Experimental Edition (Watson, 1996) have a sound theoretical and research basis in the C.D.A. Competency Goals and Objectives. The N.P.S. assess parents in the essential skills included in Table 6–1 in addition to personality characteristics, environmental resources, and interactional dynamics between parent and children.

TABLE 6–1 PARENT COMPETENCY GOALS AND FUNCTIONAL AREAS

I. Establish and maintain a safe, healthy living environment.

1. Safe: Parent provides a safe environment to prevent injuries.
2. Healthy: Parent promotes good health and nutrition and provides an environment that contributes to the prevention of illness.
3. Learning Environment: Parent uses spatial relationships, materials, and routines as resources for constructing an interesting, secure, and enjoyable environment that encourages play and exploration.

II. Advance physical and intellectual competence.

4. Physical: Parent provides a variety of equipment, activities, and opportunities to promote the physical development of children.
5. Cognitive: Provide activities and opportunities that encourage curiosity, exploration, problem-solving, and responsibilities appropriate to the developmental levels and learning styles of children.
6. Communication: Parent actively communicates with children and provides opportunities and support for children to understand, acquire, and use verbal and nonverbal means of communicating thoughts and feelings.
7. Creative: Parent provides opportunities that stimulate children to play with sound, rhythm, language, materials, space, and ideas used in individual ways to express creative skills and abilities.

III. Support social and emotional development and provide positive guidance.

8. Self: Provides physical and emotional security and helps each child to know, accept, and take pride in himself or herself and develop a sense of independence and self-esteem.
9. Social: Parent helps each child feel accepted in groups, helps children learn to communicate and get along with others, and encourages feelings of empathy and mutual respect among children and adults.
10. Guidance: Provide a supportive environment in which children can learn and practice acceptable behaviors as individuals and in groups.

IV. Maintain positive and productive relationships within the family and community.

11. Relationships: Parent maintains open, friendly, honest, and cooperative interactions with each family member, encourages involvement, and supports relationships with all family members and members of the community.

V. Ensure a well-run, purposeful home, responsive to individual needs.

12. Management: The parent is a manager who uses all available resources to ensure effective home operation. Competence in organizing, planning, and cooperating with others is demonstrated.

VI. Commitment to constructive family values.

13. Family Values: Parent makes decisions based on knowledge of sound childhood principles and practices, and sets limits and values that are in the best interest of each child as a regular priority.

A general requirement of excellent child care involves a team approach between parent, the child care program, and community resources. Initial research found that a group of eighty parents entering children in day care who took the N.P.S. worked more closely with Child Care Specialists and program goals than did parents not taking the Scales (Watson 1997). When combined with Developmental Profiles and Prescriptions for children, it appears that assessment of parent strengths and weaknesses results in a cooperative team approach consistent with child care program goals.

Four Scales were developed for each of three Developmental Levels based on the ages of the children in care:

Scale I. Parenting Skills Scales: an objective multiple choice scale measuring the essential skills in the six Goals and thirteen Functional Areas listed in Table 6–1;

Scale II. Family Values Scale: a projective assessment measuring social and moral judgement and values applied to conflict situations with children;

Scale III. Home Environment Study: a structured study of the home environment from the perspective of children for developmentally appropriate care; and

Scale IV. Parent/Child Observation and Interview: a structured observation and interview of parents with children which evaluates interaction and communication dynamics.

Quantitative results from all four scales are combined to establish a Parent Profile and a Parent Prescription detailing individual parent strengths and weaknesses and providing procedures and resources to improve caregiving skills.

Because the N.P.S. are available in a Self Administered and a Professional Version and provide Developmental Levels, from birth to eighteen years, they can be used easily by the caregiver or child care program to help parents understand their parenting strengths and weaknesses, and to ensure that developmentally appropriate activities and practices are continued in the home setting. Since parents can take the Scales home to complete, they are not threatened as they might be if they were "tested."

Results from initial research using the N.P.S. reveal four parenting styles that the caregiver can use to communicate effectively with parents. In addition to a Competent Style (CO) where parents use appropriate goals and objectives, the caregiver can determine a Selfless Style (S) where the parent doesn't consider their own needs, doesn't establish appropriate limits, abdicates inappropriate responsibilities to the children, and lacks self-respect, a Controlling Style (C) where the parent is demanding or authoritarian and lacks respect and sensitivity to children's needs, and a Detached Style (D) where the parent is not emotionally and/or behaviorally involved with children appropriate to the care situation.

Knowing the strengths and weaknesses of the parents in your group can help you communicate effectively and plan ways to extend the care program into the home to optimally enhance the development of each child.

Parents need to be informed of the particular national issues concerning child care that will impact on their children, and they need to know who to write to at local, regional, and national levels to lobby for services for their children.

Parents need to be educated how to choose a safe, developmentally correct, and growth-producing environment for their children. They need to understand the on-going responsibilities that the caregiver has for children, what constitutes a trained or certified person, and the caregiver's level of education.

Parents should have an active relationship with their caregivers. This partnership exists in order to best facilitate all the daily needs of their children.

Parents need competent parent education from someone they trust and whose experience will meaningfully impact on the decisions they make. As part of that training, they need help with setting priorities to balance all areas of their lives and to help take good care of themselves, as well as their children. They also need a designated time and place to discuss on-going concerns with other parents of similarly aged children. They need resource materials to read, listen to, and view.

The child care facility, regardless of the type of setting, can fill all these needs. Often, a parent survey will help identify which areas should be addressed first. All the measures suggested should be practical to help build a strong partnership between parents and caregivers.

Statistics indicate grandparents are taking care of children more than ever before. According to 1997 Children's Defense Fund, more than 1.4 million children lived with grandparents with a parent absent in the household during 1995. This is a 66 percent increase since 1989.

A special invitation for grandparents who are now facing the challenge of raising grandchildren as primary caregivers should be extended, since this family situation is sometimes not evident. Some grandparents are frustrated and some are isolated. Often they try to balance the demands of working full-time, and acting in the role of primary caregiver. They need encouragement and a place to confide in someone regarding their concerns. All these factors add to grandparent's increased stress. It is understandable why these caregivers often need support.

Parent-Caregiver Conferences

It is important that parent meetings and conferences have structure. Preparing an agenda and checklist, being a good listener, and keeping confidences are some of the important factors to consider (Orstein and Chapman 1988). Consideration of differences in education, language, and cultural issues is also important (Bauette and Peterson 1993).

Interpret each child's progress to parents within the framework of a Developmental Profile and Prescription to help parents understand and appreciate developmentally appropriate early childhood programs (Feeney and Kipinis 1990).

Employed parents often have difficulty scheduling formal conferences. To make the most efficient use of time, plan the conference thoroughly. Identify the major purpose of the conference. If the parent requests a conference, ask what the parent's concerns are so you can prepare for the conference. If the caregiver requests the conference, tell the parent why, so the parent has time to think about it before the conference begins. Gather background information to discuss the topic. Caregiver records of observations, both formal and informal, may be helpful. Outside sources such as articles, books, pamphlets, tapes, and filmstrips may provide information for the caregiver and share with the parent. You may also need to refer parents to organizations in your community or region.

Plan the conference agenda:

1. State the purpose for the conference.
2. If initiated by a parent, state your interest in listening to the parent.
   a. Actively listen to them.
   b. Present information that you think are appropriate and helpful to the discussion.
3. If initiated by the caregiver, state your information, ideas, and concerns.
   a. Actively listen to the parents' responses.
   b. Explain your points further if you think it will help the parent understand.
4. Provide additional outside information if needed.
5. Discuss the issue(s) with the parent.
6. Emphasize that both you and the parent are working together for the welfare of the child.

Home Visits

Home visits are a regular part of Head Start programs, but few other child care programs make them. Home visits can be valuable opportunities for the parent and the caregiver to learn more about each other and the child. The caregiver can see how the parent and child relate to each other in their own home. Home visits must be planned carefully.

Identify the purpose for the visit. It is to get acquainted? Is it to gather information? Is it to work with the parent, child, or both?

Gather background information the visit requires. Do you need to take along any forms to be filled out? Will you be sharing your program goals? If so, do you have a flyer or pamphlet or will you just tell them? Are there specific problems or concerns you want to discuss? Do you have written documentation of the child's behavior, such as daily reports or notes, to share, as well as resource and referral information which might be available?

When you make a home visit, you are a guest in the parent's home. You are there to listen and learn. Discuss the purpose of the conference. When you have finished talking about the issues, thank the parents for their interest, time, and hospitality, and then leave. A home visit is not a social visit.

Teenage Parents

"Kids Having Kids" is an important reality examined in a book with the same name (1996). A sufficient amount of life experience is necessary for the development of sound coping mechanisms and informed decision making, and raising children under the best of circumstances is frustrating and very difficult at times. Teenage parents have not had enough life experience to learn the valuable coping mechanisms necessary to competently deal with our extremely complex society, usually do not have family support, and almost always suffer from limited financial resources because they have not developed careers. Add the necessity to set aside childhood dreams and aspirations and place a baby's needs before their own, and it is no wonder that the large majority of teenage parents have emotional conflicts that decrease their ability to provide good parenting.

According to the Children's Defense Fund, "The rate of adolescent childbearing decreased in 46 states between 1991 and 1994 . . . 59.9 percent of teen births were to older teens, 37.6 percent to 15–17 year olds, and 2.5 percent to girls younger than 15." This decrease is thought to be the result of national campaigns against AIDS and the use of birth control. Even with this reduction in teenage pregnancies, nowhere is the need for a solid partnership between parents and the child care specialist more important than with teenage parents.

In order to effectively work with teen parents, the child care specialist should understand the factors that influence their parenting ability. Often mothers under 15 years of age have not received good prenatal care. "A mother less than fifteen years of age does not eat well or obtain regular medical care and is twice as likely to have a pre-term or low birth weight infant compared to a woman in her mid to late twenties" (Somers 1995). Good counseling should include a nutritional guide for teenagers such as the following from Nutrition for a Healthy Teenage Pregnancy (Somers 1997):

FOOD FAMILY	SERVINGS P/DAY
Calcium-rich group	4–5
Vegetables	6–7
Fruits	4–5
Grains	8–9
Extra lean meats and legumes	4–5
Quenchers	6–8

This guide can also be recommended for young mothers using the higher servings on the scale.

Teenage parents are still not adults and need to be accepted for who they are. Whenever possible referrals to community based organizations that can support both the father and mother should be made. It is the responsibility of the child specialist to know what resources are available in the community.

Teenage parents need healthy concepts for parenting including good information and role models. Information should include lessons about empty calories and good nutrition, handling finances, cleaning and organizing a home, and dealing with relationships. Good role models involve people in the community who can be of help to the new parent and increase the circle of support to the teenager. "Mothering the mother" and "parenting the parent" are increased responsibilities for the child care specialist working with teenage parents.

A role of the child care specialist is to support the positive qualities of teenage parents in their child care abilities and to highly praise their efforts. This requires setting aside time to empathize, actively listen, and mirror the young parent.

Involved teenage fathers should also be praised, encouraged, and offered options for further parent training within the community. One more example is the Union Industrial Home (UIH) in Trenton, New Jersey which is a 138-year-old organization which sponsors First Steps. First Steps was formed in 1992 to work with 13- to 17-year-old fathers and other at-risk youth, and provides weekly support groups to talk about fathers' roles and provide support and role models for fathering. In areas with large numbers of teenage parents, the child care program can use the First Steps model to provide supportive service to teenage fathers.

Teenage parents need good information, support, and role models that teach, through example, the daily competent care of infants and toddlers. This modeling should include the conscious application of attention, approval, and affection in addition to the mechanics of care. A competent child care professional will parent the parent by appropriately extending positive attention, affection, and approval to teenage parents.

Communicating with Staff

When more than one person works in a child care program, effective communication among staff is essential. Arranging to meet with each staff member regularly on an individual basis enhances communication. Although family child care providers often work alone in their own home, they can contact licensing staff and other family child care providers. Group family child care arrangements employ at least two people who work with a larger group of children in the home. Child care centers usually have a staff which includes a director and one or more caregivers. The size of enrollment determines the number and kind of additional staff; these may be caregivers, cooks, custodians, bus drivers, education, social service, and health personnel.

Listening to Staff

Each caregiver needs to be a listener. Staff can exchange information and discuss program issues in a reasonable way only if all are active listeners. How you listen to one another reflects how you respect each other.

Sharing with Colleagues

Share information with colleagues. Your experiences give you information, insights, and perspectives which will help others understand issues and deal with problems.

Share your feelings and actively listen while expressing your excitement and joy about working with your colleagues. As a part of a team, you all benefit from sharing pleasurable experiences. Tactfully express frustrations, disappointments, and anger. Keeping those feelings bottled up can harm all of you. Determine what is distressing you and discuss the issue. By staying within your active listening guidelines you can focus on how staff activities are affecting program goals. You will be more likely to clear up misunderstandings and misperceptions if you focus your discussion on issues rather than on personalities.

Share feedback. Both informal and formal observations provide you with information to share with your colleagues. This kind of information is called feedback. Noting how other caregivers behave with people and materials in various settings, schedules, and routines can help the entire staff evaluate the current program and make necessary adjustments. Feedback can highlight caregiver actions which are helpful and effective, but you should use tact when commenting on a situation where you believe your colleagues might act differently. Focus on what is best for the children and what changes can provide a better situation. Do not focus on what a caregiver did "wrong." Actions are more often "inappropriate" than "wrong." Since all caregivers are developing their skills, comments that make colleagues feel incompetent are not helpful. It is more productive to focus on appropriate alternative actions to learn and use.

Share responsibilities with your colleagues. Your colleagues will notice whether you are willing to carry your load. Even when people work under written job descriptions containing specific tasks, the total responsibilities often do not fit neatly into separate categories. Martha is responsible for getting snacks ready, but today she is rocking Natalie, who after crying and fussing has finally settled down but does not seem quite ready to be put down to play. If another caregiver volunteers to set up snacks, Natalie will not be disturbed again and so will not disturb the other children.

Share your expertise. Each person has special talents and unique insights to share with colleagues, children, and parents. Nobody appreciates know-it-alls, but we all benefit from people who are willing to share ideas which can be discussed, accepted, modified, or rejected.

Supporting Colleagues

Caregiving is physically and emotionally draining. Remembering and putting into practice the 3A's of caregiving presented in Chapter 2 will help you and your colleagues cope with stress. For example, assisting a colleague when extra help is needed reduces stress. You can provide positive emotional support by listening, using honest compliments, giving credit, assuring and reassuring colleagues about ideas or actions of theirs which you think are appropriate. Your colleagues' knowing that you are working with them rather than against them is in itself a powerful emotional support (see Figure 6–3).

Making Decisions

Caregivers need information to make intelligent staff decisions. Meet with other staff members regularly. Study and learn about issues when necessary so that you will be able to discuss subjects intelligently and make wise decisions. Identify the issue and factors which affect the decision. Raise questions with colleagues; listen, think, and take an active part in making decisions relating to caregiving.

Figure 6–3 Supportive relationships are necessary among caregivers who work together in a child care program.

RESOURCES FOR PARENTS AND STAFF

Governmental:
Administration for Children, Youth
   and Families
P.O. Box 1182
Washington, D.C. 20013
(202) 205-8570

Bureau of Community Health Services
Office of Maternal and Child Health
Public Health Service
U.S. Dept. of Health and Human Services
5600 Fishers Lane
Rockville, Maryland 20857
(301) 443-2170

Centers for Disease Control
1600 Clifton Road, N.E.
Atlanta, Georgia 30333
(404) 639-3311

National Hotline for AIDS
1-800-342-2437

Children's Bureau
Office of Human Development Services
Administration for Children,
   Youth and Families
U.S. Dept of Health and Human Services
Washington, D.C. 20201

Food and Nutrition Services
U.S. Dept of Agriculture
301 Park Center Drive
Alexandria, Virginia 22302
(703) 305-2286

Head Start Bureau
Office of Human Development Services
Administration for Children,
   Youth and Families
U.S. Dept of Health and Human Services
Washington, D.C. 20201

National Caries Program
National Institute of Dental Research
9000 Rockville Pike
Bethesda, Maryland 20892
(301) 496-3571

State Departments of Health

County Health Departments

State and Regional Poison
   Control Centers

State and County Cooperative
   Extension Services

Professional:
American Academy of Dermatology
930 North Meacham Road
Schaumburg, Illinois 60173-6016
(708) 330-9830

American Academy of Pediatrics
141 Northwest Point Boulevard
P.O. Box 927
Elk Grove, Illinois 60009
1-800-433-9016

American Dental Association
211 East Chicago Avenue
Chicago, Illinois 60611
(312) 440-2500

American Optometric Association
243 North Lindbergh Boulevard
St. Louis, Missouri 63141
(314) 991-4100

Health Related:
American Automobile Association
100 AAA Drive
Heathrow, Florida 32746-5063
(407) 444-7000

American Red Cross (National
Headquarters)
P.O. Box 7406
Benjamin Franklin Station
Washington, D.C. 20044-7406
1-800-279-9248

Johnson and Johnson Consumer
Products Information Center
199 Grandview Road
Skillman, New Jersey 08558
1-800-526-3967

Metropolitan Life
Health & Welfare Division
One Madison Avenue
New York, New York 10010
(212) 578-2211

National Center for Clinical Infant
Programs, Zero to Three
2000 14th Street, North #380
Arlington, Virginia 22201
(703) 528-4300

Parents' Health Report
Child Health Care Newsletter
21 Oak Shore Drive
Bayville, New York 11709

Ross Laboratories
Columbus, Ohio 43216

U.S. Consumer Product Safety
Commission
Office of Information and Public Affairs
Washington, D.C. 20207
1-800-638-2772

STUDENT ACTIVITIES

1. Review the four active listening steps in the chapter.
2. Actively listen to a parent-caregiver dialogue when the child arrives in the morning. Write down the statements and then categorize them.

	PARENT	CAREGIVER
Information		
Questions		
Affirmation		

3. Conduct one simulated parent-caregiver conference initiated by the caregiver and another initiated by the parent.
4. Interview a caregiver who has made a home visit. Determine the purpose and procedures for the visit.
5. Role-play a child care center staff meeting which is discussing problems of sharing play yard space.
6. Identify the responsibilities of a caregiver in a setting with which you are familiar. Categorize the activities according to whether the caregiver attends to them independently or in cooperation with other staff members.

TASK	ACCOMPLISHES INDEPENDENTLY	NEEDS COOPERATION OF OTHER STAFF

7. What did you learn by using the Active Listening techniques?
8. List your perceived strengths in interrelationships with parents and staff. List areas where you need to set growth goals.

CHAPTER REVIEW

1. What is active listening?
2. Why is effective communication with parents important?
3. Why is effective communication with staff important?
4. Write an agenda for a parent-caregiver conference initiated by the caregiver to discuss a child's toilet-training.
5. Describe two situations in which caregivers interact with each other. Identify the interpersonal skills needs.

SITUATION	SKILLS NEEDED: CAREGIVER 1	SKILLS CAREGIVER 2

6. How can you contribute to effective, positive staff relationships?

REFERENCES

Bautte, G., and Peterson, E. 1993. Beginning to create a multicultural classroom. *Dimensions of Early Childhood* 21(2), 11–12.

Douville-Watson, L., and Watson, M. 1998. Family Actualization through Research and Education F.A.R.E., Fourth Edition. New York: Instruction Press, 21 Oak Shore Drive, Bayville, NY 11709.

Douville-Watson, L., and Watson, M. 1988. *Family Actualization through Research and Education F.A.R.E.*, Third Edition. New York: Actualization, Inc.

Feeney, S., and Kipinis, K. 1990. *Code of Ethical Conduct & Statement of Commitment.* Washington, DC: National Association for the Education of Young Children.

Gordon, Thomas. 1976. *Parent Effectiveness Training: P.E.T.* New York: Peter H. Wyden.

Hendrix, H. 1993. *Getting the Love You Want.* New York: Institute for Relationship Therapy.

Hewlett, B. S. 1992. *Father-child Relations.* New York: Adline DeGruyter.

Lally, J. Ronald, ed. 1992. *Language Development & Communication: A Guide, Infant/Toddler Caregiving Series.* San Francisco: Far West Lab.

Lamb, M. E. 1987. *The Father's Role: Cross Cultural Perspectives.* Hillsdale, NJ: Erlbaum.

Orstein, Allan C., and Chapman, J. Karen. 1988. The parent-teacher conference. *PTA Today* V14.

Owen, M. T., and Cox, M. J. 1988. Maternal employment and the transition to parenthood. In *Maternal Employment and Children's Development: Longitudinal Research,* eds. A. E. Gottfried and A. W. Gottfried, p. 850119. New York: Plenum.

Rogers, C. 1961. *On Becoming a Person.* Boston: Houghton Mifflin.

Watson, M. A. 1996. *The National Parenting Scales: Experimental Edition.* New York: Instructional Press, 21 Oak Shore Drive, Bayville, NY 11709

Watson, M. A. 1997: "Giving & Receiving family support through using the National Parenting Scales." National Association for the Education of the Young Child (NAEYC) Annual Conference: Anaheim, CA.

Weill, J. D., and Jablonski, M. (eds.). 1997. *Children's Defense Fund: The State of America's Children: 1997 Yearbook.* Washington, DC: Children's Defense Fund.

ADDITIONAL RESOURCES

Ardell, Donald B., and Tager, Mark J. 1981. *Planning for Wellness.* Portland, OR: Wellness Media, Ltd.

Dawley, Gloria, and Sorger, James. 1982. *What To Do . . . Until the Doctor Calls Back.* Plainfield, NJ: Bayberry Books.

Greater Minneapolis Day Care Association. 1983. *Child Health Guidelines.* Minneapolis, MN: Author.

Horowitz, Alice M. 1981. *Prevent Tooth Decay: A Guide for Implementing Self-applied Fluorides in School Settings.* (NIH Publication No. 82–1196). Bethesda, MD: National Institute of Dental Research.

National Institute of Dental Research. 1983. *Snack Facts.* (NIH Publication No. 83–1680). Bethesda, MD: Author.

National Institute of Dental Research and the National Association of Community Health Centers, Inc. 1979. *Good Teeth for You and Your Baby.* (NIH Publication No. 79–1255). Bethesda, MD: Author.

National Institute of Dental Research and the National Association of Community Health Centers, Inc. 1979. *Una buena dentadura para usted y su bebe.* (NIH Publication No. 79–1465). Bethesda, MD: Author.

Public Health Service. 1980. *Healthy Children.* Effective public health practices for improving children's oral health. (DHHS Publication No. [PHS] 80–50136). Washington, DC: Author.

7

Settings for Child Care

OBJECTIVES

After completing this chapter, the child development specialist should be able to:
1. Identify characteristics of the family child care home.
2. Identify characteristics of the child care center.
3. Distinguish among the regulations of child care.
4. Categorize child care program emphases.
5. Compare caregiver support systems.

CHAPTER OUTLINE

I. Family-Based Care
   A. Staffing
   B. Unique characteristics
   C. Regulations
II. Center-Based Care
   A. Staffing
   B. Unique characteristics
   C. Regulations
III. Program Emphases
   A. Holistic
   B. Developmental
   C. Quality
IV. Program Funding
   A. Public tax support
   B. Private support
V. Support Groups
   A. Child care systems
   B. Child care networks
   C. Associations

CHILD DEVELOPMENT ASSOCIATE FUNCTIONAL AREAS

    I. 3 Learning Environment
    V. 12 Program Management
  VI. 13 Professionalism

Care outside the child's home may be provided in a family child care home or a child care center. There are some similarities and differences and some advantages and disadvantages in each place of care. Family child care homes and child care centers may be either licensed or unlicensed, depending on state regulations.

FAMILY-BASED CARE

Staffing

The family child care specialist provides care in her own home for children other than her own. The caregiver in a family child care home is usually a woman; she may be single or married, a non-parent, or parent.

The number of children one caregiver can care for varies and usually depends on the ages of the children. Many states restrict the number of infants the caregiver can include. A family child care provider with her own 3- and 5-year-old might also care for four other children (see Figure 7–1).

The group family child care home provides care for a greater number of children, often from six to ten or twelve. In some states, one caregiver may be responsible for this group of children, whereas in other states an additional caregiver is required for this number.

Figure 7–1   Several children may receive care in the familiar setting of a family child care home.

Unique Characteristics

A family child care home provides an environment for children which is home-like. Familiarity with the surroundings helps the child adjust to a new setting. The physical arrangements may resemble the child's own home. There is usually a kitchen where food is prepared; a bed or cot on which to sleep; toilet facilities; and play areas. The family child care home usually allows the child to move and play within several rooms.

The small number of children in a family child care home means the children and caregiver have time to develop close relationships. The stability and depth of this relationship contribute to the child's feelings of trust and security.

The family child care home often includes children of several ages. Two-year-old Sasha puts her arm around 6-month-old Jeremy and gives him a hug. Matthew, who is 3¹/₂, sits on the floor with 11/2-year-old Michele, putting shoes on her and fastening the Velcro tapes. Year-old toddler Suzanne follows Miss Jan into the kitchen, watches 4-year-old Larry get a drink of water, and then follows Larry into the den to pick up blocks. Multi-aged groups of children have opportunities to learn from each other. Older and younger children provide physical, emotional, social, and cognitive support and challenge to each other.

The program in a family child care home consists of the routines of living together as a "family." The cooking and pick-up-the-room times contribute to the child's development, along with the stories, the art on the kitchen table or driveway, the tapping-pan-lid noises, the snuggles and hugs, the sitting alone under the table to watch, and the on-again/off-again interaction with other children and the provider.

The family child care home usually has a flexible schedule. The daily schedule may have a few fixed times, such as lunch for children who are awake. However, it may permit flexibility in times for eating snacks, sleeping, and playing. This flexibility minimizes the pressure on children to meet other people's schedules. The home often adjusts its schedule to the child rather than requiring the child to adjust to a schedule. For example, one child can be allowed to stay in the bedroom and sleep while other children can play in other rooms of the home without disturbing the sleeping child.

Family child care providers have autonomy. They decide what they will do, when they will do it, and how they will do it. Many states now offer mentoring programs which support the independent care of home providers.

One disadvantage for family child care providers is their heavy load of responsibilities. Caring for up to six children from eight to ten hours a day, five days a week, all alone, produces a heavy physical and emotional strain. To get time off during the day for relaxation or to attend meetings requires locating and hiring a substitute, activities demanding additional time and money.

Another disadvantage is isolation from other caregivers. Working alone in their homes, family child care providers miss the informal sharing with other caregivers of ideas, frustrations, and concerns. Many communities do not have organizations which meet the emotional and educational needs of family child care providers, thus leaving them on their own to locate the support they need or to go without it. Resource and referral agencies often offer organized groups.

A major difference between family child care, group family child care, and child care centers is that often infants and toddlers are overwhelmed by large, noisy centers. In contrast, young children are very relaxed in family child care settings. The advantage of group family child care is the presence of an extra provider who helps care for the six to twelve children, which allows the director and assistant to function as a team. This helps overcome feelings of isolation and fatigue often experienced by the family child care provider who solely cares for up to six children by herself.

Regulations

For many years a state or county agency, often the welfare, health, or social services agency, has regulated family child care homes.

> The regulation of family day care involves 1) the rights of children to be protected, 2) the rights of child care providers to carry on a legitimate home business without infringement of their rights, 3) the extent to which state laws can adequately regulate ALL the homes where children are in care, 4) the ability of the states to enforce their current laws, 5) the interpretation of standards to the public, parents, and potential family day care providers, and 6) the future needs of consumers of family day care who may not be able to find child care if regulations drive providers out of business (Adams 1982, 13).

Three types of regulation of family child care homes are licensing, registration, and certification. To be licensed, the family child care home must meet the standards established by the local governmental agency. These may include the number of children to be served, physical space, equipment, and health and safety factors. In some localities zoning requirements must be met.

Many people care for children other than their own in their homes and yet remain unlicensed. It has been estimated that more than 90 percent of all family child care homes are unlicensed (Corsini, Wisensale, and Caruso 1988). A proposed alternative to licensing is registration of family child care homes. Registration in most states is a simple process of listing the family child care home with the licensing authority.

Most states now use certification of family child care homes. Certification (sometimes called approval) is a form of regulation for purchase of care. Certification standards are, in almost every state, some modification of FIDCR (Federal Interagency Day Care Requirements) standards (Walker 1992).

CENTER-BASED CARE

Staffing

A child care center provides care away from home for more than six children for some part of the day or night. Child care centers differ from family child care homes in several ways.

The child care center staff consists of a director and caregivers. It may also include a cook, custodians, bus drivers, education specialist, social services workers, health specialists, and others depending on the size, goals, and financial support of the child care center.

The number of caregivers and group sizes are regulated according to the ages of children served. Adult-child ratios vary slightly among states. Typical requirements are two adults for each of the following number of children in a group:

AGE OF CHILDREN	NUMBER IN GROUP
Up to 18 months	6 to 8
18 months to 3 years	10 to 12
3 years to 6 years	14 to 20

Unique Characteristics

The child care facility may be a house, a building converted to center use, education rooms in a church, a community center, a school, or a building especially designed as a child care center. Each room, which provides for sleeping, eating, and playing in specially arranged areas, often houses one age group of children. The play areas may have blocks in one section, a home living section, a dress-up section, and so on. Where groups of children use rooms frequently, most states require a minimum of 30 to 35 square feet of play space per child and approximately an additional 20 square feet for children under two years old for crib space. Children may remain in that room for most of the day, with other indoor play space available in some centers and outdoor play space available at most centers (see Figure 7–2).

Children in child care centers are usually grouped with those of similar age. The licensing requirements for adult-child ratios make broader multi-aged grouping costly since the group must use the ratio for the youngest child in the group.

Many toys and much equipment are needed for the number and age range of children in a center. Child care centers often can purchase expensive, sturdy play equipment and a variety of toys because the number of children using them make such purchases cost effective. The equipment, other than cribs and cots, may be used by several groups of children, and the toys may be sanitized and passed back and forth among rooms to provide variety and stimulation without undue cost.

Figure 7–2 In a child care center, a group of children may remain in one room which is divided into playing, eating, and sleeping areas.

The director and caregivers plan the program in a child care center, often with input from parents. The program should put the center's philosophy and goals into practice. These philosophies and goals should cover all aspects of the child's care, of the caregiver's roles, of parental involvement, schedules, routines, room arrangement, curriculum, assessments, and evaluations. The director determines and sets the standards of quality for the overall program and the individual caregivers are responsible for maintaining these standards of quality in their individual rooms. It is important for caregivers not to minimize the impact they each have on the individual child placed in their care.

Since a child care center has at least two caregivers, it is more conducive to the stimulation of new ideas, release of tension and frustration, and support. However, working with another adult in the same room or in the same building requires skills in getting along with others, sharing, compromising, and cooperating. Caregivers need to work constantly on maintaining and improving their working relationships with other adults. Many centers provide education and assistance through in-service education and participation in workshops and conferences, as do professional organizations such as the National Association for the Education of Young Children (NAEYC) and Child Development Associates (CDA) credentialing authorities.

Child care centers tend to have less flexible daily schedules than family child care homes. They have tended to borrow a daily schedule from schools, with fifteen- to thirty-minute time blocks which structure a young child's day. However, this kind of schedule is not appropriate for infants and toddlers who need very simple schedules of large time blocks which fit their physical needs and their own interests.

Regulations

A state agency is usually responsible for child care center licensing. Each state has developed standards for child care center administration, staff, facilities, and program as a part of government's responsibility to protect its citizens. Local governmental agencies are involved with health requirements, fire codes, and zoning ordinances. Licensing identifies a set of minimum standards which a center has met; it does not guarantee quality of care.

PROGRAM EMPHASES

Holistic

Whether care is provided in a family child care home, group family child care home, or a child care center, it must be holistic; it must consider the whole child. Physical, emotional, social, language skills, and cognitive development are all vitally important during these early years, so balance is needed to help the child properly develop (see Figure 7–3). Overemphasis in one area or limited involvement in another may create unnecessary stress or it may delay development.

Figure 7–3 Child care programs must be holistic, meeting the child's physical, emotional, social, and cognitive needs.

Young children need to experience nurturance, love, consistency, touch, movement, exploration, interactions with others, comfort, challenge, and stimulation. The child care provider should be well-versed in the 3A's of childcare. These help develop the child's feelings of security and trust, self-worth and self-identity, curiosity, creativity, and active involvement with people and the world.

Developmental

The program emphasis in both home-based care and child care centers should consider the developmental needs of each child. Each child, parent, and caregiver involved in child care is developing as an individual.

Children develop naturally. It is not helpful for anyone to push, prod, or pressure them to develop. Adults can enhance, encourage, and nurture children's development in a variety of ways by taking cues from the children and providing the appropriate "match" of materials and experiences to fit the children's needs, interests, and behaviors. Under ideal conditions a variety of age-appropriate toys are made available for the child to choose from, and caretakers structure activities around the child's interests.

Each parent is developing both as a person and as a parent. How the caregiver behaves with the parent can help or hinder the parent's development.

Each caregiver is developing as both a person and a caregiver. Caregivers who view themselves as learners continually discover things about themselves; they come to know more about others; and they increase both their skills as caregivers and the roles they assume as caregivers. Partnership between caregiver and parent for the benefit of the child should be an ongoing goal.

Quality

High-quality care is required for each child. National accreditation is being used to identify homes and centers that attain standards of quality.

The National Association for Family Day Care (NAFDC) began its Accreditation Program in 1988 to offer professional recognition and distinction to those family child care providers whose services represent high-quality child care. The accreditation process involves the provider in an in-depth self-assessment that focuses on physical provisions in the home, child care procedures and policies, and adult-child interactions. Dimensions of the family child care home that are assessed include indoor safety, health, nutrition, play environment, interaction, and professional responsibility. The provider's self-assessment is validated by a parent and a NAFDC representative (NAFDC 1988).

The National Association for the Education of Young Children established the National Academy of Early Childhood Programs to administer an accreditation system for child care centers. The academy defines a high-quality early childhood program as one that meets the needs of and promotes the physical, social, emotional, and cognitive development of the children and adults—parents, staff, and administrators—who are involved in the program. Each day of a child's life is viewed as leading toward the growth and development of a healthy, intelligent, and contributing member of society.

The criteria address all aspects of an early childhood program:

- interactions among staff and children
- curriculum
- staff and parent interactions
- administration
- staff qualifications and development
- staffing patterns
- physical environment
- health and safety
- nutrition and food service
- program evaluation (NAEYC 1992).

PROGRAM FUNDING

There are a variety of sources of financial support for child care programs. Some programs utilize only one source, such as parent tuition. Other programs may receive funds from several sources: for example, Title XX, United Way, and/or parent fees. Many corporations help subsidize centers for their employees and/or set up a Dependent Care Assistance Program (DCAP) which allows the employee to set aside up to $5,000 in pre-tax dollars for day care (Family Day Care Advisory Project 1991).

Public Tax Support

Two federal programs limited to children of low-income families are Head Start and Title XX Social Services subsidized child care. Part-time and full-time care may be available for those meeting income eligibility guidelines.

Some city, state, and federal governmental units and agencies provide child care services for their employees. These are tax subsidized through use of public buildings, utilities, employees, and so on.

Public schools are opening classrooms for full-day infant and toddler child care. The space and sometimes the utilities, personnel, and equipment may be paid for with tax support.

State vocational and technical schools, community colleges, and universities may use tax monies to support child care as a part of their instructional program or as a service to their students and/or faculty and staff.

Private Support

The majority of child care in America is provided by private licensed and unlicensed family child care homes and child care centers, and it is paid for by parents through tuition and fees.

A few corporations are now providing child care alternatives. These include on-site child care centers, corporate supported near-site child care centers and group family homes, corporate contributions to community child care, child care reimbursement, the use of pre-tax dollars to pay for care (DCAP), resource and referral services, and educational programs for parents.

Churches are "a major provider of child care in this nation" (Gormley 1995).

As the steward of substantial resources, including real estate, capital, administrative services and health and insurance benefits, the churches are in an ideal position to make child care delivery available to families. Churches taken in the aggregate are the largest single provider of child care in the United States today. Space, location, and tax exempt status contribute to the desirability of church properties for child care programs. Of course, churches will want to consider carefully the ethical implications of their fee policies for the use of space for this ministry of child care.

United Way funds are used in many communities to provide child care services or to subsidize existing community programs.

SUPPORT GROUPS

Child Care Systems

Some public and private agencies set up child care systems. When several child care centers are administered from a central office, they often gain access to greater financial support; additional education, social, and health services; toys and equipment; caregiver training; and parent education.

A single child care center or a child care center system may make arrangements with neighboring family child care homes to serve as satellites to the center. This can benefit both home and center. The family child care provider can use center staff, toys, and materials. Since these family child care homes often care for infants and toddlers, their children often transfer to the center program when they are about 3 years old. The child care center is thus able to serve families with children both below and above 3 years of age without having to provide the more costly infant service in their center.

Child Care Networks

Many communities are establishing child care information and referral networks to serve parents, providers, and community agencies. They have several features in common:

- *Matchmaking:* a commitment to parental choice in child care and respect for all parents' ability to choose the child care setting most appropriate for their own child.
- *Universality of services:* a willingness and capacity to address [the child care information and referral] needs of all parents regardless of income and family circumstance.
- *Inclusive referral system:* a capacity to work nonjudgmentally with all sectors of the provider community, including home- and center-based, public and private, profit and not-for-profit groups.
- *Community-level networking:* a cooperative relationship with community agencies and institutions that serve children and families.
- *Knowledge of child care policy and programs:* a thorough familiarity with child care regulations and public policy issues (Siegel and Lawrence 1984, 223).

Some agencies have established their own information and referral networks. One hospital, in an attempt to meet the diverse needs of its staff, developed a family child care network, "a personalized child care information service—a matching of employee child care needs with the availability of spaces in family day care homes" (Torres 1981, 45). During the decade since then, many corporations and public and private facilities have contracted with agencies and have paid a fee to make resource and referral services available for their employees (Morgan 1991).

Three basic types of child care information and referral services are (1) information and referral; (2) technical assistance: training; and (3) advocacy: community education (Siegel and Lawrence 1984). Of these, technical assistance or training is directed most specifically to caregivers. Workshops, seminars, and telephone networks can provide caregivers with information and training regarding the program and give directors help concerning administrative functions.

Family child care providers have been especially active in some areas establishing their own networks. Meeting together, they have dealt with problems specific to their situation of caring for children in their own homes.

The mentoring program described in detail in Chapter 1 discussed the advantages of mentors to all child care settings. Child care owners and directors of programs should inquire at their nearest college for information regarding area mentoring programs.

The Home Visitor assessment and certification procedure offered by the CDA Council is a valuable certification. Information concerning this certificate is available from the CDA Council, 2460 16th Street, NW, Washington, DC 20009-3575.

At the time of this writing, The Home Visitor Certificate Program offered by the CDA Council is being revised. This program is extremely valuable as it qualifies professionals interested in doing home advisory teaching. For more information regarding this program, contact the CDA Council.

The National Center for Early Childhood Workforce also has information regarding other mentoring programs. Contact them by telephone at (202) 737-7700.

Associations

Since the early 1980s, task forces have been established at the local, state, and national levels, and family child care associations address child care needs and solutions. The following quote still applies today.

At one end of the spectrum is the loosely organized group which meets mainly on a social level. . . . There is no set program, but providers use the time to air their grievances with the system in general and to discuss particular problems in their own day care businesses. . . . [The next level, meetings with the licensing agent] quickly becomes a way to get ideas filtered back into the bureaucratic system. [The next level involves a few dedicated caregivers plus an enthusiastic sponsor.] Meetings are held to discuss purposes, needs, expectations and even long-range plans. [County associations meet together to form state associations. Some state associations have met to form a national organization.] (Click 1981, 39–41).

Among the national organizations that provide resources for child care providers are the following:

Ecumenical Child Care Network
National Council of Churches
475 Riverside Drive, Room 572
New York, New York 10115
(212) 870-2511

This network links church-housed child caregivers, early childhood educators, advocates, and church leaders nationwide.

National Association for the Education of Young Children (NAEYC)
1509 16th Street, N.W.
Washington, D.C. 20009
(202) 232-8777 or 1-800-424-2460

The NAEYC publishes a journal, Young Children, and various books and pamphlets that include articles and book reviews relating to many areas of infancy and caregiving. The association has regional, state, and local affiliates.

National Association for Family Day Care
1331A Pennsylvania Avenue
Suite 348
Washington, D.C. 20004
1-800-359-3817

National Child Care Association
1029 Railroad Street
Conyers, Georgia 30207
1-800-543-7161

This organization is composed of grassroots, small business entrepreneurs who seek for all children responsibly regulated, quality child care services that are provided by public, private, and secretarian programs.

National Head Start Association
201 North Union Street
Suite 320
Alexandria, Virginia 22314
(703) 739-0875

STUDENT ACTIVITIES

1. Compare a family child care home and a child care center in your area using the following categories:

STAFFING	NUMBER AND AGES OF CHILDREN	REGULATION
Family Child Care Home		
Child Care Center		

2. Interview one family child care provider and one child care center caregiver.
   a. What are the goals of the program?
   b. What are the caregiver responsibilities?
   c. What is planned for the children?
3. Make a list of local and state organizations that provide phone contacts, meetings, workshops, or conferences for caregivers.
4. How has each addressed cultural diversity within its setting?

CHAPTER REVIEW

1. How are a family child care home and a child care center alike? How are they different?
2. Compare the responsibilities of a family child care provider and a caregiver in a child care center.
3. Describe a "holistic" child care program emphasis.
4. Describe a "developmental" child care program emphasis.

REFERENCES

Click, M. H. 1981. The growth of family day care associations. *Day Care and Early Education* 8(3), 39–41.

Corsini, D. A., Wisensale, S., and Caruso, G. 1988. Family day care: System issues and regulatory models. *Young Children* 4(6), 17–23.

Family Day Care Advisory Project. 1991. Washington, D.C.: Children's Foundation.

Gormley, W. T. 1995. *Everybody's Children: Child Care as a Public Problem.* Washington, DC: Brookings Institute.

Morgan, Gwen. 1991. Career progression in early care and education: A discussion paper. Center for Career Development, Wheelock College, Boston, Mass.

National Association for Family Day Care. 1988. *New Accreditation for Family Day Care Homes.* Washington, DC: Author.

National Association for the Education of Young Children. 1992. *Accreditation by the National Academy of Early Childhood Programs.* Washington, DC: Author.

National Council of Churches. 1984. *Policy Statement of Child Day Care.* New York: Governing Board of the National Council of Churches.

Siegel, P., and Lawrence, M. 1984. Information, referral, and resource centers. In *Making Day Care Better,* eds. J. T. Greenman and R. W. Fuqua, New York: Teachers College Press, 227–43.

Torres, Y. 1981. A hospital-based family day care network. *Day Care and Early Education* 9(1), 44–45.

Walker, J. R. 1992. New evidence on the supply of childcare: A statistical portrait of family providers and an analysis of their fees. *Journal of Human Resources* 27, 1 pp. 30–40.

8

The Indoor and Outdoor Environment

OBJECTIVES

After completing this chapter, the child development specialist should be able to:

1. Identify components of the indoor and outdoor environment.
2. Analyze the appropriateness for infants and toddlers of equipment and materials used in the indoor and outdoor environment.

CHAPTER OUTLINE

I. Room Arrangement
   A. Infant/Toddler Settings
   B. Creating Infant/Toddler Activity Areas
II. Play Yard Arrangement
   A. Designing Areas
   B. Sharing Space
   C. Safety Considerations
III. Materials
   A. Matching Goals with Materials
   B. Age-Appropriate Materials
   C. Homemade Materials
IV. Conditions Fostering Safety and Health
   A. A Quiet Zone
   B. Parent Awareness of Safety
   C. Universal Precautions
   D. Signs and Symptoms of Possible Severe Illness
   E. Immunization Schedule
   F. Fire Prevention and Emergency Numbers
   G. Human Immunodeficiency Virus (HIV) Infection
   H. SIDS: Sudden Infant Death Syndrome and the Back to Sleep Campaign

CHILD DEVELOPMENT ASSOCIATE FUNCTIONAL AREAS

I. 1   Safe
I. 3   Learning Environment
II. 4   Physical
II. 7   Creative
III. 10 Guidance
IV. 8
V. 12 Program Management

The environment for very young children must be planned carefully. The first step is to identify your program goals. The equipment and materials you select should reflect your goals and help the children develop to their fullest potential physically, emotionally, socially, perceptually, and cognitively. This requires a variety of high-quality equipment and materials. "It is the environment, in all its manifestations, that is the curriculum" (Olds 1983, 16). This chapter focuses on the tangible objects and space within the child care setting.

Dori Walther-Lee, President of the Workplace Child Care Consultants Inc. advises using contrasting colors like black and white to help develop visual discrimination in infants, as well as to stimulate interest when planning infant space for corporate centers.

Jane Healy, a noted neuropsychologist, writes that "A variety of patterns are important: contours, horizontal and vertical lines, shapes, sizes and colors, for example. Visual feature detectors are forming which will later enable the child to discriminate such complex patterns as alphabet letters or numerals when there is a good reason for learning them" (1989).

ROOM ARRANGEMENT

Infant/Toddler Settings

The child care setting includes equipment necessary for providing basic care. Child care homes often include some special equipment or they adapt available home furnishings (see Figure 8–1).

Safety remains the highest concern when utilizing space for infants and toddlers. Structures to be avoided include rooms with angles that might be potential hazards for a mobile infant or a fast-moving, mission-bound toddler.

The ideal situation is to plan your space from scratch, and create your blueprint based on activity centers and group sizes. In an ideal situation, you have the best possibility of avoiding hazards. Most areas, however, require conversion of space which is a greater challenge to creative solutions because of possible safety hazards.

Whether you create new space or convert space to fit your child care needs, there are always angles, pipes, ledges, and rough surfaces that can create hazardous drop spots where children could be injured. These should be turned

Figure 8–1 On cold or rainy days children enjoy the sensory table inside the child care center.

into storage areas or made safe in some way. Products such as Ethafoam Padding® can be used around windows, corners, and rough surfaces. This padding can lay over angled areas, reach up walls, and frame window ledges to make them safe.

By being creative and looking for every potential hazard to infants and toddlers, the child care specialist can child-proof any area so that it is safe.

Square footage requirements are always necessary when designing your child care setting. Infants and toddlers need a great deal of space, so whenever possible, additional footage above state and local regulations should be allowed.

Infants progress through all of the developmental phases to preschool utilizing some of the same equipment by using it differently at various stages and ages. For example, the "Crawly Corner" by Childcraft® is convertible equipment comprised of hard foam rubber blocks. These cubes can be used in corners or can be free-standing, and are ideal for infants who are beginning to climb, or for toddlers to build houses or do gymnastics safely. Using such equipment can provide safe exploration, imagination, and flexible uses for both infants and toddlers.

Equipment is needed to facilitate all areas of development and for all ages of children in the setting. One piece of equipment may aid development in more than one developmental area. For example, a child using a very low slide is moving physically and is also usually developing emotional responses such as pleasure, excitement, and pride in accomplishment.

Children of various ages may enjoy the same piece of equipment. Two-year-olds may use the low slide competently, while a 1-year-old may use it with caregiver assistance, and a 9-month-old may use it as a low structure to crawl on and to stand up with caregiver assistance.

Jones and Prescott emphasized that "planning space is a problem-stating as well as a problem-solving process" (1982, 18). Start with identifying the ages of the children in the program and plan your needed basic furnishings (see Table 8–1). Arrange the furnishings in the room into areas based on usage (that is, a crib area for sleeping, a high chair area for eating). Jones and Prescott offered the following suggestions to the child care staff for analyzing the setting:

1. Articulate program goals in a general fashion. What kinds of experiences and feelings do we wish to provide? What are the special needs of the children we serve?
2. What types of furnishings are necessary—for example, cribs for infants, climbing areas for toddlers (see Table 8-1).
3. Look critically and closely at how well existing arrangements work.
4. Be willing to experiment with alternative arrangements. Design does not mean fixing ideas in concrete. Rather, it is a process of devising ad hoc solutions, informally monitoring how they work, and remaining open to change if the results warrant it (1982, 18).
5. Use large pieces of furniture such as bookcases to divide areas into different activities.

Using program goals which focus on holistic development, consider some equipment not included in Table 8–1.

Playpens: Playpens are used only when necessary. The purpose of a playpen is to contain the child in a small space. There may be a variety of reasons to do this. You may wish to keep the infant or toddler away from unsafe situations. You may wish to keep a child and his or her toys together. Be aware that too many toys can create a ladder for the child to climb out. Limit the amount of toys and change them frequently.

Some caregivers believe it is easier if every child has a separate playpen. Whatever the reasons, the caregiver must evaluate the use of the playpen.

Physically, infants and toddlers need gross motor movement, which includes crawling, pushing, pulling, walking. The playpen limits the amount and types of gross motor movement. Children who spend much of their waking time in a playpen (or the crib used as a playpen) have limited opportunities for gross motor movement.

Socially and emotionally the playpen isolates rather than facilitates interactions with others. Visual and verbal exchanges must take place through the mesh of the playpen across a certain distance to the other people. Approaching others, touching, and selecting social experiences are severely limited and sometimes even eliminated when children stay in playpens. The caregiver maintains strong control, while the children have almost no control over when to get in and out of the playpen and what

TABLE 8–1 BASIC EQUIPMENT FOR INFANTS AND TODDLERS

CHILD CARE CENTER CLASSROOM	CHILD CARE HOME
Indoor	**Indoor**
EATING	*EATING*
High chairs	High chairs
	Booster seats for kitchen and dining room chairs
Low chairs and tables	Kitchen and dining room table
SLEEPING	*SLEEPING*
Rocking chair	Rocking chair
Cribs	Cribs
Cots	Family beds and sofa covered with the child's sheet and blanket for naps
TOILETING	*TOILETING*
Changing table	Changing table or counter space in the bathroom for changing diapers and storing supplies
Supply storage	
Free-standing potty	
Toilet seat adapter	Toilet seat adapter
Steps (if needed at sink)	Steps (if needed at sink)
STORAGE	*STORAGE*
Coat rack	Coat rack near door
Cubbies	
Shelves: toys, books	Especially designated shelves in the family room, living room, and/or bedroom where books and toys are kept for the child care children
RECORD KEEPING	*RECORD KEEPING*
Bulletin boards	Wall and refrigerator door space to exhibit art treasures
Record-keeping table, counter	Table, counter, drawer
Outdoor	**Outdoor**
CLIMBING STRUCTURES	*CLIMBING STRUCTURES*
Wood, tile, rubber tires, steps, tied ropes	Rubber tires, steps, tied ropes
CONTAINERS	*CONTAINERS*
Sand table or box	Large plastic trays, pools for sand and water
Water table or pool	

materials to play with. These children have little opportunity to learn to exert control over themselves and their world. For these reasons children should not be left in playpens for long periods of time. Wheeled walkers do not enhance upright development of the mobile infant. If their feet reach the floor only their toes bear body weight. Walkers put undo stress on back, legs and toes before they are developed adequately. In addition there is a serious question of the safety of use and in some cases these walkers are banned by licensing regulations (American Academy of Pediatrics 1993).

Arranging the room is not a one-time task. There are several reasons for re-arranging your room(s):

1. Activity areas are changed to offer new and novel areas.
2. Materials in the activity areas are changed to maintain challenge.
3. Modifications need to be made in equipment and placement when the age of the children changes.
4. Room arrangement is changed when the childrens' behavior shows that the room arrangement causes management problems.

Licensing regulations state minimum requirements for activity floor space per child; 35 to 55 square feet are often required, depending on whether the program serves infants and toddlers who need cribs. The ar-rangement of equipment, materials, activities, and people in this space is the responsibility of the child care staff. Though the arrangement of inside space may differ between child care homes and child care centers, some basic principles apply to all settings.

It is also very important not to neglect the needs of caregivers. Adult-sized chairs are more comfortable for adults and make working less physically stressful. Although the goal of a child care center is to be "child-centered," it is important to provide for the needs of the caregivers as well.

Creating Infant/Toddler Activity Areas

The room arrangement should also reflect program goals. In describing a de-velopmentally optimal child care center, Olds stated that ". . . a child's suc-cessful interaction with the physical environment must satisfy three basic needs: the need to move, the need to feel comfortable, and the need to feel competent". This is still applicable today.

The Need to Move
In 1983 Olds emphasized the need for movement, stating that "Sensorial and motoric experiences are the bedrock upon which all intellectual func-tions are built." This is still applicable today.

The environment can be organized to provide for a variety of activities. Olds identified five categories of activity that the setting should make possible:

1. quiet, calm activities
2. structured activities
3. craft and discovery activities
4. dramatic play activities
5. large motor activities (1983, 18)

Dalziel took the categories of wet and dry and quiet and active and related them to the arrangement of materials and space:

1. "wet-quiet" area—cooking, eating, messy media (paste, papier-mâché, etc.)
2. "wet-active" area—coats, toilet, sand, water, painting, some science materials

3. "quiet-dry" area—learning games and materials, writing, library, listening

4. "active-dry" area—large motor activities, construction (woodworking, blocks, building), dress-up, housekeeping (n.d., 2).

To provide for these activities adequately, you must design the areas carefully to allow the child to move as much as possible from one activity area to another at will.

The Need to Feel Comfortable

Olds identified the following benefits in meeting the need for comfort: "Comfortable surroundings foster playful attitudes that help lower anxiety, promote understanding, and enable children to be more open in divulging their personal responses to events and materials" (1983, 16). Olds also suggested that variations in architecture "provide pleasing changes in sensory stimulation":

- scale—small spaces and furniture for children, larger ones for adults; areas for privacy, semiprivacy, and whole group participation; materials at child-eye level and at adult height.
- floor height—raised and lowered levels, platforms, lofts, pits, climbing structures.
- ceiling height—mobiles, canopies, eaves, skylights.
- boundary height—walls, half-height dividers, low bookcases.
- visual interest—wall murals, classical art, children's paintings, views to trees and sky.
- lighting—natural, fluorescent, incandescent, local, indirect.
- auditory interest—hum of voices, mechanical gadgets, music, gerbils scratching, children laughing.
- olfactory interest—cookies baking, fresh flowers in a vase, plants in earth.
- textural interest—wood, fabric, fur, carpeting, plastic, formica, glass.
- kinesthetic interest—things to touch with different body parts; things to crawl in, under, and upon; opportunities to see the environment from different vantage points (1983, 17).

An activity area has five defining attributes: a physical **location** with visible **boundaries** indicating where it begins and ends, within which are placed **work and sitting surfaces** along with the **storage and display of materials** which are to be used on the surfaces in performing the activities for which the area is intended (Olds 1983, 19) (see Figure 8–2).

The Need to Feel Competent

To help the child develop feelings of competence, Olds asserted, "A teacher needs to provide a room which allows children to fulfill their own personal needs, execute tasks successfully, readily control their own tools and materials, make easy transitions, and control their own movements from place to place" (1983, 18).

Figure 8–2 Children of various ages may be able to use the same piece of equipment—just at a different pace.

PLAY YARD ARRANGEMENT

The play yard serves many functions as an integral part of a child care program. Just as caregivers evaluate and carefully design the indoor space to provide challenging and satisfying experiences, the outdoor space requires that same attention to program goals and design of space, equipment, and materials (see Figure 8–3).

Designing Areas

Caregivers must know the needs and interests of their children in order to design appropriate and appealing outdoor environments. Essa recommended that "more thought should go into organizing the yard into interest areas—as indoors—to include quiet and noisy spaces, social areas, places to be alone, materials to manipulate, etc." (1981, 41).

Nature provides readily available and adaptable materials in many play yards. Grass, leaves, seeds, flowers, trees, bushes, dirt, sand, and water present intriguing exploring and manipulating opportunities. Caregivers should help children gain access to these areas and should allow and encourage their creative uses of the materials.

Sharing Space

The play yard needs to be able to accommodate the children in the program. If infants and toddlers share play yard space with older children, equipment and materials especially designed for the younger children should be ar-

Figure 8–3 There are many factors to consider when selecting outdoor play equipment—appropriateness, space, and cost, to name a few.

ranged into a section in the areas of the play yard. Child care homes must utilize yards or a nearby park. With the multi-aged group of children usually present in child care homes, the caregiver must make adaptations.

Plan carefully to design shared space for use by several age groups. Establish rules which identify the way each age group can safely share the space, or have the children use the space at different times. For example, toddlers, who like to start and stop often and whose balance is sometimes unstable, may use tyke bikes on their own riding strip, and 5-year-olds may have a different riding strip, where they can ride faster and ride through more complex patterns and lanes. If there is not enough space, each group may use the same strip at different times.

Safety Considerations

The play yard must be safe to get to and to use. Licensing often requires that the play yard be fenced. Many states do not allow any roadways between the day care setting and the playground areas. Grass provides the best surface covering for infants and toddlers and should cover most of the play yard. Concrete and asphalt surfaces hold the heat on hot summer days and cannot be used then by infants who are sitting and crawling. Special attention should be paid to floor or ground surfaces under climbing toys. In some cases wood chips or sand can be used, others call for impact blocks or other types of soft material rated by the height of the climbing equipment. For instance, for every 12 inches of height, 6 inches of soft ground support is needed. As an example, most toddler slides are 22 inches high; to cushion the ground, 6 to 10 inches of soft material is piled under the slide to offer support.

MATERIALS

Matching Goals with Materials

Materials include toys, books, paper, paint, clay, sand, glue, water, boxes, tires, and other items children use in the room and play yard. Like equipment, materials help children attain program goals relating to physical, emotional, social, and cognitive development.

Jones divided the environment into several dimensions: soft or hard, open or closed, simple or complex, intrusion or seclusion, and high mobility or low mobility (1973, 1). These dimensions can be applied in the child care setting to the materials, equipment, and arrangement of space as well as to the behavior of people.

Lists of materials in a child care setting help identify materials that meet children's needs. Kate may need a toy which is intrusive, which puts her into contact with others. Another time she may need a toy which encourages seclusion so she can be by herself (see Table 8–2).

Catalog age-designations do not fit all children. Caregivers must determine when an item is appropriate for a particular child. Materials may have merit for some children but not for others. For example, a colorful mobile hanging above the crib may attract the attention of 3-month-old Sam. It would go unnoticed by 1-month-old Fred because (1) the tonic neck reflex keeps Fred's head turned to the side rather than looking up, and (2) his eyes focus best at about 7 to 9 inches and if the crib mattress is set low, the mobile will be beyond his focusing range.

Sand and water can be used both inside and outside. Their characteristics stimulate varied and satisfying experiences for children of all ages. Most children love sand.

Water and water play also fascinate children. Johnson offered these ideas:

"But why provide water play?" The reasons are numerous. Children discover the qualities of water: water flows, things float on it, it conforms to the shape of a container, it mixes with other substances, it will evaporate. Children gain skills and concepts through water play: coordination, concepts of volume and measurement, language practice and extension, competence and mastery. Finally, children perceive water as pleasurable and satisfying, and the teacher can too if plans and precautions are made to make it a wet and wonderful experience (1981, 14).

Age-Appropriate Materials

Selection of appropriate equipment and materials involves the caregiver's knowledge of the program goals, the children's needs and interests, the time

TABLE 8–2 TYPES OF EQUIPMENT AND MATERIALS

SOFT	HARD
Cloth puppets	Blocks
Cloth and soft plastic dolls	Hard plastic dolls
Dress-up clothes	Cars, trucks
Fur	Plastic curtains
Pillows	Sand
Mats	Paper
Rugs	Cardboard
Cloth curtains	Books
Water	Posters
Clay	Plastic, wood mobile
Paint	Wood
Cloth wall hangings	Linoleum
Glue	Baseball
Ribbon	Plastic bottles
Cushions	Catalogs
Cloth mobile	Magazines
Rubber balls	Buttons
Sponge balls	Metal cans
Cloth scraps	Sandpaper
Foam scraps	
Yarn	

OPEN	CLOSED
Puppet	Puzzle
Doll	Zipper
Water	Button/buttonhole
Sand	Snaps
Clay	Stacking rings
Blocks	Wind-up doll
	Wind-up mobile

SIMPLE	COMPLEX
1-piece puzzle	4-piece puzzle
Doll	Doll clothes
Clay	Clothes fasteners

INTRUSION	SECLUSION
Bike	Large box to hide in

HIGH MOBILITY	LOW MOBILITY
Bike	Sit and Spin
Toy cars, trucks	Slide
Stroller, buggy	Books
Balls	Blocks
	Clay
	Painting
	Puzzles
	Water
	Sand

and space for use, and the budget. The following guide may help caregivers decide what to get (see Table 8–3).

TABLE 8–3   GUIDE FOR ANALYZING EQUIPMENT AND MATERIALS

ANALYSIS	ITEMS (EXAMPLE)
Facilitated Development	Telephone
Physical	
Emotional	
Social	X
Cognitive	X
Age Group	
0–6 months	
6–12 months	
12–18 months	X
18–24 months	X
24–30 months	X
30–36 months	X
Senses Appealed To	
Seeing	
Hearing	X
Touching	
Tasting	
Smelling	
Number of Uses	
Single	X
Flexible	
Safety Factors	
Nontoxic	X
Sturdy	X
No sharp edges	X
Construction	
MATERIAL	
Fabric	
Paper	
Cardboard	
Rubber	
Plastic	
Wood	X
Metal	
QUALITY	
Fair	
Good	
Excellent	X
DURABILITY	
Fair	
Good	
Excellent	X
Cost—$	
Commercial	$15.00
Homemade	
Comments	

With program goals emphasizing holistic development, a variety of items facilitating physical, emotional, social, and cognitive development are needed. Use Table 8–3 to help you see graphically whether there are items in each category. Some materials attract interest at particular ages. The age groupings in the guide are approximations; an 11-month-old and a 13-month-old may use the same item. Therefore, an item may overlap more than one age grouping. The guide will help you see which items a wide age range can use and which ones only a limited age range can use. Each age group needs a variety of items.

Infants and toddlers interact with their environment through their senses and therefore need items that stimulate these senses. At different ages children can make use of their senses in different ways. In the first few months of life infants see many things and need items to stimulate their interest in seeing. They do not have much control of their hands and fingers, so touching is limited to bumping and banging and finally grasping. A limited number and kind of items are needed to stimulate touching. However, 2-year-olds actively use all their senses, and so they need a number of items to stimulate each of their senses.

Some equipment and materials can be used in only one way; others have flexible uses. Children and caregivers can adjust and adapt them in a variety of ways to facilitate development. Single-use materials are in themselves neither good nor bad, but they may be costly.

When initially purchasing equipment for all child care settings, consider buying a "choke tube," because many states require its use. The device is a tube. Toy pieces are dropped through the opening. If the pieces go through the tube they are considered a swallowable hazard and are discarded. Only the toys with pieces larger than the opening are presented to the child.

It is important to analyze how materials and equipment are constructed. What they are made of and how they are put together will determine their durability in terms of the varied ways children will use them. This in turn will determine whether the item can serve the purposes for which it was intended in the program. Poorly constructed items that fall apart are frustrating, often unsafe for children, and costly for the program.

All child care programs must consider costs. To determine whether an item is cost effective, analyze the following factors for each item:

1. the importance for program goal attainment
2. the areas of development facilitated
3. the durability of construction
4. the number of ways it can be used
5. the number of children who can use it
6. the ages of children who can use it

A $45 wooden truck that is well constructed may be used for years and years by hundreds of children. In contrast, five $9 plastic trucks will probably be damaged and have to be thrown away within a year or so. Thus, for the same amount of money, the wooden truck is more cost effective.

The cost of equipment and materials can become astronomical. Therefore, most programs must decide which commercially made items they can purchase and which items they can make themselves. Some maintain that only commercially made equipment and materials have the quality young children require. because some child care programs cannot afford to purchase all items, that the quality must be built into their homemade items or they get along without the item.

Homemade Materials

Homemade items should meet high standards for construction, durability, and safety. Some things can be more individualized than commercially prepared items to stimulate the interest and development of children in the program. for example, a cardboard-mounted colored photograph of each child in your room or home is an individual homemade item.

Diligent scrounging of free and inexpensive materials from parents, friends, and community businesses and industries can greatly reduce the cost of homemade items. One group which has developed a very creative and beneficial support system to child care programs for locating and using scrounged materials is the Maryland Committee for Children. In Baltimore, Maryland, it operates reSTORE, a recycling center for discarded or excess industrial materials which can be used by child care providers and parents to provide learning activities for children at a fraction of the usual cost.

Some books and articles are available which specifically identify homemade materials. Burtt and Kalkstein present "77 easy-to-make toys to stimulate your baby's mind" in their book, *Smart Toys* (1981), for babies from birth to age two, Douville-Watson identifies age-appropriate materials in seminar lectures, *Caregiver Training* (1997). Zeller and McFarland matched materials, ages, and skill development in their article, "Selecting Appropriate Materials for Very Young Children" (1981). In this text each of the chapters in Part III, Matching Caregiver Strategies and Infant Development, includes ideas for homemade materials (see Figure 8–4).

CONDITIONS FOSTERING SAFETY AND HEALTH

A Quiet Zone

All indoor and outdoor environments should include a quiet zone large enough for one caregiver and a child to sit comfortably. The space has multiple purposes. It is a place that a child may choose to go, where the child stays when ill, or when needing to release frustration. This space should be clean and comfortable, and not viewed as a place of punishment or isolation. Rather, it is a space in which the child can become orga-

Figure 8–4 The refrigerator door becomes a bulletin board in a family child care home.

nized and calm. A corner of the room or a tree away from active play can become a quiet zone.

Parent Awareness of Safety

In previous chapters, special techniques such as circle of safety, changing of the guard, and shadowing were discussed. These tools were presented to help give form to the concept of the child's first environmental safety, and your awareness of the impact and influences you have on children. Your ability to anticipate possible harmful situations develops more easily when you are sure that the actions you take can protect children. The most far-reaching and important issues involving children are those of health and safety

Health and safety issues surround children in all settings, and are the potential building blocks for strong caregiver-parent partnerships. Parent orientation should begin by reassuring parents that the center is a healthy and safe place to bring their child. Parents need to know that the health and safety of all the children in care is a primary directive of all center staff, and that major health and safety items are reflected in a written policy statement. This policy reflects mandates by state and federal governments. Others are health and safety recommendations established by the Department of Health and recognized professional groups such as the American Academy of Pediatrics.

The child care setting should be an ongoing example for parents to duplicate. The physical environment should be protective, well thought out and one that is designed from the viewpoint of the child.

Specific questions should be answered after observing the neighborhood. Is the neighborhood conducive to children walking around? How aware of safety concerns are the parents? Where have the child care customs come from? How do these customs impact the safety of all the children as a group? What should the written policy for the child care facility include? What parent health and safety classes should be included in the coming year? What is the average income of the parents? What community resources are available to help the center provide for all the necessary health and safety standards and policies? What organizations offer financial support to fulfill requirements for center children? The Health and Safety of the children in care are the highest priority; they are the base from which all else is built.

Starting from an empty outdoor space, a plan for development should be established. Centers in most states have a rigorous process to insure that all the federal and state regulations are followed. Home care situations are generally less rigorous and depend more on the concerned, trained eye of the Child Care Specialist.

Every addition, change, piece of equipment, and all supplies must be well thought out and put through rigorous examinations for health and safety before being used in the facility. There is no time better spent. Prevention is the major rule for health and safety. If reasonable expectations for safeguarding children are understood, written down, and followed by all staff, parents and visitors, then real work with the children and their developmental needs can follow. Managing the indoor and outdoor environments means making policies that should include the following topics:

1. Respectful care of children and treatment of staff.
2. Parental partnership with all caregivers.
3. Confidentiality of records.
4. Proper documentation of staff and children with special needs.
5. Control and prevention of injury.
6. Prevention of child abuse.
7. Staff health.
8. Prevention and control of infectious disease.
9. Promoting a safe environment.
10. Individualized perspective care.
11. Emergency care and training for staff.
12. Ill child policy.
13. Health training for children.
14. Safety training for children.
15. Transportation safety policy.
16. Food safety policy.
17. Community involvement.
18. Ongoing training for staff and parents.
19. Up-to-date medical, immunizations, emergency numbers, and a referring pediatrician.

20. Performance evaluations of staff at frequent intervals.
21. Salary and benefit plans for caregivers, a way to state grievances, and a way to make suggestions for positive changes.
22. Primary caregivers assigned to specific children. A daily log of ongoing change, and designated responsibility for each child's Developmental Prescription.
23. Health and safety notification policy for parents of a disease to which their child was exposed, including the name of the disease, signs and symptoms, mode of transmission, period of communicability, and disease prevention measures.

One staff member who is properly trained in emergency care and cardiopulmonary resuscitation (CPR) training must be present at all times. The nurse or designated health professional should be in contact with the parent, and when appropriate, the referring pediatrician in the event that illness precludes a child attending care. This person is considered the health advocate for the center. They conduct health and safety seminars, keep aware of changing health policies, and inform the staff and parents of ongoing health recommendations.

Universal Precautions

Universal precautions must be understood and used by every person in the care setting who has contact with body fluids. Rubber gloves must be worn every time body fluids are present such as when changing diapers and wiping up spills. Universal precautions are a set of procedures prescribed by the local Department of Health. It is the responsibility of each caregiver to receive the training and updates necessary to be aware of current policies.

Blood contaminants such as Hepatitis B pose a real health threat. Blood fluid (watery discharge from lacerations and cuts) pose a risk of the greatest concern. In addition, Hepatitis B can survive in a dried state in the environment for at least a week or even longer. Other fluids such as saliva contaminated with blood may contain the live virus. Procedures for handling spills of body fluids —urine, feces, blood, saliva. nasal discharge, eye discharge, and or tissue discharges—*after the specialist gloves*, are as follows:

1. For spills of vomitus, urine, and feces—the floors, wall, bathrooms, table tops, toys, kitchen countertops, and diaper-changing tables should be cleaned and disinfected.
2. For spills of blood or blood-containing body fluids, injury, and tissue discharges—the area should be cleaned and disinfected.
3. Persons involved in cleaning contaminated surfaces are to avoid exposure of open skin sores or mucous membranes to blood or blood-containing body fluids, injury, or tissue discharges by using gloves to protect hands. Illnesses may be spread in varying ways, such as coughing, sneezing, direct skin-to-skin contact, or touching an object or sur-

face with germs on it. Infectious germs may be contained in human waste (urine, feces and body fluids, saliva, nasal discharge, tissue and injury discharges, eye discharges, and blood). Because many infected people carry communicable diseases without symptoms, and many are contagious before they experience symptoms, staff need to protect themselves and the children they serve by carrying out sanitation and disinfection procedures on a routine basis that avoid every potential illness-spreading condition.

   Education of staff regarding cleaning procedures can reduce the occurrence of illness in the entire group of children. Use a solution of $1/4$ cup household liquid chlorine bleach to one gallon tap water when cleaning contaminated surfaces.

4. Mops should be cleaned, rinsed in sanitizing solution, wrung as dry as possible, and hung to dry.
5. Blood-contaminated material and diapers should be disposed of in a plastic bag with a secure tie, and labeled with a tag.
6. Sanitize, disinfect, and maintain toys and objects. Insure that frequently used rooms and items are disinfected. Nondiapered children's rooms should be cleaned weekly. Thermometers, pacifiers, and the like should be disinfected between uses. Individual children's items and travel items for personal hygiene should be sent home with parents to be cleaned weekly, or after each use if more than one child uses a crib. All equipment should be cleaned and maintained by staff. Crib mattresses should be cleaned at least weekly. Each child should have his or her own bed not to be shared with other children. Regular cleaning maintenance of the entire facility should be done weekly.

Hand-washing instructions involve modeling and assisting children in adjusting water temperature and pressure, cleaning palms and backs of hands and wrists, using liquid soap properly, cleaning nails and between fingers, drying hands properly, and paper towel disposal.

Signs and Symptoms of Possible Severe Illness

These include:

- unusual lack of movement
- uncontrolled crying
- coughing
- different breathing or wheezing
- uncontrolled diarrhea
- vomiting
- rash
- sores in the mouth
- red conjunctivitis
- head lice

- strep throat (until 24 hours after starting antibiotics)
- Chicken pox (until 6 days after onset of rash or until sores are dried and crusted)
- Influenza Hemophilus Pertussis (until 5 days placed on antibiotics)
- Mumps (until 9 days after onset of swollen glands)
- hepatitis until one week after onset of illness or as directed by health official when immune serum globulin has been administered to all other children and staff
- Measles (until 6 days after onset of rash)
- Rubella (until 6 days after onset of rash)

—(Nassau County Department of Health, 1997)

A child who exhibits any of the above symptoms, or demonstrates unusual atypical behavior in relation to any of the above symptoms, should be removed to a predetermined place of isolation where they should be supervised until the parent takes their child home. For additional information, contact The American Red Cross, National Headquarters, Health and Safety, 18th Street NW, Washington DC 20006.

Another publication available for health and safety is *Child Care Health Programs*, King County Dept. of Public Health, 110 Prefontaine Place South, #5r Seattle, WA 98104. You can also contact your local Health Department, or a local registered nurse (RN) or Pediatrician who will be happy to help you with additional library source information.

Immunization Schedule

The following schedule from the American Academy of Pediatrics (1997) may be modified in some states which approve care of children at six weeks of age. All children must be immunized before attending day care.

Recommended Schedule of Immunizations for Infants to 14 Years Old

AGE	VACCINES	DESCRIPTION
2 months	*DTP-1, OPV-1a or IPV-1, HbCV-1b	*DTP=diphtheria and tetanus
4 months	DTP-2, OPV/IPV-2, HbCV-2b	toxins with pertussis vaccine; OPV=
6 months	DTP-3, HbCV-b	oral poliovirus vaccine with attenuated
15 months	MAR-c, HbCV-b	poliovirus types 1, 2, & 3; IPV = inactivated
18 months	DAB-4, OPV/IPV-3	poliovirus vaccine with killed type 1, 2,
4–6 years	DTP-5, OPV/IPV-4	& 3; MAR = attenuated measles, mumps,
4-14 years	MAR-2	rubella viruses in combined vaccine; HbCV=H, influenza type b conjugate vaccines

Chicken Pox Vaccine will be available in 1998.

Safety issues include transporting children from one area to another. Every state has seatbelt laws to protect children. The safest place for transporting children by car is the middle of the back seat in an approved car seat. Ideally, the seat should be attached to the metal frame of the car. Because of accidental eruption of air bags, all children should be seated in back seats.

First aid kits should be in the open and visible, but out of reach of children. First aid kits should include the following items (from Health, Safety, and Nutrition for the Young Child (1997):

Basic First Aid Supplies
- activated charcoal
- adhesive tape, $1/2$- and 1-inch widths
- alcohol
- bandages, assorted sizes
- blanket
- cotton balls
- flashlight
- gauze pads, sterile, 2 x 2s, 4 x 4s
- hot water bottle
- instant ice pack or plastic bags
- needle-sewing
- roller gauze, 1- and 2-inch widths
- latex gloves
- safety pins
- scissors, blunt tipped
- soap, preferably liquid
- spirits of ammonia
- splints
- syrup of Ipecac®
- thermometers, 2
- tongue blades
- towels, large and small
- triangular bandages for slings
- tweezers
- Vaseline®
- first aid book such as *Sigh of Relief*

First aid refers to treatment administered for injuries and illnesses that are not considered life-threatening. Emergency care and first aid are based on principles that should be familiar to everyone involved in the care setting.

1. Summon emergency medical assistance (911 in many areas) for any injury or illness that requires more than simple first aid.
2. Stay calm and in control of the situation.

3. Always remain with the child. If necessary, send another adult or child for help.
4. Keep the child still until the extent of injuries or illness can be determined. If in doubt, have the child stay in the same position and await emergency medical help.
5. Quickly evaluate the child's condition, paying special attention to an open airway, breathing, and circulation.
6. Carefully plan and administer appropriate emergency care. Improper treatment can lead to other injuries.
7. Do not give any medications unless they are prescribed for certain life-saving conditions.
8. Do not offer diagnosis or medical advice. Refer the child's parents to health professionals.
9. Always inform the child's parents of the injury and first aid care that has been administered.
10. Record all the facts concerning the accident and treatment administered; file in the child's permanent folder.

In most states, legal protection is granted to individuals who administer emergency care unless their actions are judged grossly negligent or harmful. This protection is commonly known as the Good Samaritan Law. Many states require a signed Emergency Care Permission form from the parent.

Animals need to be properly immunized, clean, fed, and cared for in loving ways. Permission slips for children to have access to pets should be attained, and children with allergies should not be exposed to areas with pets.

Fire Prevention and Emergency Numbers

Fire drills should be established. A safety drill should be performed, timed, and recorded on a monthly basis. A safe place outside should be established such as a tree, building, or sign where everyone is to meet. An evacuation plan and map should be posted at all doorways.

Emergency numbers should be current and posted in a convenient place for the staff to see. New fire extinguishers should be in unlocked boxes and replaced after any use. Safety bars or windows that are shatterproof should be installed. All equipment must pass rigorous testing. All pools should have locked fences around them. Constant supervision is necessary whenever water play in initiated.

Regular fire drills are necessary. Determine the closest exit route and post on the wall a room diagram marked with your fire exit route. Talk with the children about times when all of you might need to get out of the building quickly; be careful, however, not to scare them. If you have nonwalkers, select one crib that will fit through doorways, put heavy-duty wheels on it, and put a special symbol on it. In case of fire, put your nonwalkers in this special crib and wheel the crib outside. Holding hands and talking calmly, walk the toddlers as quickly as possible out of the building.

Continue to hold hands and talk calmly as you stand outside the building at a pre-designated spot.

Materials and equipment must be selected with special care for use with infants and toddlers. Young children put everything they touch to a hard test: they bite, pinch, hit, fling, bang, pound, and tear at whatever they can. In their explorations of what they can do with the materials and equipment, young children focus on actions and do not think in terms of cause and effect so far as use is concerned. Therefore, the caregiver must take care to provide only materials and equipment which can safely withstand the child's use.

Safety is a matter to consider when analyzing the sturdiness of construction, the materials of construction, the size, the weight, the flexibility of use, and the effect the item will have on the child.

> Look for wood that doesn't splinter, wheels that won't pinch, corners and edges carefully rounded. Design, too, must be safety-conscious, stable and secure without small openings to catch fingers or limbs Community Playthings 1981,10) (see Figure 8–5).

The developmental capabilities of the child affect safety. A tyke bike may be safe for a 30-month-old but unsafe for a 9-month-old. Some equipment is safe if it is used with assistance but may be unsafe if it is used independently. For example, some children would not be able to play safely with a record player.

Aronson analyzed insurance claims for injuries in child care. She found that the following were associated with the most frequent or more severe injuries: motor vehicles, climbers, slides, hand toys, blocks, other playground

Figure 8–5 Scrap paper is a good recyclable resource for creative activities.

equipment, doors, indoor floor surfaces, swings, pebbles or rocks, and pencils (1983, 19). Aronson recommended the following:*

1. Unsafe climbers, slides, and other playground equipment should be modified or eliminated. The U.S. Consumer Product Safety Commission suggests these modifications to make safer playgrounds: place climbing structures closer to the ground, mount them over 8–12 inches loose fill material such as pea gravel, pine bark, or shredded tires; space all equipment far enough away from other structures and child traffic patterns to prevent collisions; cover sharp edges and exposed bolts; limit the number of children using equipment at one time; and teach children to play safely (see Figure 8–6).
2. Hazardous activities require closer adult supervision than activities with a lower injury rating.
3. Architectural features such as doors and indoor floor surfaces require special attention. Doors should have beveled edges and mechanisms which prevent slamming or rapid closure. Full-length-view vision panels will help assure that small children are seen before the door is opened. Changes in floor surfaces and edges which might cause tripping should be modified. Long open spaces should be interrupted to discourage running in areas where running is dangerous.

Figure 8–6 Only sterilized sand should be used in sandboxes for children.

---

*Courtesy of Susan Aronson, Ph.D., Associate Clinical Professor Pediatrics and of Community and Preventive Medicine.

4. Children must always travel in safety-approved restraints in cars, vans, and buses and follow all other safety rules.

5. Training and resources to change hazardous conditions should be made available to all staff. Injury reports should be routinely examined by trained personnel to identify and correct trouble spots. A systematic study of injury in child care centers and in home child care is needed to assist adults in making provision for the safe care of children (1983, 19–20).

The Massachusetts Department of Public Health developed a Site Safety Checklist and a Playground Safety Checklist that can be used and/or adapted for assessing and providing safe and healthy indoor and outdoor environments for infants and toddlers (see Tables 8–4 and 8–5).

Traffic safety involves safety near traffic and auto safety. Toddlers are excitable and change interests suddenly. Therefore, when walking with toddlers, one adult should be responsible for only a few children. You must be able to reach out and touch the children with whom you are walking. Many toddlers will not keep holding onto a rope or onto a child's hand five children away from you.

When traveling with children in a car or van be sure that each child is in U.S. safety-approved infant car seats or restraints. A crash at 30 miles per hour can produce a force on impact similar to falling from a three-story building (Transportation Hazards Commission 1984). Check the car seats to make sure they are securely attached to the seat belt or floor. Strap the child securely into the infant car seat. Some children do not like to ride with restraints and will wriggle around until they are twisted in the straps. Be available to help settle the children and to keep their seat restraints on correctly so they will not be injured from improper use of the restraints. Check with your local or state traffic safety department or local hospital for specific details on approved infant car seats and restraints.

In the child care home or room it is essential to be able to go out of and come into the room immediately. Evaluate the setting for fire safety, looking not only at what everything is made out of (will it burn?) but also at its location in the room. Children and adults need to be able to get out rapidly, and firemen need to come in. Therefore, doors and windows should open easily, and the space in front of them should be kept free from clutter.

Equipment must be disinfected regularly. Food containers and utensils must be washed regularly and thoroughly. Since infants put toys in their mouths, these toys should be washed daily in a solution of ¼ cup chlorine bleach to 1 gallon water, or 1 tablespoon bleach per quart of water, and left to air-dry. Toys for older children should be washed regularly. Large equipment should be sprayed and cleaned. During the cold and flu season, disinfect toys and equipment more often than at other times of the year.

The floor should be cleaned daily, with spills and spots cleaned up immediately. Vinyl flooring should be swept or vacuumed and then sponge-

TABLE 8-4   SITE SAFETY CHECKLIST

ITEM	YES/NO	CORRECTIONS/ COMMENTS	DATE MADE CORRECTION
General Environment			
Floors are smooth and have a nonskid surface			
Pipes and radiators are inaccessible to children or are covered to prevent contact			
Hot tap water temperature for hand-washing is 110°–115°F or less			
Electrical cords are out of children's reach and are kept out of doorways and traffic paths			
Unused electrical outlets are covered by furniture or shock stops			
Medicines, cleansers, and aerosols are kept in a locked place where children are unable to see and reach them			
All windows have screens that stay in place when used; expandable screens are not used			
Windows can be opened 6" or less from the bottom			
Drawers are kept closed to prevent tripping or bumps			
Trash is covered at all times			
Walls and ceilings are free of peeling paint and cracked or falling plaster; center has been inspected for lead paint			
There are no disease-bearing animals, such as turtles, parrots, or cats			
Children are always supervised			
There is no friable (crumbly) asbestos releasing into the air			
Equipment and Toys			
Toys and play equipment are checked often for sharp edges, small parts, and sharp points			
All toys are painted with lead-free paint			
Toys are put away when not in use			
Toy chests have lightweight lids or no lids			
Art materials are non-toxic, and have either the AP or the CP label			

TABLE 8-4   *(continued)*

ITEM	YES/NO	CORRECTIONS/ COMMENTS	DATE MADE CORRECTION
Art materials are stored in their original containers in a locked place			
Teaching aids (e.g., projectors) are put away when not in use			
Curtains, pillows, blankets, and soft toys are made of flame- resistant material			
Hallways and Stairs			
Stairs and stairways are free of boxes, toys, and other clutter			
Stairways are well-lit			
The right-hand railing on the stairs is at child height and does not wobble when held; there is a railing or wall on both sides of stairways			
Stairway gates are in place when appropriate			
Closed doorways to unsupervised or unsafe areas are always locked unless this prevents emergency evacuation			
Staff are able to watch for strangers entering the building			
Kitchen			
Trash is kept away from areas where food is prepared or stored			
Trash is stored away from the furnace and hot water heater			
Pest strips are NOT used; pesticides for crawling insects are applied by a certified pest control operator			
Cleansers and other poisonous products are stored in their original containers, away from food and out of children's reach			
Food preparation surfaces are clean and free of cracks and chips			
Electrical cords are placed where people will not trip over them or pull them			
There are no sharp or hazardous cooking utensils within children's reach (e.g., knives, glass)			
Pot handles are always turned in toward the back of the stove during cooking			
The fire extinguisher can be reached easily in an emergency			

TABLE 8-4   *(continued)*

ITEM	YES/NO	CORRECTIONS/ COMMENTS	DATE MADE CORRECTION
All staff know how to use the fire extinguisher correctly			
Bathrooms			
Stable step stools are available when needed			
Electrical outlets are covered with shock stops or outlet covers			
Cleaning products, soap, and disinfectant are stored in a locked place, out of children's reach			
Floors are smooth and have a nonskid surface			
The trash container is emptied daily and kept clean			
Hot water for hand-washing is 110°–115°F			
Emergency Preparation			
All staff understand their roles and responsibilities in case of emergency			
At least one staff person is always present who is certified in first aid and CPR for infants and children			
The first aid kit is checked regularly for supplies and is kept where it can be reached easily by staff in an emergency			
Smoke detectors and other alarms are checked regularly to make sure they are working			
Each room and hallway has a fire escape route posted in clear view			
Emergency procedures and telephone numbers are posted near each phone in clear view			
Children's emergency phone numbers are kept near the phone, where they can be reached quickly			
All exits are clearly marked and are free of clutter			
Doors open in the direction of all exit travel			
Cots are placed so that walkways are clear for evacuation in an emergency			

Source: Statewide Comprehensive Injury Prevention Program (SCIPP), Department of Public Health, 150 Tremont Street, Boston, Massachusetts 02111.

TABLE 8-5   PLAYGROUND SAFETY CHECKLIST

ITEM	YES/NO	CORRECTIONS/ COMMENTS	DATE MADE CORRECTION
All Equipment			
Nuts, bolts, or screws that stick out are covered with masking tape or sanded down			
Metal equipment is free from rust or chipping paint			
Wood equipment is free from splinters or rough surfaces, sharp edges, and pinch/crush parts			
Nuts and bolts are tight			
Anchors for equipment are stable and buried below level			
Equipment is in its proper place and is not bent with use			
Children who use equipment are of the age/development level for which the equipment was designed			
Ground Surface			
All play equipment has 8"–12" of shock-absorbing material underneath (e.g., pea gravel or wood chips)			
Surfaces are raked weekly to prevent them from becoming packed down and to find hidden hazards (e.g., litter, sharp objects, animal feces)			
Stagnant pools of water are not present on the surface			
There is no exposed concrete where equipment is anchored			
Spacing			
Swing sets are at least 9 feet from other equipment			
Swings are at least 1½ feet from each other			
Slides have a 2½- to 3-yard run-off space			
There is at least 8 feet between all equipment			
Boundaries between equipment are visible to children (for instance, painted lines or low bushes)			
Play areas for bike-riding, games, and boxes are separate from other equipment			

TABLE 8-5 *(continued)*

ITEM	YES/NO	CORRECTIONS/ COMMENTS	DATE MADE CORRECTION
Swing sets are at least 6 feet from walls and fences, walkways, and other play areas; there is a barrier to prevent children from getting into traffic (e.g., when chasing a ball)			
Slides			
Slides are 6 feet in height or less			
Side rims are at least 2½ inches high			
Slides have an enclosed platform at the top for children to rest and get into position for sliding			
Slide ladders have handrails on both sides and flat steps			
There is a flat surface at the bottom of the slide for slowing down			
Metal slides are shaded to prevent burns			
Wood slides are waxed, or oiled with linseed oil			
The slide incline is equal or less than a 30° angle			
Steps and rungs are 7" to 11" apart to accommodate children's leg and arm reach			
Climbing Equipment			
Ladders of different heights are available for children of different ages and sizes			
Bars stay in place when grasped			
The maximum height from which a child can fall is 7½ feet			
Climbers have regularly spaced footholds from top to bottom			
There is an easy, safe "way out" for children when they reach the top			
Equipment is dry before children are allowed to use it			
Rungs are painted in bright or contrasting colors so children will see them			
Swings			
Chair swings are available for children under age 5			
Canvas sling and saddle seats are available for older children			

TABLE 8-5   *(continued)*

ITEM	YES/NO	CORRECTIONS/ COMMENTS	DATE MADE CORRECTION
"S" or open-ended hooks have been removed			
Hanging rings are less than 5" or more than 10" diameter (smaller or larger than child's head)			
The point at which seat and chain meet is exposed			
Seesaws			
The fulcrum is enclosed or designed to prevent pinching			
Handholds stay in place when grasped, without turning or wobbling			
Wooden blocks or part of a rubber tire are placed below the seat to prevent feet from getting caught			
Sandboxes			
Sandboxes are located in a shaded spot; only sterilized sand is used.			
The frame is sanded and smooth, without splinters or rough surfaces			
The sand is raked at least every two weeks to check for debris and to provide exposure to air and sun			
The box is covered at night to protect from moisture and animal excrement			
The sandbox has proper drainage			
Poisonous plants and berries are removed from play area			
There is a source of clean drinking water available in the play area			
There is shade			
The entire play area can be seen easily for good supervision			

Source: Statewide Comprehensive Injury Prevention Program (SCIPP), Department of Public Health, 150 Tremont Street, Boston, Massachusetts 02111.

mopped with detergent and disinfectant (never combine ammonia and bleach). Carpeting should be vacuumed daily, with periodic shampooing of the whole area. The eating area needs to be swept or vacuumed after each meal.

The sleeping equipment should be cleaned and disinfected regularly. Every caregiver must use universal precautions. Every child should have an individual sheet and blanket. These should be washed at least weekly and changed immediately if soiled. Diapers should not be changed on the sheet.

The crib mattress and sides and the cots should be cleaned regularly with a disinfectant spray of 1 ounce chlorine bleach to 1 gallon water, or 1 tablespoon bleach to 1 quart water.

Toilet seats should be kept clean. Toddlers just learning to take care of their own toilet procedures often get urine and feces on the seats. Allow toddlers to be as independent as possible, and assist them when necessary with wiping, hand-washing, and clothes. Wipe the seat and spray with disinfectant afterwards. Some pediatricians recommend using an adapter seat on the toilet rather than using a potty chair. All staff should remain conscious of hand-washing procedures and wash hands after dealing directly with each individual child and help the child to wash his or her hands after toileting.

Remember that the quality of human relationships is one of your primary focuses. Your attention to cleanliness and sanitation should be an automatic procedure rather than a major obstacle to relationships. Find a balance so that the children experience a normal life. Conditions which are either dirty or overemphasize disinfecting and not touching children or materials focus undue attention on physical health while hampering emotional, social, and cognitive growth.

Human Immunodeficiency Virus (HIV) Infection

"On the basis of available data, there is no reason to believe H.I.V.-infected adults will transmit H.I.V. in the course of their normal child duties." (American Academy of Pediatrics, 1997). The HIV virus cannot be transmitted as long as there are no open sores or other blood sources existing. HIV-positive adults may care for children. However, the HIV caregiver is at great risk due to the highly contagious environment that childcare settings represent.

Parents of HIV children should be alerted to exposure of such agents as measles and chicken pox. Their pediatrician will probably inject them with an immune booster such as Immune Globulin. Universal precautions are used on every incident of spilled blood or possible blood exposure.

If an HIV-infected child leaves the center due to exposure, the decision to return will be made by the child's pediatrician or nurse practitioner, the parents, and the director of the center. This is also a procedure for a known HIV-infected caregiver. Laws from federal, state, and local authorities are designed to protect families, and confidentiality is a legal right. All information, medical records, and personal information is set aside and kept confidential. No one shall have access to this information unless the parents give written releases. Only staff who have a need to know will be informed. They also must sign a disclosure form that is kept in the child's record.

SIDS: Sudden Infant Death Syndrome and the Back To Sleep Campaign

According to the National Center for Health Statistics, 3,397 deaths occurred in 1995 (.87 per 1000 births) compared to 1996 where 2,906 deaths occurred (.74 per 1000 births) after the Back To Sleep campaign was started. The Back

To Sleep Campaign involves placing babies on their back to sleep, not smoking around them, lying them on flat surfaces, washing all bedding before using it, removing all articles from cribs, not using a pillow, and regular health check ups.

Child care professionals must take these recommendations seriously and regard them as some of the main safety procedures to use with infants. The American Academy of Pediatrics adds the warning that "It is important for caregivers to be knowledgeable about SIDS and that they take steps so they are not falsely accused of child abuse" (1997).

For additional information on SIDS, contact: The National SIDS Clearinghouse, 8201 Greensboro Drive, Suite 600, McLean, Virginia 22102, or SIDS Alliance, 10500 Little Patuxent Parkway, Suite 402, Columbia, Maryland 21044.

STUDENT ACTIVITIES

1. Identify one item in your child care setting for each category of Jone's dimensions of the environment.
2. Use the Guide for Analyzing Equipment and Materials (Table 8–3) to analyze five pieces of equipment and five materials used indoors and five pieces of equipment and five materials used outdoors in your child care setting.
3. Observe two children playing with materials. Write down the actions of each child as he or she manipulates the object(s).
4. Draw a diagram of the child care room or home showing the placement of basic equipment and activity areas.
5. Draw a detailed diagram of one activity area. Compare it to the specifications identified by Olds.
6. Draw a diagram of the play yard arrangement. Identify activity areas. List equipment and materials in each area.
7. Interview a caregiver in a child care program where age groups share the outdoor space. Describe how that program facilitates play yard use and ensures safety.
8. What important influence is the neighborhood in which the child care setting is located?

CHAPTER REVIEW

1. How can caregivers determine whether a piece of equipment or material is useful in the program?
2. When planning room arrangements, why do we distinguish between soft and hard, wet and dry, quiet and active?
3. What does it mean that the play yard is "an integral part of the program"?
4. List four safety factors which caregivers must consider in selecting toys and equipment for infants and toddlers.

5. Describe how a toy or equipment may be safe for one child and unsafe for another child.
6. List two adaptations that caregivers can make when young infants, crawlers, and toddlers share space.
7. "Go shopping" and "buy" all the fine motor equipment and materials a group of 24 months olds will need (use supply catalogues such as Child Craft, Community Playthings, etc.) and give yourself a realistic budget to work with.

REFERENCES

American Academy of Pediatrics. 1996. *Caring for Our Children: National Health and Safety Performance Standards.* American Public Health Association, Washington, DC. pp. 92-111.

American Academy of Pediatrics. 1993. *Safety for Consumers.*

Aronson, S. S. 1983. Injuries in child care. *Young Children* 38(6): 19–20.

Burtt, K. G. and Kalkstein, K. 1981. *Smart Toys.* New York: Harper & Row.

Clar, P. 1981. Industrial scraps go to school. *Day Care and Early Education* 8(3): 34–35.

Community Playthings. 1981. *Criteria for Selecting Play Equipment.* Rifton, New York: Author.

Dalziel, S. No date. *Spaces in Open Places.* Cortland, New York: SUNY. Project Change. Unpublished manuscript.

Douville-Watson. 1997. *Caregiver Training '97. Creating Boundaries Using Puppets.* New York Instructional Press, 21 Oak Shore Drive, Bayville, New York 11709.

Essa, E. L. 1981. An outdoor play area designed for learning. *Day Care and Early Education* 9(2): 37–42.

Gordon, D. M. 1981. Toward a safer playground. *Day Care and Early Education* 9(1): 46–53.

Healy, J. 1989. *Your Child's Growing Mind: A Guide to Learning and Brain Development from Birth to Adolescence.* New York: Doubleday.

Johnson, E. 1981. Water. Wet and wonderful. *Day Care and Early Education* 8(3): 12–14.

Jones, E. 1973. *Dimensions of Teaching-Learning Environments.* Pasadena, CA: Pacific Oaks.

Jones, E. and Prescott, E. 1982. Planning the physical environment in day care. *Day Care and Early Education* 9(3): 18–25.

Massachusetts Department of Public Health. *Statewide Comprehensive Injury Prevention Program.* Boston, MA: Author.

Olds, A. R. 1983. Planning a developmentally optimal day care center. *Day Care Journal* 1(1): 16–24.

Salkever, M. 1980. Don't throw it away. *Day Care and Early Education* 8(1): 55–57.

Transportation Hazards Commission, American Academy of Pediatrics. 1984. *The Perfect Gift.*

Walther-Lee, Dori. 1994. Workplace child care consultants. Bayville, New York.

Zeller, J. M. and McFarland, S. L. 1981. Selecting appropriate materials for very young children. *Day Care and Early Education* 8(4): 7–13.

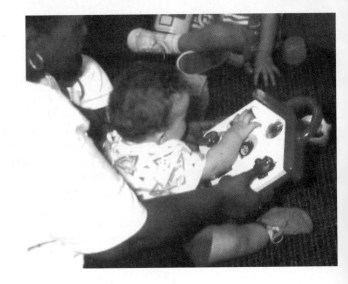

9 Designing Curriculum

OBJECTIVES

After completing this chapter, the child development specialist should be able to:
1. Identify major influences on the curriculum.
2. Examine the caregiver's role in curriculum development.
3. Write an integrated unit plan.

CHAPTER OUTLINE

    I. Infant-Toddler Curriculum
       A. Definition and Scope of Curriculum
       B. Purposes for Curriculum
   II. Influences on the Curriculum
       A. Influences of Society
       B. Corporate Child Care Advocacy
       C. Cultural Expectation
       D. Influences from the Care Setting
       E. Influences from the Child
  III. Children with Special Needs
       A. Functional Ability versus Actual Age
       B. Special Needs Children and Community Support
       C. Brain Gym
       D. New Brain Research
  IV. The Process of Curriculum Development
       A Purposes and Philosophy
       B. Goals
       C. Objectives
       D. Methods
       E. Materials
       F. Evaluation
       G. Feedback
   V. Implementing Curriculum
       A. Schedule

B. Nutrition for Young Children
C. Routines
D. Daily Written Plans

CHILD DEVELOPMENT ASSOCIATE FUNCTIONAL AREAS

I. 1–2
I. 2
I. 3 Learning Environment
II. 4
II. 4– III. 9
IV. 11 Families
IV. 11 Families
VI. 13 Professionalism

INFANT-TODDLER CURRICULUM

Definition and Scope of Curriculum

A curriculum is a course of study based upon a philosophy and goals. Specifically, a curriculum is the development of written goals, the definition of steps (in order of difficulty) necessary to achieve the goals, and the activities and materials necessary to accomplish the steps.

Infants and toddlers participate actively in selecting their curriculum and initiating their activities. When Jessie babbles sentencelike sounds and then pauses, Ms. Howard looks over at her, smiles, and answers, "Jessie, you sound happy today. That is a pretty ring in your hand." Jessie is playing with a large colored plastic ring that Ms. Howard has set near her. Jessie determines what she will do with the ring and what she will say. Her sounds stimulate Ms. Howard to respond to her (see Figure 9–1). Daily experiences can provide an integrated curriculum, for children are actively involved with themselves, and with the world around them. All are parts of the curriculum.

The five major Developmental Areas give an overall structure for defining goals. Each activity the child undertakes can then be broken down into these five areas. Next, activities involved in each area can be broken down into as specific steps in the natural developmental hierarchy as necessary to achieve this goal. This process of breaking down tasks into their natural developmental steps is called task analysis. We task analyze activities as specifically as necessary to ensure that the child has success at each step and attains the goal.

Example 1

The caregiver is holding 4-month-old Lisa, patting her, and singing and talking to her. While the infant drinks milk from her bottle, she pats the flowers on the caregiver's blouse and looks at the flowers, the buttons, her own hand, and the caregiver's face. Lisa stops eating, talks to the caregiver, smiles, and then starts eating, patting, looking, and listening again.

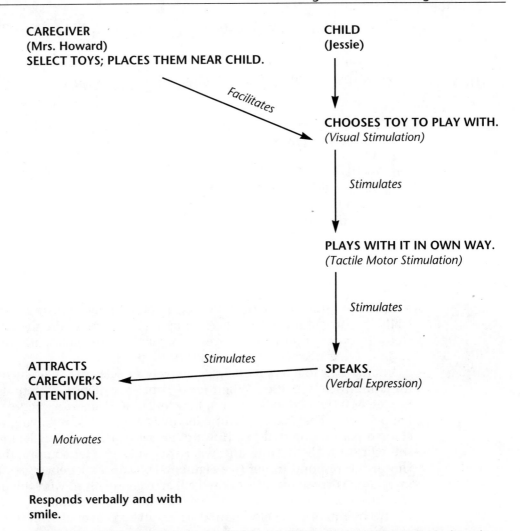

Figure 9–1   An example of caregiver-child-material interaction which individualizes the curriculum.

    Here is a task analysis of the situation described in this example using the five major Developmental Areas as a structure:

Infant Behaviors
Motor
    Drinking milk
    Reaching
    Coordinating eye and hand to pat the flowers
Seeing
    Focusing
    Changing focus
    Looking at attention-catching features

Smelling
  Smelling familiar odor of caregiver
Hearing
  Listening to caregiver's voice
  Hearing own voice
  Hearing caregiver's heartbeat
  Hearing own and caregiver's breathing
Emotional
  Satisfying self
  Touching
  Achieving closeness
  Gratifying needs
Social
  Gaining familiarity with and acceptance of another person
  Smiling
  Interacting with another person
Cognitive
  Paying attention to details
  Noticing one object, then moving on to another and another
Language
  Listening
  Talking
  Responding to another's talking, singing

Caregiver Behaviors
  Observing
  Holding
  Feeding
  Rocking
  Talking
  Singing
  Listening
  Responding

Example 2

One-month-old Roger awakens from a nap and cries with intense body jerking movements. The caregiver immediately lifts him up, holds him close, changes his diaper, prepares a bottle and feeds him, smiles and talks quietly while doing so.

Infant Behaviors
Physical
  Moves reflexively
  Begins to control movements
Emotional
  Shows distress

Calms down
Language
  Cries

Caregiver Behaviors
  Listens
  Responds to infant's cries by physically comforting him using the
    rueing technique
  Determines cause of distress
  Responds to infant's needs—need for food/comforting
  Initiates and continues interacting by looking, smiling, talking with the
    infant

Since infant and toddler curriculum involves the whole child, the child should have experiences which enhance his or her physical, emotional, social, cognitive, and perceptual skill development. The caregiver is responsible for planning and facilitating this holistic curriculum.

Each child is a distinct being, differing from others in some ways, yet sharing many of the same basic needs. *There is no one curriculum for all infants.* Caregivers have a special responsibility to design each child's curriculum by observing, thinking, planning, and putting many different skills and information together using the Developmental Areas as a structure and performing task analysis as the method.

Purposes for Curriculum

Designing curriculum serves several functions in child care.

1. The providers (caregivers) and the consumers (parents and children) contribute to the decisions on curricula.
2. The process of curriculum development helps the caregiver understand and plan so that curriculum goals and objectives are realized through daily experiences.
3. The curriculum reflects the interrelationship of the caregiver and child in determining and initiating the curriculum.
4. Task analysis of the curriculum ensures a balance and natural progression in the experiences offered to children.
5. Awareness of need levels and task analysis of the ever-changing child supports and enhances overall growth and development.

INFLUENCES ON THE CURRICULUM

Society, the setting, the child, and the caregiver all influence the infant and toddler curriculum. Each of these influences on the child is discussed in detail in the following sections.

Influences of Society

Parents

Parents place children in child care outside their own home for a variety of reasons. The majority of parents do so because they work. Their primary goal is to make sure their children are safe in a stable situation which the parents can trust. Therefore, parents are concerned about the physical environment and how it is used.

Parents may share with caregivers their expectations as parents. One aspect of curriculum is to help parents meet their needs as they relate to child-rearing and child care. Different parents have different ideas about child-rearing and parenting techniques. The following questions can stimulate varying responses from parents:

- Should a mother breast-feed or bottle-feed?
- How frequently should a parent hold and cuddle the infant?
- Should parents respond immediately to the crying infant?
- When and how should parents talk, sing, play with the infant?
- What are appropriate mothering behaviors?
- What are appropriate fathering behaviors?

Parents also look to caregivers to reinforce and extend their own child-rearing practices. They usually convey to the caregiver their expectations for their children and their attitudes concerning parenting roles and children's behaviors.

Parents view themselves in various ways. Some parents expect to be "perfect" parents. The realities of parenting often cause them to feel guilty when they fall short of perfection or when they turn the child over to the caregiver. Their frustrations may affect their attitudes about themselves and their interactions with their children and their children's caregivers. Sometimes jealousies develop. The child care staff can help these parents establish more realistic expectations.

Some parents seem very casual. They move in a very off-handed way from one parenting task to the next with seemingly little thought of goals or consequences. Some of these parents seem to place their children into child care with the attitude of "do what you want to with them; just keep them out of my hair." The caregiver may need to emphasize the worth of the child and the importance of parents and caregivers in enhancing this worth. Between these two extremes are parents who want to be good parents and who look to caregivers to assist them and their children.

Parents have ideas about what the caregiver should do. They express these positive and negative expectations verbally and nonverbally, in direct and indirect ways. Parents expect caregivers to help their children learn their values. They expect caregivers to reinforce behaviors the parents approve of. Parents expect caregivers to be competent. They place their trust in the caregiver to provide safe, healthy, reliable, affectionate, concerned, and intelligent care for their children. Parents have their own ways of judging caregiver competence.

Some judgment is intuitive, based on listening to and watching the caregiver with their child. Some judgement is based on what parents think would be responsible caregiver behavior.

Parents expect their children to cope with the child care setting. Working parents need to use child care and want it to be an arrangement where the child will have satisfying as well as safe experiences. Parents expect their children to learn socially acceptable behavior. Parents define for themselves what is socially acceptable. They do not want their children to learn behaviors which are contrary to their own values and beliefs. Obviously, parents exert more interactive than passive influences on their children, which is explained in detail in the following section.

Corporate Child Care Advocacy

The American Institute of Physics Childcare Center Inc. offers childcare services to AIP employees, and routinely assesses their infants and toddlers by utilizing the developmental profiles offered in part three of this text. Developmental prescriptions are designed to facilitate the enhancement of young children's' progression through the developmental process.

Terri Braun is an excellent professional who recognized the need to help her associates balance their concern between family and careers. As Director of Human Resources at the American Institute of Physics, she was the inspiration for award-winning, state-of-the-art child care centers.

The AIP corporate site in College Park, Maryland and one located in Woodbury, New York are outstanding examples of child care advocacy in action. Because of Terri's direct efforts, employed parents can work with peace of mind knowing their children are close by and are being cared for in an excellent manner. Both centers have received several highly acclaimed awards of excellence.

"The private sector needs to make an increasing effort to support partnerships between themselves and their employees. Child care is a national concern...The welfare of tomorrow's business depends on the services offered to today's children." President Bill Clinton (October, 1997).

Cultural Expectations

Parents feel pressures of family and society upon their own child-rearing activities. They receive comments, praise, suggestions, scolding, and ridicule on a variety of topics. Sometimes they hear mixed opinions on the same topic. Some conflicting comments they are likely to encounter include the following:

- The parent should stay home with the newborn and very young infant vs. It is acceptable for the parent of any aged child to work outside the home.

- The newborn and very young infant should stay home and not be taken visiting vs. The infant may be taken visiting occasionally.
- The parents are wasting their time when talking to and playing with a young baby vs. The parents should talk to and play with the infant.
- The infant needs lots of clothes and blankets to keep warm vs. The infant may need only moderate covering depending on the weather.
- The infant should start solid foods at 4 months of age vs. The infant should start solid food at a later age.
- The infant's solid food should be commercially prepared food vs. The infant should eat only mashed table food.

The behaviors of parents are a compromise between what society expects and what the parents feel comfortable with.

What one considers proper language and food are unique to one's subculture. The caregiver can draw attention positively to the similarities and uniquenesses of others. Expansion of language usage and food preference can be a part of the curriculum without negating the parent's cultural expectations.

Each caregiver brings unique cultural experiences and expectations to the caregiving role. Be aware of how these are similar to or different from those of the parents and other staff in order to plan and provide a curriculum acceptable to all.

For example, an infant will initiate visual, social, and language interactions but will stop if no one responds. If the caregiver feels uncomfortable or believes it is wrong to interact with the infant, that infant will gradually cease to initiate language or other interactions. But if the caregiver also initiates stimulation of visual, social, emotional, or language interactions, the infant will be challenged to respond and do the same.

Most caregivers have frequent physical contact with the infant because they feel comfortable doing it and because they know it is comforting to infants. When feeding the baby, most caregivers not only hold the infant and the bottle, but they also pat the infant and talk and sing. These activities meet several of the infant's needs: touching, holding, and patting help the infant feel secure and cared for; holding the bottle, talking and singing to the infant provide a positive interaction between the caregiver and infant which stimulates the infant to look around, listen, and talk. The infant whose culture expects limited physical contact will have different experiences from the infant who has received much physical contact. Remain aware that withholding the 3A's—attention, approval, and affection—influences the child negatively just as much as *providing* the 3A's affects the child positively.

Cultural Diversity
Cultural diversity means being sensitive to cultural differences in the children and families with whom you have contact. If you are embarrassed

about discussing differences or prejudices, you might actually help and encourage children to form biases. You could, through omission, perpetuate oppressive beliefs and behavior (Jones and Derman-Sparks 1992).

Child care settings offer many opportunities to experience cultural differences. Young children's beliefs and perceptions are only as limited as their interest in people, so plan activities and experiences that directly include multiculturalism (Turkovich and Mueller 1989).

Every culture has somewhat different customs, mores, beliefs, and attitudes toward child care. While the style and form may vary from one culture to the next, all cultures have healthy child car practices. An example of different forms is the use of unleavened bread. In the Mexican culture, corn flour is made into tortillas, Sweden and Norway call it flatbrod (flat bread), and in China and India, rice is used. An example of different styles are the bright, contrasting colors of some cultures while others prefer more subdued colors. Each style is important and valuable to the people who practice it.

Evaluation of the style and forms that exist in one culture is called bias. To successfully integrate style and form into a curriculum, the child care specialist must be aware of and examine their bias for certain styles and forms. These biases may not be obvious until they are carefully examined, and only then can they be changed.

When working with young children, it is important to be able to relate to each of them without bias or prejudice. Each infant and toddler is a unique being who develops in the same way and deserves the same positive support to remain unlimited and reach their full potential.

Some cultures do not talk to their young children as much as other cultures. Some do not smile at them or expect a response. Some carry their babies on their backs and other cultures carry them over their hearts. Father involvement is different from one culture to another, as well as how family members interact with each other. Acceptance of these differences and the ability to perceive healthy childcare practices within every culture is important for a competent child care specialist.

One way to overcome cultural bias in a child care setting is to subtly include music, artwork, and a variety of culturally defined materials into the curricula. Children are not born biased and they should grow up with positive memories which include a variety of sounds, patterns, and colors.

It is extremely important that the child care program honor individual parents' sociocultural milieu. Pacific Oaks, in Southern California, has done exemplary work in their Anti Bias Curriculum, and Merril Palmer in Chicago, Bank Street College in New York, and Delmar in Albany have developed materials which focus on cultural diversity. Other materials available for young children and adults include:

Anti Bias Curriculum: Tools for Empowering Young Children, by Louise Derman-Sparks and the A.B.C. Task Force;

Creative Resource for the Antibias Classroom (1999), by Nadia Saderman Hall. New York: Delmar Publishers;

Roots and Wings: Affirming Culture in Early Childhood Programs (1991), by Stacey York, Redleaf Press;

How to Have Intelligent and Creative Conversations with Your Kids (1994), by Jane Healy, New York: Doubleday;

Different and Wonderful Raising Black Children in a Race Conscious Society (1992), by Hapson and Hapson;

Everyday Acts Against Racism: Raising A Child in a Multicultural World (a collection) (1996), by Marian Reddy (ed.), Seattle, WA: Seal Press; and

Beyond the Whiteness of Whiteness: A White Mother of Black Sons (1996), by Jane Lazarre, Duke University Press.

It is important that child care programs represent stepping stones to the formal education system and create partnerships with parents for progressive change. Some school systems have integrated programs with great promise toward bridging the cultural gap resulting from teacher biases, and are integrating cultural differences into the curriculum. The child care specialist needs to work with the local school district to ensure that antibias techniques and tools are consistent in the transition from child care to formal education.

The national SEED Project on Inclusive Curriculum (Seeking Educational Equity and Diversity) prepares teachers to lead year-long seminars in their schools reflecting on local practices. The project helps teachers welcome and respond to all children in class and deal with student sensitivity to the complex identity matters such as race and gender.

The Celebration of Life Calendar is an effective tool to help integrate the concepts of diversity into daily activities and schedules. Tools such as this help integrate multicultural concepts and practices into the program, while providing a valuable vehicle for promoting positive parent input.

"What does make a difference when you care for children from a culture different than your own is when you listen to what their parents want for them in their day to day care. It also means potential conflict when your beliefs and values clash with those of the parents. . . . A true multicultural infant-toddler approach in such cases would be to invite parents input and then figure out what to do with it" (Mena and Eyer 1997).

Nowhere is acceptance of differences more important than in the child care setting where we grow seeds of new beginnings.

"The International Playgroups, as it was known during our New York days almost two decades ago, was the most special of special schools. . . . What a uniquely rich way for our children to begin to learn about the world, themselves and others!" Barbara Bush (1990). This statement encapsulates the understanding promoted by Childcare Director, Nancy Brown and her staff of the International Preschools, Manhattan, New York. The International Preschools are an excellent example of child care curricula for celebrating diversity with young children and their families.

Mrs. Brown described how the goals evolved so that by 1963, the mission was to help bring quality educational programs to larger numbers of international families who came to New York City through organizations such as the United Nations and the Consular Corporation hospitals and universities. In 1968, the Creche, a popular infant-toddler program serving over 100 children a year, was opened under the sponsorship of the New York City Commission for the United Nations. By 1972, over 600 children were enrolled in five different programs offered by The Creche. Over the years, more than 100 countries have been represented. In 1995, the United Association for the Education of Young Children granted the International Preschools accreditation status, recognizing the organization as a provider of high-quality programs which meet the developmental needs of young children.

"The International Preschools provides young children and their families from all over the world an opportunity to share their cultures and gain a sense of international awareness through mutual understanding and respect. We recognize that all children are individuals with unique qualities and interests. Our developmentally-based program is designed to build on each individual's strengths. Through the play experience, we seek to promote the cognitive, emotional, social and physical growth of each child within a nurturing atmosphere" Brown, N. (1995).

Guidelines for teachers include:

- Respect diversity;
- Avoid stereotyping;
- A girl can be strong and a boy can be gentle;
- Recognize and encourage prosocial behavior such as cooperation;
- Listen to children with attention and respect;
- Do not forget to enjoy the children! and
- A relaxed and happy atmosphere makes learning fun.

Some specific curriculum suggestions to handle diversity include:

- Give children a flag that represents their heritage and country;
- Design the daily curriculum and the semester's outline around different countries that the children in your class represent;
- Make a calendar representing a holiday for each child;
- Involve the children in activities;
- Have the parents come and demonstrate their native costumes;
- Encourage them to wear costumes and describe the reason for a particular celebration, and tell a story told them by their grandparents to the other parents, children, and staff; and
- Have children or parents bring native food or desserts to share with others.

One holiday the entire school (all five locations) celebrates is United Nations Day.

The following example calendar is from *Celebrating Diversity: A Multicultural Resource* (1996):

THE CELEBRATION OF LIFE CALENDAR

Month/Day	Holiday	Country
January		
1.	New Year's Day; Georgian Calendar Everyone's Birthday—all add one year	China/Asia
7.	Nandkusa Festival—honors seven plants that are believed to have medicinal powers	Japan
15.	Martin Luther King Jr.—National Holiday remembering the Afro-American minister and civil rights leader	United States
February		
5.	Constitution Day—present constitution was adopted in 1917	Mexico
11.	National Day—commemorates the fall of the shah and the takeover of Ayatollah Khomeini (1979)	Iran
19.	Independence Day—independence from the Soviet Union in 1990	Estonia
March		
(unscheduled)	Purim—Jewish Holiday commemorates Queen Esther's role in saving the Hebrews	Israel
(unscheduled)	Taiwan Al-Qudr—"the Night of Power" Muslim festival	
3.	Hinamatsuri: Doll Festival—special day for girls	Japan
17.	St. Patrick's Day— celebrates Christianity coming to Ireland	Ireland
22.	New Year Day	India
April		
(unscheduled)	Good Friday—oldest Christian celebration commemorating the day of the crucifixion	
(unscheduled)	Easter—Christian day commemorating the resurrection of Christ	
(unscheduled)	Festival of Redvan-Baha'i—holiday honoring Baba Ullah, prophet founder of the Baha'i faith	
May		
1.	National Holiday—commemorates the battle of Puebla in 1862 (also widely celebrated in the United States)	Mexico

THE CELEBRATION OF LIFE CALENDAR

Month/Day	Holiday	Country
22.	Slavery Abolition Day	French West Indies
25.	Freedom Day—commemorates the independence from foreign rule in Africa	Africa
June		
2.	Republic Day	Italy
6.	Memorial Day	Korea
12.	Independence Day	Philippines
18.	Evacuation Day	Egypt
21.	Festival of Lord Gagannath, Lord of the Universe	India
July		
4.	Independence Day	United States
	Tanabuta, or Star Festival	Japan
14.	Bastille Day—Independence Day	France
17.	World Indian Day	Eskimo
26.	Independence Day	Liberia
August		
(unscheduled)	Festival of Hungry Ghosts	China
31.	Independence Day	India
September		
(unscheduled)	Rosh Hashanah (Jewish New Year)	Israel
3.	Independence Day	Chile
8.	United Nations International Literacy Day	World
21.	World Gratitude Day—to unite all people in gratitude	
29.	Michaelmas—celebration of all angels in Greek and Roman Catholic Church	
October		
(unscheduled)	Grandparents Day	United States
(unscheduled)	White Sunday—American and Western Samoan, adults and children reverse roles	Samoa
(unscheduled)	National Book Day—Reading Day	United States
(unscheduled)	United Nations Day for the Elderly	World
17.	Black Poetry Day	United States
24.	United Nations Day—all celebrate	World

THE CELEBRATION OF LIFE CALENDAR

Month/Day	Holiday	Country
November		
(unscheduled)	World Community Day	World
(unscheduled)	Thanksgiving Day	United States
3.	Sandwich Day—celebrates the birthday of John Montague, the 4th Earl of Sandwich, and creator of the sandwich	United States
15.	Schichi-Go-San—annual children's festival honoring all three year olds, and five- and seven-year-old females	Japan
17.	National Young Readers' Day	United States
21.	World Hello Day	World
December		
6.	Independence Day	Finland
13.	Santa Lucia Day, the Festival of Lights	Sweden
25.	Christmas—Celebration of birth of Jesus Christ	
31.	New Year's Eve—Celebrates new beginning	World

Television

Influences are either interactive or passive. Interactive influences are those in which the child directly interacts and passive influences affect the child without the necessity of child interaction. For example, television is a passive influence because the communication is one-way; the television does not require interaction from the child. On the other hand, the caregiver is an interactive influence because the child is required to respond to the caregiver.

Television is the largest single passive influence on families and caregivers. Because of its passive (but effective) influences on children and parents, television should be used cautiously by caregivers. Parents see role models of what parents "ought" to do. They compare their own children to those on television. Toddlers watch television and imitate repeated language and behavior they do not understand. They lack judgment to determine whether what they are doing and saying is appropriate. Caregivers see television role models and come to expect certain adult and child behavior regarding learning, achievement, and excellence. These pressures affect their selection of curriculum.

The ease with which television becomes an instant babysitter may tempt the harried caregiver at times, but hopefully the caregiver will not give in to the temptation. The caregiver needs to be aware of how television can limit infant and toddler experience. Very few television programs are appropriate for infants and toddlers. Television does not permit the child active interaction with it, and the child under three years of age cannot understand most of what is on. Special programs should be carefully selected, and the caregiver should actively view them with the toddler. The television set should **not** be left on through adult programs. Not only is the content inappropriate for toddlers but children need times of peace and quiet when no extra noises are intruding.

The video cassette recorder (VCR) provides a valuable tool to the caregiver when used wisely. Within the last several years, educational publishers have produced many worthwhile videos that can enhance the curriculum when used by the caregiver to help children interact with material presented.

Jane Healy, in her book *The Child's Growing Mind*, states: "It's a hard parental assignment, but try to be aware of potentially anxiety-producing information to which your child is exposed, and make yourself available to help put it in perspective. TV violence and even current events are hard enough for adults to comprehend, but impossible for children. They need help and lots of reassurance in dealing with the complexities of the world."

In general, television should not be perceived as a way to keep children occupied. Only supervised programs should be allowed.

Influences from the Care Setting

Child Care Home

Influences of the setting on your curriculum are varied. Physical location, financial limitations, parent work schedules, and other factors make up the child care setting. As discussed in Chapter 3, establishing a positive learning environment is essential to quality care whatever resources and limitations you find in your particular setting. Establishing a consistent, warm, friendly environment where large doses of the "3A's" (attention, approval and affection) are administered is the way to establish the most powerful positive influence in any physical setting.

Family child care homes provide a homelike situation for the infant or toddler. Because the child must adjust to a new caregiver and a new situation, the caregiver should quickly establish the child's familiarity with a similar setting: crib, rooms, and routines of playing, eating, sleeping. A warm one-to-one relationship between the family child care provider and the child provides security in this new setting.

Child Care Center

Some child care centers care for infants 6 weeks of age and older, and a few centers are even equipped to care for newborns. The very young infant must receive special care. One caregiver in each shift needs to be responsible for the same infant each day. The caregiver should adjust routines to the infant's body schedule rather than trying to make the infant eat and sleep according to the center's schedule. The caregiver will need to work closely with parents to understand the infant's behavior and changing schedule of eating and sleeping. Consistently recording and sharing information with parents is necessary to meet infant needs and involve the parents in their child's daily experiences.

Time

The number and age of children in a group will affect the amount of time the caregiver has to give each child. The needs of the other children also affect how the time is allocated.

Schedules in the child care home or center are adjusted to the children and the parents' employment schedules. For instance, if three school-aged children arrive at 3 P.M., the infant feeding may be disrupted. But it can also mean there are three more people to talk and play with the infant.

If the parent works the 7 A.M. to 3 P.M. shift, the infant awakening from a nap at 2:45 may need special planning to be ready when the parent arrives. The quality of interaction can remain high even when time for interactions is limited. Caregivers should determine what earlier activities will let them spend more time with the infant on this nap schedule.

Influences from the Child

Every child has an internal need to grow, develop, and learn. During the first years of life children's energies are directed toward those purposes both consciously and unconsciously. Though children cannot tell you this, observers can see that both random and purposeful behaviors help children.

The children look, touch, taste, listen, smell, reach, bite, push, kick, smile, and take any other action they can in order to actively involve themselves with the world. The fact that children are sometimes unsuccessful in what they try to do does not stop them from attempting new tasks. Sometimes they may turn away to a different task, but they will keep seeking something to do.

Infants learn from the responses they get to their actions. When the caregiver consistently "answers" cries of distress immediately, infants begin to build up feelings of security (see Figure 9–2). Gradually these responses will

Figure 9–2   The caregiver facilitates each child's development by making the child feel secure.

help infants learn to exert control over their world. If caregivers let infants cry for long periods of time before going to them, the infants remain distressed longer. They may have difficulty developing a sense of security and trust. Remember to use the "unlimited child" principle that the more immediately and completely needs are fulfilled, the more securely and happily children will develop. You can't love or fulfill an infant or toddler too much. Add large measures of the "3A's" to this principle, and you will be influencing happy and secure children.

CHILDREN WITH SPECIAL NEEDS

As late as 1970, most children with birth abnormalities or learning difficulties were viewed on an individual basis with no formal procedures or laws to direct care. Educational theories and principles which would later become "Special Education" were just beginning. A landmark law was passed in 1976 called The Education of All Handicapped Children Act. This law later grew in scope and purpose and became The Individual With Disabilities Education Act.

Because this act was passed, special needs children became entitled to appropriate public education regardless of their disability. The law provided that children should have the "least restrictive environment possible" which meant that all children would be registered within the same school district and special services would be provided as necessary.

Three- to five-year olds were among the first to be serviced. Then, additional laws were passed to educate even younger children with special needs. One pediatrician, Dr. Cecilia McCarton, took exception to the accepted view that infants with special needs do not need special public assistance. In her words, "In the 70's, the usually practice was to make a diagnosis and then send the parents of these children back to their own communities for follow-up care. There was not a single place that offered a diagnosis, prescription for care and actual appointments with those supporting professionals necessary for follow up. Parents faced extremely frustrating situations, and most often were devastated to find no available people in their community to follow through with our suggestions."

In response to the need, Dr. McCarton developed one of the first comprehensive treatment centers in the United States. She has conducted research on thousands of children with low birth weight and special anomalies. For over twenty years, Dr. McCarton has been the Director of the Life Program at the Rose Kennedy Center at Beth Israel Hospital, Bronx, New York. She has done much to advance the areas of research in underweight preemies and children with special needs.

Functional Ability Verses Actual Age

Age appropriateness has a different meaning when designing curricula for special needs children. Special needs children often function at a lower level in certain areas than their actual age, so knowing the functional age of a child is essential to structure and design appropriate activities. Equally important is using attention, approval, and affection as a way of communicating and satisfying the child's needs.

Today, curricula for special needs children generally involves a didactic team approach. Specialists interact with each other on behalf of the child based on the type of special needs the child exhibits. A functional age is established in each area of development and priorities for care are set using Developmental Profiles and Prescriptions.

Special Needs Children and Community Support

Caregivers must be aware of community resources for special children. Many special needs children lack funding sources. Sometimes community groups or generous, qualified professionals donate their time and energy to ensure proper treatment for special groups. One example is the Nassau Cleft Palate Center and Dr. Pamela Gullagher, a Plastic Surgeon who volunteers her time and expertise in Long Island, New York, along with other professionals to perform cleft palate repairs for children in need. The Nassau Cleft Palate Center has materials available for concerned parents including *A Guide For Parents With A Cleft Lip and Palate*. For more information, contact The Nassau Cleft Palate Center, Long Island Plastic Surgical Group, 999 Franklin Avenue, Garden City, Long Island, New York 11530, (516) 942-3404. Call The Cleft Palate Foundation at (412) 481-1376 for literature, resources, and parent groups nationwide.

Brain Gym

The human brain has three main structures: the cerebrum, the cerebellum, and the brain stem. The control center is the cerebrum which processes all the information it receives. It is the largest part of the brain, comprising approximately 80 percent of the total area. Each of its two halves, called hemispheres, has five lobe areas. Each lobe area is responsible for specific tasks, such as recognition of visual images, bodily sensations, and emotions. The entire cerebrum is covered by a layer of gray matter called the cerebral cortex. This is where the higher intellectual functions originate, such as memory, receiving, and interpreting information from the five senses (vision, hearing, taste, smell, and touch).

The cerebellum is located at the back of the brain behind the cerebrum. This area helps maintain balance, the ability to stand upright, and coordinate muscle activity. The brain stem is the life-support system. It maintains essential functions such as heartbeat, breathing, blood pressure, swallowing, and digestion. It is the site of the communication center in humans, and regulates additional processes such as thirst and hunger, and sends information to other parts of the brain.

One difference between a newborn and an adult brain is that the newborn's left and right hemisphere have not yet defined specific tasks and functions.

Normally developed newborn infants have clearly defined brain anatomy waiting to be determined by stimuli processed from the environment.

By the end of 36 months, the hemispheres have defined functions with individual styles of integration. In normal children, the kind of experiences the environment offers will determine how well prepared the brain is for future learning, and how well the hemispheres integrate information.

Brain Gym was discovered and developed by Drs. Paul and Gail Dennison who found that, when specific body maneuvers were done by children, their attention consistently improved. Brain Gym has successfully been used with autistic and speech-impaired children, attention deficit, hyperactivity disorder, and emotionally handicapped children. All the maneuvers are designed to stimulate brain-center responses by working with connecting body parts that cross the body's midline. Debbie Neurnberger, a kinesthetic counselor who specializes in teaching Brain Gym techniques to children and adults, works at Mind Resources, Inc. in Honesdale, Pennsylvania. Brain Gym helps establish optimal learning readiness. Debbie explains, "These techniques are so easy that they are met with much skepticism. However, the results are consistently impressive. All educators should be promoting these simple techniques."

Teaching toddlers simple activities such as cross-pattern crawling, right-hand-to-left-knee exercise, Simon Says, and so forth, helps to promote focus and impacts on the focal attention of the child. The elimination of sugar and high carbohydrate foods are also recommended. It is also important to drink plenty of water.

Carla Hannsford, author of *Smart Moves: Why Learning is Not All In Your Head*, has this to say: "We must give learners mind/body integrative tools, such as Brain Gym, that allow them to stop the stress cycle and activate full sensory/hemisphere access."

New Brain Research

The child contributes to his or her own development because genetic make-up and brain potential help determine intelligence. New brain research indicates that, not only is the environmental a crucial factor for brain development, but also there are specific times, called windows of learning, when the brain must be stimulated. The following is an example of how the brain is wired:

Vision: Unless exercised early on, the visual system will not develop.
Feelings: Emotions develop in layers, each more complex than the last.
Language: Language skills are sharpest early on, but grow throughout life.
Movement: Motor-skill development moves from gross to increasingly fine.

Researchers at Baylor College of Medicine, for example, have found that "children who don't play much or are rarely touched develop brains 20 percent to 30 percent smaller than normal for their age. . . ." Not only do young rats reared in toy-strewn cages exhibit more complex behavior than rats confined to sterile, uninteresting boxes, but researches at the University of Illinois at Urbana-Champaign have found the brains of these rats contain as many as 25 percent more synapses per neuron. "The data underscore the importance of hands-on parenting, of finding the time to cuddle a baby, talk with a toddler and provide infants with stimulating experiences. . . ." There is an urgent need, say child-development experts, for preschool programs designed to boost the brain power of youngsters born into impoverished rural and inner-city households. Without such programs, they warn, the current drive to curtail welfare costs by pushing mothers with infants and toddlers into the work force may well backfire. "There is a time scale to brain development, and the most important year is the first" notes Frank Newman, president of the Education Commission of the States. "By the age of three, a child who is neglected or abused bears marks that, if not indelible, are exceedingly difficult to erase" (Nash 97).

THE PROCESS OF CURRICULUM DEVELOPMENT

Curriculum development is an ongoing process of goal setting and problem solving. As previously discussed, assessment of each child in the five major Developmental Areas provides a structure in which meaningful goals may be established. A development cycle helps ensure that the curriculum is appropriate and relevant. The process involves setting goals, selecting objectives, determining appropriate methods, using task analysis, selecting materials, evaluating the attainment of objectives, gathering feedback on the above components, and making necessary adjustments (see Figure 9–3).

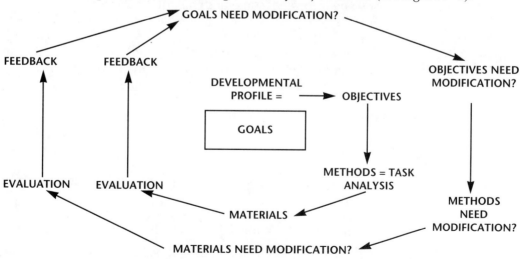

Figure 9–3 The cycle of curriculum development

Purposes and Philosophy

The purposes for providing child care and the philosophies of parents and care-givers need to be identified and discussed. This text reflects the following view:

1. The purposes of child care
    a. for children; to provide a positive and supportive environment with trained and experienced staff where children can develop to their fullest potential physically, emotionally, socially, perceptually, and cognitively.
    b. for parents; to provide a mutually supportive environment with a variety of materials and experiences and a staff with diverse abilities where parents can place their children for high-quality care and where they can also receive guidance and resources for parenting.
    c. for caregivers; to provide a work environment which addresses the needs of infants, toddlers and staff, and to create a positive team to meet the needs of the families being served.

2. The philosophy
    a. All people are viewed developmentally. From the moment of birth to the time of death every person is constantly growing in many ways. Focusing upon the positive changes resulting from growth helps maintain a positive learning environment.
        (1) Each infant and toddler is progressing through specific sequences or stages of development.
        (2) Each parent is in a phase of parenting the experiences of which contribute to the parent's knowledge and skill. Some are new parents, some are experienced, some anxious, some relaxed, some informed, some nonchalant, and some eager.
        (3) Each caregiver has his or her own level of competence. Caregivers have knowledge obtained from talking, reading, and studying; they have individual experiences with children and parents; their views and expectations of themselves as people and caregivers all contribute to their increasing competence as caregivers.
    b. Development and growth occur through active interaction with one's environment and can be observed through the five major Developmental Areas. Each person:
        (1) is an active learner.
        (2) constructs knowledge through active interactions with people and materials.
        (3) adapts previous experiences to current situations.
        (4) builds on the knowledge and skills learned from previous experiences.
        (5) initiates interactions with other people.
        (6) initiates interactions with materials in the environment.

These purposes and philosophy serve as the foundation for curriculum development. All goals, objectives, methods, materials, and evaluations are built upon them, providing a consistent, integrated program. Parents, children, and caregivers all participate in the process of curriculum development.

Goals

Goals are broad generalizations about what you want a program to provide. The program's purposes and philosophy shape determination of the goals.

As an example, the Infant and Toddler Caregiver Competencies developed for the Child Development Associate (CDA) Credential appear in Table 9–1. These competencies state the purpose or goal of the caregiver's behaviors. Program goals can be matched with goals for caregivers.

Mrs. Jalimek is an elementary school teacher with a 2-year-old son, Leon. Her caregiver is moving, so she is looking for a new child care arrangement. She has visited several child care centers and family child care homes and interviewed the directors and caregivers. She wants a program where a caregiver will provide strong emotional support for Leon, will learn about him and adjust to his needs, will help him have happy, satisfying experiences, will allow him to grow at his own rate, and will listen to her concerns and share information with her as a parent.

Mrs. Jalimek has seen situations where 2-year-olds are seated at tables working on worksheets and struggling with numeral and alphabet flashcards. She has observed classrooms and homes where the children play among themselves while the caregivers sit apart talking with other adults and only occasionally interact with the children, and then mainly to reprimand them. She finally chose a program where the caregiver stated:

> I try to make this as much like a home as possible. I am available to each child. I snuggle and love them. We play and sing and laugh and sometimes cry. We cook and help with clean-up chores. When an infant is

TABLE 9–1 CDA PROGRAM AND CAREGIVER GOALS

PROGRAM GOALS	CAREGIVER COMPETENCY GOALS
I. Safe, healthy learning environment	I. Establish and maintain a safe, healthy learning environment
II. Physical and intellectual competence	II. Enhance physical and intellectual competencies
III. Positive social and emotional development	III. Support social and emotional development of each child and provide positive guidance
IV. Positive and productive relationships with families	IV. Establish positive and productive relationships with families
V. Well-run, purposeful program	V. Ensure a well-run, purposeful program responsive to participant needs
VI. Professional relationships and development	VI. Maintain a commitment to professionalism

hungry, I feed him. The children know each other and watch, touch, hug, and talk with each other. They watch in the morning for each child to arrive and greet each with big smiles and waves. They recognize mommies and daddies and watch afternoon greetings and then wave and call out goodbyes in the language they use. The children act like they are comfortable here with me and with each other. I really enjoy them.

Objectives

Objectives describe specific achievements that lead to attainment of a goal. Several objectives may be directed toward the same goal.

The Child Development Associate (CDA) Infant and Toddler Caregiver Competencies are organized into Competency Goals I–VI, which are subdivided into Functional Areas One–Thirteen. Each of the Functional Areas lists examples of caregiver behaviors. Each behavior addresses a specific objective for the child, parent, and caregiver. (See Appendix C for the complete CDA Infant and Toddler Competency Standards.) Table 9–2 shows the interrelationships of the child's needs, parents' needs, and caregiver behaviors.

Methods

Methods are one of the means by which the curriculum occurs. The caregiver has several tasks relating to methods.

1. Knowledge:
   a. of a variety of caregiver behaviors and strategies
   b. of the child's needs
   c. of how to match caregiver behaviors and strategies to the needs of the child
2. Application:
   a. to assess the child in each major Developmental Area and to task analyze developmental tasks for specific situations
   b. to select appropriate caregiver behaviors and strategies
   c. to use selected caregiver behaviors and strategies
3. Evaluation:
   a. to judge whether caregiver behaviors and strategies "match" the child's needs appropriately

The caregiver behaviors and strategies should be consistent with the objectives, goals, and philosophy of the program. For example, one facet of the caregiver role is to act as organizer (see Chapter 4). When the caregiver views the child developmentally and as one who needs to have active interaction with materials, the caregiver may select several toys which are developmentally appropriate for the child and then allow the child to choose which toys to use. The caregiver facilitates the child's development by encouraging the child to make the choices among appropriate materials.

TABLE 9–2   RELATIONSHIP OF THE CDA OBJECTIVES TO THE CHILD, PARENT, AND CAREGIVER

FUNCTIONAL AREA	TO CHILD	TO PARENT	TO CAREGIVER
ONE: Safe	Safe environment	Reliable, safe environment for child	Provide safe environment for child
TWO: Healthy	Good health and nutrition	Healthy and nutritious environment for child	Promote good health and nutrition
THREE: Learning Environment	Access to stimulating learning environment	Appropriate, stimulating learning environment	Plan, organize, and set up appropriate stimulating learning environment
FOUR: Physical	Development and coordination of physical movements and senses	Opportunities for stimulating physical development	Provide equipment and interaction to stimulate physical development
FIVE: Cognitive	Development of thinking and problem solving	Appropriate stimulation of thinking	Provide appropriate cognitive stimulation
SIX: Communication	Communicate by verbal and nonverbal means	Active involvement in communicating	Model communication through interaction with child and adult
SEVEN: Creative	Explore sights, sounds, and materials	Individualized, flexible materials and activities	Encourage child's unique explorations and creations
Eight: Self	Emotional security	Trustworthy, responsive care for child	Provide love, affection, and security
NINE: Social	Social interactions and social awareness	Appropriate social support and stimulation for child	Model and stimulate positive social interactions
TEN: Guidance	Use acceptable behaviors	Support and reinforce child's appropriate behaviors	Establish and maintain management rules and routines and nurture child's self-control
ELEVEN: Families	Stability between environments at home and child care	Partnership with caregiver, exchanging information and support	Communicate with parent, sharing child's experiences and mutual concerns
TWELVE: Program Management	Participate in consistent, appropriate, quality	Predictable, appropriate, quality program	Plan, coordinate, implement quality program
THIRTEEN: Professionalism	Appropriate care	Informed, learning caregiver for child	Attitude and behavior seeking continued learning

Materials

Materials are a vital part of the curriculum. The infant and toddler learn by interacting with materials. The child constructs knowledge by holding, tasting, shaking, hitting, throwing, looking, smelling, and listening to objects.

Some materials provide a variety of experiences; sand has texture, weight, color, smell and can be formed, shaped, dropped, thrown, and so forth.

Other objects have very limited use; a wind-up dancing doll provides little stimulation for varied and continued use.

Materials can contribute to or impede the child's development. The caregiver's selection of appropriate materials for each child facilitates that child's development (see Part III). Materials that are too easy can be boring, and those that are too difficult can be frustrating.

Caregivers should select materials that contribute to the attainment of program goals and objectives. Currently popular materials or those labeled "educational" may or may not be appropriate and effective.

Evaluation

Curriculum evaluation is on-going in an infant and toddler program. The caregiver must continually examine the daily experiences to determine whether the curriculum is individualized, is balanced (for the whole child), is relevant, is realistic, and implements the program goals and objectives.

Evaluation should always relate to the identified goals and objectives of the program. Were the goals and objectives attained? If so, what contributed to their attainment? If not, were some or parts of them attained? Satisfactorily or unsatisfactorily? What reasons or factors caused less than full attainment?

Statements of goals and objectives for the child care home or center serve as guidelines for evaluation. Curriculum evaluation can be informal or formal. Recorded data about children and activities may be selected to provide needed information for evaluation (see Chapter 9 and Appendix A, Developmental Prescriptions).

Feedback

Feedback is a critical step in curriculum development. Feedback comes from the parents, caregivers, and the children themselves.

Feedback uses information from each of the parts of the process of curriculum development. Are the goals and objectives still appropriate? Do new influences make it necessary to modify them? Were some methods and materials more effective than others? Do they need to be changed if the goals and objectives are modified? Was the curriculum evaluated periodically and accurately, or was it a one-time evaluation that missed several influencing factors?

Feedback from the total process is necessary to determine whether changes need to be made. Feedback also provides guidance for selecting the kinds of changes that will improve the curriculum.

IMPLEMENTING CURRICULUM

Your selection of a curriculum for an infant or toddler is based on what you know about that child's development, that is, what the child can do now and what the next step is. Your caregiver strategies should reinforce the child's present level of development and challenge the child to move toward the next level. Use of Developmental Profiles (introduced in Chapter 2) to assess the child, task analysis of the natural hierarchy of steps necessary to achieve objectives, and written Developmental Prescriptions will enhance balanced development.

Schedule

Flexibility

There are two kinds of schedules:

1. The infant's schedule: each infant has an individual physical schedule.
2. The caregiver's schedule: each caregiver designs a schedule which co-ordinates caregiving duties with each infant's schedule.

Andrea arrives at 7:45 A.M.; Kevin is ready for a bottle and nap at 8:00 a.m.; Myron is alert and will play until about 9:00 A.M., when he takes a bottle and a nap; and Audrey is alert and will play all morning and take a nap immediately after lunch. As caregiver, write a list of expected activities in each time block. This also will provide you with guidelines for your time.

The daily schedule must be individualized in infant and toddler care. It focuses on the basic activities: sleeping, feeding, playing. During the first months the infant is in the process of setting a personal, internal schedule. Some infants do this easily; others seem to have more difficulty.

First of all, ask parents what the infant or toddler does at home. Write this down to serve as a guideline. Next, observe the child to see whether he or she follows the home schedule or develops a different schedule.

Time Blocks

The daily schedule in an infant and toddler program is organized around the child's physical schedule. As the infant spends more time awake, the schedule will change. Toddlers also differ in how much time they spend asleep or awake. Their morning and afternoon naps often do not fit into a rigid "nap time from 12 to 2 P.M." schedule. The caregiver can identify blocks of time for specific types of activities, but should keep in mind that no clock time fits all children.

Arrival Time   During this special time the primary caregiver greets the parent and child and receives the infant or toddler. This is the time for the caregiver should listen to the parent tell about the child's night and about any joys, problems, or concerns. The parent should write down special information on the message board, for example, "exposed to measles last night."

Arrival time is also a time to help the infant or toddler make the transition from parent to caregiver. The caregiver's relationships with the child should provide a calming, comfortable, accepting situation so the child will feel secure. Touching, holding, and talking with the child for a few minutes helps the child re-establish relations with the caregiver. When the child is settled, the caregiver may move on to whatever activity the child is ready to do.

Sleeping   Most of a newborn's time is spent sleeping, although the time awake gradually lengthens. Some infants and toddlers fall asleep easily; others need to be fed, rocked, and then held for a short time even after they are asleep. If you are responsible for several infants or toddlers, plan your time carefully so you are available to help the child fall to sleep. Provide quiet, calming holding, talking, singing, rubbing, rocking. Provide toys for the other children who are awake so they will be productively occupied.

Record the child's sleeping time. Parents need to know how long and at what time their child slept. The caregiver needs to know when each infant or toddler will usually be sleeping. Each infant or toddler in your home or room may have a different nap time.

Each month infants sleep less. This affects when they will eat and when they will be alert. As each infant changes his or her sleeping schedule, the caregiver has to change the infant's feeding and playing times.

Some infants and toddlers wake up alert and happy. Others awaken groggy and crying. You can help ease the infant or toddler into wakefulness. Some you can pick up and cuddle. Talk quietly to them, and move them around so they see other things in the room that may be interesting. Usually infants and toddlers need to have their diapers changed or need to go to the bathroom when they wake up. Some infants will be hungry and need a bottle at this time.

Eating   The very young infant may eat every 2 to 4 hours. Ask the parent how often the baby eats at home. Infants will tell you when they are hungry by fussing and crying. Learn their individual schedules, their physical and oral signals, so you can feed them before they have to cry. Record the time of feedings and the amount of milk or formula the baby drank.

Hold the infant when you are giving a bottle. This is not only feeding time; it is a time to nurture physical, emotional, social, cognitive, and language development.

Nutrition for Young Children

Parents are responsible for what their children eat. It is extremely important for caregivers to understand the nutritional needs of the children in their care. These nutritional needs vary with the age of the child. For example, breast milk or iron fortified formula is all a young infant needs to sustain adequate growth until four to six months. Breast milk also helps fight infections because of the immunity factors coming from the mother. Many working mothers are unable to breast feed for an extended a period of time.

It is the caregiver's responsibility to be aware of the special nutritional needs of the young infant. Parent education is an ongoing process, and it is the caregiver's responsibility to help parents make educated choices by bringing them necessary information. One way to make this information available is to have posters and written materials about the importance of nutrition for young children available for the parents.

Decisions on feeding schedules are ultimately up to the parent. According to current thinking, however, very young children should eat when they are hungry. This is called demand feeding. Demand feeding involves more flexibility for the caregiver and is one of the first steps to building a bond between that person and the children in his or her care. It is also the first step toward the child internalizing a sense of trust and security.

There are great advantages to consciously caring for the child. Holding, feeding, relating, maintaining eye contact, and ultimately building a secure foundation for the child are only possible through conscious caring. Being with the child and remaining silent and calm also allows the child to remain calm.

Parents are responsible for bringing new bottles of milk, breast milk, or formula every day. Bottles should be dated and labeled with the child's name. Do not store unopened formula for the child. Only whole, pasteurized milk should be given to children between six and 24 months. Low-fat milk does not provide enough calories or nutrients for children under the age of two years.

When preparing to feed an infant, be sure to thaw frozen breast milk under cold, running water. Never microwave it. Heating breast milk or bottled milk can also be done by placing the bottles in hot water for five or six minutes. Test the milk on the inside of your arm between the wrist and elbow to check its temperature. Do not feed an infant milk that is hot.

All bottles should be washed with hot, soapy water, rinsed, and washed in a dishwasher, or boiled for five minutes between uses. When feeding, never prop a bottle in the crib. It may cause the child to choke.

Nutritional needs vary as children develop. Solid foods are gradually introduced, and as children gain strength and are able to sit up, the skills to feed themselves develops. Foods for older infants should be cut into pieces no larger than a quarter of an inch. Older toddlers can have one-half-inch pieces. Children's eating time must be supervised.

Soft foods progress to harder foods as children sit up, become mobile, gain teeth, and have the ability to eat more without assistance. Small, bite-sized foods are introduced. Children love to feed themselves.

Meal time is a time for a few rules based on health and safety needs. Since eating is a time for communicating, it should be structured to allow a routine to develop that will promote an unhurried, relaxed atmosphere in a consistent place. All the children who are beginning to sit up should join in this community event, and all children should be seated.

Choice of foods is extremely important. Fruits, vegetables, grains, milk, and a variety of proteins should be offered at each meal. Children under age four are at high-risk for choking (Marotz, Cross, and Rush 1996). *Foods that must never be given to children in that age group include bubble gum, hard candies, peanuts, marshmallows, and hot dogs cut into rounds.* Staff must be well-versed in emergency procedures involving eating and choking. Children should eat frequently and always evaluate the fuel content of the food being eaten evaluated. The foods should be rated and elimination of empty calories is a must.

Many nutritional choices should be offered at one time, and children should be encouraged to choose what they like to eat. Lunches and supplemental snacks should meet at least two-thirds of the Recommended Daily Allowance (RDA).

It is acceptable if children want to skip a meal or snack occasionally. Encourage community involvement, have the children stay in the area where others are eating, or allow the child to sit on your lap as you continue your routine. Toddlers, in particular sometimes get too busy to take time to eat. Do not worry because they will eat at the next meal when their attention is on eating.

Food should never be used as a reward or punishment. Food classes for toddlers and older children should be held to educate and enrich older children. Food preparation can involve a group effort to fix a meal. This teaching, however, should be conducted outside the kitchen, keeping children away from potential kitchen hazards (see cooking activity in Chapter 16, Fun in the Kitchen).

Elimination   Often infants need their diapers changed after eating. Check an infant's diaper after you have cleaned up from feeding. Check periodically during the time the child is awake. Talk and sing while you are changing the infant. Make this a pleasant time for both of you. Your positive feelings about diapering are communicated to the child. The toddler who is being toilet-trained may need special attention after meals, nap, and during play. Toilet-trained children can be helped to anticipate when they will need to go to the bathroom (for example, after the nap).

Alert Time   In between sleeping and eating, infants and toddlers have times when they are very alert and attracted to the world around them. This is the time when the caregiver does special activities with them (see Part III for suggestions). The infant or toddler discovers him- or herself, plays, and talks and interacts with you and others. Children have fun at this time of day as they actively involve themselves in the world.

Determine the times when the infants and toddlers in your care are alert. Decide which times each individual child will spend alone with appropriate materials you have selected and which times you will spend with each. Each infant or toddler needs some time during each day playing with his or her primary caregiver. This play time is in addition to the time you spend changing diapers, feeding the child, and helping the child get to sleep.

As you play with the infant or toddler, you will discover how long that child remains interested. Stop before the child gets tired. The child is just learning how to interact with others and needs rest times and unpressured times in between highly attentive times. With an infant you might play a reaching-grasping game for a couple of minutes, a visual focusing activity for about a minute, a directional sound activity for about a minute, and a standing-bouncing-singing game for a minute. Watch the infant's reactions to determine when to extend to two minutes, five minutes, and so on. Alternate interactive times with playing-alone times. Infants will stay awake and alert longer if they have some times of stimulation and interaction.

Toddlers spend increasing amounts of time in play. There should be opportunities for self-directed play as well as challenge and interaction with the caregiver. Toddlers also need quiet, uninterrupted time during their day. Constant activity is emotionally and physically wearing on them.

End of the Day   At the end of the child's day in your care, collect your thoughts to decide what to share with the child's parent. To help you remember, or to gather information from caregivers working earlier in the day, review the notes on the message board or on the report sheets for the parent. This sharing time puts the parent into the child's day and provides a transition for the child from you to the parent.

Routines

Purposes

Routines give the infant or toddler a sense of security. The infant learns to trust repetition and lack of change. The child may not think about these routines but does feel the security of familiar activities.

Implementation

Many daily routines foster physical health, particularly those related to cleaning hands, face, teeth; to eating, sleeping, and toileting. With infants and toddlers the caregiver must care for or assist with these needs. With washing routines, the task is to remove all dirt and microorganisms as well as possible. Excellent charts and suggestions are provided in the manual, *What YOU Can Do to Stop Disease in the Child Day Care Centers* (Centers for Disease Control 1984).

Face Washing   Wet a paper towel or clean washcloth with warm water. Add soap. Liquid soap in a dispenser is more sanitary than a bar of soap because dirt and germs may remain on the soap bar. Keep dirt off the dispenser plunger. Wipe the face gently. Rinse the paper towel or washcloth thoroughly in warm water. Wipe the face gently, patting areas around the eyes.

Hand washing   Hand washing is a procedure directly related to health and the occurrence of illness. Hand-washing procedures should be thorough. A quick rinse through clear water does not remove microorganisms. Frequent handwashing is a vital routine for caregivers and children to establish.

   1. Caregiver:
      a. Wash hands before
          (1) Working with children at the beginning of the day

          (2)   Handling bottles, food, feeding utensils
          (3)   Assisting child with face and handwashing
          (4)   Assisting child with brushing teeth
          (5)   Changing a diaper (after rubber gloves are removed)
      b. Wash hands after
          (1)   Feeding
          (2)   Cleaning up
          (3)   Diapering (rubber gloves are removed first)
          (4)   Assisting with toileting (rubber gloves are removed first)
          (5)   Wiping or assisting with a runny nose (rubber gloves are removed first)
          (6)   Working with wet, sticky, dirty items (rubber gloves are removed first)

2. Child:
    a. Wash hands before
        (1)   Handling food, food utensils
        (2)   Brushing teeth
    b. Wash hands after
        (1)   Eating
        (2)   Diapering or toileting
        (3)   Playing with set, sticky, dirty (sand, mud, etc.) items

Wet the whole hand with warm water, soap it, and rub the whole hand—palm, back, between fingers, and around fingernails. Rinse with clean water, rubbing the skin to help remove the microorganisms and soap. Dry hands on a disposable paper towel which has no colored dyes in it. Throw away the towel so others do not have to handle it. You can also use small washcloths as towels, with each child using his own once and then putting it in the laundry basket.

Toddlers who can stand on a stepstool at the sink can be assisted in washing their own hands. You can turn on the water, push the soap dispenser, verbally encourage them to use their hands to wash and rinse each other, turn off the water, and if necessary hand them a towel.

Toothbrushing Help toddlers step up on the stepstool at the sink if they need assistance. Turn on the faucet so a small stream of water is running. Wash your hands. Assist in the child's handwashing.

Allow the toddlers to wet their own toothbrush. Shut off the water. Put a small amount of toothpaste on the toothbrush and then encourage toddlers to brush all their teeth (not just the front ones).

Fill a paper or plastic cup half full of water. Encourage the toddlers to rinse their mouths well. Give them more water if needed. Turn on the faucet and allow the toddlers to rinse their own toothbrush and rinse out the plastic cup. Have the children wipe off their mouths with a tissue. Return the toothbrush and plastic cup to their proper place or throw away the paper cup.

Eating Eating routines should have a positive effect on children physically, emotionally, socially, and cognitively.

Bibs protect infants' clothes when they are drooling during the first year or so of life. A little cloth bib can be changed during the day when it becomes wet and soiled. These bibs should be laundered rather than just rinsed out.

Infants and toddlers eating solid food need to wear bibs to protect their clothes and the area around them. Bibs with pockets to catch the spills are helpful. Each child needs a separate bib. The bib should be wide enough to cover the child's shoulders and reach the child's sides. It should be long enough to reach the lap; however, if it is too long, it will wrinkle the pocket so spills will not be caught. Plastic bibs should be immersed in soapy water, rinsed, and towel or air dried. Fabric bibs should be shaken, and if wet or soiled, they should be put in the laundry.

Bottle procedures are simple and need to be consistent. Infants let you know when they are hungry. Wash your hands and the infant's face and hands. Prepare a bottle (ask the parent whether it should be warm or cold). Put a bib on the infant. Hold the infant while giving the bottle. Emotionally the baby needs your closeness. Also, choking, tooth decay, and ear infection are more prevalent among babies who lie down when drinking from the bottle. Never prop up a bottle to allow a baby to drink unsupervised.

Stop periodically to burp the baby. Support the infant's head until the infant has enough neck strength to control head movements. Set the infant upright or up to your shoulder. Press firmly upward or pat on the baby's back until the burp comes. Because the baby may spit up when burping, keep a towel under the infant's mouth to keep both of you dry and to wipe off the baby's mouth. When the baby has finished drinking and burping, remove the bib if it is soiled.

An unfinished bottle should be refrigerated immediately. It may not be saved for use the next day.

After feeding infants a bottle, hold them to put them to sleep, or play with them, or put them down to play with toys and watch or play with other children.

Baby food requires one bowl and spoon per baby. If you anticipate that the baby will not eat a full jar, spoon the desired amount into a dish and put the remainder in the covered jar into the refrigerator. If the spoon is dipped into the jar during feeding, the spoon leaves saliva in the food which can contaminate the rest of the jar of food.

Wash your hands and the infant's face and hands. Put a bib on the infant.

Plan something to keep the infant's hands busy: use one of your hands to play with the baby's hands or give the child a small toy or feeding tool to grasp. Infant muscular coordination is still erratic, so waving arms and grasping hands often collide with a spoonful of food. The infant does not mind the mess, but gradually you may become frustrated, and the infant can sense your negative feelings.

When food is spilled (hit, tipped, etc.), don't spoon it up to feed to the infant. The tray and clothes surfaces are not kept as clean as the dishes and spoons; they have dirt and germs which would be spooned up with the spilled food. When infants stop eating, stop trying to feed them. *Do not force food!*

Wash the infant's face and hands while you talk and sing to the child, take off the bib, and put the child down to play. Put the dish, spoon, and bib in the kitchen to be washed. Wash off the tray with soapy water and rinse. Wash spills off surfaces.

Finger food affects space as well as eating. Prepare the area by clearing the table and clearing or covering surrounding floor space. Wash your hands and the infant's face and hands. Put a bib on the child. Wash the eating surface; finger foods often are pushed off plates and bowls onto the tray or table.

Set the finger food in front of the infant, say what it is, and encourage the baby to take the first bite. Talk with the infant, using descriptive words as the child eats. Praise the child's competence. Emphasize how special it is that the child can feed him- or herself (see Figure 9–4).

Wash the infant's face and hands, take off the bib, and put the child down to play when he or she has stopped eating. Pick up any remaining food on the tray, table, and floor. Take dish and bib to the kitchen to be washed. Wash the eating surface. Sweep or vacuum the floor. Wash your hands.

Table food is prepared for the young child. Wash your hands and assist the toddler to do likewise. Put a bib on the child. Serve small portions of food. Cut up meat and firm foods into bite sizes of about a half inch.

Figure 9–4 The young child soon becomes adept at eating finger foods.

Allow the child to pick up and use a child-size spoon with whatever hand the child chooses. Since most people are right-handed, you can place the spoon on the right side of the plate. But if the child puts the spoon in the left hand, leave it there. Provide a child-sized spoon and help the child grasp it with palm and fingers. The toddler will use both hands when eating. The hand without the spoon is sometimes used to put food in the mouth and sometimes to put food on the spoon. Do not try to keep one hand in the child's lap. When children develop the coordination needed to use utensils, they use their whole body by leaning, twisting, pushing, and grasping. Muscular control must develop before manners can be stressed.

Do not put dropped food back on the child's plate. This food should be thrown away.

Talk with children when they are eating. Name foods, tastes, and textures. Praise the children's competence in eating. Listen and enjoy their talk with you and with others.

When a child has stopped eating, wash the infant's face and hands and help the toddler to do this job.

Remove the bib and allow the child to leave the eating area and go to a play area while you complete the remaining tasks. Put the dishes, utensils, and bibs on a cart or in the kitchen to be washed. Pick up dropped food. Wash the eating surface and table and chair surfaces where sticky hands and food have touched. Sweep or vacuum under the eating area. Wash your hands.

Sleeping You control the sleeping conditions of the infant and toddler. Each child has preferences which you need to learn.

Each infant needs a separate crib with a sheet and blanket. If another infant sleeps in the crib later in the day, remove the sheet and blanket of the first child and store them or put them into the laundry. Spray the crib with disinfectant before putting on the sheet and blanket of the next child. Keep the sheet and blanket sets in cubbies or on a labeled shelf.

Licensing requirements will indicate the space needed between cribs. Many states require two feet of space between cribs.

"Cribs and playpens with slats spaced no wider than $2\,^3/_8$ inches apart must be used. Crib sides must remain up at all times and cover at least $^3/_4$ of the child's height. The mattress must fit the crib snugly. If there is more than one inch between the crib sides or ends and mattress, the mattress is too small. Bumper pads must extend around the entire crib and tie into place with at least six ties; they need to be used until four months of age" (Greater Minneapolis Day Care Association 1989). Check older cribs to cover slats that are too far apart.

Some infants will be sleeping while others are awake. Use sheets or blankets to hang over the crib side to create a visual barrier if you use the room for sleeping and playing.

Infants have their own schedules for sleeping. Ask parents what schedule their infants had before coming to child care. Allow children to sleep when they indicate they are sleepy.

Some infants awaken at dawn and may be ready for a morning nap by 8:30 or 9:00 A.M. As they get older, nap times change to later and later in the morning. At some point it is necessary to adjust so that nap time and lunchtime do not coincide, or you will find the infant falling asleep in his lunch. During these months either feed the infant before the nap or postpone lunch until after the child awakens. Falling asleep in the potatoes is no fun. In the process of being cleaned up the infant usually awakens and cries and fusses at the interrupted nap.

Some infants and toddlers like to be rocked to sleep; some enjoy back rubs. Some prefer to lie on their stomachs to go to sleep; some prefer to lie on their backs. Ask parents what their children prefer. Coordinate your routines with what is done at home. Share information with parents about how the infant or toddler responds with you.

Allow infants or toddlers to awaken on their own schedule and give them time to adjust to wakefulness. Change their diapers, take them to the bathroom, and talk softly to them, helping them make the transition gently. Some children are "on the move" immediately upon awakening. Provide a place and quiet activities for them.

Cribs are for sleeping; they are not play pens. When infants wake up, they should be removed from the crib to enjoy activities in other parts of the room.

Record the time the child slept. The time of day and length of time are important information for you during the day and for parents in planning activities and in noting symptoms of possible sleep problems.

If the sheet is wet or soiled, change it now so it will be ready when the child needs to sleep again.

Infants' afternoon naps depend on the time and length of their morning nap. Some infants may be awake and ready to play while the other infants and toddlers are napping. Provide space and time for these infants to be involved in meaningful activities.

Afternoon nap time may be similar for many toddlers. After lunch and diapering or toileting, toddlers can remove their shoes and lie down on a cot with their own sheets and blankets. Put the shoes in the same place under the cot each day so each toddler learns where to put them and where to look for them. If possible, reduce the light and noise level at least slightly.

Some toddlers like to have their backs rubbed or arms or legs stroked. Some like to listen to music. Hum or play quiet music without words so children can relax rather than remain alert to the words (see Figure 9–5).

Toddlers will wake up at different times. Assist with diapering or toileting and putting on shoes. Designate a room or an area of the sleeping room as a quiet play area until others awaken.

Some infants and toddlers have difficulty relaxing and falling asleep. Schumann (1982) has described relaxation techniques she has used with

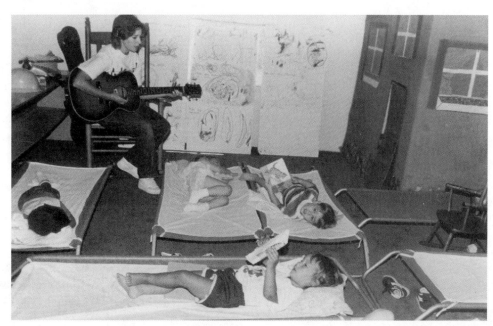

Figure 9–5   The caregiver can assist children who need help relaxing by playing soothing music.

children as young as 18 months old. After creating an environment conducive to sleep, she uses the following procedures. A quiet, steady voice along with stroking facilitate relaxation even when the child may not understand all the words being used.

Use a quiet even voice to help the children relax each part of their bodies. Repeatedly (six to eight times) state that the body part is "heavy." For some children it may help to stroke firmly with two hands over the body part to be relaxed. Begin with the toes and work up the body in the following fashion: toes, feet, legs, back (or abdomen, depending on position), fingers, hands, arms, shoulders, neck, eyes, lips, and chin. After relaxing each body part, check it to see how successful each child has been. Tenseness is indicated by a raised bulging or rigid muscles or by movement of a muscle or body part. Using firm hands, strive for being able to move the body part yourself at the joint without the child's helping or keeping the area stiff. Give POSITIVE reinforcement for the way you want the body part to be. Explain to the children to let the feet stay "heavy" while you are checking that part. As you move from talking about one body part to the next, keep your voice a continuous monotone rather than pausing. After doing two or three body parts, repeat the idea that the previous ones are still "heavy" also.

For example, "Your toes are heavy. Your toes are heavy. Your toes are heavy. Your toes are heavy." (Check for relaxation, insert positive reinforcement) "Your feet are heavy. Your feet are relaxed. Your feet are heavy. Your feet are heavy." (Check for relaxation, insert positive reinforcement) "Your toes are heavy. Your feet are heavy. Your legs are heavy." By the time each child is told his eyes are heavy, it is likely that he will either already have them closed or be willing to close them at your request. . . . If a child still seems fairly alert at the end of the toe-to-head release sequence, try repeating the sequence but eliminating touch and checking of the body for relaxation. Some children might require or seek more body contact than others (pp. 17–18).

Toileting   Diapering requires planning. If you use a changing table, have all supplies within reach. It is desirable to have the changing table next to a sink with hot and cold running water. If you do not use a changing table, use a piece of heavy plastic large enough to hold the infant's back and legs as well as the container with the supplies and a place to put the soiled diaper. Glove with latex gloves.Remove the infant's clothes or pull them up to chest level. Remove the soiled diaper. Put a disposable diaper in a covered, plastic-bag-lined container. Put a cloth diaper in a plastic bag which will be closed with a twisty when you are finished.

Keep one hand on the infant at all times.

Wipe off bowel movement with toilet tissue, going from front to back. Put the tissue on the soiled diaper or drop it into the toilet stool if it is next to your changing area. Use separate toweling or tissue when turning the faucet on and off so feces will not contaminate the faucet. Use a plain paper towel or washcloth with warm water and soap to wash the infant's bottom thoroughly. Rinse the towel or cloth and rinse the baby's bottom. Throw the paper towel away, or put the washcloth in the laundry. Pretreated paper wipes are not necessary, and they sometimes irritate an infant's skin.

Put on a clean diaper, fitting it snugly around the legs and waist. Redress the infant, wash the child's face and hands, and take the child to the next activity. Wash off the changing table or plastic sheet and spray with disinfectant. Remove gloves, *wash your hands thoroughly* before you do anything else.

Record the time and consistency of bowel movements. You and the parents need this information to determine patterns of normalcy and to look for causes of irregularity.

Toilet-training may begin when the toddler is ready. Toddlers will indicate when they are ready to be toilet-trained. Their diapers may be dry for a few hours; they may tell you they have urinated or had a bowel movement after they have; they may watch other children use the big toilet—a motivation available when you have children who are already toilet-trained (see Figure 9–6).

Discuss the timing with the toddler's parents. Both the home and child care program need to begin at the same time and use the same procedures. Frequent, regular dialogue between parents and caregivers is needed to deter-

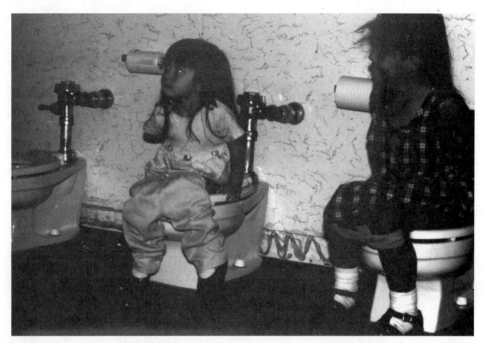

Figure 9–6 Already toilet-trained children can help motivate younger children to use the toilet.

mine whether to continue toilet-training or to stop and begin again a few months later.

It is often difficult for parents to resist cultural pressures for early toilet-training even when they know the toddler is not ready and is unsuccessful in attempts. The caregiver can help parents understand the needs and development of their toddler.

The toddler needs two major functions for toilet-training—biofeedback and muscular control. Toddlers learn to recognize the feelings their bodies have before they urinate or have a bowel movement. They can use this biofeedback to decide what to do. At first they seem to "observe" the feelings and afterward label what has happened. When they decide to go into the bathroom *before* elimination, they need to use muscular control until they are safely on the toilet. Timing and control must be coordinated. Toddlers may have some control but not enough to last as long as it takes to get into the bathroom, get clothes out of the way, and get seated or standing. Through trial and error, feedback and adjustments, toddlers learn what their bodies are doing and what they can control and plan.

When the child starts toilet-training, use training pants at home and at the child care program. Do *not* put diapers on the toddler during nap time. Outer clothes must be loose or easily removed to facilitate self-help.

Take the toddler to the bathroom and instruct how to pull down necessary clothes and how to get seated on the adapter seat or potty chair. For the boy who can reach standing, determine where he should stand and where he should direct his penis. Glove before proceeding. Wait until the child goes to the toilet, or wait a few minutes. Teach how to get toilet paper and how to wipe from the front to back. Then let the child try to do it alone. Check to see if assistance is needed in cleaning the child's bottom. Assist in getting clothes back up. Assist in washing the child's hands with soap and water.

Wipe off the toilet seat and spray with disinfectant if there is urine or feces on the seat or sides.

Remove gloves and wash your hands thoroughly before doing anything else.

Occasionally during play time ask children whether they need to go to the bathroom. Ask them to go after lunch and before nap time. As soon as they get up from their naps, have them go to the bathroom.

Toilet-training should be a positive developmental experience. It should take a very short period of time. Problems in toilet-training most often arise when adults do not pay attention to the child's lack of readiness. They pressure the child through weeks of unsuccessful experiences during which they blame the child for the failure rather than blaming themselves for wrong timing. Help parents understand that timing for toilet-training is individual, as is learning to walk. There is no *right* age by which all children should be toilet-trained. According to many experts, children will train themselves with help when they are ready to give up diapers. Girls often are trained between 30–36 months of age and boys by 36–42 months (Carr 1993).

Daily Activities   Routines are ready guides for caregivers so that important details of caregiving are attended to. Some routine tasks can be accomplished by the toddler alone, some can only be accomplished by the caregiver, while some tasks involve the caregiver's facilitating the toddler.

Hang outside clothes on a hook or put in the cubbie. Leave those clothes there until it is time to go back outside.

Encourage children to hold books with both clean hands and to turn the pages carefully. Help them learn to put the book back on the shelf or table when they finish looking at it.

Encourage children to take out, or off the shelf, only the toy they are going to play with. At clean-up time before lunch and before going home, have the children help put the toys where they belong.

Have the children put on a smock when painting or gluing (they should ask for help if they need it). Have them stand at the easel or table while working, and keep the supplies at the easel or table. Teach them to wash their hands while the smock is still on (in a nearby sink or in a water-filled basin or pail at the table). They should then dry their hands and throw away the towel in the nearby wastebasket. The children can then take off the smock (asking for help if they need it).

Daily Written Plans

You now have the basis to establish individualized curricula for each child in care. Appendix A presents Developmental Prescriptions that can be used to assess each child's development in the five major Developmental Areas. Additional sources that help establish age expectations can also be used, such as *The First Twelve Months of Life* (Caplan 1978) and *The Second Twelve Months of Life* (Caplan and Caplan 1980). Next, copy the Developmental Profile form in Appendix B. Use the sample profile to plot a profile for each child in care. Finally, task analyze the steps necessary to help the child achieve proficiency in behaviors and skills at his or her present level. This structure can then be translated into daily and weekly plans.

Daily and Weekly Plans

Plans should be both daily and weekly. To make a daily plan, decide after your special time with the infant or toddler which of the things you did together today you can build on tomorrow. Review and if necessary revise the plans you had made for tomorrow. Weekly plans should provide task analyzed experiences in all five major areas of development. You can add additional information during the week so that you adequately reinforce the behaviors which actually occur during that week (see Table 9–3).

Look at the child's Developmental Prescription (see Appendix A) to determine which behavior is new and to select one behavior to reinforce. List the appropriate materials and strategies to use with the child (see Part III).

Unit Plans

Long-term planning involves your choosing appropriate themes for the next weeks and months. When you have selected your themes, you can collect

TABLE 9-3   WEEKLY PLAN FOR AN INDIVIDUAL CHILD

EXAMPLE:

CHILD'S NAME:			WEEK:
	Area of Development*	Materials	Caregiver Strategies and Comments
T	Physical: Vision	Red Ribbon	Hold bow where infant can focus. Slowly
U	R: Visual tracking	bow	move bow to side, to front, to other side.
E			Observe eyes holding focus. Stop. Talk
S			to infant. Repeat moving bow.
D			
A	N: Changing focus	Red and blue	Hold red bow where infant can focus.
Y		blue ribbon	Lift up blue bow and hold a few inches
			to side of red bow. Observe eyes
			changing focus. Continue changing
			positions with both bows.

*Behavior: R = Reinforced, N = New

materials and decide on activities long before you will need to use them. Careful long-term planning means you do not have to rush to get the information and material you need for your daily and weekly plans.

When you write down your unit plan, you can think more clearly about your ideas, add to them, revise them, and get yourself, your materials, and your room organized before you begin the unit with the children. The following outline has five major parts which must relate to each other. The materials, preparation, procedures, and evaluation all must implement the objectives. If you have a clever idea or some cute material, but they do not fit the unit objectives, do not include them in that unit.

1. Unit Objectives
2. Materials
    a. Select equipment, furniture.
    b. Select manipulatives, art, books, toys.
3. Preparation
    a. Identify materials which need to be ordered or made.
    b. Collect and organize materials and space.
    c. Set up Learning Centers, if used.
    d. Determine caregiver's schedule for specific involvement with individual children.
4. Procedures
    a. Facilitate individual child's involvement with materials and children.
    b. Facilitate the child's use of new behaviors.
    c. Interact with the child or children.
5. Evaluation
    a. Of learning
        (1) Observe each child's behaviors and compare to the unit objectives.
    b. Of the unit
        (1) Observe each child's behaviors to determine whether the unit objectives, materials, and procedures matched the child's ability to learn physically, emotionally, socially, and cognitively.
        (2) Observe each child's beginning, continuing, and failing interest in the topic.

Thematic Units

Unit themes can be planned to provide new and interesting experiences for the children. You must give much thought to whether the topic is one the children can deal with physically, emotionally, socially, and cognitively.

Objectives Unit objectives for infants and toddlers differ from objectives for older children. Objectives for infants and toddlers focus on involving the child with materials and people so that the child can construct knowledge. Children of this age derive much of the information from the material itself rather than from being told something about it by or telling something about it to the adult. Therefore, the materials themselves and the child's actual use of them are more important than "making" and "talking about" something.

A thematic unit may have some objectives which are appropriate for all children and some which are appropriate for specific children. A Bumpy Unit may have the objective that the child will touch and hold bumpy and smooth objects. Both a 9-month-old and a 27-month-old can do this. An additional objective for the 27-month-old may be to say verbally which object is bumpy and to find another bumpy object.

A theme or topic may last a week or be extended as interest continues. It can be integrated into many experiences.

The Environment   Room arrangement may reflect the theme. Furniture placement and tape on the floor can enrich a unit. You can arrange chairs in rows like a bus or train. A large cardboard box can be painted to look like a house when you talk about families. Use wall and hanging space for pictures, mobiles, floor-to-ceiling projects, bulletin boards, and displays.

Learning Centers   Learning centers integrate a theme by organizing the room and materials, and encouraging specific uses of a particular space. Tables, shelves, containers, floor and wall space all form part of a learning center. You can change learning centers to fit new themes.

For infants and toddlers you can organize learn centers in several ways. These children use their senses to gather information to construct knowledge, so the senses can become the focus for the learning centers—you can set up a Seeing Center, Hearing Center, Touching and Feeling Center, Smelling Center, and Tasting Center. Any or all sense centers may be used in a thematic unit. For a Bumpy Unit a Touching Center could contain bumpy objects. A Hearing Center could have bumpy and smooth objects and items which make contrasting sounds when rubbed. A Seeing Center could have clear plastic bags of gravel, corn, and flour to look at and then feel.

You can also organize centers around room-use areas. You can have a Quiet Zone, a Construction Center, a Wet Center, a Reading and Listening Center, or a Home Center. The use of themes in each learning center area for infants and toddlers is an extremely important aspect of curriculum development. Several excellent resources for learning center ideas and themes are currently available (Cataldo 1983).

Materials   The theme will stimulate ideas for materials. A Bumpy Unit would need all kinds of materials which are bumpy and a few materials which are smooth.

Many household items make good materials for infant and toddler units. Each chapter in Part III contains several ideas for easy-to-make materials.

Books related to the theme can be read to one or a few children at a time when they show interest in hearing a story. For toddlers most books become more meaningful when they are talked about. The caregiver may choose to tell the story in her own words rather than read the printed storyline. She can direct attention to pictures, ask questions about them, and ask the child or children to tell what they are thinking about the story. If children lose interest, put the book down; a child may choose to use the book again at a later time either with you or alone.

Strategies   Most of your strategies should focus on helping the individual child become involved. Few toddlers are ready for group experiences. The young child constructs knowledge by actively using materials and engaging in a limited amount of verbal naming of the materials.

   Sample Thematic Unit   The sample thematic unit presented here shows the planning, preparation, and relationships of the unit parts. To put this unit into actual practice, you would need to match the suggested activities with the interests and needs of your children. Be sure to refer to The Celebration of Life Calender in this Chapter.

Sample Thematic Unit on Riding

Riding is physical knowledge. The child constructs this knowledge by physically experiencing riding rather than being told about riding. If your children do not ride the subway (or train, airplane, etc.), do not include those activities in your unit.

1. Objectives
   a. The child shall ride in wheeled equipment.
   b. The child shall ride on wheeled toys.
   c. The child shall show pleasure when riding.
   d. The child shall be exposed to representations of riding: toys with riders, pictures, and oral language.
   e. The child shall identify riding.

2. Webbing

   Unit objectives are fostered by activities which help the child develop and use the desired concepts. Webbing is useful to help you think about the many possible concepts for a unit. Creating the webbing picture shows you the relationships of concepts to the central theme and often stimulates the development of other concepts (see Figure 9–7).

3. Learning Environment

Centers	Materials	Additional Materials

a. Riding
    (1) Set boundaries
	(1) Tyke bike
	(2) Sit and spin
	(3) Wagon
		(1) Pictures of children, families
		    riding in car, city bus, etc.
		    (Display at 2-year-old's eye level.)

b. Dramatic Play	(1) Empty
	    cardboard
	    boxes large
	    enough to
	    seat 1–2
	    children
	(2) Toy and/or
	    child-sized
	    stroller
	(3) Pick-up
		(1) Floor-to-ceiling hanging: car
		    (made from paper sacks cut and
		    taped together and painted with
		    tempera by children. The "door"
		    opens to allow a child to enter
		    and sit down.)

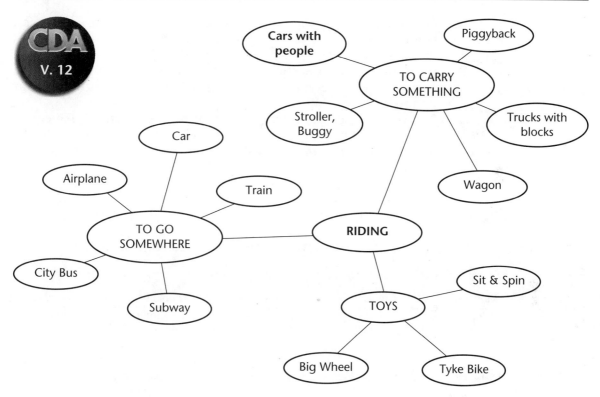

Figure 9–7   An example of webbing for a riding unit

   c. Language
      (1) Books (about riding on or in objects familiar to the child)
      (2) Records (songs and sounds of riding familiar to the child)
      (3) Song cards (for caregiver)
      (4) Newsprint
      (5) Paper and markers (for child's "drawings" and stories)
      (Other areas may contribute to the theme. A child playing with
      blocks may call a block a car and in sing-song fashion tell where he
      is "riding" as he pushes the "car" around.)
  4. Possible Caregiver-Initiated Activities
    a. Labeling: Use descriptive words to describe a child's actions. For ex-
       ample, "Maria is riding in the stroller"; "Nathan is giving his babies
       a ride in his wagon"; "Sasha is riding the big wheel." Name objects
       in pictures on the wall and in books.
    b. Reading: Talk about pictures from magazines, wordless picture
       books. Use picture books. Children can draw their own pictures to
       accompany their story.

   c. Listening: Listen to each child. Listen to how they make sounds and words. Respond to feelings they show. Provide verbal labels, ask questions, and listen some more.

   d. Questioning: Ask questions. For example, "Who are you giving a ride?" "Where are you going riding?" "Can that box ride in your wagon?"

   e. Singing: Make up your own songs to fit a child's actions. For example, "Li is riding, riding, riding. Li is riding her tyke bike." If you cannot make up a tune, say the words in sing-song fashion.

TABLE 9–4   WEEKLY GROUP RECORD OF CURRICULUM EMPHASIS IN CAREGIVER-CHILD PLANNED INTERACTIONS

DATES:	THEME: Riding				
	Monday	Tuesday	Wednesday	Thursday	Friday
CHILD:	Development Area:	Development Area:	Development Area:	Development Area:	Development Area:
	Cognitive Recall Problem-Solving				
	Materials:	Materials:	Materials:	Materials:	Materials:
	Baby Stroller Toy Truck				
CHILD:	Development Area:	Development Area:	Development Area:	Development Area:	Development Area:
	Physical Large motor-riding				
	Materials:	Materials:	Materials:	Materials:	Materials:
	Tyke bike				
CHILD:	Development Area:	Development Area:	Development Area:	Development Area:	Development Area:
	Language Labeling				
	Materials:	Materials:	Materials:	Materials:	Materials:
	Pictures of objects to ride in				
CHILD:	Development Area:	Development Area:	Development Area:	Development Area:	Development Area:
	Cognitive Creative				
	Materials:	Materials:	Materials:	Materials:	Materials:
	Paper, tempera, paint				

TABLE 9–4 *(continued)*

CHILD:	Development Area:	Development Area:	Development Area:	Development Area:	Development Area:
	Cognitive listening, labeling				
	Materials:	Materials:	Materials:	Materials:	Materials:
	Record, tape of sounds of car, train, airplane				
CHILD:	Development Area:	Development Area:	Development Area:	Development Area:	Development Area:
	Social Independence				
	Materials:	Materials:	Materials:	Materials:	Materials:
	Stroller Dolls				

Your record of each child's involvement provides assurance that the child has a balanced curriculum in the formal, planned times with you. Your informal times with each child are also important parts of the curriculum. Both the planned and informal involvement should provide a holistic, supporting, nurturing curriculum for each child in your care.

STUDENT ACTIVITIES

1. Obtain a written statement of the goals of a child care program. Identify the purposes and philosophy of the program.
2. Identify the time blocks in one child care program.
3. List the sequence of activities in two daily routines.
4. Use one child's developmental profile as the basis for writing a daily lesson plan.
5. Select one group of children and write one thematic unit for them.

CHAPTER REVIEW

1. Write a statement for a new caregiver explaining why flexibility in schedules is important in an infant and toddler program.
2. List three daily routines. Explain how each routine may be helpful to a child.

	ROUTINE	HELPFUL
1.		
2.		
3.		

3. List two reasons for written daily plans.
4. List the five major parts of the unit plan.
   1.
   2.
   3.
   4.
   5.
5. How can a thematic unit involve the child physically?
   emotionally?
   socially?
   cognitively?

REFERENCES

Bagnato, S. J., Kontos, S., and Neisworth, J. T. 1987. Integrated day care as special education: Profiles of programs and children. *Topics in Early Childhood Special Education* 7(1), 28–47.

Caplan. F. 1978. *The First Twelve Months of Life.* New York: Bantam/Grosset and Dunlap, Inc.

Caplan, F., and Caplan, T. 1980. *The Second Twelve Months of Life.* New York: Bantam/Grosset and Dunlap, Inc.

Caring for Our Children 1996. *National Health and Safety performance Standards: Guidelines for Out-of-Home Child Care Programs.* American Academy of Pediatrics/American Public Health Association.

Carr, Linda. 1993. Toilet training toddlers. Lecture Series to Suffolk County "Mommy & Me Parent Trainers," Selden, New York.

Castellanos, L., & Watson, L. 1997. Infant Assessment-Developmental Profiles, Prescriptions and Outcomes. *National Conference Association for Education of the Young Child.* Anneheim, CA.

Cataldo, Christine Z. 1983. *Infants and Toddlers Programs: A Guide to Very Early Childhood Education.* Reading, MA: Addison-Wesley Publishing Co.

Clegg, L., Miller, E., and Vanderhoof, Jr., W. H. 1995. *Celebrating Diversity: A Multicultural Resource.* Albany, NY: Delmar ITP.

Clinton, President W. 1997. NBC Broadcast, National Child Care Forum: Washington, DC.

Centers for Disease Control. 1984. *What YOU Can Do to Stop Disease in the Child Day Care Centers.* Atlanta, GA: Author.

Council for Early Childhood Professional Recognition, CDA National Credentialing Program. (1987). *Child Development Associate Assessment System and Competency Standards Infant/Toddler Caregivers in Center-Based Programs.* Washington, DC: Author.

Greater Minneapolis Day Care Association. 1989. Minneapolis, MN.

Hannaford, C. 1995. *Smart Moves: Why Learning Is Not All In Your Head.* Arlington, VA: Great Ocean Publishing, Inc.

Jones, E., and Derman-Sparks, L. 1992. Meeting the challenge of diversity. *Young Children* 47(2), 12–17.

Nash, J. 1997. *Fertile Minds*. Special Report: How a child's brain develops and what it means for child care and welfare reform. New York: *Time* Magazine.

Schumann, M. J. 1982. Children in daycare: Settling them for sleep. *Day Care and Early Education* 9(4): 14–18.

Turkovich, M., and Mueller, P. 1989. The multicultural factor: A curriculum multiplier. *Social Studies and the Young Learner* 1(4), 9–12.

Part **III**

Matching Caregiver Strategies and Child Development

The chapters in Part III present how the caregiver works with infants and toddlers at specific age ranges. Each chapter refers to the developmental profiles and characteristics of children in a specific age range, lists materials, and presents examples of caregiver strategies which may be used with individual children. Refer to each chapter which contains information relevant to the children with whom you work. As your children develop, refer back to these chapters for additional information to help you meet the changes.

The *sequence* of development presented is common to all infants and toddlers. The time behaviors occur or the rate of development may differ. Two eleven-month-olds may be at different levels of development. Concentrate on each child as an individual rather than comparing them and deciding that one is faster than another or better than another. Compare infants and toddlers to themselves. Look at their individual records to see where they are making progress; gradually developing new, more complex skills and behaviors, or where they seem to be stuck at one level. Check to see where progress of development is appropriate.

Remember that infants and toddlers make spurts of growth. When one area is in a spurt, the other areas seem to slow down. For example, an infant's talking may increase dramatically for several weeks. Then you notice repetition of old sounds but nothing new for a while. But you may also see during this lull in language the infant is beginning to creep. His or her energies seem to have turned away from language and toward creeping. This is a common pattern for infants. They seem to have one major area of development at a time.

Appendix A contains a complete list of Developmental Prescriptions. Begin using this with each child in your program. It is cumulative, with information added regularly, so refer to Chapter 5, What is Development and Learning? for a more complete picture of where a phase of development fits into a child's ongoing total development.

Use the Developmental Prescription and Profile to discover what the child presently *can* do. Concentrate on the child's accomplishments. Reflect to the child your enthusiasm about his or her development and report to the parent how the child is developing. Your enthusiasm helps everyone feel good about the child.

You need information from the Developmental Prescriptions and Profiles to plan appropriately for the child. Total program planning of curriculum, schedule, routines, and space should be based on the information from the Developmental Prescription and Profile for each child in your program. The Developmental Prescription is divided into major areas of development: physical, emotional, social, cognitive, and language. These are listed separately to help you with observations and planning. You should remember that these five areas are integrated in the child's life.

Age expectations are included in the Developmental Prescriptions and Profiles. These are approximations, since all children develop at their own rates. Use the age designations to examine the chapters in Part III which present suggestions of materials and caregiver strategies.

Many child care specialist strategies enhance development. In order to understand the importance of what the child and caregiver is doing, several areas of child development will be examined. It is necessary to remember, however, that the purpose for looking at the parts of the picture is to understand the whole picture better. Areas of development are *interrelated* and *interdependent*.

The crucial issue in looking at Developmental Prescriptions and Profiles is to task analyze (break into logical steps from simple to complex) and become familiar with the *sequence* and *pattern* of development. The age at which a particular behavior appears and the time it takes to develop varies from child to child. The caregiver must look at the goals and objectives of the program; there is no one curriculum or teaching strategy for all infants and toddlers everywhere. There are, however, some situations which have generally been very effective in helping individual children reach their potential.

Infants and toddlers are growing and developing rapidly. As their alert time and playtime lengthen, they become ready for more involvement with people and materials. Selection of materials is determined by the interest and development of each child. You can use the materials identified in each chapter with many children in that age range. Let the child's developmental profile help you determine which materials will be appropriate for that child. The materials listed are suggestions and need not be used with all children. You can also add other materials to fit the particular child's development.

Child care homes and centers plan to use part of their budget for the purchase of high-quality toys and equipment. However, the wide range of ages of children in the program often means that each year only a few sturdy toys can be purchased for different developmental levels of children. Each chapter in Part III includes a list of homemade materials so that a variety of materials can be available for limited cost.

There is no one best way to care for children. Therefore, the caregiver must constantly make choices. The child's development, the society, and the setting provide possibilities and limits on the caregiver. All of these become a part of the reasoning for the caregiver's decisions and actions.

It is important to realize that caregiving is, first of all, a relationship between caregiver and child. Everything in the infant's and toddler's curriculum occurs in a context which interrelates physical, emotional, social, and cognitive development. Even though each of the outlines in this section focuses on one area of development, the other areas are also involved.

10

The Child from Birth to Four Months of Age

OBJECTIVES

After completing this chapter, the child development specialist should be able to:

1. Identify and record sequences of change in the physical, emotional, social, cognitive, and language development of infants from birth to 4 months of age.
2. Select materials appropriate to that age-level infant's development.
3. Devise strategies appropriate to that age-level infant's development.

CHAPTER OUTLINE

I. Materials and Activities
   A. Types of Materials
   B. Examples of Homemade Materials
II. Caregiver Strategies to Enhance Development
   A. Developmental Profile
   B. Physical Development
   C. Emotional Development
   D. Social Development
   E. Cognitive Development
   F. Learning Skills/Language Development

CHILD DEVELOPMENT ASSOCIATE FUNCTIONAL AREAS

All CDA functional areas are integrated into the caregiver decisions and behaviors.

Use Appendix A, the Developmental Prescriptions, and Appendix B, the Developmental Profile, with each infant. Children follow a *sequence* of development. There are often ranges in the *rate* of development.

Kiera, 2½ months old, has just arrived at the child care home. She sits in her infant seat, which is on the floor by the sofa. Kiera's fists are closed and her arms and legs make jerky movements. As each of the other children arrive, they smile and "talk" to her, with the caregiver watching close by. Kiera looks at each child, and after a few minutes she starts to whimper, then cry. Bill, the caregiver, picks her up and says, "Are you getting sleepy? Do you want a nap?" Bill takes Kiera into the bedroom and puts her in her crib where she promptly falls asleep (see Figure 10–1).

MATERIALS AND ACTIVITIES

Materials used with infants of this age must be safe and challenging. Every object these infants can grasp and lift will go into their mouths. *Before* you allow an infant to touch a toy, determine whether it is safe. Each toy should pass *all* the following criteria:

1. It is too big to swallow (use a "choke tube" to measure smaller objects).
2. It has no sharp points or edges to cut or puncture the skin or eyes.
3. It can be cleaned.

Figure 10–1 The caregiver anticipates and provides for the newborn's needs.

4. It has no movable parts that can pinch.
5. Painted surfaces have nontoxic paint.
6. It is sturdy enough to withstand biting, banging, and throwing.

To be challenging for the young infant, materials should do the following:

1. Catch the infant's attention so the infant will want to interact with it in some way, for example, reach, push, grasp, look, taste, turn, and practice these movements over and over again.
2. Be movable enough so the infant can use arms, legs, hands, eyes, ears, or mouth to successfully manipulate the object and respond to it.
3. Be able to be used at several levels of complexity so that the infant can use it with progressively more skill.

Look for toys and materials which the infant can use in several different ways. These provide greater opportunities for the infant to practice and develop new skills. Change the toys often so they seem new and interesting. An infant seems to get bored using the same toy for months.

Types of Materials

Crib gyms
Mobiles
Rattles
Yarn or texture balls

Small toys to grasp
Sound toys
Pictures, designs
Mirrors

Examples of Homemade Materials

Materials may be homemade or commercially made. The following are suggestions for making some of your own materials:

CRIB GYM

Tie a sturdy cotton rope from the short side of the crib to the other. Tie on three different objects (these can be changed regularly) so they hang just at the end of the infant's reach. Poke a small hole in the bottom of a small colored plastic margarine tub; thread and knot it on one rope. It will swing when the infant hits it.

RATTLES

Film canister (plastic or metal): Put in one teaspoon uncooked cereal. Replace the cap and tape it on with colored tape.

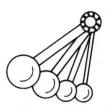

Plastic tablespoons: tie together on a circle of strong yarn.

YARN BALLS

Roll up balls of washable yarn. Tuck the loose end inside. Make the balls different sizes and different colors.

Wrap yarn around the palm of your hand until you have a thick mitt. Carefully slide it off your hand and tie a short piece of yarn tightly around the middle of the "mitt." Cut the ends apart. Pull the loose ends around to shape a ball.

FABRIC TWIRLS

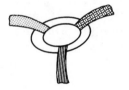

Cut out the center of a lid from a margarine tub. Cut carefully, leaving a clean, smooth edge. Use the remaining rim ring. Sew on three strips of printed washable fabric 3 inches long by 2 inches wide. Hang from the crib gym or put on the infant's wrist.

DESIGNS

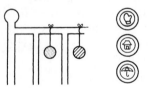

Cut faces, wallpaper, pictures, and contrasting colored fabric to fit inside the lids of margarine tubs. Glue one piece in each lid. Hang some from the sides of the crib or give several to the infant to play with.

CAREGIVER STRATEGIES TO ENHANCE DEVELOPMENT

Developmental Profile

Perhaps the single most difficult task of caregiving is assessing the developmental strengths and weaknesses of children. References, scales, and a step-by-step format such as the Prescriptions in Appendix A give only general guidelines to milestones and expectations. The caregiver still must make estimates based upon observations of behavior, past experience, cultural mores, and comparisons with other children. Further, judgments of what is considered "average," "normal," and "appropriate" differ depending upon the age of children. For example, a 3-month-old who is 2 months below age level in a skill may have a significant deficit, whereas a 30-month-old who is 2 months below expectations is probably within normal limits.

Because of the difficulties inherent in assessing what is expected of young children, some authorities advise caregivers not to assess children at all! This practice is not only impossible, but results in care without any clear goals. The best approach, then, is to formally observe children often and make frequent adjustments in activities based upon their continuous growth.

Now, turn to the Developmental Profile for 10-week-old Kiera in Figure 10–2, and be cautious as you read it not to view it as a "test" or "diagnosis." Developmental Profiles are pictures of skill *estimates* and *trends* and should be used to help direct activities in major areas of skill development.

Kiera is a healthy and normal 10-week-old who was observed over a five-day period using the Child Behaviors in each of the five major areas from the Developmental Prescriptions, birth to 4 months. The Profile shows that her skills fall within expected ranges, with her lowest skill estimate being 8 weeks and the highest estimates being 14 weeks.

In the Physical Area (I), Kiera exhibits 100 percent of the "reflexes," successfully demonstrates 75 percent of "muscle control" behaviors, and functions as expected in "eating," "sleeping," and "elimination." She is estimated to be a little above age in "muscle control" (12 weeks) because her muscle control is more like that of a 3-month-old than of a 2½-month-old.

Within the Emotional Area (II), Kiera exhibits 100 percent of "types of feelings," 75 percent of "control of feelings" (she doesn't increase sounds with conversations yet), and expected "activity level" and "regularity of temperament." Displaying all types of feelings is more like a 14-week-old, and not increasing sounds with conversation is more like an 8-week-old.

Within the Social Area (III), Kiera has a little difficulty with "attachment" to her caregiver, but is very aware of herself and others for her age. Because she has a little trouble with attachment, Kiera is estimated to be a little below expectations in that area (8 weeks), but is above expectancy in awareness of self and others (11 and 12 weeks).

Kiera demonstrates skills in the Cognitive Area (IV) which are expected for her age. She functions in "sensory-motor levels 1 and 2" and "permanence" as expected for her age of 10 weeks.

Finally, Kiera exhibits Learning Skills (V) at age in visual and speech development, above average in auditory development, and slightly less than expected eye-hand coordination; that is, she doesn't "move her arms or reach her hands toward objects." Therefore, her "seeing," "hearing," and "sounds" are estimated at 11 and 12 weeks, and her "eye-hand coordination" is a little below age at 8 weeks.

Using this Profile and the Materials and Caregiver Strategies listed below, attention should be focused on those tasks and activities in less-developed areas while maintaining activities in all other skills. In this way, the caregiver encourages balanced development in all areas important to Kiera's growth.

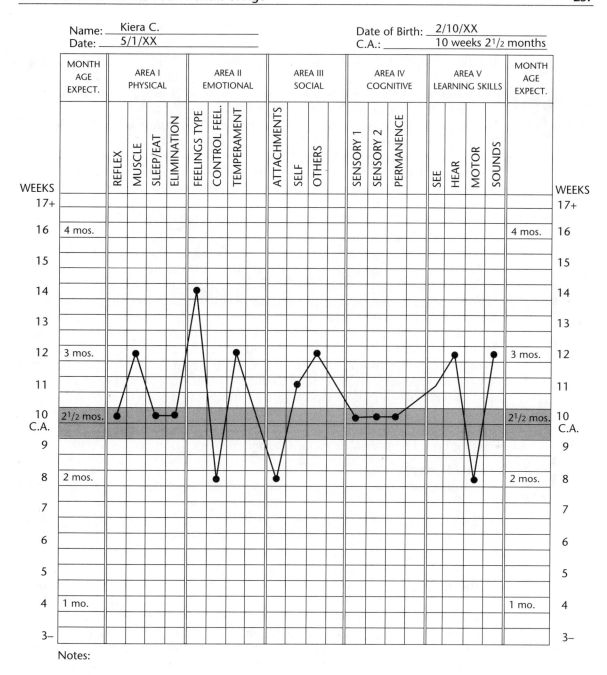

Figure 10–2 Developmental Profile, Kiera C.

Physical Development

Infants from birth to 4 months of age show a very rapid rate of physical development, which varies widely from infant to infant. One baby may turn from stomach to back early and another may reach for objects early and turn over late. Starting at birth with reflexive movements, infants rapidly gain an increasing level of muscular control over much of their bodies. In general, development moves from the simple to the more complex movements.

The control moves from their heads and necks to their shoulders, backs, waists, and legs. For example, they first lift their heads up before they have the muscular control to sit and they sit before they can use their legs for standing.

Muscular control also develops from mid-body out to the hands and feet. Gradually infants are able to control to some degree their arm and leg movements before they develop control of their hands, and to control their hands before they can grasp or pick up things with their fingers.

Infants also increase their ability to notice differences and experience their world through seeing, hearing, touching, smelling, and tasting. While these perceptual senses are listed in the Prescription in Appendix A under the "Physical" area, they are placed within the "Learning Skills" area on the Profile because learning skills, as well as physical acuity, are necessary for normal development. In newborns, only acuity of senses is measured, but after the first six months, perceptual skills such as auditory, memory, visual discrimination, and so forth play an important part in learning and development.

Readiness is important in infant development. The child should set the pace. Caregivers should not expect the child to do something the child is not ready to do. The specialist should honor the uniqueness of each child.

Visual Perception

In earlier times, it was believed that infants were sightless; later theories held that they were able to see only forms. It is now accepted that infants can see and that they learn very quickly to differentiate objects and interpret nonverbal cues. They spend most of their early months just looking, and they prefer faces to all other objects.

A newborn baby focuses best on objects that are between 8 and 14 inches away from his eyes, a range that seems to have been selected by nature . . . it being the distance at which a nursing infant sees his mother's face . . . he will spend most of his time looking to his right or to his left, rarely focusing straight ahead . . . Most young babies like to study faces . . . prefer black-and-white patterns to bright colors; complex objects to simple ones. They love looking at light . . . (Eisenberg et al. 1989, 97).

The basic Developmental Learning Skills of Visual/Motor Control, Visual Memory, Visual Discrimination, and Visual Association are beginning to be established during the first months of life.

Hearing

Newborns can hear sounds. In fact, they could hear sounds before they were born. They respond to almost any type of sound. By moving their heads they show they can identify the direction of the sound. They do better locating sound coming from either side than from above or below, or in front or behind them. In the first few months they can discriminate between many speech sounds.

> Most babies will react to loud noise—in early infancy by startling, at about three months by blinking, at about four months by turning toward the source of the sound (Eisenberg et al. 1989, 96).

The basic Developmental Learning Skills of Auditory Discrimination, Auditory Memory, Auditory Association, and Auditory/Visual Association are established during the first months of life.

Taste

Newborns can distinguish between water and sugar water. They prefer sugar water to plain water. They can distinguish between sweet, salty, and bitter solutions and prefer the sweet ones. Later, taste will become another sense used in exploring the world and almost anything they come in contact with will end up in their mouths.

Smell

Newborns can distinguish odors and respond positively or negatively to them. The sense of smell is another way they learn about their world.

An infant's well-developed sense of smell has implications for caregivers. Some babies may do better in adjusting to a childcare setting if the mother or primary caregiver leaves an article of clothing for the baby to be wrapped up in or snuggle up with. The consistent, familiar odor can ease the transition from mother to caregiver. A child care specialist should consider not wearing cologne.

Touch

The baby's most valuable tool for learning about the world is touching and being touched. The infant can feel different textures and identify elements and people through the differences in softness, roughness, and so forth.

Babies who are not touched may fail to grow normally. Further, infants have preferences for types of touching and stroking, and most babies love and need to be held and cuddled.

Movements

Newborns' movements are reflexive; they occur without the infants' control or direction. Through growth and learning infants begin to control their movements.

In the first few months infants learn to use many movements well but they have not yet coordinated the movements. Bruner and his colleagues observed, recorded, and analyzed infant behavior. They found that infants learn to control their sucking in the first month of life and that sucking is used for relieving distress, holding attention, and exploration as well as for feeding. Infants may require being held more than older children which is why it is important to hold a baby while feeding instead of simply propping up a bottle.

Reflexive hand and arm movements develop into a grasping-groping action which can be independent of vision. Within the first four months "this slow reaching has the mouth as its inevitable terminus. There is an invariant sequence: activation, reach, capture, retrieval to the mouth, and mouthing" (Bruner 1968, 38) (see Figure 10–3). In the next year these hand and arm movements will become directed voluntary activity, which may be visually controlled.

Stability

The newborn's head moves reflexively from side to side. When upright, the neck cannot yet support the head. Within the first month infants can lift their heads when lying on their stomachs. By the third month they are using their arms to push against the floor or bed to raise their heads and chests.

During these first three months infants are also busy with their legs. The legs have been kicking and pushing in the air and against anything within range. The infants roll and kick their legs from side to side. Their upper and lower back muscles are developing so that one day when they kick and roll to one side, they keep going right onto their backs or their stomachs. The baby has rolled over!

Many caregiving strategies at this time involve providing appropriate space so infants can move as they want to. The caregiver does not tell the in-

Figure 10–3   When an infant brings an object to his mouth, he is learning about the world around him.

fants to arch their backs, kick their legs, or wave their arms wildly. Infants do this naturally. The caregiver facilitates infant movement by making sure their clothes do not limit movement, by providing a circle of safety, and by offering the infant materials and toys that are safe and appropriate.

Sleep

Most newborns sleep between fourteen and seventeen hours a day. There will be times when they are actually awake, though their eyes are closed, and they will respond to stimulation. Newborns are relatively light sleepers, and deep sleep periods are only about 20 minutes long. The longest sleep period is usually four or five hours.

Sleep patterns will usually be consistent with a baby's other patterns. For example, a baby who is active and noisy when awake will also be active and make noises in his sleep.

Gradually the sleep patterns become more regular and shorter as the baby spends more time being alert and attentive. Eisenberg, Murkoff, and Hathaway (1989) give detailed information and tips on patterns, better sleep, sleep positions, and so forth.

Suggestions for Implementing Curriculum

Physical development can be encouraged by providing opportunities for physical activity, changing the baby's position, and motivating movement without instilling "pressure to perform" (Eisenberg et al. 1989).

The caregiver can employ several strategies to enhance the infant's *muscular control*.

1. Place infants in positions where they can practice developing muscular control. For example, when you lay them on their stomachs, they can keep trying to lift their heads, shoulders, and trunks. Never place infants on their stomachs to sleep.
2. Until infants can roll over, sit up, and stand by themselves, they will need to be moved into those different positions several times each day during their waking hours.
3. Interact with the infant using yourself as a stimulator. Grasp the infant's hands and slowly lift the child upright. Hold your hands in different places so the infant will look around and reach for you. Gently snap your fingers behind, beside, and in front of the infant and watch the child turn his or her head to locate the sound.
4. Use toys and materials to play with the infant; offer some for the infant to use independently.

   Place objects within the vision and reach of the infant. Select toys the infant can grasp. First there is a gross, grabbing movement. Later a more refined finger-thumb or pincer grasp is used.

CHILD BEHAVIOR	MATERIALS	EXAMPLES OF CAREGIVER STRATEGIES
Reflex*		
Grasp reflex (hand closes).	Finger, rattle.	Lift infant's body slightly. Place object in palm of infant's hand.
Startle reflex.		Touch, hold infant to calm him.
Tonic neck reflex (head facing one side or other, not facing up).	Mirror, mobile, toys, designs.	Place objects at side of crib, not above middle of crib.
Muscular Control		
(Develops from head to feet.)		
HEAD AND NECK		
Turns head.	Stuffed toy.	Place infant on back or stomach. Place toy to one side.
Holds head upright with support.		Support infant's head when holding infant upright.
Lifts head slightly when on stomach.		Place infant on stomach.
Holds head to sides and middle.		Place infant on stomach.
Holds up head when on back and on stomach.		Place infant on stomach or back.
Holds head without support.		Set and hold infant upright.
TRUNK		
Holds up chest.		Place infant on stomach.
Sits with support. May attempt to raise self. May fuss if left lying down with little chance to sit up.		Place infant in sitting position. Support head and back with arm or pillow. Lengthen sitting time as infant is able.
Holds up chest and shoulders.		Place infant on stomach.
LEG		
Rolls from stomach to back.		Place infant on flat surface where infant cannot roll off.
Muscular Control		
(Develops from mid-body to limbs.)		
ARM		
Moves randomly.	Toys.	Place objects within reach of infant.
Reaches.	Bright toys that make noise.	Place objects slightly beyond reach of infant; give to infant when child reaches for it.
HAND		
Opens and closes.	Toys with handles, which fit in fist.	Place handle in fist; help infant close fist around object.

CHILD BEHAVIOR	MATERIALS	EXAMPLES OF CAREGIVER STRATEGIES
Keeps hands open.		
Plays with hands.	Colorful plastic bracelet.	Place colorful objects which attract infant's attention on infant's hands, fingers (must be safe to go in mouth).
Uses hand to grasp object. Whole hand and fingers against thumb.	Toys with bumps to hold onto.	Place object within reach of infant.
Thumb and forefinger.	Toys which can be grasped with one hand.	Place object within reach of infant.
Holds and moves object.	Toys which can be pushed, pulled, or lifted with hands; toys which make noise.	Place toy on flat surface free from obstructions.
EYE-HAND COORDINATION		
Moves arm toward object; may miss it.	Toy, bottle.	Place within reach of infant.
Reaches hand to object; may grab or miss it.	Toy, bottle.	Place within reach of infant.

The caregiver can use several strategies to enhance the infant's *seeing*.

1. Place the infant or objects at the correct distance so the infant can focus to see people or objects. The newborn focuses at about 8 to 14 inches. When infants are about 4 months old, they can adjust focal distance as adults do. The caregiver can place materials at the proper focusing distance. These should attract the infant's attention (see Figure 10–4).

2. Select eye-catching materials. Contrasts seem to interest infants: designs, patterns, shapes, colors. Faces also attract their attention.

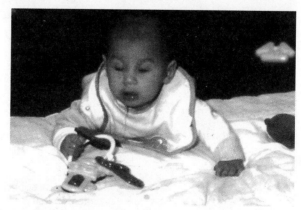

Figure 10–4   The caregiver moves a toy where the infant can see and reach for it.

CHILD BEHAVIOR	MATERIALS	EXAMPLES OF CAREGIVER STRATEGIES
Seeing		
Focuses 2 inches from eyes.	Mirror, mobile, toys, pictures, designs (e.g., patterns, faces)	Place object 8 inches from infant's face.
Follows with eyes.	Mobile, toys, hand.	Move object slowly after infant focuses on object.
Stares. Sees objects beyond 8 inches.	People, pictures, toys.	Attract attention by shape, color, movement.
Looks from object to object.	Toys, mobile, designs, pictures.	Provide two or more objects of interest to infant.
Looks around; stops to focus on object which has caught attention; then looks at something else; continual visual searching.		Provide eye-catching items in room: faces, patterned designs, contrasting colors in objects, and pictures.

The caregiver can use several strategies to enhance the infant's *hearing*.

1. Newborns respond to sound. The caregiver can produce and select sounds which help infants differentiate between voices as well as among other sounds.
2. Provide a variety of sounds. Tie a bell to the infant's wrist to catch the child's listening attention as the child moves his or her arm. Music can calm or excite infants. Clicking, clucking, snapping, humming, or singing all can provide opportunities for listening. Infants gradually learn to search for and identify the source of the sound. Later they also may try to reproduce the sound (see Figure 10–5).

CHILD BEHAVIOR	MATERIALS	EXAMPLES OF CAREGIVER STRATEGIES
Hearing		
Responds to voice.		Talk to infant. Answer him or her.
Hears range of sounds.	Music, singing, caregiver movements.	Talk, sing to infant. Answer him or her. Enter and leave room.
Calms while hearing low-pitched sounds.	Humming, singing, records.	Select quiet, gentle music to calm infant.
Becomes agitated while hearing high-pitched sounds.	Singing, records.	Select songs to sing to calm infant. Sing with infant; let him or her lead.
Locates sound.	Mechanical sounds, voices, music, musical toys.	Move sound around so infant searches for source.

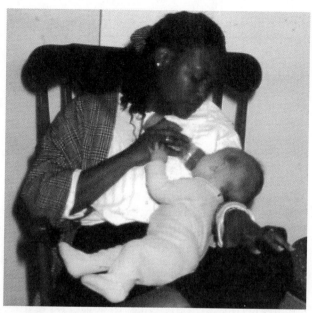

Figure 10–5   The caregiver talks and listens to the infant.

The caregiver can use several strategies to enhance the infant's *sleeping*. Anticipate when the infant probably will take a nap. Plan very calming time and activities for the infant just before nap time so the infant can get in a mood to sleep. Sitting with the infant in a rocking chair and humming a lullaby often prove very effective.

CHILD BEHAVIOR	MATERIALS	EXAMPLES OF CAREGIVER STRATEGIES
Sleeping		
Sleeps much of the day and night.	Flat, firm mattress.	Provide restful environment, moderate temperature, free from sudden loud noises.
Takes a long morning nap and a long afternoon nap.		Adjust routines to fit infant's changing sleep schedule.
May have irregular sleep habits.		Shorten or lengthen activities with infant to assist establishing some pattern for sleeping.

The caregiver can use several strategies to enhance the infant's *eating*. Parents and pediatricians determine what and how much infants are fed during their first four months. The caregiver is responsible for making eating a happy, successful time for the infant. Organize your time so you can hold each infant when bottle feeding. Eye focusing, eye-hand coordination, as well as emotional bonding, language, and communication all occur while holding the infant for feeding.

CHILD BEHAVIOR	MATERIALS	EXAMPLES OF CAREGIVER STRATEGIES
Eating		
Takes bottle on demand.	Formula and bottle.	Determine formula with parent. Determine schedule with parent. Hold infant when bottle feeding. Tilt bottle so milk fills the nipple to prevent infant's swallowing excess air. Burp the infant. Put infant straw in bottle.

The caregiver can use several strategies for *elimination*. Two important caregiver responsibilities are to change the infant's diaper frequently and to record the time and any abnormalities of bowel movements. Eating schedules affect the time infants have bowel movements. As they establish eating schedules, some infants develop predictable elimination patterns. Cleanliness is critical for the infant and the caregiver.

The infant's bowel movement reflects the child's health. Ask the parent what color, texture, and frequency are normal for the infant. Record the frequency daily. Record any differences in color and texture and inform the parent.

CHILD BEHAVIOR	MATERIALS	EXAMPLES OF CAREGIVER STRATEGIES
Elimination		
Begins to establish predictable eating and elimination schedules.	Diapers, cleansing supplies.	Put on disposable gloves. Remove soiled diaper and dispose of it. Wipe infant's bottom with warm, soapy wash cloth. Rinse. Dry. Put on dry diaper. Disinfect the changing surface. Remove gloves. **Wash your hands with soap.**
Establishes regular time for bowel movement.		Record time of bowel movement. Note changes in times of bowel movements.
May suffer from diarrhea or constipation (both problems call for attention).		Record type of bowel movement. Record changes in type of bowel movement. Discuss with parent. If diarrhea, notify parent immediately. Do not wait until the end of the day; the baby can dehydrate rapidly and may need medical care.

Emotional Development

Philip S. Riback, M.D., F.A.A.P. and assistant professor of neurology and pediatrics at Albany Medical College in Albany, New York states "Repeating tasks—sending the same messages to the brain over and over again—seems to result in certain chemical and anatomical changes that actually help a baby retain something she has learned. . . . Here's how a baby's brain develops best times to learn new skills . . . the first two years of life are considered a critical period for laying down the circuits necessary for acquiring motor skills . . . the connection between emotions and brain development is an area of considerable interest to pediatricians and child-development experts . . . feelings experienced by the child can affect the brain and lay the groundwork for later emotions."

During the first months of life infants develop their basic feelings of security. There seems to be little "catch-up" time for emotional security. If the infant does not develop these feelings of security now, it is difficult to develop them as adequately later. Along with the parents the caregiver plays a key role in providing the kinds of relationships and experiences which enable the infant to develop this basic security.

Feelings of security and trust develop out of relations with others. Infants cannot develop these on their own. They develop these feelings from the way other people treat them. Parents and the primary caregiver are probably the most influential people in the lives of young infants in child care. Therefore, the caregiver is very directly responsible and involved in helping the infant feel secure.

Two caregiver behaviors of special importance are responding immediately to the infant's distress signals and responding constantly to the infant's signals of stress, need, or pleasure.

Temperament, the infant's basic style of behavior, gradually emerges in the first four months. Some styles are easily recognized, whereas others may be more difficult to observe.

The activity level of infants is obvious. They may kick and wriggle and squirm a great deal or they may lie quietly while either asleep or awake. Highly active infants may kick their covers off consistently and get tangled in their clothes. Their bodies get plenty of activity. They may need to be checked frequently to be sure they can move freely. A blanket may be more of a bother than it is worth, since it seldom covers the infant. Infant suits or long smocks and socks may keep the active infant just as warm. Very quiet infants may seem easy to care for. They seldom kick off their covers or need their clothes adjusted. They may, however, need to be picked up and moved around to stimulate their physical movement.

Infants' living patterns usually take on regularity in the first months of life. The infant who establishes a regular, though slowly changing, schedule for eating and sleeping creates a predictable world into which the caregiver can easily fit. Infants whose feeding and sleeping times remain erratic create stress for themselves and their caregiver.

Differing levels of sensory threshold are apparent in young infants. One infant will awaken when a light is turned on or a person steps into the room. Another infant will sleep in a brightly lit room with the record play on.

When several children are in one room, special adjustments need to be made for the sleeping infant who reacts negatively to light and sound.

Infants characteristically use differing levels of energy when responding to stimuli. One infant will cry loudly whenever he or she cries. Another infant will whimper and fuss and occasionally cry more loudly when very distressed. The caregiver, when responding to the infant's cries, will need to learn cues other than loudness to determine the type and severity of stress. The caregiver may need to check infants who fuss and cry quietly to make sure their needs are being met.

The caregiver can use several strategies to enhance the infant's *emotional development*. Whereas physical development can be enhanced by moving the infant, toys, and oneself around, emotional development demands more than manipulation.

When relating to the infant, the 3A's—Attention, Approval, and Affection—play a most crucial part in the daily emotional development of the child (see Figure 10–6). The following strategies will help the caregiver to be conscious of the 3A's while performing tasks such as diapering and feeding:

Use your relationship with the child.
Focus your attention on the child's needs.
Engage the child—make eye-to-eye contact.
Move slowly and with intention.
Make meaningful physical contact.
Actively listen to his or her whole body message.
Reflect back to him his vocal expressions, sounds.

Figure 10–6   Gentle touching and cuddling comfort the infant.

Try to sense how the child is feeling—is the child excited, happy, frustrated?

Try to judge the amount of stimulation the child prefers.

Try to get in rhythm with the child. Let him lead you vocally.

Talk and sing, hum and smile.

Place him where he can observe room activity.

Involve him in activity.

When leaving the infant, tell him where you'll be in the room if he needs you.

Suggestions for Implementing Curriculum

CHILD BEHAVIOR	MATERIALS	EXAMPLES OF CAREGIVER STRATEGIES
Types of Emotions-Feelings		
Shows excitement.	Attention-catching objects.	Use voice and facial expression to reflect back excitement.
Shows stress.	Calming touch, talk, music, singing. Rueing	Determine cause. Change situation to reduce stress, e.g., change diaper; change position; talk to infant (child may be bored).
Shows enjoyment.	Interesting, challenging toys, objects.	Provide pleasant experiences, e.g., give infant a bath; snuggle; converse; smile.
Shows anger or frustration.	Rueing	Determine cause. Remove or reduce cause. Divert infant's attention, e.g., turn infant around to look at something else.
Shows fear.	Rueing	Hold, comfort infant. Remove fear-producing object or change situation, e.g., hold infant startled by sudden loud noise, remove source of pain.
Protests.		Determine what infant is protesting about. Eliminate activity or do it a different way, e.g., change how you wash infant's face. If continues, ask another caregiver to take child for you.
Control of Emotions-Feelings		
Seems to occur automatically.		
Decreases crying.	Activities, toys which catch infant's attention and which infant likes.	Involve infant in an activity.
Increases sounds (talking).		Initiate "conversations" and respond to infant's talking.

CHILD BEHAVIOR	MATERIALS	EXAMPLES OF CAREGIVER STRATEGIES
Reflects feelings in sounds (talking).		Respond to the feelings expressed, e.g., comfort whining child; change situation.
Comforted by holding.		Consistently hold, caress, cuddle, and comfort when infant needs it.
Temperament		
Activity level.		Observe and identify where infant is in a range of behaviors. List adjustments you need to make to fit infant's temperament.
Regularity.		
Approach or withdrawal as a characteristic response to a new situation.		
Adaptability to change in routine.		
Level of sensory threshold.		
Positive or negative mood.		
Intensity of response.		
Distractibility.		
Persistence and attention span.		

Social Development

The caregiver must become emotionally involved with the infant. Just as infants develop a unique attachment to their mothers, they can develop an additional attachment to their own primary caregivers. Many of the caregiver strategies which build this emotional relationship involve frequent use of looking and touching.

Attachment theory and research have identified phases in the development of attachment. Ainsworth identified infants' social behaviors during the first few months of life which relate to developing attachment.

Phase 1: Undiscriminating Social Responsiveness
first two-to-three months
orienting behaviors: visual fixation, visual tracking, listening, rooting, postural adjustment when held
sucking and grasping to gain or maintain contact
signaling behaviors: smiling, crying, and other vocalizations to bring caregiver into proximity or contact (1982, 139).

Infants from birth to 4 months are egocentric; they have only their point of view. They use their senses to begin to develop a global concept of self. They need to see, hear, smell, touch, and taste themselves. People and objects are familiar insofar as they interact with the infant's sense experiences. For infants at this level people and objects do not exist as separate objects.

The caregiver can use several strategies to enhance social development. The caregiver can respond quickly to the infant's needs and can initiate interactions by looking, holding, stroking, talking, playing, carrying, and rocking the infant.

The caregiver arranges time and selects materials which help infants learn about themselves. Mirrors fascinate infants. Dots on bare feet and hands extend the infant's interest in his or her body. The caregiver arranges for the infant to interact with other people and with playthings.

Suggestions for Implementing Curriculum

CHILD BEHAVIOR	MATERIALS	EXAMPLES OF CAREGIVER STRATEGIES
Attachment		
Shows special closeness to parent; differentiates response to parent—voice, touch, presence, absence.		Accept that the infant will respond differently to you than to parent. Closely observe the parent-infant interaction and then model some of the caregiving behaviors, sounds, and other characteristics of the parent.
Develops familiarity with one primary caregiver (significant other).		Same caregiver provides most of infant's care, although other caregivers may share responsibility occasionally.
		Provide consistent care of infant: feed; comfort; change diapers and clothes; talk and sing and play with infant; rock and hold; put to bed; pick up when awake; respond to infant's special needs, likes, and dislikes. Touch, hold, caress, cuddle the infant.
Self		
Becomes aware of hands and feet.	Bright clothes, materials for hands, feet; bare feet sometimes.	Provide clothes which allow freedom of movement. Occasionally put bright colors, dots on hands, feet, to attract infant's attention.
Smiles spontaneously, sometimes immediately at birth.		
Smiles at self in mirror.	Mirror	Smile with infant.
Others		
Establishes eye contact with another person.		Hold infant so the caregiver is in infant's range of vision. Engage infant in eye contact.

CHILD BEHAVIOR	MATERIALS	EXAMPLES OF CAREGIVER STRATEGIES
Recognizes voice of parent.		
Smiles at people (social smile).		Hold infant. Smile, talk with infant.
Watches people.		Place infant where you can be seen moving about. Carry infant around to see others.
Talks (coos) to people.		Respond and initiate talking, singing with infant.
Shows longer attentiveness when involved with people.		Spend time during infant's alert times interacting with infant.
Recognizes parent visually.		
Recognizes individual people.		Provide daily care, interactions with a few persons other than parent.
Behaves differently with parent than with others.		Accept different responses.
Interacts with people.		Initiate interactions, respond; place, carry infant where infant can meet people.
Laughs.		Play with infant; laugh with infant; respond to infant's laugh.
Differentiates self from parent.		
Initiates talking to others.		Answer infant's talk.
Plays with toys.	Toys that attract infant's attention, challenge infant.	Provide toys; change toys to renew interest.

Cognitive Development

Child caregivers are teachers and they need to know the importance of infant stimulation. Neuropsychologist Jane Healy discusses brain development of an infant in her book *Your Child's Growing Mind* (1989):

> Amazingly, although the number of cells remains almost the same, brain weight can double during the first year of life . . . as stimuli seen, heard, felt and tasted are received . . . they build new physical connections . . . During the first six months active sensory messages bombard the infant brain . . . these connections where learning begins are enriched by repeated use—Every response to sights, sounds, feelings, smells, and tastes make more connections. The weight and the thinking power of the brain increase in an elaborate geometric progression. The more work the brain does, the more it becomes capable of doing.

This means that caregivers take every opportunity to teach, knowing that to increase an infant's stimulation is to increase ultimate human intelligence.

Piaget's theory of cognitive development categorizes the first four months of life as a part of the sensorimotor stage. Infants get information in this stage through their senses and motor activity. When infants interact with their environment, they are *doing* something. Infants use all their senses. With experience they refine their capacities for seeing, hearing, smelling, tasting, and touching. Moving themselves, moving others, and handling objects become coordinated with their senses. For example, when hearing a sound, infants turn their heads in the direction of the sound.

> Sensorimotor intelligence is primarily focused on action, not on classification and organization. . . . the knowledge that young infants have of objects is in terms of the sensorimotor impressions the objects leave on them and the sensory and motor adjustments the objects require. For young infants objects do not have an existence independent of their reactions to them (Anisfeld 1984, 15).*

The sensorimotor stage has been divided into six substages; the first two are evident in the first four months. In each stage the infant develops new behaviors.

In Stage One the newborn's behavior is reflexive. Infants quickly start to change their behavior from passive reactions to active searching. Each of the senses operates independently.

During Stage Two infants begin to coordinate their senses. They begin to develop hand-mouth coordination, eye coordination, and eye-ear coordination. One behavior can stimulate another; for example, a reflexively waving arm may attract the infant's attention so that the child visually focuses on his or her hand.

The caregiver uses several strategies to enhance cognitive development. Selecting items for and arranging an attention-catching environment stimulates the infant to respond in any way possible at his or her particular stage. Repeating and reinforcing the infant's behaviors pleases and stimulates the infant.

Suggestions for Implementing Curriculum

CHILD BEHAVIOR	MATERIALS	EXAMPLES OF CAREGIVER STRATEGIES
Piaget's Stages of Sensorimotor Development		
STAGE 1 (*Reflex*)		
Carries out reflexive actions—sucking, eye movements, hand and body movements.		Provide nonrestricting clothes, uncluttered crib, which allow freedom of movement.
Moves from passive to active search.	Visually attractive crib, walls next to crib, objects; occasional music, singing, talking, chimes.	Provide environment which commands attention during infant's period of alertness.

*From *Language Development from Birth to Three*, (15) by Moshe Anisfeld 1984, Hillsdale, New Jersey: Lawrence Erlbaum. Copyright by Lawrence Erlbaum. Reprinted by permission.

CHILD BEHAVIOR	MATERIALS	EXAMPLES OF CAREGIVER STRATEGIES
STAGE 2 (*Differentiation*)		
Makes small, gradual changes which come from repetition.		Provide change for infant; carry infant around, hold infant, place infant in crib. Observe, discuss, record changes.
Coordinates behaviors, e.g., a sound stimulates looking.	Face and voice, musical toy, musical mobile, rattle.	Turn on musical toy; place where infant can see it.
Puts hand, object in mouth and sucks on it.	Objects infant can grasp and which are safe to go in mouth.	Place objects in hand or within reach. Infants attempt to put *everything* in their mouths. Make sure they get only safe objects.
Moves hand, object where can see it.	Objects which infant can grasp and lift.	Provide clothes which allow freedom of movement. Place objects in hand or within reach.
Produces a pleasurable motor activity and repeats activity.		Provide time, space for repetition.
Piaget's Concept of Object Permanence*		
SENSORIMOTOR STAGES 1 AND 2		
Follows moving objects with eyes until object disappears. Looks where object has disappeared. Loses interest and turns away. Does not search for it.	Toys, objects which attract visual attention.	Place object in range of infant's vision. Allow time for infant to focus on object. Move object slowly back and forth within child's field of vision. Move object where infant cannot see it, e.g., ball which rolls behind infant.

Object or person exists when out of sight or touch.

Learning Skills/Language Development

Language is a tool one uses to communicate with oneself and with others. Crying is one way infants communicate with others. Even newborns cry in different ways depending on whether they are startled or uncomfortable.

Prelinguistic vocalizations contribute to the infant's developing ability to speak. In the first 8 weeks vocalizations are of two kinds: One category consists of vegetative sounds and includes burping, swallowing, spitting up, and the like. The other category consists of discomfort sounds and includes reflexive crying and fussing (Anisfeld 1984, 221).

Infants produce sounds as they use their mouths and throats. These sounds are the infants' "talk." At first they seem unaware of their sounds, and then gradually they begin to repeat their own sounds. Infants will talk to themselves for the pleasure of making the sounds and hearing themselves talk.

Infants use several kinds of sounds as part of their language. They produce sounds as they eat and as they play with their tongues and mouths. They use their throats, saliva, tongues, mouths, and lips to produce gurgling, squealing, smacking, and spitting noises. Gradually they produce sounds which can be classified as "cooing," which resemble vowellike sounds. A second stage of vocalization occurs between 9 and 20 weeks. "It is characterized by cooing and laughter; sustained laughter occurs at 16 weeks" (Anisfeld 1984, 222).

When infants hear someone talk to them, it stimulates them to talk. This dialogue is very important. Effective dialogue can occur when the caregiver looks at the infant while alternately listening to and answering the child's talk. The one-to-one dialogue is what stimulates the infant. Talking not directed to the infant personally is not as effective a stimulator. Adults conversing with each other in the presence of the child, or a radio or television program turned on do not involve the child in language dialogue.

Suggestions for Implementing Curriculum

The caregiver can use several strategies to enhance the infant's *language*.

1. Talk: Sounds, words, sentences, nursery rhymes, reading stories, books, and pictures with faces of many different races.
2. Sing: Humming; original songs or talking set to your own music; nursery rhymes; lullabies; songs; African drums; and bagpipe music.
3. Listen and respond: Infants will make sounds by themselves for a few months. This talk will decrease if the infants do not have someone to listen to them and to "answer" them.
4. Initiate conversation: Almost every encounter with an infant is an opportunity for conversation. Routine physical care like feeding, changing diapers, and rocking all present the necessary one-to-one situations where you and the infant are interacting. It is not necessary nor helpful to talk all the time or to be quiet all the time. The infant needs times for language and conversation and times for quiet.

CHILD BEHAVIOR	MATERIALS	EXAMPLES OF CAREGIVER STRATEGIES
Physical Components Involved in Language Communication		
Back of throat.		Observe, record infant's use of sound.
Nose.		
Mouth cavity.		Record repetitions, changes, new sounds.
Front of mouth.		Record mood of infant when infant is making longer repetitions of sounds.

CHILD BEHAVIOR	MATERIALS	EXAMPLES OF CAREGIVER STRATEGIES
Tongue.		
Lips.		
Saliva.		
Actions Involved in Language Communication		
Changes air flow: through nose; through mouth.		
Uses tongue to manipulate air flow, saliva.		
Plays with tongue—twists, turns, sticks it out, sucks on it.		
Uses saliva in various places and changes sounds: gurgle in back of throat; bubbling in center of mouth; hissing, spitting with partially closed lips and tongue.		
Initiating-Responding		
	Rattle, objects which make sounds or noises, music box, music, talking, singing	Talk, sing to infant while feeding, changing diapers and clothes, holding, carrying around, rocking. Carry on normal conversation with infant—talking, listening, silence.
Initiates making sounds.		"Answer" infant with sounds or words.
Responds vocally to another person.		Hold infant: look at infant eye-to-eye; make sounds, talk, sing to infant; listen to infant's response; talk, sing again; listen, etc.
Makes sound, repeats sound, continues practicing sound a few minutes and lengthening to longer blocks of time.		Talk with infant, show interest, look at infant.
Imitates sounds already knows.		Repeat sound infant has just made; listen to infant make sound; repeat it again, etc.
Experiments with sounds.		
Crying		
Cries apparently automatically in distress, frustration.		Rue with the infant. Respond to infant's crying immediately and consistently.
Cries differently to express hunger, discomfort, anger.		Attend to the need infant expressed by crying.
Cries to gain attention.		Find out what infant wants.

CHILD BEHAVIOR	MATERIALS	EXAMPLES OF CAREGIVER STRATEGIES
Cries less as vocalizing increases.		
Cooing		
Coos in vowellike sounds.		Imitate, respond, talk to infant.
Adds pitch.		

STUDENT ACTIVITIES

1. List the child's behaviors you see in a picture of an infant under 4 months of age (see pp. 211 and 213).
2. Observe one infant under 4 months of age. Record the infant's behavior in two five-minute sequences. Transfer the descriptions to the Developmental Profile.
3. Select toys from catalogs and newspaper ads which are stated to be appropriate for an infant under 4 months of age. Read the toy description. Match it to the category and level of development of a specific infant.
4. Select one category of the Developmental Profiles (for example, physical development). Observe a caregiver and classify the strategies (see Chapter 9) the caregiver used in that category (for example, physical support: holds hand behind infant's head and neck).
5. List five strategies which you competently use with infants from birth to 4 months.
6. List strategies you need to develop and list ways you intend to develop them.

CHAPTER REVIEW

1. In each area state a purpose for using the Developmental Profiles with infants from birth to 4 months of age.

AREA	PURPOSE
a. Physical	
b. Emotional	
c. Social	
d. Cognitive	
e. Language	

2. Describe how you get information about the infant's developmental levels.
3. List three toys or materials which can be used with infants from birth to 4 months of age. List the area(s) of development which each can enhance.

TOY/MATERIAL	AREA(S) OF DEVELOPMENT
a.	
b.	
c.	

4. State two reasons why it is helpful to the infant to have the caregiver talk to him or her.

REFERENCES

Ainsworth, Mary D. 1982. The development of infant-mother attachment. In *In the Beginning: Readings on Infancy*, ed. J. Belsky. New York: Columbia University Press.

Anisfeld, Moshe. 1984. *Language Development from Birth to Three*. Hillsdale, NJ: Lawrence Erlbaum Associates.

Bruner, Jerome S. 1968. *Processes of Cognitive Growth: Infancy*. Clark University Press.

Eisenberg, Arlene, Murkoff, Heidi E., and Hathaway, Sandee E. 1989. *What to Expect the First Year*. New York: Workman Publishing.

Healy, Jane. 1989. *Your Child's Growing Mind: A Guide to Learning and Brain Development from Birth to Adolescence*. New York: Doubleday.

Preller, M. B. 7-97. *Health Kids*. New York: K-111 Magazine Co.

11

The Child from Four to Eight Months of Age

OBJECTIVES

After completing this chapter, the child development specialist should be able to:

1. Identify and record sequences of change in the physical, emotional, social, cognitive, and language development of infants from four to eight months of age.
2. Select materials appropriate to that age-level infant's development.
3. Devise strategies appropriate to that age-level infant's development.

CHAPTER OUTLINE

   I. Materials and Activities
     A. Types of Materials
     B. Examples of Homemade Materials
  II. Caregiver Strategies to Enhance Development
     A. Developmental Profile
     B. Physical Development
     C. Emotional Development
     D. Social Development
     E. Cognitive Development
     F. Learning Skills/Language Development

CHILD DEVELOPMENT ASSOCIATE FUNCTIONAL AREAS

All CDA functional areas are integrated into the caregiver decisions and behaviors.

Use Appendix A, the Developmental Prescriptions, and Appendix B, the Developmental Profile, with each infant. Children follow a *sequence* of development. There are often ranges in the *rate* of development.

Theresa, six months old, is lying on her stomach on the floor, kicking her legs and waving her arms. She looks at a toy radio and drools. She fingers the toy radio. She chews and drools. She "sings" with the music. Ellie, the caregiver, winds up the toy radio. Theresa kicks her feet and smiles. She watches the radio and kicks her feet. Ellie smiles at Theresa and Theresa smiles back. She kicks her feet rapidly. Theresa looks at Wayne, another infant. Ellie speaks to Theresa. Theresa tries to lift herself by pushing on the floor with her arms. She turns herself around, still on her tummy. She kicks her feet and keeps trying to lift herself up onto her knees to a crawling position. She presses her feet against furniture. During this time she has turned about 180 degrees.

MATERIALS AND ACTIVITIES

Materials for this age group must be safe for the infants to mouth and hit and bang on themselves. These infants have developed some manual skills but their limited control of their arm and hand muscles causes them to be rather rough on their toys and themselves. Attention-catching toys stimulate the interest of these infants and lengthen their playtime.

Types of Materials

Foam toys   Toys safe to bang and hit
Small toys and objects to grasp   Low material and equipment to climb
Soft balls   on and over
Sound toys   Mirror
Toys safe to throw   Teething toys

Examples of Homemade Materials

BLOCKS

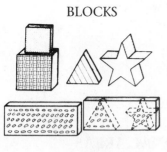

Cut foam rubber into squares, circles, rectangles, triangles, and other shapes. Cover the foam with printed fabric sewn to fit the shapes. Large shapes can be stacked as blocks.

Cut 1-inch-thick sponges into shapes. Make sure the finished pieces are a good size to handle but too big to swallow.

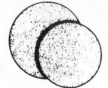

Cover foam ball with washable pattern fabric.

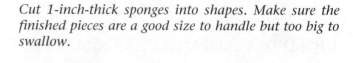

CRIB GYM

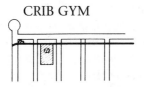

Tie a colorful 3-inch-wide strip of fabric in between the slats. Make individual cloth toys that will move when the infant pulls the ties.

RATTLES

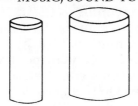

Empty and wash childproof clear plastic medicine bottles. Put in uncooked cereal—one teaspoon white, one teaspoon red (dyed in food coloring). Use sturdy glue to fasten cap tightly.

MUSIC, SOUND TOYS

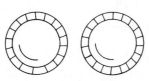

Use empty round cans with lids (oatmeal, potato chip). Put jingle bells or loose items like blocks inside. Glue the lid on security and tape around the edges. When the infant pushes and rolls it, the bells or blocks will make a noise.

POT PIE FOIL PANS

Place disposable pie pans near infant to use for mirror, for grasping and for banging. Check frequently. If sharp edge or tear develops, discard.

BEAN BAG

Sew together along three sides two double layers of 3-inch-square colorful terrycloth fabric. Turn right side out. Fill the pouch half-full with aquarium rocks which have been boiled to sanitize them. Sew the fourth side shut.

BRACELET

Sew a 4-inch length of elastic together to make a circle. Sew on several yarn pompoms. Place on wrist or ankle for infant to watch while waving arms, kicking feet.

SOCK DOLL

Use a child's sock. Make eyes, nose, and mouth with permanent nontoxic marker or sew features with embroidery thread. Sew on short yard hair. Stuff with foam or nylon scraps. Sew closed at bottom (top of sock). Caution: Make sure the "hair" is secured and cannot pull out.

CAREGIVER STRATEGIES TO ENHANCE DEVELOPMENT

Developmental Profile

Please refer to the Developmental Profile in Figure 11–1 for Theresa, a healthy infant with a C.A. of 6 months, 0 days. Theresa was observed over a two-week period and estimates were made of her skill development in the Child Behaviors from the Prescriptions in Appendix A. The profile indicates her lowest skill to be "teeth" (5 months) and her highest estimates to be "attachment" and "visual-motor control" (8 months).

Specifically, Theresa can perform behaviors in the Physical Area (I) under "muscular control" indicative of an 8-month-old, such as sitting unsupported for short times and pulling herself to a standing position. Because two upper and two lower teeth are not through her gums yet, she is estimated at the 5-month rather than the 6-month level in that area.

Theresa was estimated in the Emotional Area (II) to be a little above C.A. (7 months) in "temperament" because she has a very good attention span and persistence for her age.

Regarding the Social Area (III), Theresa is estimated at the 8-month level because she differentiates well between people and exhibits strong attachments to people she cares about.

The Cognitive Area (IV) was estimated to be at C.A., except that Theresa "misses special toys," which suggests a little higher level of "object permanence" (7 months).

Within the Learning Skills Area (V), Theresa's language development is as expected, but she exhibits better eye-hand coordination (8 months) and visual skills (seeing; 7 months) than many children her age. The skills of "eye-hand coordination," "seeing," and "hearing" are placed within the Learning Skills Area (V) although they appear within the Physical Area (I) in the Prescription. This is done because higher levels of visual and auditory perception skills, and visual-motor control are essential for pre-academic skills such as letter and number recognition, and so forth.

To summarize, Theresa is a healthy 6-month-old who exhibits average to above skills in all areas with the exception of "teeth." The caregiver should design activities for all developmental areas and focus specific tasks, for example, teething ring, chewing things, and so forth on teething. In this way, Theresa is assured of a balanced developmental program.

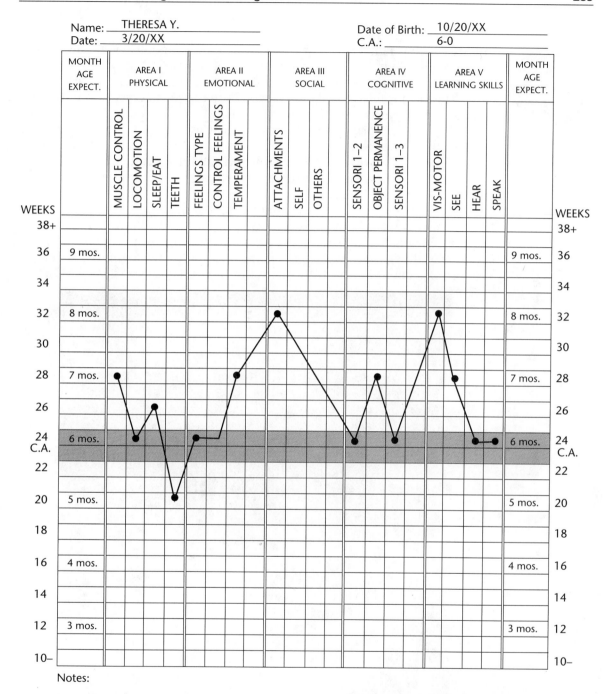

Figure 11–1 Developmental Profile, Theresa Y.

Physical Development

Infants develop rapidly during this four-month period. They are awake and alert longer. They are becoming more coordinated. They can sit when propped and are developing the ability to sit alone and can sit in a high-chair. They can roll over and may creep. They can grasp objects intentionally and move and bang them purposefully.

The head, neck, arm, chest and back muscles are used to maintain a sitting position. These are developing from the pushing and pulling and kicking and rolling the infant does. Even when the infant can sit when propped or can sit alone, these muscles tire easily, so care must be taken to allow the infant to change positions.

By the middle of the first year infants can stand on their legs. The muscles in their heads, necks, arms, chests, backs, and legs are all functioning but are not yet coordinated. With the aid of people and furniture infants can stay standing and begin to take steps. Their ankle, foot, and toe muscles develop strength and coordination with the rest of their bodies (see Figure 11–2).

Figure 11–2 The caregiver smiles, talks, and encourages the infant's movements.

Locomotion

While infants are developing some stability in relation to the force of gravity (sitting, standing), they are also attempting to move forward (locomotion).

Between the fourth and fifth months, the infant will roll from stomach to back and, by the sixth month, from back to stomach for most. Creeping is the first locomotor movement, which starts around the sixth month (refer to Physical Development in Developmental Prescription). Regan is lying on her stomach, reaching for a toy. She twists her body, pulls with her arms, and pushes with her legs. Slowly she moves forward to the toy. To accomplish this major task Regan used her head, neck, back, arm, and leg muscles to move and to lift the top part of her body up and down without tipping over. She may even get up on her hands and knees and rock. Infants can be encouraged to move at this stage by placing toys just out of reach.

By the seventh month she may actually be able to crawl about on her hands and knees and may pull herself to a standing position. By the eighth month she may put one foot in front of the other when held in a standing position.

Manipulation

Manipulation involves reaching, grasping, and releasing. In the first year infants move from reflexive to voluntarily controlled manipulation. During the first six months infants develop from erratic waving to carefully controlled reaching. They use shoulder, elbow, wrist, and hand movements to coordinate with what they see in order to reach purposefully and successfully to an object. Control of reaching is necessary to accompany the task of grasping.

Newborns grasp reflexively. For the next few months their hands will close on anything that touches them. They will grasp objects with either hand. Gradually infants begin to open their hands and use the whole hand to "palm" a toy. Around the end of the fourth month, the child will be able to move toys from one hand to the other. By the end of the first year, an infant will be able to use thumb and forefinger to assist in grasping objects (see "Hand" in Developmental Prescription).

Seeing

By the fourth month, vision has pretty much matured. When visually following a moving object (that is, tracking), the baby's eye and head movements are as coordinated as an adult's. The infant is visually attracted by colorful objects and will show preferences for specific colors. Infants at this age are also attracted by faces, shapes, and designs, and may reach for a favorite toy or object. By five months many infants will smile at themselves in a mirror.

To encourage visual stimulation, hang pictures and objects at eye level, near the floor or at crib level, where infants can observe them. Put up new pictures and mobiles frequently and provide a safety mirror to stimulate new interest.

Elementary skills of Visual Memory, Visual Discrimination, Visual Association, and Visual-Motor Control can be enhanced through simple "games."

Hearing
Infants enjoy making sounds and playing with sounds. Imitate infants' sounds back to them. Hearing and seeing and hearing and reaching are becoming more coordinated. While more is known about vision than the other senses, it is believed that all the other senses develop at about the same time as vision. Elementary Developmental Learning Skills of Auditory Discrimination, Auditory Memory, Auditory Association, and Auditory/Visual Association can be enhanced through simple "games" at this age.

Eating
Many pediatricians recommend that infants begin solid foods at about 6 months of age. Mouthing and swallowing solid foods involves a coordination of muscles different from those used for sucking. Begin solid foods when the parents request it. Use the same kind of spoon the parents use so the infants do not have to adjust to different sizes and shapes of spoons while they learn to retrieve food from a spoon and swallow the food without spitting it out or choking.

Feeding time presents an opportunity to socialize and the infant may be distracted from eating to coo and gurgle with his caregiver between eating spurts. This social exchange is very important to later social development.

By the sixth month, the infant may insist on holding the bottle or may try drinking from a cup, even though not yet being ready to give up the bottle. By the seventh month, even though it is too early to use a spoon, the infant will want to feed himself by showing resistance to being fed. It's time to let the child try it! At this time finger foods are developmentally appropriate. The experience of eating with fingers is an important one.

Teething
Infants will usually begin teething at this age. Infants react differently to teething. Sometimes an emerging tooth will cause an infant to be very fussy and irritable, while other times a new tooth just seems to appear with the infant behaving no differently at all. Teething infants often like to bite on something. They use teething rings as well as anything else they can put into their mouths. If an infant seems to be hurting, a cold teething ring or crushed ice in a clean cloth provides coldness as well as hardness for the child's gums. Teething infants may drool profusely. They may need to wear a bib all day, and it may need to be changed frequently to keep their clothes dry.

Suggestions for Implementing Curriculum

CHILD BEHAVIOR	MATERIALS	EXAMPLES OF CAREGIVER STRATEGIES
Muscular Control		
HEAD AND NECK		
Holds head up independently.		Allow infant to lift head. Keep hand near to provide support.
Holds head in midline position.	Mobiles, crib gyms.	Put some objects above center of crib
Holds head up when on back, stomach, and sitting.		Place infant where child can safely look around.
TRUNK		
Holds up chest, shoulders; arches back, hips.		Provide clothes that allow freedom for pushing up, kicking, and wriggling. Check area for safety.
Sits with support. May attempt to raise self; may fuss if left lying down with little chance to sit up.		Provide pillows, firm items to prop infant against. Hold infant in sitting position.
Leans back and forth.	Place toys within reach.	Keep area around infant free of sharp objects. Infant topples over easily.
Sits in a chair	Chair with back.	Use chair strap for safety. Let infant sit in chair, but for a short time, for the infant's muscles tire quickly.
Sits unsupported for short time.	Safe, flat sitting space.	Place in safe area where infant can sit and play or watch. Infant will tire soon and will lie down.
Pushes self to sitting position.	Flat sitting space.	Provide uncluttered space where infant can roll around and push with arms and legs to sit up alone.
LEG		
Lifts legs when on back and stomach.		Provide clothes which allow free kicking.
Rolls from stomach to back.		Place where infant can move freely and safely. Keep crib sides up. Keep hand on infant while changing diapers.
Straightens legs when standing.		Hold infant in standing position for short periods. Hold infant's sides firmly when child bounces.
Stamps feet when standing.		Firmly hold infant upright and provide flat surface for infant to push and move feet against.
Rolls from back to stomach.		Place where infant can move freely and safely. Keep crib sides up. Keep hand on infant while changing diapers

CHILD BEHAVIOR	MATERIALS	EXAMPLES OF CAREGIVER STRATEGIES
Raises to hands and knees.		Place on flat, firm surface
Stands with support.		Hold infant's sides or hands while infant is standing on flat surface.
Pulls self to standing position.		Hold infant's hands and allow infant to use own muscles to pull self up. Check furniture and shelving to make sure neither will tip over when infant pulls on them to stand up.
LOCOMOTION		
Kicks against surface to move.	Floor space, sturdy furniture.	Provide area where there is safe resistance, e.g., carpeting which helps traction, bare feet on vinyl, furniture to push against.
Rocks on hands and knees.	Blanket on floor.	Provide clear, safe area where infant can safely raise self up and rock, then lurch forward and fall on face. Praise infant for success in getting to hands and knees.
Creeps on stomach.	Blanket on floor.	Provide clear safe area where infant can creep. Place toy slightly out of reach to motivate creeping. Encourage and praise creeping.
Uses legs to pull, push self when sitting.	Floor space.	Sit a short distance from infant. Call child's name. Encourage infant to come to you. Show excitement and give praise.
ARM		
Visually directs reaching, hitting.	Crib toys, movable toys.	Provide toys that infant can reach and hit. Provide large toys infant can accurately hit against.
Throws objects.	Soft, light toys; objects.	Select toys which are light and will not go far and hit other children. Place infant in an area where child can safely throw objects.
HAND		
Grasps objects with whole hand and fingers against thumb.	Clutch ball.	Provide toys that allow infant to wrap hand around some part. Flat surfaces slip out of grasp.
Uses thumb and forefinger.	Small toys of any shape.	Make sure toys are too big to be swallowed. Infant will pick up anything, even mouth it.
Picks up object with one hand; passes it to the other hand.	Small toys of any shape.	Place toys around infant so child will use both hands. Ask for toy from one hand. Give toy to each hand.

CHILD BEHAVIOR	MATERIALS	EXAMPLES OF CAREGIVER STRATEGIES
Uses objects in both hands.	Banging toys.	Play banging game with blocks, bells, balls.
Grasps and releases objects.	Toys which fit in hand or have handles.	Play game, "Put it here." You put one toy in a pile. Infant picks up and puts down a toy in the same place.
Drops objects.	Unbreakable toys and objects, pail.	Provide space for dropping. Play game, "Drop it." Stand up and drop toy into pail. Infant stands against chair and drops toys into pail.

Seeing

Focuses on objects near and far.	Designs, pictures, wall space.	Regularly change pictures, floor-to-ceiling projects, and bulletin boards to stimulate new looking.
Distinguishes color, distance; depth perception.	Colorful objects.	Provide colorful items. Put materials with reach so infant can succeed. Respect infant's resistance to moving where child does not feel safe.
Distinguishes visually attractive objects.	Faces, designs, shapes, color in room's materials and space.	Note preferences for faces, designs, shapes. Make frequent changes.
Has visual preferences.	Favorite faces, pictures, objects.	Observe infant's reactions to pictures, objects. Provide access to favorites by displaying them again later.

Hearing

Listens to own voice.		Provide quiet space where infant can enjoy hearing own voice.
Listens to others' voices.		Place near other infants and caregivers. Direct your talking to the infant.
Looks around to locate sound.	Sounding toys, cans, bells.	Play game: shake can beside infant. Wait for child to turn around and find you shaking the can. Shake bells beside you. Wait for infant to locate the ringing bells. Talk and sing with the infant.

Sleeping

Takes a long morning nap and a long afternoon nap.		Adjust routines to fit infant's changing sleep schedule.

Eating

6 months begins solid foods.		
Eats baby food (new tongue and swallowing technique).	Mashed foods, baby spoon,	Clean up infant and self for feeding time. Check with

CHILD BEHAVIOR	MATERIALS	EXAMPLES OF CAREGIVER STRATEGIES
	heated dish, plastic-lined bib, washcloth	parent about desired food. Feed patiently while infant learns to eat from a spoon. Talk calmly. Praise infant's accomplishments. Clean up.
Drinks from cup (new tongue and swallowing technique).	Cup with special cover to control flow of milk, juice	Hold cup for infant. Tilt up and back to give infant time to swallow before next drink. Allow infant to help hold cup.
Eats at "mealtimes" with solid foods, milk, juice.	Food grinder.	Provide milk or juice in cup and solid foods at regular mealtimes to fit into the infant's sleep and play schedule.
Feeds self finger foods.	Bite-size food.	Clean up infant, self, and eating area. Provide food and time to eat it. Minimize distractions. Talk with infant, encourage infant, label food and actions. Clean up.

Teeth

First teeth emerge. 2 middle lower. 2 middle upper.	Hard teething rings: firm, safe objects to bite, cold objects to bite.	Provide objects safe for infant to bite on hard. May occasionally put ice in sterile cheesecloth for infant to bite on.

Elimination

Decreases number of times of urination and bowel movements.	Daily report form.	Check diapers frequently; may be dry longer. Record bowel movements

Emotional Development

Infants now express a wider range of emotions. Pleasure, happiness, fear, and frustration are displayed in a variety of sounds, such as gurgles, coos, wails, cries, along with physical movements like kicking rapidly, waving arms, bouncing, rocking self, and smiling.

Fear

Many infants experience what is called stranger anxiety, especially between 5 and 7 months of age. People whom the infant doesn't know or does know but does not often see may find the infant afraid of them. The infant may cry, cringe, hide, or move away. This very normal infant behavior occurs at a time when the infant is beginning to construct the idea of self as separate from others. It is important that "strangers" not feel something is "wrong" with them. A substitute caregiver may experience this infant withdrawal because the infant has established familiarity and attachment to the primary caregiver, whereas the substitute is different.

It is also during this period of time that the infant may demonstrate anxiety at being separated from mother and/or the caregiver. The infant may become nervous or distraught if the caregiver is too far away or out of sight. Take every opportunity to verbally tell the child that you will leave and will return. Introduce the substitute caregiver and explain that this person will take good care of him until you return. It is important to tell the infant when you have returned.

Temperament

Activity Level   The "high active" infant may kick and wriggle and jerk, and therefore tip over when sitting propped more often than the "low active" infant. High active infants need sitting times even though they need more caregiver assistance. On the other hand, low active children are easy to leave in a sitting position longer than may be good for their muscles because they may not fuss and move enough to tip over. These children need to be moved from sitting to lying on their stomachs, to holding, to sitting (see Figure 11–3).

Approach or Withdrawal as a Characteristic Response to a New Situation   Infants from 4 to 8 months of age are experiencing many new situations. They are introduced to solid foods and probably will be encouraged to try various vegetables, fruits, and meats. They are beginning to creep and move into room areas on their own, sometimes into areas not meant for them. Those infants who characteristically encounter newness easily may take in stride new foods

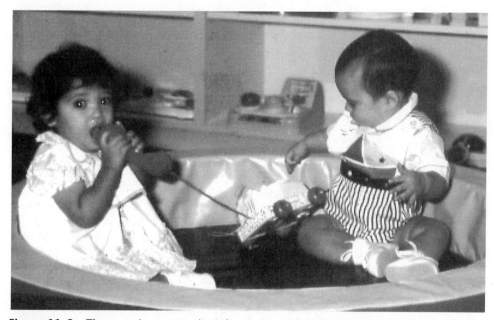

Figure 11–3   The caregiver props the infant into a sitting position for only short periods of time.

and new spaces. They will have food preferences, but the act of trying something new usually will not distress then. Those infants who characteristically hesitate or withdraw in new situations will need new experiences presented slowly. Allow time for the infant to become familiar with one kind of food before introducing a new one. Allow the infant to seek new floor spaces and gain familiarity with them; do not move the infant around from new space to new space.

Suggestions for Implementing Curriculum

CHILD BEHAVIOR	MATERIALS	EXAMPLES OF CAREGIVER STRATEGIES
Types of Emotional Feelings		
Shows pleasure in watching others.		Place infant where child can see others playing.
Shows pleasure in repetitive play.	Favorite toys.	Provide favorite toys. Share pleasure in repetitive actions e.g., clapping hands.
Shows depression.		Discuss possible causes with parent. Provide consistent loving touching, holding, playing whenever possible.
Shows fear		
of strangers.		Introduce strangers carefully. Do not let stranger hover closely. Give the infant time to become accustomed to the stranger at a distance. Use Rueing
of falling down.		When infant is standing and falling, keep area safe. Comfort when needed and then encourage infant and praise infant's standing.
Shows frustration with stimulation overload.		Provide quiet space and time for the infant. Constant visual and auditory stimulation is nerve-racking. Comfort, hold, talk softly to frustrated infant.
Shows happiness, delight, joy; humor expressed with laughs, giggles, grins.		Share laughing, giggling. Play funny games, e.g., "Touch your nose"—hold your finger by your head and slowly move it to touch the infant's nose while you say excitedly, "I'm going to touch your nose."
Shows rage.		Allow infant to kick legs, flail arms, scream and cry for a short time. Determine the cause of the rage. Reduce or eliminate the

CHILD BEHAVIOR	MATERIALS	EXAMPLES OF CAREGIVER STRATEGIES
		cause if possible. Use touching, rocking, soothing talk to help the infant calm down.
		Verbally affirm and acknowledge the infant's anger and distress. Remain calm and present soothing support.
Control of Emotions-Feelings		
Sometimes stops crying when talked to, sung to.		Talk calmly, soothingly to crying infant. Use Rueing.
Temperament		
Activity level.		List two of the infant's behaviors in each category which indicate the infant's basic style. List adjustments you need to make to help the infant cope with daily situations.
Regularity.		
Approach or withdrawal as a characteristic response to a new situation.		
Adaptability to change in routine.		
Level of sensory threshold.		
Positive or negative mood.		Follow the strategies of applying the 3A's, make eye-to-eye contact, move deliberately with purpose, talk consistently, use your senses to determine how much stimulation the child requires; hold, cuddle, and soothe.
Intensity of response.		
Distractibility.		
Persistence and attention span.		

Social Development

Infants are now developing definite and strong attachments to parents and the primary caregiver. The primary caregiver's presence, consistent care, and emotional involvement with the infant reinforce the attachment.

Infants are engaged in several new social experiences. Their developing physical skills of manipulating objects and moving themselves around contribute to their cognitive development of constructing a concept of self and not-self. During this time from 4 to 8 months of age, many infants relate more frequently with other adults and children. Their interest and mobility contribute to their initiating and responding in interactions with others (see Figure 11–4).

Ainsworth identified several social behaviors during this age range.

Phase 2:   Discriminating Social Responsiveness
                   6 months or more.
                   discriminates between familiar and unfamiliar persons.
                   Responds differently to them.
                   differential smiling, vocalization, crying.

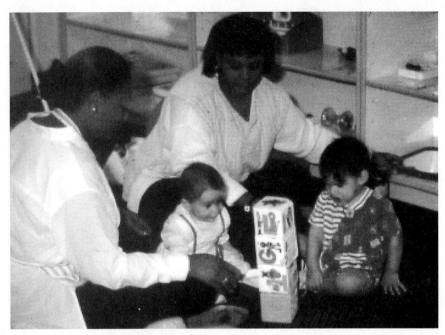

Figure 11–4   The caregiver encourages the infant to play.

Phase 3:   Active Initiative in Seeking Proximity and Contact
                  around 7 months.
                  signals intended to evoke response from mother or
                  attachment figure.
                  locomotion facilitates proximity seeking.
                  voluntary movements of hands and arms.
                  following, approaching, clinging—active contact behaviors
                  (1982, 139–41).

Suggestions for Implementing Curriculum

CHILD BEHAVIOR	MATERIALS	EXAMPLES OF CAREGIVER STRATEGIES
Attachment		
Shows strong attachment to parent.		Reinforce attachment to parent.
Differentiates response to parent.		
Shows familiarity with one specific caregiver		Assign a specific, primary caregiver to a specific infant. One caregiver can be a primary person (significant other) to several infants. Primary caregiver assumes responsibility for

CHILD BEHAVIOR	MATERIALS	EXAMPLES OF CAREGIVER STRATEGIES
		emotional involvement with the infant while providing care for the whole child.
Shows intense pleasure and frustration with person to whom attached		Accept, share pleasure; calm, soothe, stroke, sing during infant's frustration periods.
Self		
Recognizes self in mirror.	Foil, metal, or plastic shatterproof mirrors.	Provide hand mirror for the infant to see self. Provide full-size mirror for infant to see self and others.
Seeks independence in actions.		Allow infant to accomplish tasks by self when possible, e.g., creeping to toy, pulling self up.
Plays self-designed games.		Allow infant to play own game. Do not distract infant or make infant change and play your game.
Others		
Observers others.		Place the infant where child can observer other's activities.
Imitates others.		Play games with the infant. Imitate each other, e.g., open mouth wide, stick out tongue.
Recognizes children.		Allow infant to touch, "talk to" other children. Stay close so each is safe from pinching, hitting.
Plays with people.		Let older children and other adults play looking, hearing, touching games with the infant.
Seeks parent's and caregiver's attention by movement, sounds, smiles, cries.		Respond immediately and consistently to happy, sad, angry pleas for attention.
Follows parent and caregiver to be in the same room.		Arrange room so infant can see you from any place the infant is in the room.
Resists pressures from others regarding feeding, eating.		Encourage but do not force the infant to eat. Adjust the time to stop and start according to the infant's rhythm.
Acts shy with some strangers.		Hold, provide security to the infant when meeting a stranger. Allow the infant time to hear and see the stranger before the stranger touches the infant or even gets too close.

Cognitive Development

Infants in sensorimotor substage 3 are constructing the beginnings of the concept of objects separate from themselves. When an object they are watching disappears, they will visually search for it, but they will not manually search for it. When an object they are holding disappears, they will search manually for it. Their senses still strongly control their actions (see Figure 11–5). As Dr. Healy said in her book *Your Child's Growing Mind*,

> Each child must build individual networks for thinking; this development comes from within, using outside stimuli as materials for growth. A baby will give explicit clues about what kind of input is needed and let you know when it isn't interesting anymore. Babies come equipped with the "need to know"; our job is to give them love, acceptance, and the raw material or appropriate stimulation at each level of development. Your own common sense, augmented by current knowledge, is the best guide (Healy 1989).

Figure 11–5   The caregiver holds the blocks near the infant so the infant can focus on them and reach for them.

Suggestions for Implementing Curriculum

CHILD BEHAVIOR	MATERIALS	EXAMPLES OF CAREGIVER STRATEGIES
Piaget's Stages of Sensorimotor Development		
STAGE 3 (REPRODUCTION)		
Produces a motor activity, catches interest, and intentionally repeats the activity over and over.	Objects which attract attention: contrasting colors, changes in sounds, variety of textures, designs.	Watch movements the infant repeats. Waving arm may hit the crib gym; the infant may wave arm more to hit the crib gym again. Watch which movements the infant repeats. Provide materials which facilitate, e.g., new items on the crib gym.
Repeats interesting action.		The infant may pound fists on legs. Watch to see that child's actions are safe.
Develops hand-eye coordination further. Looks for object, reaches for it, and accurately touches it.	Toys.	Place blocks, dolls, balls, other toys near the infant where child can reach them.
Imitates behavior that is seen or heard.	Toy, food, body.	Initiate action; wait for infant to imitate it; repeat action, e.g., smile, open mouth.
Piaget's Concept of Object Performance		
SENSORIMOTOR STAGE 3		
Visually follows object.	Toys, bottle, objects which attract visual attention.	Show infant a toy. Play with it a minute and then hide the toy. Bring it out and play with it again. (You will not "teach" the infant to look for the toy. Enjoy playing with the infant and toy.)
Searches visually for short time when object disappears.		
Does not search manually.		
Sees part of object; looks for whole object.	Familiar toy, bottle, rattle teething ring, ball, doll.	Cover up part of object with a blanket or paper. Infant will pull object out or push off blanket, e.g., with person: play peek-a-boo.

Learning Skills/Language Development

The crying, cooing, and babbling of the infant help develop the physical mechanisms which produce speech (see Figure 11–6).

Following the cooing period there is an extended period in which infants engage in babbling. Babbling continues the diversification of sounds begun in cooing. The main difference between the two is in function. Whereas cooing seems to have the function of expressing feelings of comfort, babbling is primarily sound play (Anisfeld 1984, 221–22).

Figure 11–6   The caregiver talks and listens to the infant's new sounds.

Infants seem to produce sounds first and then "discover" them to reproduce over and over again. They experiment with these sounds and begin to
make changes in them. The difference may consist of the same sound made
from a different part of the mouth. For instance, when infants play with a
voiced sound and the tongue and saliva at the back of their mouths, they
produce a gurgle. With the same sound, tongue, and saliva at the front of
the mouth they produce a hissing or spitting sound. Infants listen to themselves and seem to enjoy their vocal play.

Babbling is playing with speech sounds. It is spontaneously produced
rather than intentionally planned. Infants in their babbling use and learn to
control their physical speech mechanisms. They babble different speech
sounds, combine them into two- and three-syllablelike sounds. They control
air flow to produce wordlike sounds and change the intensity, volume,
pitch, and rhythm of their babbling sound play.

Infants also listen to the sounds around them. When you repeat the
sound infants have just made, they may imitate your sound. This stimulation and repetition encourages their practice and the result is increased control over their language. This stimulation also helps infants begin the
two-way communication process of talking-listening-talking. They are finding that when they talk, you will listen; infants make you talk to them.
Cooing and babbling sounds are used to provide pleasure as well as to convey feelings. Conversations include pitch and volume added to strings of

sounds which seem like syllables or words. Infants imitate and initiate private and social talking.

Suggestions for Implementing Curriculum

CHILD BEHAVIOR	MATERIALS	EXAMPLES OF CAREGIVER STRATEGIES
Coos vowellike sounds for many minutes.		Respond with talk.
Babbles syllablelike sounds.		Respond with talk.
Responds to talking by cooing, babbling, smiling.		Talk directly to infant.
Imitates sounds.		Make sounds, talk, sing to infant.
Initiates sounds.		Listen and respond.
Makes vowel sounds.		
Looks for person speaking.		Place yourself so that the infant can see you when you converse together.
Looks when name is called.		Call the infant by name and talk with child.
Makes consonant sounds.		
Babbles conversation with others.		Respond with talking.
Reflects happiness, unhappiness in sounds made.		Let your voice reflect response to mood.
Babbles 2- and 3-syllable sounds.		Respond with talking.
Uses intensity, volume, pitch, rhythm.		Use normal speaking patterns and tones when talking to the infant.

STUDENT ACTIVITIES

1. Listen to the "talk" of one infant between 4 and 8 months of age. Write down the sounds you hear (they may be strings of vowels or syllables, e.g., aaaa; bababababa).
2. Observe a caregiver talking to an infant who is this age. Write down what the caregiver says and what the infant says.
3. Observe one infant from 4 to 8 months of age. Record the infant's behavior in two five-minute sequences, using narrative description. Transfer the descriptions to the Developmental Profile.
4. Examine the written records of one infant from 4 to 8 months of age. List the Wednesday nap times for eight weeks. Identify any changes in nap times.
5. Observe one infant who is creeping. Write a description of the infant's physical movements.

6. List five strategies which you competently use with infant from 4 to 8 months of age.
7. List strategies you need to develop and list ways you intend to develop them.

CHAPTER REVIEW

1. When an infant can roll from stomach to back and from back to stomach, what additional caregiver strategies are needed? Explain three.
2. Deborah, a 5-month-old, is sitting up against a pillow on the floor. She is looking at the toy she has just thrown out of her reach. She leans forward, tips over, and cries. Describe what you would do next. Explain why you would do it.
3. List three caregiver strategies that facilitate the emotional development of the infant between 4 and 8 months.
4. Describe the changes in eye-hand coordination of an infant between 4 and 8 months.

REFERENCES

Ainsworth, Mary D. 1982. The development of infant-mother attachment. In *In the Beginning: Readings on Infancy*, Jay Belsky, ed. New York: Columbia University Press.

Anisfeld, Moshe. 1984. *Language Development from Birth to Three*. Hillsdale, NJ: Lawrence Erlbaum Associates.

Healy, Jane. 1989. *Your Child's Growing Mind: A Guide to Learning and Brain Development from Birth to Adolescence*. New York: Doubleday.

12

The Child from Eight to Twelve Months of Age

OBJECTIVES

After completing this chapter, the child development specialist should be able to:

1. Identify and record sequences of change in the physical, emotional, social, cognitive, and language development of infants from 8 to 12 months of age.
2. Select materials appropriate to that age-level infant's development.
3. Devise strategies appropriate to that age-level infant's development.

CHAPTER OUTLINE

I. Materials and Activities
   A. Types of Materials
   B. Examples of Homemade Materials
II. Caregiver Strategies to Enhance Development
   A. Developmental Profile
   B. Physical Development
   C. Emotional Development
   D. Social Development
   E. Cognitive Development
   F. Learning Skills/Language Development

CHILD DEVELOPMENT ASSOCIATE FUNCTIONAL AREAS

All CDA functional areas are integrated into the caregiver decisions and behaviors.

Review Chapter 5. Use Appendix A, the Developmental Prescriptions, and Appendix B, the Developmental Profile, with each infant. Children follow a *sequence* of development. There are often ranges in the *rate* of development.

Leroy, eight months old, is sitting on the floor with several toys in front of him that Miss Virginia, the caregiver, has just placed there. He picks up a pink toy elephant, lifts it up and down in his right hand and says, "Ahh. Ah, Ah, Yah, Ahya." He picks up lock blocks, saying, "Eee, Ahh, Ahh." He throws down the blocks and then picks up blocks and twirls one in his left hand. He puts down the blocks and crawls away to another part of the room and sits up to watch a child run cars. He crawls to Miss Virginia, who pulls him up to his knees. He stares at her and says, "Ayy." He crawls to the toys, sits back, and then pulls to the train. He pulls up on his knees to the toys and pats the ball. He starts to stand up and goes back to his knees. He pushes the train and it goes forward; his eyes get big. Miss Virginia pulls him up. Leroy stands and goes up on his toes as he holds her hands. Miss Virginia picks him up and holds him in her lap a minute.

MATERIALS AND ACTIVITIES

Infants in this age range are mobile and will encounter an expanded world. All objects within reach must be safe to taste and touch and move. These infants need space as they continue to develop control of gross motor movements like crawling, standing, pulling, and throwing objects. Materials to manipulate must be small enough to grasp with the palm and fingers, as well as some items small enough for infants to pick up using their thumbs and forefingers, but not small enough for them to swallow. Attention-catching materials stimulate infants to select and use those materials (see Figure 12–1). The Celebration of Life Calendar in Chapter 9 has additional ideas you can integrate to use with this age level and share with parents.

Types of Materials

Very low materials to climb over	Stroking, textured objects
Sturdy furniture to pull self up next to and walk around	Sound toys
	Mirrors
Balls to clutch	Crayons
Stacking objects	Puppets
Nesting objects	Pictures
Pail and small objects to drop into it	1-piece puzzle

Examples of Homemade Materials

CLUTCH BALL

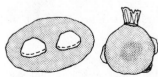

Cut a circle of colorful, washable fabric. Put polyester filling on one part of the fabric and sew around it, creating a lump. Repeat, making a second lump. Baste stitch around the edge of the circle and pull the circle almost closed. Stuff in polyester filling to pad the ball. Sew through the fabric and wind thread around the gathered end, creating a tuft of fabric.

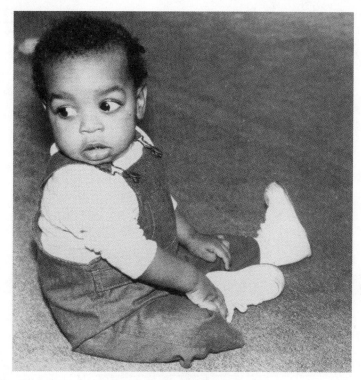

Figure 12–1 Sounds and objects attract the infant's attention.

NESTING TOYS

Select three containers of different sizes: plastic margarine tubs; cardboard tubes.

PUZZLE

Glue a picture of one simple object on a piece of thick cardboard (use white glue and water mixture to cover the whole picture and cardboard). Cut out the object, making a simple shape. Place the object into the matching frame.

PUPPET

On a child-sized white sock, use a nontoxic waterproof marker to draw a face on one side, hair on the other side.

CAREGIVER STRATEGIES TO ENHANCE DEVELOPMENT

Developmental Profile

Marcel, an eight-month-old, was observed over a three-day period and the following Developmental Profile in Figure 12–2 was the outcome. The Child

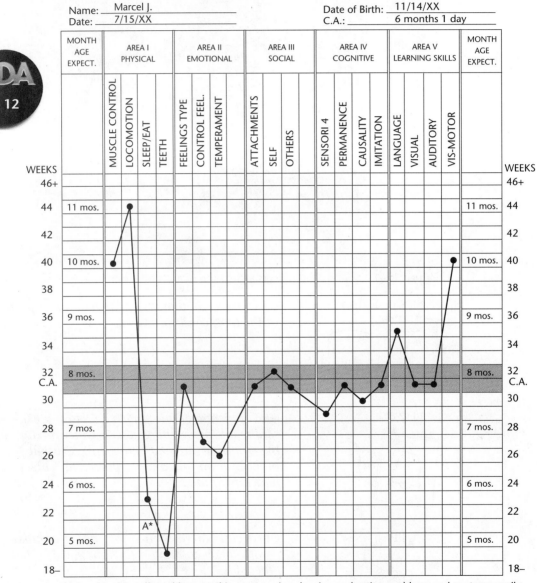

Name: Marcel J.
Date: 7/15/XX

Date of Birth: 11/14/XX
C.A.: 6 months 1 day

Notes: A* = Marcel's problems teething are causing sleeping and eating problems and are temporarily affecting temperament.

Figure 12–2   Developmental Profile, Marcel J.

Behaviors from the Prescriptions in Appendix A were used to make estimates of Marcel's skills in each major area of development. His highest estimate is 11 months in "locomotion" and the lowest estimate is 5 months in "teeth." This range may suggest significant strengths and weaknesses in Henry's development at this time.

Within the Physical Area (I), Marcel exhibits strength in his "muscle control" and "locomotion." Estimates of 10 and 11 months are based on his skills for climbing on furniture, walking, and standing without assistance. The low score in "teeth" (5 months) came about because Marcel is having pain and a hard time teething. This is also affecting his eating and sleeping patterns and his temperament (6 months).

Estimates in the Emotional Area (II) are at age in "types of feelings" (8 months), slightly below age in "control of feelings" (7 months), and "temperament" (6 months). His difficulty teething causes him to be "cranky" and lose control of his feelings more easily.

Marcel exhibits Social (III) and Cognitive (IV) development near his age level with no significant strengths or weaknesses being observed.

Within the Learning Skills Area (V), Marcel shows "language," "visual," and "auditory" skills at age expectancy. Because he can stack blocks and take off his clothes, the estimate for visual-motor control (eye-hand coordination) is above age at 10 months.

Marcel exhibits strengths in his Physical and Visual-Motor development and problems with sleeping, eating, emotional control, and temperament as the result of teething problems. While these problems are temporary, the caregiver should design activities and tasks to help with these problems, including discussing solutions with Marcel's parents and pediatrician.

Physical Development

Infants of this age are rapidly developing muscular control. They learn to sit alone. They crawl, stand with support, and walk with help. Creeping evolves into crawling, where the arms and legs are used in opposition. On hands and knees the infant first slowly moves one limb and then another. With increased control, crawling can become a very fast and efficient means of locomotion, providing the infant with a new world of possible experiences.

When infants have gained stability in standing upright, they can turn their efforts toward moving forward (walking). Ryan is standing next to a chair watching a bright toy on the floor sparkle in the sunshine. He leans toward it and reaches for it, but he cannot reach it. He takes one step away from the chair while still holding on to the chair. He still cannot reach it. He takes another step, and his hand slips off the chair. He is now on his own. He takes another step, stops, weaves, takes another step, and then falls down. Ryan is beginning to walk. His first attempts at locomotion are filled with standing, stepping, weaving, sitting or falling down, pushing himself back up to standing, and trying again. Ryan will repeat this cycle thousands of times, a process which strengthens his muscles and develops his coordination. To accomplish this task Ryan needs open floor space where he can walk without bumping into furniture or having to step on or over toys on the floor.

Many months of movement precede the actual accomplishment of walking. Shirley identified four stages:

1. An early period of stepping, in which slight forward progress is made (3–6 months).
2. A period of standing with help (6–10 months).
3. A period of walking when led (9–12 months).
4. A period of walking alone (12–15 months) (1931).

All infants proceed through these levels of locomotion, though the age will vary among infants. A formerly quiet baby may show a sudden spurt of activity during this time.

Although the baby starts practicing muscle control almost immediately, integrating reflex motor movements into controlled patterns takes a long time. The baby needs many things to see and to touch with body, mouth and hands. Initially the infant's movements seem random, but as he gets the feel of his own body in space, connections build to help the child organize his muscles around independent plans of action. Most children enjoy being stroked with a variety of pleasant textures— for example, velvet, a feather, a soft-bristled brush, or cotton—or having their limbs gently manipulated (Healy 1989).

The accomplishment of unassisted walking is the product of both maturation and appropriate experiences. No one can hasten a child's walking if the child is not ready. We can, however, facilitate a child's movements. Infants need adequate floor space where they can roll, crawl, climb, reach, stand, and walk. Caregivers should be cautious in the equipment they use. Playpens can very easily become prisons that restrict movement. Wheeled walkers can put undue strain on the infant's back, restricting the development and coordination of head, neck, arm, chest, back, leg, and foot muscles, while putting too much emphasis on leg movement.

Infants of this age use their thumb and fingers to grasp objects. Using this skill often, they continue to develop their finger muscles and eye-hand coordination. Because they do not have good control of the strength of the pinch, they may sometimes pinch another child hard enough to hurt.

Holding a finger straight, infants poke at themselves and objects around them. They push and pull and may keep repeating their actions.

These infants are developing control of their arms, so now they can clap and bring both hands to mid-body repeatedly. Their hands can grasp some objects, so they may bang objects together. They can hold crayons and make marks with them (refer to Developmental Prescription: Muscle, Hand).

These children are beginning to use each hand for different tasks. They may pick up a toy with one hand, transfer it to the other hand to hold, and then pick up another toy. They may reach out and stack one block, transfer the other toy to that hand, and stack the second block.

Infants are now beginning to be able to stroke objects, controlling their arm and hand movements so that they can touch lightly over the surface of an object. They can explore objects now by touching lightly rather than by pinching.

Infants now can hold their own bottles if they are still using one. Allow the child this independence. Help the infant grasp the cup and then allow the child to drink by him- or herself, assisting only if necessary.

An infant's soft palate is important in making sounds and later in forming words to speak. To guard against the infant's soft palate becoming mis-shapen Daniel Garliner, Speech Pathologist at his Institute for Myofunctional Therapy in Coral Gables, Florida, recommends "placing a straw in hard plastic bottles. This prevents the child from sucking too hard."

Infants now use both fingers and a spoon to eat and may use them at the same time. They are developing finger and arm control which helps in using a spoon and in picking up food with their fingers. Infants want to get the food into their mouths, and they use every way they can to ac-complish this task.

Infants use their new teeth to bite anything put into their mouths. Check toys, materials, and utensils a child uses to determine that they can with-stand biting.

Sleep patterns continue to change gradually. At this age infants take a morning and afternoon nap but have more awake time in which to be alert to play. Each infant has a personal sleep schedule. It is affected by the child's own body needs for sleep as well as by the sleep routines at home. If the infant is awakened at 5:00 A.M. to get ready to come to child care, that child may need a morning nap earlier than an infant who was allowed to sleep until 7:00 A.M.

Suggestions for Implementing Curriculum

CHILD BEHAVIOR	MATERIALS	EXAMPLES OF CAREGIVER STRATEGIES
Muscular Control		
TRUNK, LEG		
Raises self to sitting position.	Flat surface.	Keep area clear of objects which would hurt the infant if child falls on them.
Sits alone.		Provide short time to sit. Infant may tire soon.
Stands holding on to furniture or hand.	Sturdy chair, bench, table.	Remove furniture which could tip over on infant.
Stands without assistance.	Flat surface.	Allow infant to stand alone.

CHILD BEHAVIOR	MATERIALS	EXAMPLES OF CAREGIVER STRATEGIES
Sits from standing.		Keep area clear of objects which could hurt infant. Infant often falls down when trying to sit down from standing.
Squats and stands.		Watch sharp-cornered furniture.
		Pad corners as needed. Infant often stands up underneath furniture (tables) and bumps head.
LOCOMOTION		
Crawls.	Obstacle-free space.	Allow infant to crawl. Play with infant to stimulate crawling. Place toys slightly beyond reach to stimulate crawling.
Steps forward.	Obstacle-free space.	Hold infant's hand, provide furniture to lean on for support when stepping forward.
Crawls up steps.	Low 2–4 step equipment.	Allow infant to crawl up steps.
		Watch so you can assist infant's getting back down safely. Barricade any steps you do not want the infant to use.
Steps sideways.	Equipment, furniture to hold onto.	Allow infant to stand and step around furniture. Keep chairs, toys away from path.
Walks with help.	Obstacle-free area.	Hold infant's hand(s). Slowly walk around allowing infant to step and balance as he or she needs to. Infant's swaying body will give you clues for stopping and starting.
Climbs on furniture.	Low, sturdy furniture.	Infant can climb but has not learned how much space his or her body takes up so may climb into areas where the child does not fit. Watch, caution, and assist when necessary.
HAND		
Used thumb and forefinger.	Toys, dolls.	Provide objects small enough to pinch and lift.
Uses thumb and two fingers.	Toys, dolls.	Provide objects small enough to pinch and lift.
Brings both hands to middle of body.	Banging objects, pot pie pans, blocks.	Play clapping, banging games with infant. Play pat-a-cake game.

CHILD BEHAVIOR	MATERIALS	EXAMPLES OF CAREGIVER STRATEGIES
Uses finger to poke.	Pillow, ball, small box.	Provide soft objects to poke into.
		Watch carefully because infant may poke other children's face, eyes, etc.
Carries objects in hands.	Attractive objects small enough to grasp but too big to swallow.	Provide objects which can be carried.
Holds and uses pen, crayon.	Flat surface, fat felt marker, fat crayon, paper.	Provide materials and space. Demonstrate where marks go (on paper, not floor or table). Remain with infant when child is using marker or crayon. Allow child to make the kind and number of marks he or she wants to. Praise child for the interest and effort. Put materials away when child decides he or she is finished.
Reaches, touches, strokes object.	Textured objects.	Provide objects of different textures. Infants can stroke, not just grasp and pinch. Demonstrate gentle stroking. Describe the texture, e.g., "the feather is soft." Allow infant to gently stroke many objects.
Uses one hand to hold object, one hand to reach and explore.	Objects small enough to grasp.	Provide several objects at once which stimulate infant's interest.
Stacks blocks with dominant hand.	Blocks, small objects.	Allow infant to choose which hand to use in stacking objects.
Takes off clothes.	Own clothes with big buttonholes, zippers.	Infant's fingers are beginning to handle buttons, zippers. Allow infant to play with these. Infant does not understand when to undress and when to keep clothes on. Discourage undressing when you want infant to stay dressed.

Sleeping

May have trouble sleeping.	Calming music, musical toy.	Provide adequate time to spend with infant preparing for sleep. Rock, sing, talk, stroke.
		Respond immediately if infant awakens during regular sleep time. Rub child's back, talk quietly as you attempt to help infant go to sleep again.

CHILD BEHAVIOR	MATERIALS	EXAMPLES OF CAREGIVER STRATEGIES
Takes morning nap and afternoon nap.	Quiet, dim, clean sleeping space.	Determine infant's preferences for going to sleep. Feed, hold and rock, rub infant's back, hum and sing to help get the infant to sleep.
Seeks parent or caregiver presence.		Primary caregiver should prepare infant for sleep, put infant to bed, respond if sleep is interrupted, and get infant up from nap.
Eating		
Holds bottle.	Bottle.	Allow infant to hold bottle while you hold infant.
Holds cup.	Cup with special cover.	Allow infant to hold own cup.
		Assist when necessary, e.g., the spout is at infants nose rather than mouth.
Holds and uses spoon.	Child-size spoon.	Provide food which can fit on spoon. Allow infant to use spoon to feed self. Assist when necessary with difficult food. Praise infants efforts and successes. Child will hold spoon in one hand and eat with fingers of other hand.
Uses fingers to eat most food.	Finger food.	Wash hands and face *before* eating.
		Allow infant to use fingers to pick up food. Wash hands, face, chair, and whole area after eating time.
Starts establishing food preferences.		Identify and record infant's food likes and dislikes. Plan a balanced diet for child emphasizing foods child likes. Do not force foods child does not like.
May eat less.		Do not force eating. Infant's body may need less. Children make adjustments in the amount they eat.
		Be sure children have food available they like so they can make choices about *amount* rather than *kinds* of foods.
Teeth		
Begins to get teeth.	Teething ring, cold hard objects to bite, bib.	Provide objects safe to bite. Cold soothes the gums. Change bib as needed since drooling increases.

Emotional Development

Positive interactions with caregivers help infants develop good feelings about themselves. Infants express their happiness in many ways. They also express their anxiety and fears.

Out of fear and/or uncertainty an infant may regress temporarily to an earlier stage. Understanding this regression helps the caregiver to be aware that the child may need more reassurance than is given to a younger infant. The caregiver should be alert and notice when the child is feeling confident once more and able to function at age level again.

At this age infants are developing preferences. Providing toys they like not only adds to their pleasure in playing with the toys but also enhances their feelings of asserting some control over their world.

Developing physical skills make infants more independent in feeding and dressing themselves. Allowing them to accomplish as many tasks as possible on their own helps them strengthen their sense of independence.

External influences like a verbal "no" or a firm look may sometimes cause infants to limit or change their behavior. Follow up your restrictive words or looks with an explanation. For example, when an infant throws food on the floor, the caregiver can say, "No. You need the carrots up here in your dish. Let's see you put a carrot in your mouth." Sometimes infants will stop their own negative action. You may see them pick up food or a toy, start to throw, and then stop their arm movement and put the object down carefully. This early self-restriction may be caused by distraction rather than self-control. Nevertheless, praise such actions to reinforce acceptable behavior.

As soon as the child has minimal verbal skills, Positive Perspective and applying the 3A's will elicit positive emotions. Remember that the most powerful way to promote positive feelings is to reward appropriate behavior and remove reward from behavior and reactions that are unwanted. Removing attention for negative behavior works better than drawing attention to it. Be sure to trust the child's motives. Children are doing the best they can at all times.

The temperaments of infants produce varying responses to experiences. The high active infant who is crawling will spend much time and energy trying to crawl wherever you allow the child to go. His or her whole body is moving and developing physically. These children move into new areas and may keep changing their place in the environment frequently. The changing environment in turn stimulates their senses and their involvement with the world. The low active infant who is crawling will initiate crawling but move around less than a high active infant. These children may have the ability to move their whole bodies but may choose instead to use their eyes and hands and arms to search and interact in their space (see Figure 12–3).

Some infants approach new situations openly. When new solid foods and finger foods are introduced, they try them. They accept and eat many of the foods, and those they reject, they reject with minimal fussing. Other infants are hesitant or resist new situations. Each new food causes these infants to

Figure 12–3   Crawling enables the infant to explore a wide new world.

pull back and at first reject the new food. With encouragement, these infants may taste the new food and then determine whether they like it or not. Sometimes they so actively resist a new food that it is difficult to get them to eat enough of it to develop an acceptance of it.

Variation in intensity of response often shows up when infants are pulling themselves up and falling down. Falling down, whether toppling forward or sitting down hard on their bottoms, always surprises infants. It is also sometimes painful. One infant will scream and cry loudly. Another may cry quietly or whimper or perhaps look surprised and upset but will not verbalize his or her discomfort.

Persistence at trying to stand upright and step forward leads toward walking. Very persistent infants will try again and again to stand or step. Falling down becomes a deterrent only after many tries. Other infants persist only a few times, then stop their efforts and change to some new task or interest.

Suggestions for Implementing Curriculum

CHILD BEHAVIOR	MATERIALS	EXAMPLES OF CAREGIVER STRATEGIES
Types of Emotions-Feelings		
Shows happiness, joy, pleasure.		Share infant's feelings. Reflect back smile, positive tone of voice; hug, pat.

CHILD BEHAVIOR	MATERIALS	EXAMPLES OF CAREGIVER STRATEGIES
Shows anxiety.		Use calm, quiet talking, singing. Cuddle, stroke. Remove from situation if necessary.
Shows fear.		Determine and remove cause of fear if possible. Use calm, quiet talking, singing. Cuddle, stroke.
Shows anger, frustration; has tantrums.		Determine and remove cause if possible. Use calm talking, may sometimes hold and soothe infant.
		Help infant start a new activity. May sometimes ignore a tantrum.
Rejects items, situations.		Allow infant to make choices. Figure out alternative choices for situations he really needs, e.g., time or place choices.
Develops preferences with toys, people.		Identify and record infant's preferences. Make sure these toys are available frequently.
Shows independence—helps with feeding and dressing self.	Cup, spoon, clothes child can manipulate.	Allow infant to help feed and dress self. This takes much time and patience. Lengthen eating time to adjust to self-feeding skills.
Shows affection.		Accept and return affection with smile, hug, cuddle.
Begins developing self-esteem.		Provide positive affirmation of infant through your tone of voice, looks, touch.
Control of Emotions-Feelings		
Begins to learn to obey "No."		Use "No" sparingly so infants can determine important situations when they must control their behavior. Use firm, not angry, voice. Use firm, not smiling, look on face.
Sometimes inhibits own behavior.		Praise infant for self-control; e.g., infant raised arm to throw book and then put it down on table.
Obeys commands: No-No; Stop.		Use commands sparingly. Praise infants when they obey.
Temperament		
Activity level.		List two of the infant's behaviors in each category which indicate the infant's basic style.
Approach or withdrawal as a characteristic response to a new situation.		List adjustments you need to make to help the infant cope with daily situations.

CHILD BEHAVIOR	MATERIALS	EXAMPLES OF CAREGIVER STRATEGIES
Adaptability to change routine.		
Level of sensory threshold.		
Positive or negative mood.		
Intensity of response.		
Distractibility.		
Persistence and attention span.		

Social Development

Interactions with others are increasing. The mobility infants now have enables them to encounter different people and to move away from them. These infants initiate interactions with others and respond to others' interactions with them (see Figure 12–4).

The infant's egocentric perspective is evident. These infants do not clearly separate others' desires and needs from their own. Therefore, they often do not consider or respond to someone else's requests. They are very possessive of materials and people. Such materials and people still seem part of the infant, not completely separate, and thus they seem to belong to the infant.

The caregiver is familiar to the infant and fosters a sense of security. The infant therefore tries to keep the caregiver in sight, reinforcing his or her feelings of security.

Figure 12–4 The crawling infant encounters other children.

Suggestions for Implementing Curriculum

CHILD BEHAVIOR	MATERIALS	EXAMPLES OF CAREGIVER STRATEGIES
Others		
Initiates interactions with others.		Respond to infant's behavior. Talk, play with infant. Allow infant access to other children and adults.
Responds.		Initiate talking and playing with infant.
May fear strangers.		Keep strangers from forcing themselves on infant, who may not want to be held by stranger.
Keeps parent or caregiver in sight.		Allow infant to follow you around.
		Arrange room so infant can see you from different areas of the room.
Initiates play.		Respond and play infant's game, e.g., pat-a-cake.
Becomes assertive; initiates action to fill needs.		Encourage infant's assertiveness.
		Observe to determine whether infant is getting aggressive and will need cautions.
Wants own pleasure; may not consider others.		Verbalize limits and help infant choose other activities, materials.
Initiates play.		Play games with infant, e.g., "Can you do this?" Wave hand, clap hands, etc.
Is possessive of people.		Verbally assure infant you will be here and will come back to talk, play with infant again.
Is possessive of materials.	Many toys.	Provide enough toys and materials so infant does not need to share.
May become shy, clinging.		Hold, hug, pat; allow infant to remain close; verbally assure infant you are here.
May demand attention.		Provide positive verbal attention even though you may be busy with another child.

Cognitive Development

Assimilation and accommodation begin to operate independently. Infants of this age are beginning to separate their thinking about what they want to accomplish from how they can accomplish it.

The establishment of object permanence is the major development during this age range. The infants remember events, people, and objects for an increasingly longer period of time. Awareness of object permanence forms the basis for rapid development of representations in play and language.

These infants are constructing a concept of self separate from all other entities. People and toys will become real entities which continue to exist even when the infants cannot see them (see Figure 12–5). With this concept, infants now actively search visually and manually for people or objects which are no longer visible. These infants are mentally constructing a representation of the person or object. This mental representation of the real entity forms the foundation for increasingly complex forms of representation. Along with thinking about other people as separate from themselves, these infants also begin to determine that others can cause actions. They will incorporate others' actions into their own play.

At this stage infants imitate people and things that are not present. They have established sufficient auditory and visual Developmental Learning Skills to remember and reproduce things they have seen and heard: ". . . early imitation serves a learning function, that is, infants imitate to advance their comprehension and mastery of behaviors that interest them" (Anisfeld 1984, 44).

Figure 12–5 Other people and toys are beginning to be perceived as "not self" by the developing infant.

Suggestions for Implementing Curriculum

CHILD BEHAVIOR	MATERIALS	EXAMPLES OF CAREGIVER STRATEGIES
Piaget's Stages of Sensorimotor Development		
STAGE 4 (coordination)		
Differentiates goals. Can focus on reaching and focus on toy.	Toys, visually attractive objects.	Place objects near infant.
Piaget's Concept of Object Permanence		
Establishes object permanence; object exists when it is no longer visible; child seeks toy that rolls behind box.		Play hiding games, e.g., hide the doll under the blanket; place the block behind you.
Causality		
Learns that others cause actions.		Verbalize caregiver's own actions, e.g., "I put the ball behind me."
Imitation and play		
Imitates other's actions; uses actions as play.		Introduce new copy games. Allow time and space for infant to play.

Learning Skills/Language Development

Infants at this age use combinations of sounds, babbling, and words to converse with themselves and others (Wilson 1989). "Just as the sensorimotor exploration of objects lays the groundwork for object representation, so the sensorimotor exploration of speech lays the groundwork for speech representation" (Anisfeld 1984, 224).

Newborns can distinguish frequency and pitch, but finer discriminations aren't possible until about 1 year. Sounds from the environment, music, and human speech are all necessary for a well-balanced auditory diet—perhaps even before birth. Soothing, pleasant and interesting sounds inspire curiosity and a receptive attitude toward language. A noisy and confusing environment can be detrimental to development (Healy 1989).

Anisfeld identified levels of meaning, characterizing the first level as presymbolic uses of words. "The early words have a sign character. . . . They are *context bound*" (1984, 67). Infants learn to associate a word with a particular object or action. They respond to the word in that context but cannot identify it in other contexts. For example, each day the caregiver says "Sit in your chair" as she gets the infants ready for lunch. When told to "sit in your chair," Beverly looks at her chair. She does not look at other chairs around the room. "Chair" relates to a specific chair, not to a class of objects called "chairs." ". . . [C]hildren's early words are nonsymbolic because they function primarily as responses to specific stimulus contexts" (Anisfeld 1984, 69). An infant says the word in association with the context in which it was learned: ". . . the context-boundness of the first level results from a conceptual limitation. The child does not automatically conceive of words as independent of the specific contexts of their use" (Anisfeld 1984, 70).

Reading aloud to infants facilitates their language development. Linda Lamme recommends in *Growing Up Reading* that

> Pointing to things in pictures and labeling them orally is especially important in the first year when your infant, though not yet talking, is acquiring so much language. Relate what is in the book to your infant's experience. "You have a ball just like that one!" Repetition is important also. After seeing a page several times, your infant will begin to recognize the pictures. You'll quickly come to realize your infant has distinct book preferences.
>
> The last guideline is: The earlier you begin to read aloud, the better. If your child can become used to having stories read aloud before he or she starts walking, reading-aloud sessions can be sustained during those mobile, early walking times. Children who are learning to walk have a hard time sitting still to listen to a story if they have not previously become hooked on book reading (1985, 51).

Scribbling is related to the language/reading/writing processes which the infant is developing. In her earlier work on infants, *Growing Up Writing*, Lamme (1984)

> Well before his first birthday, your child is ready to make marks on paper or chalkboard. Those first marks will be random scribbles. Your child won't even be watching as he is making the mark and will not see the connection between the mark on paper and the writing tool in his hand. The first stage of development is called "uncontrolled scribbling."
>
> The outstanding feature of these early writing attempts is that they are more than random marks; they represent your child's intentions to create something. Scribbling has been termed "gesturing with a pencil." The role of scribbling in writing development has been compared with babbling in oral language development. In each case, there is probably some random sound or scribble made but, in both cases, your child is intending to communicate (1984, 38).

Suggestions for Implementing Curriculum

CHILD BEHAVIOR	MATERIALS	EXAMPLES OF CAREGIVER STRATEGIES
Babbles.		Respond with talk.
Shouts.		Respond to infant's feelings.

CHILD BEHAVIOR	MATERIALS	EXAMPLES OF CAREGIVER STRATEGIES
Labels object sounds.	Bell, rattle.	Name important objects. Use one word. Then use in a sentence, e.g., "Bell" (while pointing to it). "Ramon has a bell."
Uses names: Mama, Dada.		Reinforce by talking about Mama and Dada.
Responds to familiar sounds.		Provide familiar music, routine changes. Acknowledge infant's response, e.g., "Tasha heard the spoons being put on the table."
Responds to familiar words.		Frequently use names or labels which infant is learning, e.g., ball, shoe, coat.
Responds to own name.		Use infant's name when you start talking with that child.
Makes sounds which reflect emotions.		Respond to the infant's message about how he or she feels. Name the emotions, e.g., "Garrett is angry."
Repeats syllables, words, e.g., bye-bye.		Label frequent behaviors and respond to infant's use, e.g., say "bye-bye" and wave; repeat occasionally.
Makes sounds like conversation.		Respond verbally to infant's "conversation," e.g., "Holly is talking to her truck."
Repeats, practices word over and over.		Allow infant to play with words. Respond and praise occasionally.
Connects words with objects, e.g., says "kitty"—points to kitty.	Familiar toys, objects.	Point or touch objects you verbally label. Word is representing that particular object.
Chooses books.	Picture books of familiar objects.	Point to picture of object and say name of object. Repeat often.
Scribbles randomly.	Paper, markers.	Provide writing space and materials.

STUDENT ACTIVITIES

1. Observe one infant who is walking with support. Identify the following:
    a. what infant held onto for support.
    b. where infant walked.
    c. what you think caused infant to sit or fall down (lost balance, got tired, lost interest, wanted to get somewhere else fast).

2. Use narrative description to record your observations of one caregiver for five minutes. Then categorize the caregiver's behavior which relate to social development.

INITIATING BEHAVIOR		RESPONDING BEHAVIORS	
Caregiver Behavior	Infant's Response	Infant's Initiating Behavior	Caregiver's Response

3. Observe one infant between 8 and 12 months of age. Record the infant's behavior in two five-minute sequences using narrative description. Transfer the descriptions to the Developmental Profile.
4. List five strategies that you competently use with infants between 8 and 12 months of age.
5. List strategies you need to develop and list ways you intend to develop them.

CHAPTER REVIEW

1. Why is sharing difficult for the infant between 8 and 12 months of age?
2. List five strategies you can use to facilitate the physical development of an infant in this age range; use this format:

CAREGIVER STRATEGY	SPECIFIC PHYSICAL DEVELOPMENT
1.	
2.	
3.	
4.	
5.	

3. An 11-month-old is responding to labels of objects. Describe a game you can play with this child to stimulate the child's understanding and use of language.
4. Identify four ways an infant in this age range asserts independence.

REFERENCES

Anisfeld, Moshe. 1984. *Language Development from Birth to Three.* Hillsdale, NJ: Lawrence Erlbaum Associates.

Healy, Jane. 1989. Your Child's Growing Mind: *A Guide to Learning and Brain Development from Birth to Adolescence.* New York: Doubleday.

Lamme, Linda Leonard. 1984. *Growing Up Writing*. Washington, DC: Acropolis Books Ltd.

Lamme, Linda Leonard, 1985. *Growing Up Reading*. Washington, DC: Acropolis Books Ltd.

Shirley, M. M. 1931. The first two years: A study of twenty-five babies. *Postural and Locomotor Development*, Volume 1. Minneapolis: University of Minnesota Press.

Wilson, L. C. 1989. Sounding off! *Pre-K Today* 3(6): 51–53.

13

The Child from Twelve to Eighteen Months of Age

OBJECTIVES

After completing this chapter, the child development specialist should be able to:

1. Identify and record sequences of change in the physical, emotional, social, cognitive, and language development of toddlers between 12 and 18 months of age.
2. Select materials appropriate to that age-level toddler's development.
3. Devise strategies appropriate to that age-level toddler's development.

CHAPTER OUTLINE

    A. Caregivers of Toddlers
    B. The Toddler
 I. Materials and Activities
    A. Types of Materials
    B. Examples of Homemade Materials
II. Caregiver Strategies to Enhance Development
    A. Developmental Profile
    B. Physical Development
    C. Emotional Development
    D. Social Development
    E. Cognitive Development
    F. Learning Skills/Language Development

CHILD DEVELOPMENT ASSOCIATE FUNCTIONAL AREAS

All CDA functional areas are integrated into the caregiver decisions and behaviors.

Review Chapter 5. Use Appendix A, the Developmental Prescriptions, and Appendix B, the Developmental Profile, with each child. Children follow a sequence of development. There are often ranges in the rate of development.

Caregivers of Toddlers

Caregivers or teachers who are in charge of toddler programs strive to be

- empowered facilitators who structure environments to minimize conflicts and maximize explorations.
- practiced in the 3A's of Child Care—Attention, Approval, and Affection.
- skillful, patient observers who help with problem solving and promote positive propaganda.
- organized and imaginative.
- knowledgeable in Toddler Development so that they may understand toddlers' daily struggles and enjoy their daily triumphs.
- consistent, gentle and firm natured.
- easily amused.
- genuinely fond of toddlers (Douville-Watson 1979).

The Toddler

Andrea, 15 months old, stands looking around. She walks over to 2-year-old Jenny who is sitting on the sofa. She stands between Jenny's legs and bounces up and down to Hokey Pokey music from the record player. Andrea and Jenny dance around. Jenny lies down on the floor and Andrea crawls on top of her. Jenny moves and Andrea follows. They both lie quietly for a minute. Andrea walks to the toys. She picks up a toy plastic milk bottle and lifts it to her mouth to drink. She sits down and puts three lock blocks in the bottle. Allen, the caregiver, says, "Shake it, Andrea." She shakes the bottle, and it makes a noise. She shakes it again. She puts a pail over her head and walks around peeking under the edge of the pail and "talking." Andrea climbs into a child's rocking chair, turns around to sit down, and starts rocking. She "talks" and rocks and then climbs out of the chair and walks around, following Allen.

Toddlers solve problems on a physical level. Watch toddlers at play for just 5 minutes and you will see them walk (which looks like wandering), climb, carry things around, drop things, and continually dump whatever they can find. These large-muscle activities are not done to irritate adults—they are the legitimate activity of toddlers. Piaget calls this the sensorimotor stage of development (1952, 1954), (Gonzalez-Mena 1986).

MATERIALS AND ACTIVITIES

Walking is a major development for toddlers at this age. They are fascinated with toys to pull or push as they toddle around (see Figure 13–1). They climb over objects. They may ride wheeled toys. They grasp and throw and drop objects again and again. They are moving into imaginative play and need materials that can facilitate their play.

Figure 13–1   Toddlers need toys and space that encourage walking, jumping, and other physical activities.

Types of Materials

Pull toys
Push toys
Trucks, cars
Low, riding wheel toys
Low, 3-step stairs to climb
Blocks
Pail with objects to put in and take out
Water and sand toys and area

Soft objects to throw
Mirrors
Dolls
Puppets
Puzzles
Picture books and cards
Paper, nontoxic markers, crayons
Audio records and tapes

Examples of Homemade Materials

The Celebration of Life Calendar can add suggestions for classroom themes.

PULL TOY

Use plain or painted empty spools. Thread and knot spools on a length of clothesline rope.

SOUND/SIGHT BOTTLE

Use a clear plastic liter bottle (soft drink). Wash it thoroughly and allow to dry inside. Put inside material or objects which will make noise (sand, wooden or plastic blocks, metal bottle caps). Add confetti for color interest. Screw on bottle cap and glue securely. Tape over rough edges of cap.

TOSS BOX

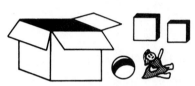

Collect several small, soft toys and place in a cardboard box. Show child how to take out objects, stand away from the box, and throw the objects into the box. Paint the inside of the box to attract the child's attention as a "target."

EXPLORING TUBS

Place one solid object in a margarine tub. Put lid on. When children shake it, they hear a noise. Encourage the children to take off lid to discover what is inside. Put lid back on. Have several tubs available with different objects inside, e.g., plastic clothes pins, large wooden thread spools.

PICTURE CARD

Use a square of 2- or 3-ply cardboard. Place a photograph of a child on the cardboard and cover the whole square (front, back, and sides) with contact paper or laminating film. Also use colorful pictures cut from magazines. Select pictures which are simple and show one object, e.g., car, cat, flower, bird. Select pictures of objects the child is familiar with.

CLOTHING FRAME BOARD

Cover wood 12" x 12" x 2" with fabric. Glue one piece of fabric to each side of wooden frame with fabric opening at center of frame. Sew buttons on one side at center, buttonholes on other side. Or put on large snaps. Or sew in large-toothed zipper.

CAREGIVER STRATEGIES TO ENHANCE DEVELOPMENT

Developmental Profile

Andrea's Developmental Profile is presented in Figure 13–2. She was observed over a two-week period on the child behaviors listed in the Developmental Prescription (Appendix A), and is 3 months below C.A. in Social Development, "self," and 3 months above expectations in "others." Overall, Andrea shows healthy, normal development.

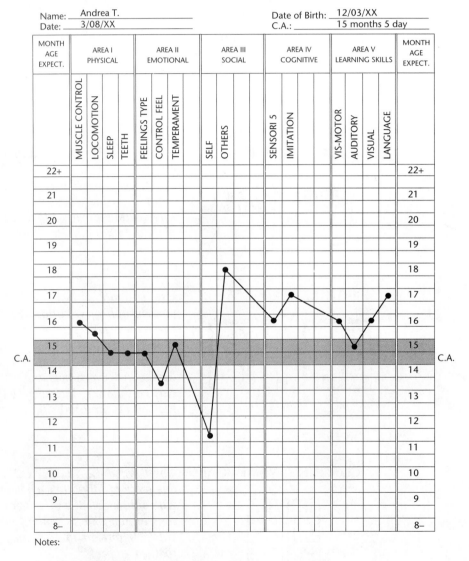

Figure 13–2 Developmental Profile, Andrea T.

In terms of the Physical Area (I) and the Emotional Area (II), Andrea is estimated to be within expected behavior. However, she seems to not focus attention on herself or her needs, and is much more concerned about gaining attention and the needs of others. As a result, she is estimated to be below age in "self" development (12 months), and above age in "others" (18 months).

The minor problem of her not considering her needs and being overly concerned about others might be related to a slightly higher "imitation" estimate in Cognitive Development (IV) and "language" (sounds) in Learning Skills (V) (17 months). Visual and auditory learning skills are slightly advanced.

In general, Andrea exhibits expected development except for the problems in not considering herself and needing other people to be happy for her to feel secure.

The caregiver should design tasks and activities using Materials and Caregiver Strategies to help Andrea feel special and make her needs more important than the needs of others when it is appropriate. Adding these activities to ones designed for all other areas will ensure a balanced program for Andrea.

Physical Development

They toddle about their own environment not necessarily to get from one part of it to another, but because they are up on their feet and it is satisfying to practice walking. Chairs become things to push and carry because pushing and carrying are also newly obtained skills a toddler delights in practicing. Chairs can also be climbed into and later, if the chairs are an appropriate size, two-year-olds may discover they can back up to them and sit down, apparently an exciting achievement when you are just learning how to do it (Brickmeyer 1978).

Erickson included toddlers in his second stage of development, Autonomy (1963). Piaget's "ages and stages" are outlined for toddlers between twelve and eighteen months: Stage 5 (Twelve to Eighteen Months). This stage marks the onset of experimentation. The child begins deliberately to invent new actions she has never tried before and to explore the novel and unique features of objects. She tries to find what will happen if she uses objects in new ways. She combines objects with other objects to create new ways of doing things and uses trial-and-error approaches to discover new solutions to problems.

Piaget labeled young children's need to gather information by shaking, grasping, listening, feeling, and tasting as "schematic." This schemata of information gathering continues throughout life (see Figure 13–3).

Toddlers learn with their whole bodies—not just their heads. They learn more through their hands than they do through their ears. They learn by doing, not only by just thinking. They learn by touching, mouthing, and trying out, not by being told . . .

Toddlers can become absorbed in discovering the world around them. If you are convinced that toddlers have short attention spans, just watch them with

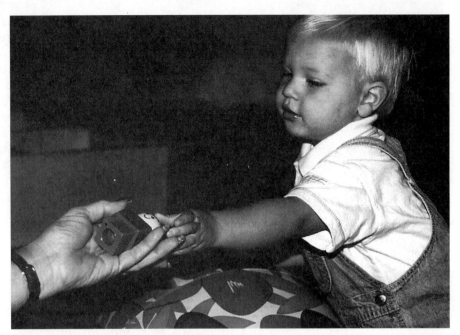

Figure 13–3 Grasping is a way to gather information.

running water and a piece of soap. Hand washing can become the main activity of the morning! Eating is another major activity, as many toddlers switch from neat to very messy in a short time. Filling and dumping are great skills to use with food or water. Of course, toddlers do put things in as part of the process, but they are more likely to end with dumping! (Gonzalez-Mena 1986)

Ambulator fourteen-month-olds like to combine emptying with transporting things. They find favorite spots or hiding places: under the bed, in the wastebasket, or even in the sink and toilet bowl. Because emptying can be a nuisance, parents put things "off limits" or temporarily out of reach. A better way to counteract a toddler's emptying game is to provide baskets that can be filled and emptied endlessly (Caplan and Caplan 1980).

An expanding world opens up to toddlers as they become mobile. They walk, lurch, run, fall, bump into things, and keep persisting in moving around in their world. They are unstable when they walk. They may topple over from stepping on an object or by leaning too far or walking too fast. They are learning to make adjustments so that they can remain upright. Their muscles are developing and coordinating gradually so in the next months their walking will become more stable (Wilson 1988).

Suggestions for Implementing Curriculum

CHILD BEHAVIOR	MATERIALS	EXAMPLES OF CAREGIVER STRATEGIES
Muscular Control		
TRUNK		
Shows high energy, is active, moves from one activity to another.		Provide a variety of materials and activities so the child can change activities and play objects often. These toddlers frequently do not "make" anything or complete an activity. Schedule clean-up and help put away toys at end of playtime.
Raises self to standing.	Sturdy furniture to grasp; flat surface.	Provide space where toddlers can stand up safely. Caution them about standing up under furniture.
LOCOMOTION		
May prefer crawling to walking.		Allow toddler to crawl when child wants to. It is faster than walking when the child is just beginning to walk.
Walks alone.		Allow toddler to walk alone when child wants to. Provide a hand to hold onto when child seeks help.
Climbs up stairs with help.	Stairs.	Provide handrail or your hand to assist child with balance.
Climbs down stairs with help.	Stairs.	Provide handrail *and* your hand. Balance is still poor when walking down stairs.
Climbs over objects.	Low, sturdy furniture, equipment, boxes.	Provide low climbing equipment, furniture, e.g., stuffed footstool, sturdy cardboard boxes, covered foam incline.
HAND		
Uses thumb against fingers.	Small toys, crayons, pens.	Provide materials toddler can grasp.
Shows hand preference.		Allow toddler to use whichever hand he or she chooses.
Points with finger.	Pictures, books, objects.	Play pointing game, e.g., open picture book—"Point to the tree."
Carries, exchanges objects in hands.	Small toys.	Ask toddler to carry toys to another part of the room. Hand toddler another toy to carry.
Throws objects.	Soft, small objects.	Provide a place and target where toddler can throw objects.
Rolls and catches objects.	Large, small balls.	Sit on floor with legs open and outstretched and roll ball back and forth with toddler.

CHILD BEHAVIOR	MATERIALS	EXAMPLES OF CAREGIVER STRATEGIES
EYE-HAND COORDINATION		
Reaches and grasps accurately.	Toys, objects which hand can grasp.	Provide toys and objects in places where toddler can safely reach, grasp, lift, and move them.
Scribbles.	Paper, nontoxic markers, crayons.	Provide flat surface for toddler to use paper and marker or pen. Admire and praise the marks the toddler makes.
Helps in dressing, undressing.	Buttons, snaps, zipper cards, books, clothing frame board, large dolls with clothes.	Allow toddler to do as much as possible. Assist when toddler needs help.
Seeing		
Watches people, objects, actions.	Space with few visual obstructions.	Provide space where people are visible to toddler. Allow toddler to choose what to watch.
Bends, looks from different directions.		Place toys, materials in different places. Allow toddler to move materials. Toddler may look up from the floor, look down between legs, look sideways under a table.
Visually scans area around.		Allow toddler to look around. Toddler may gaze around for periods of time. Provide interesting visual stimuli.
Visually searches.		Toddler may look for specific object, person. Assist if child non-verbally or verbally requests your help.
Sleeping		
Begins to move from morning and afternoon nap to afternoon nap. May fall asleep during lunch.		Adjust eating and nap schedule so toddler does not miss lunch.
Eating		
Eats three meals.		Determine mealtime. Make adjustments for individual children as necessary.
Feeds self: uses cup, spoon, and fingers.	Food, plate, cup, spoon.	Allow toddler to feed self as much as possible. Assist when necessary.

CHILD BEHAVIOR	MATERIALS	EXAMPLES OF CAREGIVER STRATEGIES
Expresses food likes and dislikes.		Record food preferences. Provide foods child likes. Introduce new foods gradually. Combine foods child does not like with ones child does like to provide needed nutrition.
May eat less food.		Do not force eating. Make food as attractive as possible.

Emotional Development

Toddlers seek both dependence and independence. most fears at this stage are learned from adults. This is why caregivers must take an inventory of themselves and recognize what emotional messages they are conveying to an impressionable toddler. It is the continued responsibility of the caregiver to promote a positive learning environment.

For many tasks toddlers need help. The caregiver can provide toddlers with emotional strength and security, accepting toddlers' very real dependence (Wilson 1987). Toddlers are also trying to become independent. Emotionally they need support that affirms their importance as individuals who can make some choices and accomplish some tasks all by themselves. Their growing sense of achievement enhances their developing positive feelings of self-worth (see Figure 13–4).

Toddlers' anger and frustration may come out as temper tantrums. Distinguish between kinds of tantrums. Frustration tantrums may respond to changing the conditions which caused the child's frustration. Toddlers sometimes have tantrums in order to get their own way. Toddlers' manipulation tantrums sometimes need to be ignored because they are seeking negative attention. Giving attention during the tantrum may reward the toddler and encourage future outbursts. Instead, the caregiver should provide positive attention soon after the tantrum is over.

Toddler negativism may be expressed by "No!" or in tantrums. Their pursuit of independence may carry over into doing the opposite of what was requested. Rephrase command statements and refocus attention to something of interest to the toddler. For example, you might rephrase "Put the doll away" to "Mary Jane, where can you find a place to put the doll down? She needs to go to sleep."

Children learn concepts of right and wrong from adults. Toddlers are just beginning to use words, and they respond to some labels and commands. But words alone will not control their behavior until they construct concepts of rightness and wrongness. These concepts are constantly being revised and expanded as the toddlers compare their behavior with adults' reaction to that behavior. At this age toddlers cannot separate themselves from their actions

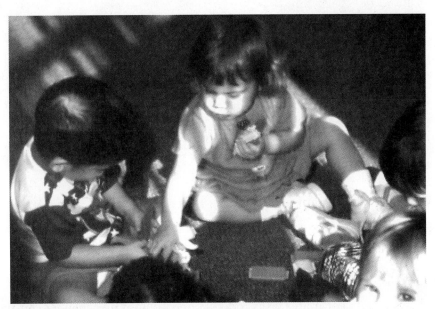

Figure 13–4   The caregiver lets toddlers concentrate on exploring toys by themselves.

enough to understand the idea, "I like you but I do not like what you are doing." Therefore, caregivers need to find ways to help toddlers discriminate between right and wrong while still accepting each child as a worthy person no matter what his or her behavior.

Direct behavior gently, but physically. Don't depend on words alone. Prevent dangerous behavior before it occurs—hold a threatening arm before it has a chance to hit. Lead a child by the hand back to the table to finish a snack. Don't let children get in trouble and then yell at them. If you find yourself saying "I knew that was going to happen," next time don't predict; prevent it . . . (Gonzalez-Mena 1986).

Children's ability to adapt to change in routine during this time of negativism may create problems. The toddler who is very adaptable may change routines easily or with a little fussing. For example, putting that toddler's chair in a different place in the room may create interest for the child. A toddler who has difficulty adapting to change may react negatively, resisting the moving of the chair by fussing or crying or even having a tantrum. This child may combine resistance to change with negativism.

"A good technique to use with any toddler is to catch the child being "good" and praise his or her behavior. Consistently using the 3A's of caregiving—Attention, Approval, and Affection—when the child has behaved correctly will help the child know what is right. Allowing the child to choose between two positive outcomes helps the child to learn to make decisions as well as to have more control over his or her environment" (Douville-Watson 1988).

Suggestions for Implementing Curriculum

CHILD BEHAVIOR	MATERIALS	EXAMPLES OF CAREGIVER STRATEGIES
Types of Emotions-Feelings		
Expresses emotions in behavior and language.		Determine and respond to toddler's emotions.
Recognizes emotions in others.		Be consistent in showing emotions, e.g., happiness—smile and laugh; anger—firm voice, no smile.
May fear strangeness.		Introduce new people, new experiences to toddler. Caution others not to "rush" the child. Allow child to approach or withdraw at own rate.
Shows excitement, delight.		Respond with similar excitement, e.g., touching a pretty flower, an animal.
Expresses sense of humor.		Giggle and laugh with toddler.
Shows affection.		Accept and return physical and verbal show of affection.
Displays negativism.		Provide honest, workable choices, e.g., "Do you want to run or walk to the table?"
Has tantrums.		Determine and remove cause if possible. Sometimes ignore. Proceed calmly with involvement with other children, activities.
Uses play to express emotions, resolve conflicts.	Blocks, dolls, home living, clothes, toy animals.	Provide props for acting out fear, frustration, insecurity, joy.
Seeks dependency, security with parent and caregiver.		Provide touching, holding, stroking interactions; respond quickly and consistently to toddler's needs.
Seeks to expand independence.		Allow toddler to attempt activities by him- or herself. Do not take over if toddler can be successful without you.
Control of Emotions-Feelings		
Begins to learn right and wrong.		Verbalize which behavior is right and which behavior is wrong. Give reasons. Since toddlers are only just beginning to conceptualize "right-wrong," they only occasionally can apply concept to control their own behavior.

CHILD BEHAVIOR	MATERIALS	EXAMPLES OF CAREGIVER STRATEGIES
Reinforces desired behavior.		Praise toddler for controlling own behavior.
Temperament		
Activity level.		List two of the toddler's behaviors in each category which indicate the toddler's basic style. List adjustments you need to make to help the toddler cope with daily situations.
Regularity.		
Approach or withdrawal as a characteristic response to a new situation.		
Adaptability to change in routine.		
Level of sensory threshold.		
Positive or negative mood.		
Intensity of response.		
Distractibility.		
Persistence and attention span.		

Social Development

Toddlers are egocentric; they see the world from their own point of view. In the first year and a half of life their bodies and the objects they play with are perceived to be part of "self." Gradually, as the concept of object permanence develops, they differentiate "self" from other objects and people, which become "not self." This major development in toddlers provides the basis for life-long expansion of their concept of self and their interactions with others and provides the child with one of his earliest experiences with self-image. "Caregiver acceptance is extremely important at any stage of development. This acceptance is internalized and becomes one with the child's self" (Douville-Watson 1979).

Toddlers behave differently toward different people. They recognize differences in people and adjust their interactions with them. They may be eager and excited with a familiar caregiver and quiet and withdrawn with a substitute.

Toddlers play with toys and materials and sing and talk usually by themselves in solitary play (see Figure 13–5). They may look at other children and play near them, but they do not interact with them in play. Toddlers now engage in solitary play (playing alone) and parallel play (playing near but not with other children); they decide what kind of interaction they want with others. At this age the toddler is more adept at dealing with older children and adults than with peers.

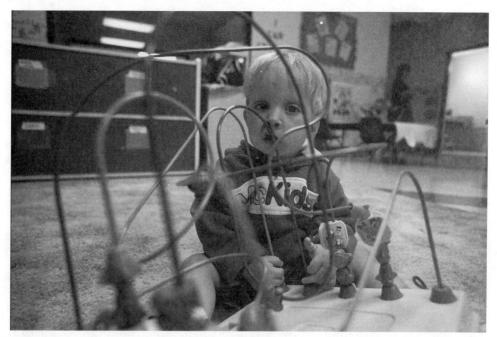

Figure 13–5 The caregiver lets toddlers concentrate on exploring toys by themselves.

Suggestions for Implementing Curriculum

CHILD BEHAVIOR	MATERIALS	EXAMPLES OF CAREGIVER STRATEGIES
Self		
Has concept of self.		Positively reinforce toddler as an individual.
Is egocentric: understands only own viewpoint.		Do not expect toddler to "feel sorry for" someone toddler has hurt. Toddler assumes everyone thinks and feels the way he or she does.
Others		
Seeks presence of parent or caregiver.		Allow toddler to follow you around. Tell child when you are going out of sight.
Plays games.		Play games with toddler. Respond and play child's games.
Occasionally shares.		Provide enough materials and equipment so sharing can be encouraged but not required.
Acts differently toward different people		Expect different responses to different people. Accept toddler's choices.

CHILD BEHAVIOR	MATERIALS	EXAMPLES OF CAREGIVER STRATEGIES
Uses variety of behaviors to gain attention.		Identify toddler's usual behaviors to gain attention. Respond to any of those behaviors as quickly as possible.
May be shy with some people.		Do not force toddler to interact with all people. Allow child to keep a distance and watch.
Engages in parallel play.		Provide materials and space so toddlers can play with own materials but near each other.

Cognitive Development

This is a time for learning, so opportunities to learn should be provided, including learning how to learn.

> Too often adults give children answers to remember rather than problems to solve. This is a grave mistake. Unless children develop the art of problem solving . . . their brains will remain underdeveloped (Princeton 1989, 63).

Providing stimulation to the learning toddler influences his development now and in the future.

Object permanence becomes more firmly established. At this age toddlers may search for an object they have seen moved and hidden again.

Toddlers of this age are interested in observing the effects of their own and other's actions. Exploration is done using trial and error. These little explorers try, and probe, and practice activities and observe the results of their actions. Logical reasoning is not a part of trying an action a different way (see Figure 13–6).

Figure 13–6   Toddlers learn about their physical world by putting themselves in different spaces.

Now that toddlers are aware that others cause actions to occur, imitation of others' behaviors becomes a part of their play. They use some play behaviors repeatedly in the same pattern and develop their own ritual play. Researchers have found that stimulating playthings are more important for cognitive development after age one than in earlier months.

Availability of interesting and challenging play materials in children's environment after the first year correlates with later IQ and school achievement in reading and math (Healy 1989).

Suggestions for Implementing Curriculum

CHILD BEHAVIOR	MATERIALS	EXAMPLES OF CAREGIVER STRATEGIES
Piaget's Stages of Sensorimotor Development		
STAGE 5 (Experimentation)		
Object Permanence		
Watches toy hid and moved. Looks for it where it was moved.	Blanket, paper, toys, dolls, spoon, interesting objects.	Play game with child. Hide the object while child watches. Let child watch you move the object to a different place under the blanket. Ask, "Where is it? Can you find it?" Observe and allow child to find the object. Praise child for good watching and thinking.
Causality		
Investigates cause and effect.		Allow and encourage child to search, identify relationship between an action and the effect of it, e.g., "What made the ball go under the table?"
Sees self as causal agent.		Verbally identify the child as cause of the action, e.g., "Laquata kicked the ball."
Explores various ways things happen.	Water toys, water basin.	Allow child time to play with the water and toys to discover different actions of water and of the objects in the water.
Employs active trial-and-error to solve problems.	Narrow-neck milk carton, different sizes and shapes of objects.	Provide time and materials which stimulate child to think and try out ideas. Ask questions but do not tell answers or show child.
Experiments.		Provide open-ended toys and materials which encourage several uses. Encourage child to see how many ways child can use them. Ask questions and allow time for child to experiment; ask "what happens?"

CHILD BEHAVIOR	MATERIALS	EXAMPLES OF CAREGIVER STRATEGIES
IMITATION AND PLAY		
Copies behaviors of others.		Encourage child to pretend: to drink from a pretend bottle like baby Gwen, to march like Pearl, to pick up toys. Think about your own behaviors; child will copy what you do. Be sure your actions are the kind of actions you feel comfortable seeing the child copy.
Turns play with imitation into rituals.		Allow child to repeat own play develop own preferences. For and example, child may see you hug a child who comes in the morning and imitate your hugging. Child may repeat this imitation and develop the ritual of hugging the child who has just arrived.

Learning Skills/Language Development

Language in toddlers of this age expands from less reliance on sounds and babbling to more use of recognizable words. Many word approximations are used and reinforced and become a usable part of toddlers' expressive vocabulary.

Toddlers use a word for many different things. "Wawa" may mean anything to drink. "Mama" may mean any woman. Word meaning is usually flexible. The toddler may call anything that is round a "ball."

This is the time the vocabulary of the toddler can be expanded by your use of words to label actions and objects. It is also a time to make them more aware of the world around them by pointing out sounds to listen to and naming what they are. By eighteen months the toddler will be asking what things and sounds are as they categorize their world.

Eighteen months to two years of age is a period of rapid language growth. By the second birthday, vocabulary has increased to at least fifty words. At this time, we see the emergence of the ability to form sentences. This begins with two-word combinations, such as "Eat cookie" or "Go bye-bye." By age three, the child is a real conversationalist, producing three- to four-word sentences, answering simple questions, and even relating events of the day! (Soman 1994).

Reading and books can provide enjoyable experiences for toddlers. Several different kinds of children's literature interest toddlers.

Point-and-say books have pictures of familiar objects and little text. The object of reading this type of literature is to increase your child's vocabulary, to compare pictures in a book with known items in the environment, to familiarize the child with books, and to show your baby that books have meaning.

Nursery rhymes, chants, poems, and songs are best chanted or sung throughout the day rather than just presented at read-aloud sessions. Then, at a later time, it can be thrilling to watch your infant associate the rhymes that he or she already knows with the picture representing that rhyme in a book. Nursery rhymes help your child become familiar with the sounds of language. They assist the transition from telegraphic speech, where one word represents a sentence, to mature language, where each word is pronounced (Lamme 1985, 57–58).

Writing can be encouraged by allowing children to watch you as you write names, labels, and notes. The interrelationships among language, reading, and writing are evident at an early age.

At what age can you begin assisting your child in becoming a writer? You can begin by reading to your child at birth. All the reading you do during the first years aids writing development by exposing your child to writing. Just before one year of age, your baby can be given (under supervision) his first writing tools—water-soluble markers and large sheets of paper. His writing experiences will have begun (Lamme 1984, 17–18).

Suggestions for Implementing Curriculum

CHILD BEHAVIOR	MATERIALS	EXAMPLES OF CAREGIVER STRATEGIES
Uses intonation.		Use intonation in your talk with toddler.
Babbles sentences.		Respond to toddler's babbling.
Repeats, practices words.		Repeat toddler's word. Occasionally expand into a sentence, e.g., "gone-gone"; "The milk is all gone."
Imitates sounds of other people, objects.		Enjoy toddler's sounds. Play sounds game—point to objects and make sound of object, e.g., dog barking.
Responds to word and gesture conversation.		Become very familiar with toddler's words and gestures. You often have to guess what toddler is saying. Make a statement or ask a question to determine if you interpret correctly, e.g., "Taylor wants to go outside."
Responds to many questions and commands child cannot say.		Choose a few questions and commands which you can use often and consistently. The toddler will learn what they mean through many experiences, e.g., "Go get your coat."

Basic visual and auditory perceptual skills are extremely important to be taught before letter and word recognition.

CHILD BEHAVIOR	MATERIALS	EXAMPLES OF CAREGIVER STRATEGIES
Uses word approximations for some words.		Watch the toddler's behavior to help you determine what the toddler is saying. What to see where child is looking, pointing, reaching. Say a word or sentence to test whether you are interpreting the word correctly.
Uses words in immediate context.		Notice what the toddler is doing, saying, needing right now. Toddler's talk is about immediate needs and desires, not past or future situations.
Identifies familiar pictures.	Pictures, picture book.	Orally label objects. Ask toddler to point to or name familiar picture.
Uses markers, chalk.	Markers, paper, chalk.	Provide table space and materials. Write labels, sentences for child.

STUDENT ACTIVITIES

1. Interview one caregiver. Ask the caregiver to describe the following:
   (a) behaviors of a toddler between 12 and 18 months who is angry, and
   (b) behaviors of the caregiver who is responding to the toddler's angry behavior.
   Write the caregiver's descriptions and then put an X beside the descriptions of the *physical* behaviors of the toddler and the caregiver.

BEHAVIOR OF ANGRY TODDLER	RESPONDING BEHAVIORS OF CAREGIVER

2. Listen to one toddler. Make a list of the child's words and "sentences." Watch the child's body language and nonverbals. Then write down the complete sentences you think the child meant (you must think about the context in which the toddler was talking).

WORDS, PHRASES	MEANING
Gone-gone	It is all gone; or, She went away.

3. Write one lesson plan to use with one toddler to help reinforce a word the toddler uses and to expand its use with sentences.
Use the plan with the toddler.
Evaluate the toddler's involvement.
Evaluate the written lesson plan.

4. Observe one toddler between 12 and 18 months of age. Record the toddler's behavior in two five-minute sequences, using narrative description. Transfer the descriptions to the Developmental Profile.

5. List five strategies which you competently use with toddlers between 12 and 18 months of age.

6. List strategies you need to develop and list ways you intend to develop them.

7. Use The Celebration of Life Calendar to set up a holiday theme for your classroom.

CHAPTER REVIEW

1. If the toddler cannot say the name of an object or person, but you think the child understands the object-name match, how can you find out whether the child has connected the correct name with the correct object or person?

2. Describe something Juanita would do which shows you that she has developed the concept of the permanent object.

3. Describe two situations where the toddler interacts with others. Describe two situations where the toddler plays alone.
With others
1.
2.
Alone
1.
2.

4. List five safety precautions you need to take with the toddler between 12 and 18 months of age.

5. With the development of eye-hand coordination, what can toddlers do now that they could not do as well several months earlier?

6. Review "Discipline" in your curriculum chapter.

REFERENCES

Brickmeyer, Jennifer. 1978. *Guidelines for Day Care Programs for Migrant Infants and Toddlers.* New York: Bankstreet College.

Caplan, F., and Caplan, T. 1980. *The Second Twelve Months of Life.* New York: Bantam/Grosset and Dunlap, Inc.

Douville-Watson, L. 1979. Child Development Lecture Series II, Bellmore-Merrick School District II, Merrick, New York.

Douville-Watson, L. 1988. Child care lecture series. *The 3A's of Child Care: Attention, Approval and Affection.* Oyster Bay, New York: Lifeskills Institute.

Erickson (1963). *Childhood and Society* (2nd ed). New York: Norton.

Gonzalez-Mena, J. 1986. *Toddlers: What to Expect.* Washington, DC: NAEYC.

Healy, Jane. 1989. *Your Child's Growing Mind: A Guide to Learning and Brain Development from Birth to Adolescence.* New York: Doubleday.

Lamme, Linda Leonard. 1984. *Growing Up Writing.* Washington, DC: Acropolis Books Ltd.

Lamme, Linda Leonard. 1985. *Growing up Reading.* Washington, DC: Acropolis Books Ltd.

Piaget, J. (1952). *The Origins of Intelligence in Children* (M. Cook, trans.) New York: International Universities Press.

Piaget, J. (1954). *The Construction of Reality in the Child* (M. Cook, trans.) New York: BASIC.

Princeton Center for Infancy and Early Childhood, The. 1978. *The Second Twelve Months of Life: Your Baby's Growth Month by Month.* New York: Bantam Books.

Soman, Bonnie. 1994. Lecture series. *The Development of Communication Skills.* Garden City, New York: Adelphi University Center for Communication Disorders.

Wilson, L. C. 1987. Mommy, don't go! *Pre-K Today* 2(1): 38–40.

Wilson, L. C. 1988. Gross-motor activities for toddlers. *Pre-K Today* 2(7): 34–35.

14

The Child from Eighteen to Twenty-Four Months of Age

OBJECTIVES

After completing this chapter, the child development specialist should be able to:

1. Identify and record sequences of change in the physical, emotional, social, cognitive, and language development of children from 18 to 24 months of age.
2. Select materials appropriate to that age-level child's development.
3. Devise strategies appropriate to that age-level child's development.

CHAPTER OUTLINE

I. Materials and Activities
   A. Types of Materials
   B. Examples of Homemade Materials
II. Caregiver Strategies to Enhance Development
   A. Developmental Profile
   B. Physical Development
   C. Emotional Development
   D. Social Development
   E. Cognitive Development
   F. Learning Skills/Language Development

Review Chapter 5. Use Appendix A, the Developmental Prescriptions, and Appendix B, the Developmental Profile, with each child. Children follow a *sequence* of development. There are often ranges in the *rate* of development.

CHILD DEVELOPMENT ASSOCIATE FUNCTIONAL AREAS

All CDA functional areas are integrated into the caregiver decisions and behaviors.

Leonard, 23 months old, walks to a child-sized rocking chair, backs up to it and sits down. He rocks and watches the other children. He gets off the chair and sits on his legs to pick up blocks. He picks up a block wagon, stands up, and walks around. He holds the block wagon in his left hand, tries to put on another block with his right hand, and succeeds. He puts the wagon on the floor and pushes it. He takes off one block and then takes off five blocks; he puts them back on. Jasper walks past and Leonard says, "No, Jasper. That mine." Tracey takes the block wagon. Leonard reaches for it and says, "That mine." Leonard picks up the wagon and begins putting blocks in it. He picks up the block wagon and a block bag, gets up and walks around, talking to himself.

MATERIALS AND ACTIVITIES

Walking, climbing, and riding materials and activities are enjoyable for children at this age. They are practicing their gross motor skills and developing increased competence in using them. Their finger and wrist muscles are developing so they can manipulate more complex objects. Their imaginations are expanding as they construct internal representations of their world. The Celebration of Life Calendar will help you celebrate diversity with this age group.

Types of Materials

Textures	Tunnel
Snap toys	Riding toys and cycles
Large stringing beads	Water play equipment
Blocks	Sand play equipment
Toy people	Soap paint
Caps or lids to twist off containers	Finger paint
Toys to throw	Tempera paint
Tools: hammer, broom, shovel	Puzzles
Cars, trucks	Books
Zippers	Telephones
Hairbrush	Dolls
Toothbrush	Stuffed animals
Low, wide balance beam	Puppets
Sliding board	Music: records, tapes
Pull and push toys	Modeling dough
Balls	Markers, crayons, chalk, pens
Low stairs	Containers to fill and empty

Examples of Homemade Materials

TUNNEL

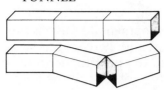

Use sturdy long rectangular cardboard box large enough for child to crawl through. Cut out ends and tape edges to keep from scraping child and also tearing box. Place several boxes end-to-end or in a square or zig-zag pattern.

PUPPET

Use a paper plate. The child tears colored paper and yarn and pastes the pieces on the paper plate. These puppets are safer without a wooden stick handle.

TARGET

Use a plastic pail (empty ice cream or peanut butter container). Place tennis balls, yarn balls in pail. Use a piece of yarn to mark where child will stand to throw objects into the pail.

CLAY DOUGH RECIPE

2 C plain flour
2 C water
1 C salt
3 tsp. Cream of Tartar
2 Tb. oil
food coloring

Combine flour, salt, and Cream of Tartar. Combine oil, food coloring and water. Pour liquids into flour-salt mixture. Stir to get pie dough consistency. Cook, stirring over medium heat until ball forms. Store in a covered container.

BOOK

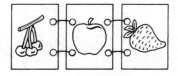

Cut three pieces of sturdy cardboard, Select three magazine pictures which make a sequence, or have something in common (e.g., they are all red). Glue one picture on each piece of cardboard. Cover the pictures and cardboard with contact film. Connect the pieces by punching holes in the side of the cardboard and tying together with yarn.

CAREGIVER STRATEGIES TO ENHANCE DEVELOPMENT

Developmental Profile

Lennie is a 23-month-old whose Developmental Profile is presented in Figure 14–1. His C.A. was actually 22 months and 29 days, but because the days are more than 15, the C.A. is rounded to the next higher month. Inspection of the Profile reveals that Lennie exhibits problems in the Emotional and Social Areas and is within age expectations in other areas.

| Name: Leonard C. | | | | | | | | | | | | | | | | | | Date of Birth: 7/29/XX | |
| Date: 10/18/XX | | | | | | | | | | | | | | | | | | C.A.: 22 months 29 days | |

MONTH AGE EXPECT.	AREA I PHYSICAL				AREA II EMOTIONAL			AREA III SOCIAL			AREA IV COGNITIVE				AREA V LEARNING SKILLS				MONTH AGE EXPECT.
	MUSCLE CONTROL	LOCOMOTION	SLEEP	TEETH/TOILET	FEELINGS TYPE	CONTROL FEEL	TEMPERAMENT	SELF	OTHERS		SENSORI 6	OBJECT	SYMBOL/PLAY	IMITATION	VIS-MOTOR	AUDITORY	VISUAL	LANGUAGE	
30+																			30+
29																			29
28																			28
27																			27
26																			26
25																			25
24		●									●		●	●		●		●	24
23																			23
22 (C.A.)		●	●		●							●			●				22 (C.A.)
21	●																		21
20									●										20
19																			19
18					●	●				●									18
					A*														
17																			17
16–																			16–

Notes: A* Lennie bites others and has tantrums each day.

Figure 14–1 Developmental Profile, Leonard C.

Specifically, Lennie is estimated at age level in the Physical Area (I), the Cognitive Area (IV), and the Learning Skills Area (V). He is estimated to be significantly below age in the Emotional Area (II)—"control of feelings" and "temperament" (18 months)—and the Social Area (III)—"self" (20 months) and "others" (18 months). These estimates are low because Lennie exhibits an average of two temper tantrums and bites other children between three and four times per day. Upon closer examination, it appears that Lennie has tantrums in response to being told that he can't do something by caregivers, and he bites when other children have toys or things he wants. For some children this age biting is commonly experienced.

In general, Lennie is a 23-month-old who exhibits normal development except for having temper tantrums and biting behavior. These aggressive and anti-social behaviors must be limited by the caregiver to ensure the safe care of Lennie and the other children. In addition to using the Caregiver Strategies described below, complete withdrawal of the 3A's, diverting attention away from the negative behavior, and attending to children who are being appropriate are all techniques which can effectively reduce tantrums and biting behaviors. Furthermore, the caregiver can "catch the child being good" and give approval when Lennie accepts "no" and shares appropriately with others. Also, role playing how to accept "not having your own way" and "how to share" can also help eliminate these inappropriate behaviors. A specific plan to reduce and eliminate tantrums and biting should be added to other Caregiver Strategies to provide Lennie with a comprehensive balanced program.

Physical Development

Children of this age are gaining much more stability and coordination. They can stand up, squat, reach over, and stand upright again without toppling. They climb on just about everything and, when they are around 18 months old, they try climbing out of their cribs. They will soon succeed. They climb up and down stairs by holding onto a rail or hand to maintain balance, but still do not alternate their feet. They move rapidly, both walking and running. They jump with both feet. They become increasingly more adept at kicking a ball and by around 22 months they can pedal a cycle such as a Big Wheel and they love to push and pull toys and objects (see Figure 14–2). They can throw objects at targets rather than randomly throwing and tossing, though they seldom hit the intended target.

These children's fine motor muscles are developing so they have increased control of their fingers and wrists. They probe and twist and turn objects (see Figure 14–3). They now can more easily release the objects they have grasped. The muscles relax, allowing them to drop or throw an object when they choose to. They also are more accurate in directing the dropped or thrown object.

At eighteen months many children can turn the pages of a book several at a time, but by twenty-four months they will be able to turn pages one at a time.

Figure 14–2 Toddlers can push and pull objects around the room.

Figure 14–3 The caregiver provides a variety of toys to promote fine motor development.

Some children may be favoring one hand preference over the other at this time. Determine each child's dominant hand and allow the child to use it. The child may occasionally use the other hand when using a spoon, for example; if the child occasionally chooses to do so, this will not be harmful. The caregiver should allow the child to develop and maintain the handedness which is comfortable. Do not attempt to make a left-handed child use utensils and toys with the right hand. That child's neurological patterns have developed with his or her left-handedness. Attempting to change a child's handedness may cause both neurological and muscular stress.

Suggestions for Implementing Curriculum

CHILD BEHAVIOR	MATERIALS	EXAMPLES OF CAREGIVER STRATEGIES
Muscular Control		
LOCOMOTION		
Walks forward. Walks backward.	Flat floor, ground, clear of toys.	Keep area clear of toys or caution child about obstacles.
Walks sideways.	Area clear of toys.	Play with child: walk sideways, forward, backward.
Runs with stops and starts.	Clear area.	Provide *flat* running space. On incline child may run down too fast and fall on face.

Suggestions for Implementing Curriculum

CHILD BEHAVIOR	MATERIALS	EXAMPLES OF CAREGIVER STRATEGIES
Jumps with both feet.	Low steps, box, block, plastic crate.	Keep other children away from jumping spot when one child is jumping to the floor. Sometimes catch child as he or she jumps. Release and steady child so he or she can climb and jump again.
Kicks object.	Large ball: beach ball, nerf ball, soccer ball, volleyball, rubber ball.	Provide space where child can kick the ball and it will not go too far, e.g., into a big cardboard box or into a corner.
Walks up stairs holding railing; walks down stairs holding railing.	Steps and rail.	Provide equipment and time for child to safely walk up and down.
Pushes and pulls objects while walking.	Small wagon, strollers, pull toys, push toys which make noise, attract visual attention.	Provide clear space for walking where pushed and pulled toys have room to move without bumping and catching on equipment, furniture, rug.
Climbs.	Sturdy box, cubes, footstool, low climbing gym.	Provide equipment. Remain close by to assist getting down if needed.
Pedals cycle.	Low riding cycle; not high tricycle.	Provide space for fast and slow riding, for turning curves and in circles. Keep away children on foot.
ARM		
Throws object at target.	Bean bag; ball, box, cardboard or wood shape with large holes cut in it.	Place target at edge of play area so object is thrown away from children.
HAND		
Grasps and releases with developing finger muscles.	Small toys, objects, pail, box.	Provide objects for game of pick-up-and-drop.
Pulls zippers.	Zipper board, book, clothes with large zipper with tab.	Provide large zipper with tab large enough for small fingers to pinch and pull. Demonstrate where to hold fabric in other hand.
Helps dress and undress self.		Allow child to do as much as possible. Plan ahead to provide enough time for child who dresses and undresses slowly.
Scribbles.	Paper, pens, crayons, markers, pencils, flat hard surface.	Provide space and time to scribble. Show scribbling boundaries (edges of paper, not beyond edges).

CHILD BEHAVIOR	MATERIALS	EXAMPLES OF CAREGIVER STRATEGIES
Increases wrist flexibility; turns wrist to turn object.	Small objects to twist and turn; jars and screw-on lids.	Provide toys which stimulate manipulating, e.g., attractive, textured on several sides. Demonstrate twisting jar lid on and off.
Establishes right-or left-handedness.		Allow child to pick up objects and use them with hand child chooses. Do not change object into other hand.
Turns book pages.	Sturdy pages in books.	Read to child, carefully turning each page by grasping the upper right-hand corner and moving hand down to middle of page to gently turn the page.
Digs with tool.	Shovel, scoop, spoon; sand, dirt.	Provide tools which are not sharp and will not bend. Provide space designated for digging. Demonstrate where sand or dirt may and may not go.
Makes individual marks with crayon or pen.	Paper, pen, crayon, marker.	Listen if child talks about his or her marks. Praise child.

Sleeping

May move from crib to bed or cot.	Firm cot, mattress.	Talk about the change *before* it happens. Emphasize child is getting bigger and now can use a *bigger* bed. Demonstrate where shoes go, where blanket is. Provide quiet talk, music, touch familiar to child.

Eating

Controls cup and spoon better.		Emphasize how well child is using cup, spoon. Be patient with spills.
May eat anything, then change to picky eating.		Allow child to change eating behavior. Don't fuss at or push child. Child usually will get adequate nutrition if variety of foods are provided.

Teeth

Has most baby teeth. Uses toothbrush.	Toothbrush, toothpaste, cup of water.	Assist when necessary with applying toothpaste and cleaning face afterwards.

Elimination

May show interest in and readiness for toilet training.	Potty chair, training pants; slacks, leggings easy to remove.	Show child where potty chair is. Encourage child to use it. Praise child when he or she does. Do not push child. Many show

CHILD BEHAVIOR	MATERIALS	EXAMPLES OF CAREGIVER STRATEGIES
		interest in potty chair months before they are ready for actual transition to toilet-training. See Chapter 6 for the child who is ready for consistent toilet-training.

Emotional Development

Children of this age are continuing to develop positive and negative feelings about themselves. They interpret responses from caregivers and children as reflecting their self-worth.

Children's fantasies increase at this age. They are very real and may sometimes be frightening. Brickmeyer's comments are noteable today.

> Caregivers must be made aware that sudden fears occur often in toddlers and that caregivers must be prepared to deal with the child lovingly and warmly, in a fashion that does not communicate to the child that the fears are remarkable, outrageous, funny or unreasonable. Sometimes a child can be reassured by a good look at the cause of his or her fright while being held by a loved and trusted caregiver. The caregiver should encourage but not force the child to make a careful examination of the feared object, offering labels and explanations while the child examines it. Occasionally, an articulate toddler can explain his fear: . . . Occasionally, particularly if the cause of the fear is unremovable—a place in a room, for example—after experimenting with changes of furniture or of light and shadow, caregivers may have to resign themselves to offering comfort and the security of laps and arms to help the child weather it out (Brickmeyer 1978).

At this stage, children's feelings are hurt by criticism and they are afraid of disapproval or rejection. They become easily frustrated and are able to communicate some feelings and desires. It is important to consciously use the 3A's and Positive Propaganda at this stage of development.

Emotions are reflected in intense behaviors. These children can swing between extremes, e.g., smiling, laughing—screaming, crying. Their basic pattern of intensity of response is affected by their swings into even more intensive behaviors. Those children who usually respond loudly may now scream and yell or laugh shrilly. The children who have a low intensity of response may use more energy and respond more loudly or actively than usual.

As toddlers approach their second birthdays, they are aware that they have a "self" and that they are separate from the world of other people and things. They now want to act like separate social beings. Becoming a separate psychological being is one of the most complicated tasks a toddler has to face. During the two years starting from birth, the child establishes a very strong attachment to the mother. When dependence on her begins to diminish, separation follows. The more enjoyable and secure the relationship with the mother has been, the easier the separation process (Caplan and Caplan 1980). This is also true of the primary caregiver who often spends more time with the child than a parent.

Suggestions for Implementing Curriculum

CHILD BEHAVIOR	EXAMPLES OF CAREGIVER STRATEGIES
Types of Emotions-Feelings	
Views internal feelings and external behavior as same.	Recognize that child does not feel angry and yet acts inappropriately.
Shows one or more emotions at same time.	Identify child's emotions. Respond to child's needs.
Continues to develop feelings about self.	Provide consistent behavior and feedback which helps child feel good about self; help child know he or she is a worthy person.
Changes feelings about self.	Reflect to child that child is still a loved person when child reflects negative or angry feelings about self.
Seeks approval.	Provide verbal and nonverbal approval of child as a person and of child's behavior when it is positive.
May develop new fears.	Listen to child's fears. Accept them as real. Comfort child. Reassure child of your concern and of your presence. May demonstrate object is harmless, e.g., siren toy. If you cannot convince child, remove the toy.
Increases fantasy.	Listen to child's fantasies. Accept them as real to child. Enjoy funny, happy fantasies. Comfort, reassure child of his or her safety when child has scary fantasies, e.g., "There's a monster in the kitchen."
May increase aggressiveness.	Remain nearby to caution, remind, and sometimes remove object or child from situation.
Seeks security in routines.	Provide consistent routines which child can use by self as child increases competence and seeks independence.
May become shy again.	Allow child to hold back or withdraw. Provide time for child to observe without having to enter into interactions with others.
Sometimes rejects parent or caregiver.	Allow child to express rejection in words and behaviors. Continue to express your affection for child.
Control of Emotions-Feelings	
Uses reactions of others as a controller of own behavior.	Use words, facial expressions, gestures to indicate approval and disapproval of child's behavior.

CHILD BEHAVIOR	EXAMPLES OF CAREGIVER STRATEGIES
May resist change.	Explain change *before it* happens. Provide reason for the change. Motivate by emphasizing specialness of the child who now is allowed to do something else. Remember development is a process not a product. Give time for lessons to be learned.
Moves to extremes, from lovable to demanding and stubborn.	Allow child to express swings in behavior. Show acceptance of child as a person. Help child work on his or her demands and stubbornness by suggesting alternatives in behavior.
Temperament	
Activity level.	List two of the child's behaviors in each category
Regularity.	which indicate the child's basic style. List
Approach or withdrawal as a characteristic response to a new situation.	adjustments you need to make to help the child cope with daily situations.
Adaptability to change in routine.	
Level of sensory threshold.	
Positive or negative mood.	
Intensity of response.	
Distractibility.	
Persistence and attention span.	

Social Development

Children of this age are continuing to develop a sense of self. They use words which identify them as separate people, e.g., "I, mine, me, you." These children are also expanding their relationships with others. They are beginning to recognize other people's feelings and they are experimenting mentally as they begin to develop an inner sense of empathy.

One child will hit the other and produce howls of pain and rage; the child may be so intrigued by the dramatic results of hitting that he or she will hit again, just to see if the results are as interesting as those produced by the first blow. All too often adults who observe this kind of behavior are horrified and react loudly, "Naughty; that's bad; say you are sorry; you shouldn't hit people!" Confused by the intensity of the adult reaction, he or she usually mumbles the magic word "sorry," getting the toddler off the hook, but offering little or no understanding of what he or she did to deserve the scolding. Because a toddler has little understanding that the feelings he or she experiences are also experienced by other people, adults should concentrate on the child who is hurt, saying briefly to the offender: "Hitting hurts. I feel sorry that _____ has been hurt." Thus, the offender is told that hitting is not allowed because it hurts the person who is hit and that the adult is sorry that someone is hurt (Brickmeyer 1978).

Although toddlers still have difficulty sharing toys (see Figure 14–4), children imitate the behavior of others. While they demand more personal attention, they also can accept shared attention. They try to please others and may help in situations where they are praised.

The 3A's of caregiving—Attention, Approval, and Affection—used together appropriately can now be seen as imitated in one child's relationship with another.

Suggestion for Implementing Curriculum

CHILD BEHAVIOR	EXAMPLES OF CAREGIVER STRATEGIES
Self	
Is egocentric, sees things from own point of view.	Recognize that child thinks others think and feel the way he or she does. Help child identify own ideas and feelings.
May change identity of self from day to day.	Provide feedback to child about self so child can identify consistency within self.
Identifies materials as belonging to self.	Recognize and allow ownership of toys.
Uses I, mine, me, you.	Verbally respond to child's use of pronouns, reinforcing distinction child makes between self and others.

Figure 14–4 Toddlers do not share toys easily, so the caregiver should provide enough toys of a similar nature for them to use.

CHILD BEHAVIOR	EXAMPLES OF CAREGIVER STRATEGIES
Others	
Demands attention.	Both initiate and respond to child to provide attention to child's needs. Share looks, touch, words with child when you may be busy with another child.
Begins to be aware of others' feelings.	Help child identify and verbalize others' feelings which appear in their behavior, e.g., "Allen is crying; he is sad."
Believes people have changes in identity—change in role changes person.	Identify yourself in your different tasks, e.g., when you sweep and clean, when you cook, when you rock a child.
Expands social relationships.	Encourage child to interact with others. Be present and provide your support when child encounters a new child or adult.
Looks to others for help.	Consistently provide assistance when needed. Praise child for seeking help with something child would not be able to do for self, e.g., puts on shoe and then seeks help for tying laces instead of fussing and crying.
Imitates tasks of others.	Allow and enjoy child's watching you and others. Enjoy the imitations and don't be concerned that the imitation might be incomplete or inaccurate. The child will continue to watch and imitate.
Wants to help, assist with tasks, clean-up.	Encourage the child to help put toys away, clean up, etc. Work along with child. Child can be a very good helper if he or she sees how you do it.
May do opposite of what is requested.	Carefully word your requests. The child's negativism comes out in a frequent "no." Think of different ways to produce desired behavior without saying, "Do this."
Has difficulty sharing.	Provide enough toys and materials so child does not have to share. Suggest allowing another child to play with toy when child finishes. Provide alternative toys to child who must wait for desired toy.
Engages in parallel play.	Provide toys, materials, space for children to play near each other. Allow them to talk with each other. You talk to each of them. Allow them to choose if they want to trade toys or do something else.

Cognitive Development

Children of this age are gradually using mental trial and error. This is much faster than the sensorimotor trial and error where the children had to manipulate objects.

Object permanence is established. These children know that an object or person exists even when they cannot see it and they remember where objects belong. They know that they exist separate from other people and objects (Wilson 1987).

Children of this age imitate past events. They remember the ideas by internal representation and reproduce them at a later time. For example, the caregiver washing the child's face is imitated later by the child as the child washes a doll's face.

Symbolic play is children's representation of objects or feelings or ideas. They will imitate housework and enjoy helping. Symbolic play serves several functions: Children can express conflicts and work them out in the pretend world. They can seek gratification of unsatisfied needs they feel they have, e.g., they play the baby to get extra nurturing they desire. They can pretend to be other people or objects, thereby reflecting their understanding of other people or objects as separate from themselves and trying behaviors similar to or different from their own.

At around twenty-two to twenty-four months, a caregiver can determine what is cognitively going on with a child by role playing with puppets or dolls. Often the troubled child explains very clearly to the caregiver a situation that might have been disturbing.

This is a good way for the child to get feedback in a positive way; a good place to use the 3A's and Positive Propaganda; and a good way to help them problem solve and help to continue to develop good *self-esteem* in the child.

Suggestions for Implementing Curriculum

CHILD BEHAVIOR	EXAMPLES OF CAREGIVER STRATEGIES
Piaget's Stages of Sensorimotor Development	
STAGE 6 (Representation)	
Mental trial and error	
Tries out ideas mentally, based on past concrete experiences.	Allow child time to figure out solutions. If child seeks assistance, help child think about the problem, e.g., "What can you use to reach that block?"
Object permanence	
Sees object disappear, mentally remembers object, and figures out where it went.	Allow child to think and search for object. Give clues, ask questions only after child has acted and still needs assistance.
Deferred imitation and symbolization	
Imitates past events.	Observe child's representations. Identify the ideas which seem very important to the child.
Symbolic play	
Resolves conflicts.	Allow child to act out conflict in play with toys and materials. Observe how child works out conflict so he or she feels better.

CHILD BEHAVIOR	EXAMPLES OF CAREGIVER STRATEGIES
Compensates for unsatisfied needs.	Observe child's play. Identify consistent themes in child's play, e.g., child's talk and actions about being a good or a naughty child.
Tries roles.	Provide clothes, materials which help child pretend to be someone else.

Learning Skills/Language Development

Teach basic learning skills; visual memory, auditory discrimination, etc. daily. Language throughout life is clearly linked with emotion, and it is important to remember that children who get enough cuddling and unconditional love have a better chance at learning language—and everything else (Healy 1989).

Caregivers must be careful not to criticize children's speech patterns. Good grammatical structure is learned by children when adults set good examples and repeatedly use words correctly. Remember to use the 3A's when speech is used correctly as well as to encourage children when they have verbalized.

At this age children's vocabulary is expanding rapidly as they label objects which they now recognize as separate entities (see Figure 14–5). Children construct the principle that

> words are labels for socially defined classes of objects and events. This achievement is reflected in more systematic and productive extension of

Figure 14–5 The caregiver uses familiar objects to play choosing and naming games with toddlers.

words and in accelerated growth of vocabulary. . . . This is the time when children may tire their caregivers by constantly asking for the names of things (e.g., what's this?). They eagerly utter the words they hear and explore their uses (Anisfeld 1984, 86) (see Figure 14–6).

Children use their language to express needs and to direct others. They question as they seek to learn about their word (Wilson 1988).

Children of this age use nouns, verbs, and pronouns as they combine their words into two- and three-word sentences. These children produce word sequences, several words in sequence which convey a thought or action but are not regular sentence patterns. For example, Cameron says, "Key go car" when he sees his mother take the key ring out of her purse. She responds, "Yes, I have the key. We are going in the car."

These children follow simple one- and two-step oral directions. There are two broad classes of language functions: "the *cognitive function*—to name, indicate, describe, and comment; and the *instrumental function*—to request, reject, manipulate, and express desires. . . . [W]ords are used for cognitive purposes before they are used for instrumental purposes" (Anisfeld 1984, 91).

Caregivers and children use words to classify objects and actions. Words help children organize what they see and hear and do. Anisfeld reported that when adults do the following things they help young children develop proper language:

- The adult speaks to children in short sentences.
- The adult articulates more clearly to young children than to others.

Figure 14–6 Outdoor activities provide many opportunities for the caregiver to observe, question, label, and praise toddlers' actions.

- The adult talks about the situation in which the child is involved.
- The adult expands what the child says: ". . . fills in the missing words as she echoes the child's utterance. . . ."
- The adult extends what the child says: ". . . continues a thought started by a child. . . ."
- The adult imitates what the child says: ". . . repeats all or part of what the child had said."

Pictures, books, and storytelling stimulate language interactions among caregivers and children. Lamme related several experiences which involved toddlers in the reading process.

> Pointing out things in pictures and encouraging your toddler to participate in the "reading" helps your child become more active in the reading process. Maybe you have tried to skip a page or shorten a story in an effort to speed up the bedtime ritual. Has your toddler surprised you by noticing and demanding the whole story? Even at these young ages, toddlers are actively listening to stories and remembering them word for word!
>
> Because reading sessions with your toddler are likely to be so short, it is important to read aloud frequently—several times during the day (1985, 52).

Choose reading materials for young children carefully. Stimulate the toddlers' interests in "reading" and hearing stories often.

> Your toddler will enjoy the classic fairy tales read over and over again. Stories like "The Three Little Pigs" or "The Three Billy Goats Gruff" will encourage your child to chant the repetitive parts as he or she sings and plays around the house. You and your toddler can act out the tales. If you make a flannel board with characters of these familiar stories or have puppets for the story characters, your child can experience the stories in lots of ways other than just by hearing them. Active involvement in the story plot is a real key for toddlers.
>
> Your toddler will enjoy books that are small in size because they are easy to carry around the house. . . .
>
> Your toddler will still enjoy much of the literature that appealed to him or her as an infant—nursery rhymes especially. Some toddlers can proceed through a favorite Mother Goose collection and chant each rhyme.
>
> Your toddler will also enjoy bigger books which are "two laps wide" for lap reading. Many children's picture books are wider than they are long so that you can spread the book out and see the pictures (Lamme 1985, 58–59).

Toddlers experiment with markers, chalk, and crayons as their interest in scribbling continues. Encourage their scribbling by providing time and attention to their use and enjoyment of writing.

> Your child may be far more interested in the process of making scribbles than in the product produced by those scribbles. You, however, may want

to write your child's name in the corner of the picture, letting him watch as you write. As scribble pictures get framed, mounted or displayed, your youngster soon learns that his scribble pictures are valued. He will want to draw more, not only because scribbling is so innately pleasurable but also because his scribbling attracts your positive attention.

Don't ask your child what his scribbles are. The scribbles at this stage do not represent anything. Rather, comment on what is apparent—lines from top to bottom or across the page, dots, and colors. You might say, "I like your orange and brown picture," or "What beautiful blue lines!" (Lamme 1984, 39).

Suggestions for Implementing Curriculum

CHILD BEHAVIOR	MATERIALS	EXAMPLES OF CAREGIVER STRATEGIES
Uses language to reflect own meaning; expects others to have same meaning.		Recognize limited meaning of child's use of words. Be careful not to read extra meaning into what the child says.
Expands vocabulary rapidly, labeling objects.		Verbally label and also point, touch objects and actions in child's world. Also expand the label into a sentence, e.g., "Ball. Michael has a ball."
Points to objects and pictures named by others.		Play games, look at pictures, read books; say, "Point to the bird" or "Where is the car?"
Learns social words—hello, please, thank you.		Consistently use social words in their correct context. Say "please" and "thank you" to the child. When child requests item, repeat request and add the word "please," e.g., "Carrot please."
Uses language to express needs, desires.		Listen to child's expression of needs. Verbally respond so child knows that his or her words get your attention and you understand them. Use words and actions to meet child's needs or explain why you cannot meet them, e.g., "The milk is all gone."
Uses language to direct others.		Listen to child's commands. Respond verbally and with action following child's directions or explain why you are not, e.g., "Here is a napkin" when child asks for one.

CHILD BEHAVIOR	MATERIALS	EXAMPLES OF CAREGIVER STRATEGIES
Questions, asks "What's that?"		Answer child's occasional and persistent questions. This is how the child learns labels and other information about the world. Provide simple answers, not complicated ones, e.g., "That is a flower" rather than a description of petals, leaves, stem, etc.
Uses nouns, verbs, pronouns.		Speak normally with the child so child can hear complete sentence patterns.
Is learning prepositions.		Use in natural contexts, e.g., "The ball rolled under the table"; "Put the book on the shelf."
Calls self by name.		Use the child's name when talking directly to child.
Follows one-step direction.		Use simple directions and praise when the child follows them, e.g., "Please put the truck here."
Follows two-step direction.		Make sure child is aware you are giving directions. Use simple directions, e.g., "Please pick up this book and put it on the shelf."
Makes two- and three-word sentences		Use both short and long sentences with the child. Praise child and respond to child's sentences, e.g., Child: "Coat on?" Caregiver: "Yes, you need your coat on."
Looks at books.	Cloth or paper or cardboard picture books.	Read books with child. Demonstrate proper care of books. Allow child to look at books alone.
Listens to stories and rhymes.		Tell stories which child can understand. Use rhymes, poems.
Scribbles.	Markers, chalk, crayons, paper.	Provide writing space and materials. Show interest and approval of scribbling. Share scribbling with others.

STUDENT ACTIVITIES

1. Observe one caregiver for ten minutes. Use narrative description to write down everything caregiver does and says. Then categorize the behavior:

CAREGIVER BEHAVIOR (WHAT CAREGIVER DID)	CAREGIVER INITIATED	WITH WHOM?	CAREGIVER RESPONDED	TO WHOM?	AREA(S) OF CHILD DEVELOPMENT INVOLVED

2. Identify one characteristic temperament of one child (by records, caregiver information, or your own observation). Observe to see how the caregiver makes adjustments in the routine or expectations of the child to the situation and how the caregiver helps the child make adjustments. For example, the caregiver may tell a low active child several minutes early that it is time for the child to put on outdoor clothing.

3. Make one toy and allow two children this age to use it. Observe and write down how they used it, what they said, and your judgment about whether they seemed interested, challenged, or bored using it. Also evaluate the toy's construction.

TOY	HOW USED?	CHILD'S COMMENTS	INTERESTING/ CHALLENGING/ BORING?	STURDY, TORN, BROKEN?

4. Observe one child between 18 and 24 months of age. Record the child's behavior in two five-minute sequences, using narrative description. Transfer the descriptions to the Developmental Profile.

5. List five strategies which you competently use with children between 18 and 24 months of age.

6. List strategies you need to develop and list ways you intend to develop them.

7. Develop a theme for the month using The Celebration of Life Calendar.

CHAPTER REVIEW

1. List three physical changes which enable the child to become more independent.
2. Chris and Marlin both pick up a car and start pulling on it. What can you do and what can you say that shows appropriate understanding of their needs and desires?
3. List three ways symbolic play helps a child.
4. Identify two possible developments in the child's language and state two strategies for each that a caregiver can use to facilitate that development.

CHILD'S DEVELOPMENT OF LANGUAGE	CAREGIVER STRATEGIES
1.	1.
	2.
2.	1.
	2.

REFERENCES

Anisfeld, Moshe. 1984. *Language Development from Birth to Three.* Hillsdale, NJ: Lawrence Erlbaum Associates.

Brickmeyer, J. 1978. *Guidelines for Day Care Programs for Migrant Infants and Toddlers.* New York: Bankstreet College.

Caplan, F., and Caplan, T. 1980. *The Second Twelve Months of Life.* New York: Bantam/Grosset and Dunlap, Inc.

Healy, Jane. 1989. *Your Child's Growing Mind: A Guide to Learning and Brain Development from Birth to Adolescence.* New York: Doubleday.

Lamme, Linda Leonard. 1984. *Growing Up Writing.* Washington, DC: Acropolis Books Ltd.

Lamme, Linda Leonard. 1985. *Growing Up Reading.* Washington, DC: Acropolis Books Ltd.

Wilson, L. C. 1987. Peek-a-boo . . . I see you! *Pre-K Today* 1(6): 32–33.

Wilson, L. C. 1988. What's in the box? *Pre-K Today* 2(4): 38–39.

15

The Child from Twenty-Four to Thirty Months of Age

OBJECTIVES

After completing this chapter, the child development specialist should be able to:

1. Identify and record sequences of change in the physical, emotional, social, cognitive, and language development of children from 24 to 30 months of age.
2. Select materials appropriate to that age-level child's development.
3. Devise strategies appropriate to that age-level child's development.

CHAPTER OUTLINE

I. Materials and Activities
   A. Types of Materials
   B. Examples of Homemade Materials
   C. Activities ideas
II. Caregiver Strategies to Enhance Development
   A. Developmental Profile
   B. Physical Development
   C. Emotional Development
   D. Social Development
   E. Cognitive Development
   F. Learning Skills/Language Development

Review Chapter 5. Use Appendix A, the Developmental Prescriptions, and Appendix B, the Developmental Profile, with each child. Children follow a *sequence* of development. There are often ranges in the *rate* of development.

CHILD DEVELOPMENT ASSOCIATE FUNCTIONAL AREAS

All CDA functional areas are integrated into the caregiver decisions and behaviors.

Twenty-six-month-old Cathy picks up a fire truck and walks up on the porch with it. She pushes it around on the floor, then picks it up and takes it out into the yard. Ms. Susan asks her what she has. Cathy responds, "A truck," and smiles. Ms. Susan asks what kind of truck. Cathy says, "Red," and smiles. Cathy picks up a ball and says, "Watch me throw it." She moves the fire truck and tells Ms. Susan "Cant' find ladder." Ms. Susan gives her the ladder and starts to put it on the fire truck. Cathy requests, "Let me do it." Cathy puts a toy fireman in the truck and plays with it. She says to Ms. Susan, "See the truck," and then, "See if it goes?" As Cathy plays with the fire truck, the ladder falls off again and she says, "Oh, no," and looks at Ms. Susan. She takes the truck to Ms. Susan to fix the ladder, saying "It fall off" and pointing to the ladder. She watches Ms. Susan fix the ladder and plays with it again. Another child gets the fire truck and begins to play with it. Cathy tells the child, "I want the truck, Bill." Bill gives the fire truck back to Cathy, who says, "Thank you, Bill."

MATERIALS AND ACTIVITIES

Riding toys are favorites at this age (see Figure 15–1). The children also use climbing and jumping equipment frequently. Kicking and throwing are more accurate than before and are enjoyed by the children. Finger, hand, and wrist movements are not only grasp and release, but also coordinate with vision, enabling the children to string beads and to use crayons and other drawing and writing tools. Children take pleasure in manipulating objects and materials. They focus on the process rather than on producing a product. They respond to and also create music. They enjoy symbolic play. They can find meaning in pictures and books representing ideas with which they are familiar.

Most adults who work with toddlers wonder when and how children begin to be able to look at situations from another person's viewpoint. Some toddlers may seem to behave in a sympathetic fashion occasionally or briefly, but such behavior is probably indicative of actions they have observed rather than an expression of understanding for what someone else is feeling. A toddler may, for example, look concerned if another child cries, may rush over to pat the unhappy one, offer a cracker or toy, or may even burst into tears. More commonly, however, toddlers pursue their own important affairs with little or no regard for what their playmates are doing or feeling. A toddler who is pushing a doll carriage around the room may push the carriage over any obstacles, including people, with little recognition that this may hurt the unfortunate person in his path (Brickmeyer 1978).

Figure 15–1   The caregiver provides riding toys of different sizes for young children.

Types of Materials

Balance beam

Climbing equipment

Bouncing equipment

Rocking boat

Wagon

Cycles

Wheeled toys

Items to throw

Balls

Blocks

Trucks, cars

Dolls, people, animals

Jars with twist lids

Items to put together or pull apart

Knobs

Large pegs and boards

Large beads and string

Markers, crayons, pens, chalk

Modeling dough

Construction material: wood, styrofoam, glue

Rhythm instruments

Records

Tape recordings

Puppets

Dress-up clothes

Pictures

Books

Puzzles

Matching games

Examples of Homemade Materials

Themes and ideas are available in The Celebration of Life Calendar in Chapter 9.

BALANCE BEAM

Tape masking tape on the floor to indicate the line where the child can walk.

In the yard partially bury a tree trunk so that several inches remain above ground. Place so that no branch stubs are on the top walking surface.

PEG BOARD

Cut a piece of heavy cardboard to fit in the bottom of a box (shoe, gift, hamburger). Cut holes in the cardboard. Cut ½-inch dowel rod into 1½–2-inch lengths. Paint if desired. Store cardboard and pegs in the box and put on lid.

RHYTHM INSTRUMENTS
MARACAS

Collect gourds in the fall. Allow to dry. The seeds will rattle when the gourd is shaken.

DRUM

Poke a hole through both ends of an oatmeal box. Pull a strong string through the box and both ends and extend 12–24 inches (measure on one of your children). Tape the box lid onto the box. Tie a knot or leave the ends loose and tie a bow each time you put it around a child's neck.

SOAP PAINT

Use 1 part soap flakes, 1 part water, and food coloring. Beat the mixture with a hand eggbeater. Skim off soap suds to paint on table top or shelf paper or freezer paper.

FINGER PAINT

Use liquid starch, dry tempera paint, and soap flakes. Pour out about a tablespoon of liquid starch on shelf or freezer paper. Sprinkle dry paint on starch. Sprinkle soap flakes on starch. Children mix ingredients as they paint.

TEMPERA PAINT

Mix ½ cup dry tempera paint and ½ cup dry detergent. Add water until mixture is thick but not runny. Keep in covered jar.

PUPPETS

Use paper sandwich bags. Child can use crayons or glue on paper to decorate puppet. Help child fit hand in bottom of sack.

CLOTH BOOK

Use pinking shears to cut heavy cloth to make several pieces the same size. Stack the pieces and sew down the middle by machine or by hand. Cut out colored pictures from magazines or cards. Glue one picture per page. Make a theme book, e.g., children riding, or use pictures of different objects or activities.

GROUP BOOK

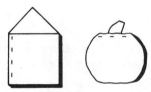

Make a group book. Children can tear out magazine pictures of objects; the pictures may fit a theme. Glue to pieces of paper. Staple the pages together. Write the title page. Write what children dictate to you for the other pages. (Paper may first be cut into a shape that matches the theme, e.g., pumpkin; leaf.)

PUZZLE

Cut out one uncluttered colored picture from a magazine.
a. Glue it to the center of the cardboard.
b. Cover the picture and cardboard with contact film. Pencil the picture into three to five sections which are visually recognizable (head, legs, tail). Cut around the picture, being careful to cut only the picture and not the cardboard.
c. Cut the remaining hole slightly larger.
d. Glue the remainder of the cardboard onto a second piece of cardboard the same size. Fit the puzzle pieces into place. If necessary, trim so the pieces come out easily.

MATCHING GAME

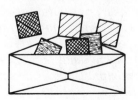

Cut two 2-inch squares from pages of a wallpaper sample book. Make about six sets, using different pages. Store the pieces in an envelope. To play, mix up the pieces and then select squares which match.

MATCHING GAME   *Select four picture sets of objects which are alike, e.g., two cardinals, two mice, two daisies, two German Shepherds. Glue one of each set onto the bottom of a styrofoam tray. Glue the other four pictures onto cardboard and cut into small squares. Glue part of an envelope in the tray to hold the loose cardboard pieces. Randomly pick pieces that match the pictures on the tray. Ask child to point to matching object.*

Activities Ideas

The following are examples of activities that help the children construct knowledge.

EXPLORATION		
Cooking		
Recipe chart	Stir	See
Oral language	Beat	Hear
Measure	Smell	Taste
Sift	Feel	
Growing Plants		
Carrot	Bean sprouts	Observations
Sweet potato	Food	Comparisons
Beans	Care	Charting
Lettuce	Rate of growth	

REPRESENTATIONS		
Oral Language		
Conversation	Poetry	Singing and rhythms
Information gathering	Nursery rhymes	Dramatic play
Story telling	Fingerplays	

Objects

Painting rocks, seeds, pine cones

Creating prints with potatoes, carrots, celery; footprints, handprints, fingerprints

Pictures

Magazines, photographs

Art media: crayons, painting, tear and paste

Books

Wordless picture books

Naming objects books

Books with a storyline to read or tell in your own words

CAREGIVER STRATEGIES TO ENHANCE DEVELOPMENT

Developmental Profile

Refer to Figure 15–2, which shows Cathy's Developmental Profile, based upon a 10-day observation of the Child Behaviors from the Developmental Prescription in Appendix A.

| Name: Cathy R. | Date of Birth: 04/06/XX |
| Date: 06/08/XX | C.A.: 26 months 2 days |

MONTH AGE EXPECT.	AREA I PHYSICAL				AREA II EMOTIONAL			AREA III SOCIAL			AREA IV COGNITIVE				AREA V LEARNING SKILLS				MONTH AGE EXPECT.
	MUSCLE CONTROL	EAT	TEETH	ELIMINATION	FEELINGS TYPE	CONTROL FEEL	TEMPERAMENT	SELF	OTHERS		PRE-CONCEPT	VERBAL	QUANTITY	SPACE-TIME	VIS-MOTOR	AUDITORY	VISUAL	LANGUAGE	
40+																			40+
38																			38
36																			36
34																			34
32																			32
30																			30
28																			28
26			●		●														26
24 (C.A.)		●				●	●												24 (C.A.)
22	●																		22
20																●			20
18				●				●							●		●		18
16									●		●							●	16
14									A*										14
12–													●						12–

Notes: A* = Generally low profile suggests developmental delays—further evaluation necessary.

Figure 15–2 Developmental Profile, Cathy R.

Cathy exhibits a generally low profile in all areas except for the Emotional Area (II), where estimates suggest near age level expectancies.

Within the Physical Area (I), Cathy is estimated to be 4 months below C.A. in "muscle control" because she can't stand on one foot yet and tends to be physically "clumsy" for her age. She is also having difficulty with toilet-training and isn't ready for training pants yet, therefore achieving an estimate of 18 months.

Cathy has a quiet, accepting temperament, displays positive and negative self-worth, and therefore functions near C.A. in the Emotional Area (II).

Socially (III), Cathy does not realize her skills and abilities and does not show independence. She does whatever other children or adults tell her to do. As a result, she is estimated to be at the 16- to 18-month level socially.

Cognitively (IV), Cathy functions more like an 18-month-old than a 26-month-old. She has trouble classifying, labeling, and understanding concepts such as up, down, more, and now.

Within the Learning Skills Area (V), Cathy exhibits low visual-motor control (23 months), auditory skills (21 months), visual skills (18 months), and language skills (16 months). She appears to learn better from auditory than visual information, but her overall perceptual and language development is estimated to be almost a year below age expectations.

In summary, Cathy exhibits general developmental lags in most of the important areas. She is estimated to be almost a year below age expectancy in both cognitive and learning skills. These deficits are considered extreme for her age and are cause for further evaluation. The caregiver should hold a conference with Cathy's parents to explore whether formal evaluations by a psychologist and her pediatrician should be done to help determine the causes of these lags.

Physical Development

The two-year-old can stand, bend, walk, run, and jump. Riding toys are favorites at this age (see Figure 15–1). The children also use climbing and jumping equipment frequently. Kicking and throwing are more accurate than before and are enjoyed by the children. Toddlers are more flexible and stable in their movements than before (see Figure 15–3). Their eye-hand coordination is more accurate so they can reach and grasp objects, but they still have difficulty using hands and fingers independently. They are able to fit objects together and like to put them together and pull them apart. Toddlers may use either their right or left hand, but most still have not established handedness. These children are visually fascinated with some new items. They spend more time observing. They use a spoon when eating and are learning to use a fork. Some children this age have all twenty baby teeth. These children may learn to brush their teeth. Many children this age are ready for toilet-training and may even train themselves if the opportunity is provided.

Figure 15–3 The young child is becoming more coordinated and can stoop and stand easily.

Suggestions for Implementing Curriculum

CHILD BEHAVIOR	MATERIALS	EXAMPLES OF CAREGIVER STRATEGIES
Muscular Control		
MOVEMENT		
Bends at waist.	Dropping and picking up objects: pail and plastic rings.	Play game with child. Observe appropriateness of materials, interest of child.
Climbs.	Low objects: steps up to slide, tires.	Select safe materials and safe height.
Jumps.	Two- to three-step equipment.	Keep floor or ground space clear where jumping. Block off higher levels so jump is safe distance for muscles and balance.
Stands on one foot.	Song for lifting one foot.	Make up rhyme or song about standing on one foot. Child will stand on one foot for only a few seconds. Praise child. Encourage child to try again.
ARM		
Throws.	Target—large paper sack or plastic basin. Nerf ball, yarn ball.	Provide space for child to throw objects at target. Decorate target so child is aiming at hoop or door.

CHILD BEHAVIOR	MATERIALS	EXAMPLES OF CAREGIVER STRATEGIES
HAND		
Touches.	Textured objects: sandpaper, fur, corduroy, egg, carton bottom, juice can.	Make feely box. Allow child to pull out object to touch and see. Label object for child. Label texture for child.
Twists.	Jars and cans with lids; large plastic nuts and bolts.	Provide objects which twist on and off easily.
Eating		
Uses spoon.	Spoon that fits child's hand.	Provide food which can be spooned easily.
Is learning to use fork.	Fork that fits child's hand.	Provide food which will stay on fork.
Uses fingers.		Cut solid food in small pieces so it can be picked up with fingers.
Teeth		
Has all twenty baby teeth.		
Brushes teeth.	Toothbrush, toothpaste.	Assist with toothpaste and water.
Elimination		
Is learning to use toilet.	Training pants, potty chair or adapter seat.	Ask whether child needs to go to toilet. Assist with clothes. Assist with hand washing. Glove hands. Clean up potty chair or toilet seat. *Wash your hands.*
Has completed toilet training.	Training pants, potty chair or toilet.	Ask whether child needs to go to toilet before and after nap, before outside play. Assist with clothes as needed. Assist with hand washing. Clean up, and *wash your hands.*

Emotional Development

Feelings about the self continue to develop: positive and negative self-image, competence, acceptance. Children this age are becoming more independent at the same time they recognize their need for help. They attempt to please and show affection. At twenty-four months they make less demands and have a better ability to express themselves. However, by thirty months these easier-going children suddenly fall into what has been termed the "terrible twos." They become more demanding and more possessive about their things. They become frustrated, say "no" to almost everything and have "temper tantrums." They may suddenly want help with things they previously could do and want to do things they are not able to do. They may be aggressive, then shy, then "act like a baby." They cannot handle choices and demand sameness and consistency. In fact, their need for sameness may well be the best way to handle the thirty-month-old. Routines provide children this age with consistency and security. They may be affectionate (see Figure 15–4) at one time and want no affection the next.

Here, the caregiver's skills of being well organized, consistent, and flexible (as discussed earlier in Chapter 10) may be challenged. Be sure to use plenty of the 3A's for your own benefit, as well as directly with the children.

We have tried to point out some of the behavioral components of healthy development in toddlerhood, a stage in which a child attempts to become an autonomous being capable of competently functioning in an environment appropriately geared to his or her needs and abilities. It should be clear that children who are given sufficient opportunities to explore, to use their senses, to be physically active, to use expressive materials, and to develop language skills may often—through the very nature of these activities—be destructive, messy, noisy, impudent, and defiant.

Figure 15–4   Friends show affection for each other.

Suggestions for Implementing Curriculum

CHILD BEHAVIOR	EXAMPLES OF CAREGIVER STRATEGIES
Types of Emotions-Feelings	
Feels comfortable with self.	Provide experiences where child can succeed often, feel pleasure with self.
Feels positive self-worth.	Provide child positive feedback. Reinforce other people's reflections of child as a worthy person.
Feels negative self-worth.	Be sensitive to child's frustrations with tasks and with social encounters. Provide reassurance of child's worth.
Control of Emotions-Feelings	
Expresses emotions.	Accept child's feelings as honest rather than manipulative.
Temperament	
Activity level.	List two of the child's behaviors in each category which indicate the child's basic
Regularity.	style. List adjustments you need to make to help the child cope with daily situations.
Approach or withdrawal as a characteristic response to a new situation.	
Adaptability to change in routine.	
Level of sensory threshold.	
Positive or negative mood.	
Intensity of response.	
Distractibility.	
Persistence and attention span.	

Social Development

Twenty-four-month-olds enjoy the company of other children, they are beginning to interact. Because toddlers still have some difficulty sharing, they often engage in parallel play. It is possible to involve this age child in group interest centers, such as sitting at the same table and playing with play dough on an individual basis. Toddlers recognize emotions in others and may help with tasks. By 30 months these children will interact with each other, but often may quarrel over possessions rather than participate in a co-operative effort. They may help with some chores. Following a routine may allow the caregiver to gain some cooperation in tasks and cleaning up.

Suggestions for Implementing Curriculum

CHILD BEHAVIOR	EXAMPLES OF CAREGIVER STRATEGIES
Self	
Realizes own skills.	Provide materials and equipment which child can use to own satisfaction. Provide challenging materials which child can use.

CHILD BEHAVIOR	EXAMPLES OF CAREGIVER STRATEGIES
Others	
Shows independence.	Allow child to accomplish as many tasks as possible by self. Assist when asked or when you anticipate you are needed.
Acts to please adult.	Provide verbal and nonverbal positive feed back to child. Recognize child's need for your attention and approval. Plan activities child can help you with (clean-up).
Shows feelings to others.	Show feelings to child. Show appropriate actions with feelings, e.g., happy—laugh, physical excitement; sad—hug, pat, listen. Praise child when child uses those behaviors.
Recognizes emotions in others.	Label children's behaviors. Verbalize about feelings of others. Provide appropriate responses to behaviors. Praise child when child identifies others' emotions. Praise when child responds to others' emotions.
Understands "mine," "yours."	Reinforce possession by child and others. It is "mine" while using it.
Shares some.	Provide materials and equipment so some sharing is necessary. Praise child who shares. Verbalize reasons for sharing. Recognize, however, that not all children can share yet.
Helps others.	Provide opportunities for purposeful helping—clean up, passing out items, assisting with clothing. Praise and thank for helping behaviors.
Engages in parallel play.	Plan space and materials so child can play close to others without having to interact in play.

Cognitive Development

Many children between 24 and 30 months are entering Piaget's preoperational stage of cognitive development. The first substage of the preoperational stage is the *preconceptual*, which occurs from about 2 to 4 years of age. These children can mentally sort some objects and actions. The mental symbols are partly detached from experience. Early nonverbal classifications are called graphic collections, where the children focus on figurative properties. These children form some verbal preconcepts. But the meaning of words may fluctuate from one time to another. Verbal reasoning is from particular to particular.

Preconceptual children are constructing and organizing knowledge about a wide range of areas in their world. They are beginning to classify objects and to develop very limited ideas of quantity, number, space, and time. Due to their preference for routines and sameness, time will be based more on what happens after an event rather than on an understanding of "later" or minutes of time passage.

The development of the symbolic function occurs in the preconceptual stage. It involves the following mental representations, presented here in increasing complexity. In the child's *search for hidden objects* the object remains permanent (does not cease to exist) in the child's thinking even when the child cannot see it. These experiences form the bases for more specific representational thinking. In *deferred imitation* the child imitates another person's behavior even when that person is no longer present. A child engaged in *symbolic play* may give the caregiver a stone and tell the caregiver to eat this apple; the stone represents the real object. The child's *drawings* may be scribbles, experiments with the media, or they may begin to be representations; a child may point to a mark he or she has made on a piece of paper and say his or her own name. *Mental images* are pictures in the mind with which children can carry out action sequences internally. *Language* (words) represent objects or behaviors. As children develop language, they use their mental images which verbally represent thoughts (Wadsworth 1978, 64).

Children at this age are active explorers, seeking information through manipulating and observing their world. As problem-solvers, they now move beyond trial and error to mental manipulation of ideas and physical manipulation of objects to construct their reasoning.

When there is only "one right way" to play, opportunities for experimentations and new discovery are limited. Common household objects, tools, cooking utensils, and gadgets are particularly fascinating because adults use them. Nesting and stacking toys and objects, as well as containers for dumping and pouring are examples of good mental stimulators. They require active handling and teach about relationships, top, middle, bottom, small, big, bigger, biggest. Blocks of different sizes are the best toys of all (Healy 1989).

Suggestions for Implementing Curriculum

CHILD BEHAVIOR	EXAMPLES OF CAREGIVER STRATEGIES
Piaget's Preoperational Stage, Preconceptual Substage.	
NONVERBAL CLASSIFICATION	
Makes graphic collections.	Allow child to create own classifications.
VERBAL PRECONCEPTS	
Uses words differently at different times.	Listen and ask for clarification of words used differently.
Uses words with private meanings.	Listen to child's words in context; reword or question to find meaning.
Begins to label classes of objects.	Repeat and identify class of object. Extend child's label to include other objects.
Focuses on one attribute.	Reinforce classifications. Child has not yet formed stable classes of objects.

CHILD BEHAVIOR	EXAMPLES OF CAREGIVER STRATEGIES
VERBAL REASONING	
Reasons from particular to particular.	Understand and accept child's classification of behaviors which seem alike. Ask for clarification if needed.
QUANTITY	
Understands some, more, gone, big.	Use quantity words in context with objects, Respond and expand child's use.
NUMBER	
Understands more.	Use objects to identify "more."
SPACE	
Understands up, down, behind, under, over.	Use spatial-position words with actions, e.g., "I will lift you up. I am putting you down on the floor."
TIME	
Understands now, soon.	Label actions in terms of time, e.g., "Let's wash your hands now."

Learning Skills/Language Development

Auditory and visual learning skills are the foundation of language. Children of this age are rapidly increasing their vocabulary. Their vocabulary may include as many as two to three hundred words. This is a time for space words.

> . . . more new space words are added to the child's vocabulary in the six-month period from Two to Two-and-a-half than in any other six-month period . . . The increase in use of two space words combined gives exactness to location: "right home," "way up," "in here," "under the table" (Ames and Ilg 1980, 89).

Building on their use of language to name objects with single words, they proceed to a more complex structuring of language, the sentence. Anisfeld says that they *construct* sentences; they do not reproduce sentences from memory (1984, 113). Thus, the child has to think and select words which express the child's ideas in ways others can understand.

Anisfeld has identified several types in the child's development of mental associations:

Demonstrative naming: The first word in a demonstrative-naming phrase points out an object; the second names it, e.g., "this ball" or "here spoon."

Attribution: Children give objects a specific attribute, often using an adjective-noun combination, e.g., blue shoes. The attribute "blue" distinguishes one particular pair of shoes from all other items in a class of things called "shoes."

Possession: Children make special associations between a person and an object, often using a two-word sentence, e.g., "mommy chair."

Action: Action sentences separate the action from the actor and from the object and explore the relations among these three. Children's descriptions of their own or other's actions at this age include sentences like "ride big-wheel" and "I jump."

Recurrence: A recurrence sentence tells of a thing or event which happens again. Children often use "more" to express this, e.g., "more juice," "more ride."

Negation: The negative sentences of children this age usually say that something desired or expected is not there or has disappeared or that the child cannot, is not permitted to, or does not want to do something. A child may say, "no car" or "no hit."

Children use many sentences which contain specific word patterns. They hear others use word patterns and then use these same word patterns over and over in their process of constructing language (see Figure 15–5). Thus they learn to use word-order patterns common to their language, but they cannot tell you the basic rule or principle of word order they are using.

Another kind of patterning which children learn is rhyme patterning. They learn emphasis and rhythm of word parts, words, and sentences along with the words themselves and syntax. For example, *"MY* ball" means something different from "my *ball."* Children learn to use the appropriate stress and intonation to express their specific ideas.

Many sentences young children use are incomplete. Very young children use subject-and-verb and verb-and-object sentences but seldom use subject-verb-and-object sentences. They also often omit function words like *on, in, a,*

Figure 15–5 The repetitive lyrics of a song help a child learn proper word patterns.

and *the*. This is because they have to plan and coordinate all the parts (words) of their sentences. The more words they use, the more difficult it is for them to construct a sentence.

Children also extend their construction of language to include two ways of forming new words. They begin to use the plural and the past tense forms of words. By now children understand that there is more than one hand, or eye, or foot. They listen to others talking and learn that the word changes when referring to more than one hand. They then construct their words to include plurals, for example, hands, eyes, and so forth. However, at this age they apply the same plural rule to all words, making possible words like "foots." Applying the same kind of pluralization to all words is called over-regularization or overgeneralization. When children can distinguish between what is happening now and what has happened previously, they can begin to use some words which are in the past tense, such as "I jumped." They also overregularize past tense forms, constructing words like "goed" and "seed."

Books contain language patterns which serve as examples to children who are busily constructing language; therefore, you should read to children often. Children also can read books with pictures. These experiences provide practice in putting thoughts into oral language. Books will soon be selected frequently by toddlers.

"Play, according to many American child-development experts, offers children a way to discover who they are and who they can be (for example, see the 1980 book *Who Am I in the Lives of Children?* by Feeney et al.; Bergen's 1988 book *Play as a Medium for Learning and Development*; and Vivian Paley's 1986 *Boys and Girls: Superheros in the Doll Corner*). Children given the chance to enjoy a variety of experiences of play—role-playing, make-believe play, social play with peers, individual creative and artistic play, dyadic play with an adult—not only develop cognitively and socially but also become self-actualized" (Tobin, Will, and Davidson 97).

Written language is becoming more a part of the children's world. They see print at home, along the highway, and in other homes or centers. They look at the print in a book as the caregiver reads the story or tells the story-line. They see their own names on each of their own papers. They are eager to make their own marks. Writing opportunities can be provided to them in several ways.

Find or make a chalkboard—the larger the better for very young children. You can make one by painting a large, very sturdy piece of cardboard with chalkboard paint. Since your youngster is standing up and using pressure to write and draw, make the board very sturdy. One that bounces will be hard to write on and may frustrate children.

Put the chalkboard in a central location where it will get lots of use. A hallway or a child's room is a good place. Buy thick, soft chalk because regular-size chalk breaks easily. Although it's messier, soft chalk makes dark marks more easily than hard chalk.

Some children may be doing controlled scribbling which has several characteristics.

Gradually, after much playing around with markers, chalk, and crayons, your child's scribbles become more controlled. He begins to see the relationship between the marks he is making on paper and the writing utensil in his hand. His scribbles are more systematic. . . . The lines go up and down . . . or in circles. Dots may surround the picture. . . . He systematically scribbles with each marker in the box. . . . Later, as part of the scribble pattern, circles, triangles, arrows, and squares may emerge (Lamme 1984, 39–40).

Suggestions for Implementing Curriculum

CHILD BEHAVIOR	MATERIALS	EXAMPLES OF CAREGIVER STRATEGIES
Uses demonstrative naming.	Toys, objects.	Point to and label objects, e.g., "a foot," "a hand," "a nose." Extend to sentence: "Mary has a foot; Myron has a foot."
Uses attribution.	Toys, objects.	Combine labels, e.g., "red car," "big book." Extend to sentence: "Ray has the red car; Twila has the green car."
Uses possession.	Toys, objects.	Identify and label. "Roger's shoe, Jenny's shoe."
Uses action.	Toys, objects.	Identify and label own and child's actions: "Urvi sits on the floor." "Stewart is eating."
Uses recurrence.		Use word patterns which indicate repeating or additional, e.g., At snack ask each child if he or she wants *more* apple.
Uses negation.		Use "no" with action, e.g., "No hitting; no kicking." Follow up commands with reasons.
Learns word order.		Use proper word order, e.g., "The truck moves." Extend child's "Move truck" to "Yes, the truck moves."
Learns prosodic patterning.		Use expression when talking. Accent the proper syllables. Child will imitate you.
Uses subject-verb pattern.		Use whole sentences. Expand child's sentences.
Uses verb-object pattern.		Use whole sentences. Expand child's sentences.
Omits function words.		Use whole sentences. Expand child's sentences.

CHILD BEHAVIOR	MATERIALS	EXAMPLES OF CAREGIVER STRATEGIES
Selects and uses books.	Picture books, story books.	Read aloud. Listen to child "read."
Controls scribbling.	Markers, crayons, chalk, chalkboard, paper.	Provide materials and space. Write labels, notes to child. Share child's scribbling.

STUDENT ACTIVITIES

1. Observe a child this age for fifteen minutes during play time. Write a narrative description.
   a. Categorize the child's social behaviors.
   b. List behaviors which indicate preconceptual classifications.
   c. Categorize the child's speech using the above types of syntax.
   d. List the kinds of representations the child used.
2. Make a theme picture book. Use it with a child. Observe the child's emotional reactions. Observe the child's language. Involve the child in rereading the book.
3. Make a puppet with a child using the theme ideas from The Celebration of Life Calendar that best relates to the child.

CHAPTER REVIEW

1. List two developing physical accomplishments of a child this age.
2. Describe a situation where the child is asserting independence.
3. Write an example of the following language patterns:
   a. demonstrative naming
   b. attribution
   c. possession
   d. action
   e. recurrence
   f. negation

REFERENCES

Ames, Louise Bates, and Ilg, Frances L. 1980. *Your Two-Year-Old: Terrible or Tender.* New York: Delacorte Press.

Anisfeld, Moshe. 1984. *Language Development from Birth to Three.* Hillsdale, NJ: Lawrence Erlbaum Associates.

Brickmeyer, Jennifer. 1978. *Guidelines for Day Care Programs for Migrant Infants and Toddlers.* New York: Bankstreet College.

Healy, Jane. 1989. *The Child's Growing Mind: A Guide to Learning and Brain Development from Birth to Adolescence.* New York: Doubleday.

Lamme, Linda Leonard. 1984. *Growing Up Writing.* Washington, DC: Acropolis Books Ltd.

Stone, L. J., and Church, J. 1973. *Childhood and Adolescence* (3rd Edition). New York: Random House.

Tobin, W., and Davidson. 1989. *Preschool in Three Cultures.* New Haven, CT: Yale University.

Wadsworth, Barry J. 1978. *Piaget for the Classroom Teacher.* New York: Longman.

Wilson, L. C. 1988. When toddlers play. *Pre-K Today* 2(5): 36–37.

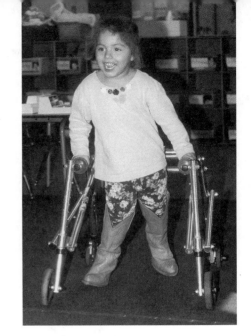

16

The Child from Thirty to Thirty-Six Months of Age

OBJECTIVES

After completing this chapter, the child development specialist should be able to:

1. Identify and record sequences of change in the physical, emotional, social, cognitive, and language development of children from 30 to 36 months of age.
2. Select materials appropriate to that age-level child's development.
3. Devise strategies appropriate to that age-level child's development.

CHAPTER OUTLINE

   I. Materials and Activities
      A. Types of Materials
      B. Examples of Homemade Materials
      C. Activities ideas
  II. Caregiver Strategies to Enhance Development
      A. Developmental Profile
      B. Physical Development
      C. Emotional Development
      D. Social Development
      E. Cognitive Development
      F. Learning Skills/Language Development

Review Chapter 5. Use Appendix A, the Developmental Prescriptions, and Appendix B, the Developmental Profile, with each child. Children follow a *sequence* of development. There are often ranges in the *rate* of development.

CHILD DEVELOPMENT ASSOCIATE FUNCTIONAL AREAS

All CDA functional areas are integrated into the caregiver decisions and behaviors.

Juan, 35 months old, is playing in the play yard. He sits on a bigwheel and rolls backward, gets off and runs around with other children, picks at the ground and finds a grub which he takes to show the caregiver, walks around showing the grub to others, sits on a small trike, takes the grub and puts him by a tree trunk, sits on the ground, climbs a tree, climbs down and runs after a soccer ball, plops on a bigwheel, and then kicks a soccer ball back and forth with another child. At another time he again plays with a grub. When asked where the grub is, he stops, puts his hands up in the air and says, "He's dead." He finds another grub and shows it to the caregiver, saying, "He might be sleeping. Wake up grub." The bug moves and rolls up again. Juan says, "He went to sleep again."

MATERIALS AND ACTIVITIES

Children this age are active, eager learners. They practice newly acquired skills and develop new ones. They like large muscle activity and are developing their fine muscles for more controlled manipulation of objects. They enjoy imaginative play. Their play incorporates their imagination, their language, and their understanding of themselves and others. They explore their world. They represent their ideas not only in play and language, but they also recognize pictures. They construct sentences to share their ideas (see Figure 16–1). They listen to stories and enjoy and participate in rhymes, fingerplays, music, and singing. This age integrates well with themes for cultural diversity. Use The Celebration of Life Calendar for ideas.

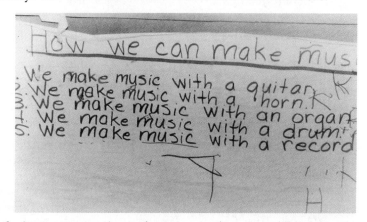

Figure 16–1 Language experience charts expose the young child to the process of writing what is spoken.

Types of Materials

Riding toys	Markers, crayons, chalk, pens
Wagon	Wooden beads and string
Trucks for hauling	Rhythm instruments
Rocking boat	Records
Tunnel, barrel to crawl through and on	Tapes
Cardboard blocks	Dramatic play props
Wooden unit block set	Puppets
Wooden people	Books
Wooden animals	Materials to explore—feel, measure, use

Examples of Homemade Materials

PROP BOXES

Gather props for one specific story or role. For example, put a stethoscope, white shirt, and small pad of paper in a shoebox for doctor props. In a larger box put a child-sized fire fighter's hat, boots, and poncho.

PUPPETS

Use cardboard tubes from paper towels. Cut paper to make face. Child uses markers or crayon to make face and clothes features. Glue face on tube.

BOOK: JOURNAL

Sew or staple sheets of unlined paper together. Each morning ask child to identify one toy or activity he or she wants to play with. Write a sentence identifying what the child chose. Allow the child to scribble, draw on the page. Read sentence to child. Label book "Juan's book," "Orelia's book." Send home each Friday.

WOODEN PEOPLE OR ANIMALS

Draw or cut out of a magazine pictures of people: infants, children, adults; fire fighter, police officer, doctor; or of animals or other objects: cars, houses, etc.

Glue picture on a piece of 1-inch thick white pine board. With a jigsaw, cut around the outside of the picture on three sides, cutting the bottom straight across. Sand the edges smooth. Apply two coats of nontoxic sealer. The object will stand up by itself.

Activities Ideas

Keeping records of informal observations as well as on the Developmental Profiles will assist you in planning appropriate experiences for each child. Plan for a holistic curriculum. Identify your children's interests. Use these to focus your thematic units. Plan mostly individual activities. Some short small-group activities may be included, for example, reading or telling a story, singing a song, saying a rhyme or fingerplay. Each small-group activity is appropriate also for use with individuals.

Children construct physical knowledge by moving objects and observing changes in objects. They observe the effects of their pulling, pushing, rolling, kicking, jumping, blowing, sucking, throwing, swinging, twirling, balancing, and dropping objects. They observe changes in objects: for example, when they put a drop of blue food coloring in a clear glass of water. Offer materials and activities that help children discover the physical characteristics of objects.

Children construct logico-mathematical knowledge by inventing relationships among objects. Comparisons of quantity, number, space, and time are explorations into relating two or more objects or events in a new and abstract way. Children can seek relationships among any kinds of materials. Games and activities which use the invented relationships help stimulate and reinforce their constructions. For example, a bulletin board of all the children's handprints provides opportunities for each child to place his or her hands over other children's handprints and make comparisons.

Children learn social-arbitrary knowledge from other people. They learn language from people. They learn the names of objects, meanings of words, intonations in pronouncing words, and word order and syntax from others. They learn the rules for living from others. They learn valuing from others. The caregiver bears the major responsibility in the child care program for providing this information and helping the child construct social-arbitrary knowledge. The child's physical, emotional, social, and cognitive development are all involved in constructing social-arbitrary knowledge.

CAREGIVER STRATEGIES TO ENHANCE DEVELOPMENT

Developmental Profile

Juan was observed over a five-day period as he performed the Child Behaviors of the Developmental Prescription in Appendix A. The resulting Developmental Profile is presented in Figure 16–2 and indicates that Juan functions at or above age expectancies in all areas except Learning Skills (V), where he is estimated to function 7 to 8 months below age.

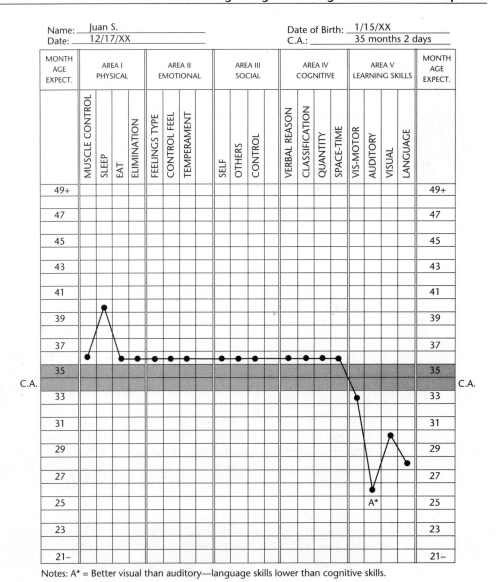

Notes: A* = Better visual than auditory—language skills lower than cognitive skills.

Figure 16–2 Developmental Profile, Juan S.

Specifically, Juan exhibits skills slightly above age expectancies in "muscle control" (36 months) and "sleeping" (40 months) within the Physical Area (I).

He also exhibits age level skills in Emotional (II), Social (III), and Cognitive (IV) Areas. In fact, his Cognitive skills in "verbal responding," "classification," and "quality" are slightly above age expectancies.

However, Juan exhibits some significant perceptual and language skill delays. His "visual-motor control" is slightly below age (33 months), and "auditory skills" (26 months), "visual skills" (30 months), and "language skills" (29 months) are significantly low. Juan has difficulty verbally expressing himself, recalling what he sees and hears (visual and auditory memory), discriminating differences between pictures and words (visual and auditory discrimination), and perceiving similarities in what he sees and hears (visual and auditory association). He is a somewhat better visual than auditory learner, although both channels are below age expectancies.

In summary, Juan is a healthy 35-month-old who functions at or above age level in all areas except Learning Skills (V). Juan exhibits significant enough lags in visual, auditory, and language skills to warrant further evaluation for possible learning disabilities. The caregiver should have a conference with the parents to go over the profile and discuss the need for further evaluations in learning skills and language areas.

A specific program of Caregiver Strategies to improve visual, auditory, and language skills should be combined with tasks and activities in all other areas to ensure a balanced program for Juan.

Physical Development

Children of this age are increasing their stability in both fast and slow movements. They walk evenly both quickly and slowly. They can walk backwards. They run quickly and usually maintain their balance. They can alternate feet going upstairs. They can master a tricycle. They jump up and down. They jump off objects. And they jump forward. They can twist and turn to dress and undress. And they can use their small muscles to hold clothes and attempt buttoning, snapping, and zippering. They practice their physical skills. Right- or left-handedness is now established, though children use both hands in many activities (see Figure 16–3).

Figure 16–3 The caregiver allows the child to use crayons in either or both hands even though handedness may be established.

At this age children can establish sleep routines which they can do themselves. Before nap they can go to the bathroom and wash their hands. They can sit on their cots, take their own shoes off, and put the shoes under the cot. They can lie down with their heads near their name tapes. When they awaken, they can go to the bathroom and return to put on their shoes. If others are still sleeping, they can choose a quiet activity, for example, looking at books or listening to a story or music with earphones.

Most children have completed toilet-training by 36 months of age. They need to wear clothes which they can remove quickly and easily. They need easy access to the bathroom. And they need occasional questions and reminders to go to the bathroom.

Suggestions for Implementing Curriculum

CHILD BEHAVIOR	EXAMPLES OF CAREGIVER STRATEGIES
Muscular Control	
MOVEMENT AND COORDINATION	
Walks evenly.	Provide uncluttered floor space.
Runs.	Provide space and games for appropriate running.
Jumps in place and forward.	Play games, sing songs which encourage jumping.
Dresses and undresses self with assistance.	Allow time for child to manipulate clothes.
	Demonstrate how to hold button and buttonholes, zipper and cloth, etc.
Uses fine motor coordination.	Turns one page at a time.
HAND	
Has established handedness.	Allow child to select hand to use.
Sleeping	
Assists with preparation routines.	Plan time in schedule for children to do as much of routines as possible. It takes longer for a child to wash and dry hands than if you help, but child needs to be independent and to develop skills.
	Help with tight snaps, etc.
Elimination	
Is in process of or has completed	Provide assistance when needed. Assist with clothes, hand washing when needed. Clean up area. *Wash your hands.*

Emotional Development

Children of this age express their emotions and feelings strongly. They let you know how they feel and then may move beyond their anger or happiness and soon express a different feeling.

These children's negativism is expressed in several ways. Sometimes negative behavior is a way of asserting themselves and their independence.

These children are enthusiastic learners, enjoying themselves and their discoveries. Their developing mastery of skills enhances their feelings of competence, self-worth, and acceptance of self (see Figure 16–4).

These children may become physically aggressive. Their widening world presents many new experiences. They may use aggression in their attempts to feel they have some control of their world.

At about 33 months they will begin to think in terms of their own past and may pretend to be a baby again. This regression may be a need based on their own development or perhaps there is a new baby in the family. Whatever the cause, these toddlers need lots of the 3A's and the time and patience to regain their proper place in their environment.

Persistence in continuing a task enables these children to discover many things. As they explore, their persistence will probably enable them to accomplish enough so that they have the feeling that "I did it" or "See what I found out." Children generally learn the love of learning when they are offered developmentally correct choices and are positively praised for their decisions by the caregiver who combines the 3A's of Child Care: Attention, Approval, and Affection. This love of learning is obvious when the child has a long attention span and displays much persistence for finishing a task. A short attention span, however, limits a child's exposure and involvement in many activities.

Figure 16–4 When young children continually make new discoveries, they become enthusiastic learners.

Suggestions for Implementing Curriculum

CHILD BEHAVIOR	EXAMPLES OF CAREGIVER STRATEGIES
Types of Emotions-Feelings	
Reacts strongly.	Accept child's initial response. Help child keep within bounds of appropriate behavior, e.g., let child express anger by vigorously riding a bigwheel for a while, or drawing an angry picture, or punching a pillow.
Acts negatively.	Rephrase suggestions to child. Stimulate interest in a different activity.
Learns enthusiastically.	Reinforce child's excitement with learning. Provide opportunities for challenging experiences.
Is mastering skills.	Provide toys, equipment, materials which child needs to use often to master skills.
Control of Emotions-Feelings	
Is physically aggressive.	Provide activities for child to work out feelings and need to control, such as: Using a puppet for imaginary play, let the child be a leader in structured activity. Paint, draw, use clay, dance or, if possible, be out of doors to run, jump, and yell.
Temperament	
Activity level.	List two of the child's behaviors in each category which indicate the child's basic style. List adjustments you need to make to help the child cope with daily situations
Regularity.	
Approach or withdrawal as a characteristic.	
Adaptability to change in routine.	
Level of sensory threshold.	
Positive or negative mood.	
Intensity of response.	
Distractibility.	
Persistence and attention span.	

Social Development

Egocentrism continues to be present in the preconceptual substage. Even though young children can distinguish themselves from others, they are only slowly developing the ideas that follow from this. They are just beginning to understand that others have feelings. They assume that when they speak, everyone understands the exact meaning of their words; they do not realize that others may give different meanings to the same words or experiences.

Young children interpret changes in appearance to mean changes in the basic object or person. "Preconceptual children generally do not see things or people as having a core and consistent identity over time" (Cowen 1978, 133). This fluctuation includes their concepts of self. "They seem to have little idea that their 'self' of a few days ago is relevant to what is happening now, today" (Cowen 1978, 133).

Children continue to identify their selfness within their world. Their toys are a part of themselves, and they remain very possessive of the toys and materials they are using. However, their strengthening sense of self also provides a foundation for expanding interactions with others. These children are increasingly aware of others as individuals. They use adults as resources, seeking assistance from them when they decide they need help (see Figure 16–5). They become directive with others, exerting control over people, animals, and toys as they learn ways to control their world. Children this age sometimes recognize others' needs and may help with tasks or initiate or respond with assistance.

These children's self-control is increasing. Their desire for instant gratification is being modified, so they sometimes accept delayed gratification. They may take turns occasionally. At times they may decide to share. And they may play cooperatively for short periods of time. The research strongly suggests that it is the felt experience, over and over and over again, of being cooperated with; the experience of having an important adult put aside his or her own needs to meet the child's very real needs; the experience of that important adult showing empathy, concern, respect, and nurturance toward the baby or toddler that begins to ingrain in that child the deepest sense of what these prosocial qualities are like (Wolf 1986).

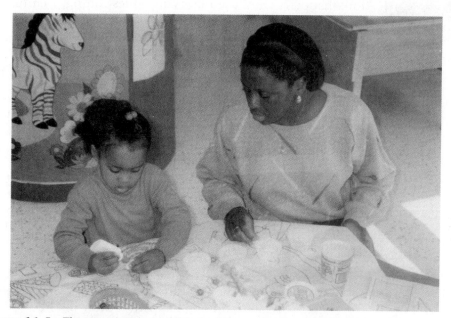

Figure 16–5   The caregiver is available to share materials and attention.

Suggestions for Implementing Curriculum

CHILD BEHAVIOR	EXAMPLES OF CAREGIVER STRATEGIES
Self	
Acts possessive.	Provide enough toys and materials so child can control use of some for a period of time.
Others	
Seeks assistance.	Allow child to use you as a resource. Help where needed. Do not take over.
Directs others.	Provide opportunities for child to exert acceptable control over others.
Helps others.	Praise child's spontaneous helping. Ask for assistance so child can help with routines, etc.
Control of Self	
Plays cooperatively.	Provide toys, materials, and time.
Shares.	Encourage by providing opportunities to share, e.g., eating orange or apple slices.
Takes turns.	Use daily routines to help control wait time, e.g., taking turns to wash hands.

Cognitive Development

Children at this age are curious, exploring problem-solvers. They are seeking to discover what makes things tick, what objects are made of, and how actions happen. They use observing, questioning, manipulating, classifying, and measuring to learn about their world.

In the preconceptual stage children may attempt to put objects in an order, like biggest to smallest buttons, but unless the materials present cues, such as fitting together, the children are not able to determine the logic of ordering. Arranging objects in a series is guesswork for young children because they do not understand the relationships in a series of objects.

These children continue to construct physical knowledge about the properties of objects (see Figure 16–6). They construct logico-mathematical knowledge about relationships. And they construct social-arbitrary knowledge about language and social rules and values.

Adults and children understand experiences differently. Even if both a child and an adult were present during the same experience, each would learn and experience something different.

Jane Healy, in her book Your Child's Growing Mind (1989), gives several ways to help "bridge the schema" (fill-in) gaps.

1. As you solve problems together, talk through your own questions. "I wonder how I should start?" "Could I put them together?" "Is it working?" "What's going to happen?" "How did I do?"
2. Ask your child similar questions.

Figure 16–6 Blocks, pegs, and other manipulatives provide cues to young children for matching shapes.

3. Phrase them simply and give the child plenty of time to think and answer.
4. Let the child repeat each solution several times to understand it.
5. Encourage understanding. Ask "Why do you think that happened?" "Why did/didn't that work?"

Around 36 months, depending upon temperament, children calm down. They become less resistant and use words like "yes" and "will" to replace the earlier "no" and "won't." The three-year-old is generally a happy, secure and somewhat conforming person, for a few months at least. Often you will hear the child repeat back to you the 3A's that you have given him over and over again.

Suggestions for Implementing Curriculum

CHILD BEHAVIOR	EXAMPLES OF CAREGIVER STRATEGIES
Piaget's Preoperational Stage, Preconceptual Substage	
NONVERBAL CLASSIFICATION	
Makes graphic collections.	Encourage child to use art media to represent. Listen to child's explanation of own classification system.

CHILD BEHAVIOR	EXAMPLES OF CAREGIVER STRATEGIES
VERBAL PRECONCEPTS	
Uses words differently at different times.	Observe context of talk. Ask for clarification of meaning if necessary.
Labels objects in one class.	Remember that child's meaning may not be as inclusive as yours. Determine exactly what child meant.
VERBAL REASONING	
Thinks one action is like another action.	Observe the behavior which precedes a child's talking. Determine how child is drawing relationships among his or her actions.
Reasons from effect to cause.	Think backward from action to previous action to understand child's reasoning.
QUANTITY	
Understands some, more, gone, big.	Use words labeling quantity. They are a part of the daily experiences.
NUMBER	
Understands more.	Use words labeling number as a comparative. Use daily situations, e.g., "There are more rocks in this pail than in that pail."
SPACE	
Understands up, down, behind, under, over.	Label child's actions when child is moving into different positions in space, e.g., "Merrilee is behind the box. Ashton is under the box."
TIME	
Understands now, soon, before, after.	Use time words in daily experiences, e.g., "We wash our hands before we eat." "We go to the the bathroom after naptime."

Learning Skills/Language Development

Visual and auditory perceptual skills should be learned daily. Children this age continue to increase their vocabulary. Their daily experiences provide opportunities for them to construct meanings of new objects and to extend previously learned concepts. The labeling process is now part of children's construction of the identity of objects.

These children continue to overregularize words. However, more and more of their plural words are formed correctly. These children are very gradually constructing concepts of time and most of their new time words come during this period. The past is still an abstraction they are attempting to understand. They still overregularize past tense words, saying things like, "Jim bited me" and "I bringed these out."

Sentence length increases as the children increase their use and familiarity with frequently used vocabulary, word-order patterns, and stress and intonation patterns. They speak more complete sentences and are able to express several ideas in a sequence of sentences.

Dramatic play provides opportunities to combine language with imagination. These children can describe their actions and say what they think others might say. They are practicing their language and fitting it into a social context.

Books play an increasingly important role. Reading aloud provides book language patterns. Reading the pictures encourages self-expression. And talking about the story or the pictures facilitates comprehension of the language (see Figure 16–7).

Scribbling continues as the child is involved in the writing process. Each child is developing scribbling at his or her own rate.

> Children are scribblers from the time they hold a writing tool until after they learn to write their names. There is a progression to their scribbles which moves from random scribbling, to controlled scribbling, to the naming of scribbling, to writing mock letters and words, to learning, finally, how to write. It is important not to underestimate the value of scribbling as a foundation for writing (Lamme 1984, 37).

Caroline Columbus, nationally recognized forensic handwriting analyst, discusses the importance of encouraging children to express themselves through scribbling.

> With the advent of computers the written word is being replaced by the printed word. It is important to allow children to develop their own

Figure 16–7 Books stimulate involvement in making and reading familiar stories.

writing integrity by encouraging scribbling which by its simple free nature will later develop into handwriting skills (Columbus 98).

You model many uses of writing for children. You write their names. You write a note to their parents. You write sentences on their art work papers. You write dictated sentences on their pages of scribbling. You write charts about daily experiences; for example, planting beans and writing on the chart what they look like each day. In this way, the children experience meaningful uses of writing.

Suggestions for Implementing Curriculum

CHILD BEHAVIOR	MATERIALS	EXAMPLES OF CAREGIVER STRATEGIES
Increases vocabulary		
Associates word and object.		Introduce new objects to see and feel and use. Label objects and actions with single words and use in sentences.
Improves syntax		
Word order.		Repeat child's sentence, using proper word order.
Two- and three-word sentences.		Respond to child's meaning. Extend his sentence.
Longer sentences.		Respond to child's meaning. Commend his ideas.
Improves word forms		
Uses plurals.		Use correct plural form. When child says "foots," restate "See your feet."
Uses past tense.		Use correct past tense. When child says "He bited me," restate, "He bit you? Show me where he bit you."
Improves reading skills		
Listens to stories, "reads" pictures, storybooks.	Records, pictures, picture books.	Read aloud. Listen to child "read." Use expression. Tell or read story line.
Uses controlled scribbling.	Markers, chalk, crayons, pencil, paper.	Write to child. Write notes to child and others. Label objects. Write dictated sentences.

Fun in the Kitchen

Activity—30–36 Months
Teaching about food, cooking, and kitchen safety is fun and important. Even nonverbal, very young children should be told what they are eating—

why it is important and what shape, color, and category of food it is—to encourage a healthy respect for the needs of the body, the joys of taste, smell, and texture, and the ability to share and have a growth experience.

The following two examples can be adapted to other teaching experiences, depending on the age of the children.

Ground Rules:

- All participants must wash their hands well before doing this food-related activity.
- No child with a cold (or symptoms of any kind), cuts, or abrasions may have direct contact with food.
- Children who touch their nose during the activity must stop and wash their hands again before continuing.
- All children should have a job, and a place to sit or stand.
- All participants should take turns.
- No one talks when someone else is talking.
- Everyone reaps the rewards of the end product.

Making Pancakes—20 minutes

The caregiver prepares all cups, spoons, plates, and ingredients before children are invited to participate. No styrofoam products of any kind should be used.

- Each person does one thing to facilitate batter preparation.
- A low-heat electric pan is used in front of children. All children watch the demonstration. Heat, electric, and cooking safety are discussed. Children watch at arm's distance from the hot pan.
- All help set the table.
- Everyone enjoys eating the finished pancakes.

Other Food Activities

Hold a tea party, using real decaffeinated herb teas. Each tea has a different color, smell, and taste.

To acquaint the child with vegetables, use the tops of broccoli. Pretend they are trees and the children are giants. Dip the tree into vanilla yogurt (each child has a separate portion). Discuss the color, texture, variety, and importance of vegetables. You can use other vegetables as well (jicama, slightly steamed sweet potato, for example).

Both food lessons should use the time to discuss how different people from different parts of the world have different vegetables, fruits, and foods. Involve one mother at a time; ask her and her child to bring in their family's favorite foods or different ethnic favorite foods and snack. Discuss this concept with the other children.

Remember that you are promoting successful future eating habits. A well-balanced diet is essential. The concept of "no garbage" in our bodies is important to help children choose the best fuel to obtain healthy bodies, calm minds, and an at-ease' state of well-being.

STUDENT ACTIVITIES

1. Observe one child for ten minutes in a play yard. Write a list of the activities the child does. Identify equipment and materials used.
2. Observe one child for ten minutes in a play yard. Tally the times the child shares a toy or equipment. Tally the times the child plays *with* another child.
3. Observe a caregiver for five minutes. Write down the dialogue the caregiver has with a child or with several children. Categorize the caregiver's statements which mirror, support, or respond to the child's statements.
4. Observe children at play. List their language and actions which indicate their developing concepts of quantity, number, space, and time.
5. Plan and use one activity with a child to facilitate the child's constructing physical knowledge.
6. Plan and use one activity with a child to facilitate the child' constructing logico-mathematical knowledge.
7. Plan and use one activity with a child to facilitate the child's constructing social-arbitrary knowledge.

CHAPTER REVIEW

1. List three tasks children this age can complete by themselves.
2. List four tasks children can assist you with.
3. Describe one way to deal with an angry child.
4. Write one example of a child's statement that uses a word to which the child has given a meaning different from that which adults give the word.
5. Compare how children learn physical knowledge, logico-mathematical knowledge, and social-arbitrary knowledge.

REFERENCES

Cohen, J. 1997. *Program for Social and Emotional Learning.* New York, NY: Teachers College, Columbia University.

Columbus, Carol. 1998. *Open Discussion on Handwriting Analysis.* Raymond, NH.

Cowen, Philip A. 1978. *Piaget with Feeling.* New York: Holt, Rinehart & Winston.

Healy, Jane. 1989. *Your Child's Growing Mind: A Guide to Learning and Brain Development from Birth to Adolescence.* New York: Doubleday.

Lamme, Linda Leonard. 1984. *Growing Up Writing.* Washington, D.C.: Acropolis Books Ltd.

White, Burton L. 1973. *The First Three Years of Life.* Englewood Cliffs, NJ: Prentice-Hall.

Wolf, Dennie Palmer. 1986. Washington: Exchange Press.

AUTHORS' CLOSING NOTE

As this book goes to print, the American people are concerned about several recent incidents reported in the national media regarding children as young as twelve years of age exhibiting deadly violence against teachers and school-mates in various parts of the country. Like many early childhood educators, we recognize the tremendous developmental lag between the social and emotional growth compared with the intellectual and technical information available to our youth today. It is painfully obvious that education regarding successful social and emotional development and functioning must be undertaken by our educational systems, including child care.

Jonathon Cohen has given a beginning to a curriculum to teach humane life skills which he calls "emotional intelligence." While there is no generally agreed upon definition of emotional or social intelligence, the goal of a curriculum for children is to monitor and manage one's own feelings; develop a positive and realistic self-image, empathize with others, listen and communicate verbally and nonverbally, and recognize and channel emotional experience in a way that furthers prosocial problem-solving and creative thinking. By placing importance on the emotional and social development of children, we can help create a social structure where compassion, understanding, and ethical behavior is valued (Cohen, J. 98).

We believe that you, the caregivers of children from infancy through toddlerhood, are in the most ideal and important position in our society to set the foundation for what is called emotional or social intelligence, and that your ability to sensitively care for the needs of young children will determine the course of our development as individuals and a world society in the Twenty First Century.

Congratulations on your choice of such an important career!

—Linda and Mike Watson

Appendix

Developmental Prescriptions

APPROXIMATELY BIRTH TO FOUR MONTHS OF AGE

CHILD BEHAVIOR	DATE FIRST OBSERVED	PRACTICING	PROFICIENT
Physical Development			
MUSCULAR CONTROL			
Reflex			
Grasp reflex.			
Startle reflex.			
Tonic neck reflex.			
Head and neck			
Turns head.			
Holds head upright with support.			
Lifts head slightly when on stomach.			
Holds head to sides and middle.			
Holds up head when on back and on stomach.			
Holds head without support.			
Trunk			
Holds up chest.			
Sits with support.			
May attempt to raise self.			
May fuss if left lying down with little chance to sit up.			
Holds up chest and shoulders.			
Leg			
Rolls from stomach to back.			

CHILD BEHAVIOR	DATE FIRST OBSERVED	PRACTICING	PROFICIENT
Arm			
Moves randomly.			
Reaches.			
Hand			
Opens and closes.			
Keeps hands open.			
Plays with hands.			
Uses hands to grasp object.			
Whole hand and fingers against thumb.			
Thumb and forefinger.			
Holds and moves object.			
Eye-hand coordination			
Moves arm toward object: may miss it.			
Reaches hand to object: may grab or miss it.			
SEEING			
Focuses 8 inches from eyes.			
Follows with eyes.			
Stares.			
See objects beyond 8 inches.			
Looks from object to object.			
Looks around; stops to focus on object which has caught attention; then looks at something else; continual visual searching.			
HEARING			
Responds to voice.			
Hears range of sounds.			
Calms while hearing low-pitched sounds.			
Becomes agitated while hearing high-pitched sounds.			
Locates sound.			
SLEEPING			
Sleeps much of the day and night.			
Takes a long morning nap and a long afternoon nap.			
May have irregular sleep habits.			
EATING			
Takes bottle on demand.			
ELIMINATION			
Begins to establish predictable eating and elimination pattern.			
Establishes regular time for bowel movements.			

CHILD BEHAVIOR	DATE FIRST OBSERVED	PRACTICING	PROFICIENT
Emotional Development			
TYPES OF EMOTIONS-FEELINGS			
Shows excitement.			
Shows stress.			
Shows enjoyment.			
Shows anger.			
Shows fear.			
Protests.			
CONTROL OF EMOTIONS-FEELINGS			
Seems to occur automatically.			
Decreases crying.			
Increases sounds (talking).			
Reflects sounds (talking).			
Comforted by holding.			
TEMPERAMENT (List two behaviors which indicate basic style)			
Activity level.			
Regularity.			
Approach or withdrawal as a characteristic response to a new situation.			
Adaptability to change in routine.			
Level of sensory threshold.			
Positive or negative mood.			
Intensity of response.			
Distractibility.			
Persistence and attention span.			
Social Development			
ATTACHMENT			
Shows special closeness to parent.			
Develops familiarity with one primary caregiver.			
SELF			
Becomes aware of hands and feet.			
Smiles spontaneously.			
Smiles at self in mirror.			
OTHERS			
Establishes eye contact with another person.			
Recognizes voice of parent.			
Smiles at people (social smile).			
Watches people.			
Talks (cooing) to people.			

CHILD BEHAVIOR	DATE FIRST OBSERVED	PRACTICING	PROFICIENT
Shows longer attentiveness when involved with people.			
Recognizes parent visually.			
Recognizes individual people.			
Behaves differently with parent than with others.			
Interacts with people.			
Laughs.			
Differentiates self from parent.			
Initiates talking to others.			
Plays with toys.			

Cognitive Development

SENSORIMOTOR STAGE 1

Reflexive actions.

Passive to active search.

SENSORIMOTOR STAGE 2

Small, gradual changes come from repetition.

Coordination of behaviors, e.g., sound-looking. Puts hand, object in mouth and sucks on it.

Moves hand, object where can see it.

Produces a pleasurable motor activity and repeats activity.

OBJECT PERMANENCE

Follows moving object with eyes until object disappears. Looks where object disappeared.

Loses interest and turns away.

Does not search for it.

Language Development

PHYSICAL COMPONENTS INVOLVED IN LANGUAGE COMMUNICATION

Back of throat.

Nose.

Mouth cavity.

Front of mouth.

Tongue.

Lips.

Saliva.

ACTIONS INVOLVED IN LANGUAGE COMMUNICATION

Changes air flow: through nose; through mouth.

Uses tongue to manipulate air flow, saliva.

Plays with tongue—twists, turns, sticks it out, sucks on it.

CHILD BEHAVIOR	DATE FIRST OBSERVED	PRACTICING	PROFICIENT
Uses saliva in various places and changes sounds: gurgle in back of throat; bubbling in center of mouth; hissing, spitting with partially closed lips and tongue.			
INITIATION–RESPONDING			
Initiates making sounds.			
Responds vocally to another person.			
Makes sound, repeats sound, continues practicing sound and lengthening to longer amounts of time.			
Imitates a few sounds he or she already knows.			
Experiments with sounds.			
CRYING			
Cries apparently automatically in distress, frustration.			
Cries differently to express hunger, discomfort, anger.			
Cries to gain attention.			
Cries less as vocalizing increases.			
COOING			
Coos in vowel-like sounds.			
Adds pitch.			

APPROXIMATELY FOUR TO EIGHT MONTHS OF AGE

CHILD BEHAVIOR	DATE FIRST OBSERVED	PRACTICING	PROFICIENT
Physical Development			
MUSCULAR CONTROL			
Head and neck			
Holds head up independently.			
Holds head in midline position.			
Holds head up when on back, stomach, and sitting.			
Trunk			
Holds up chest, shoulders; arches back, hips.			
Sits with support.			
May attempt to raise self.			
May fuss if left lying down with little chance to sit up.			

CHILD BEHAVIOR	DATE FIRST OBSERVED	PRACTICING	PROFICIENT
Leans back and forth.			
Sits in a chair.			
Sits unsupported for short time.			
Pushes self to sitting position.			

Leg

Lifts legs when on back and stomach.			
Rolls from stomach to back.			
Straightens legs when standing.			
Stamps feet when standing.			
Rolls from back to stomach.			
Raises self to hands and knees.			
Stands with support.			
Pulls self to standing.			

Locomotion

Kicks against surface to move.			
Rocks on hands and knees.			
Creeps on stomach.			
Uses legs to pull, push self when sitting.			

Arm

Visually directs reaching, hitting.			
Throws objects.			

Hand

Grasps objects with whole hand and fingers against thumb.			
Uses thumb and forefinger.			
Picks up object with one hand; passes it to the other hand.			
Uses objects in both hands.			
Grasps and releases objects.			
Drops objects.			

SEEING

Focuses on objects near and far.			
Distinguishes color, distance; depth perception.			
Distinguishes visually attractive objects.			
Has visual preferences.			

HEARING

Listens to own voice.			
Listens to others' voices.			
Looks around to locate sound.			

CHILD BEHAVIOR	DATE FIRST OBSERVED	PRACTICING	PROFICIENT
SLEEPING			
Takes a long morning nap and a long afternoon nap.			
EATING			
Begins solid foods (new tongue and swallowing technique).			
Drinks from cup (new tongue and swallowing technique).			
Eats at "mealtimes"—solid foods, milk, juice.			
Feeds self finger foods.			
TEETH			
First teeth emerge: 2 middle lower, 2 middle upper.			
ELIMINATION			
Decreases number of times of urination and bowel movements.			
Emotional Development			
TYPES OF EMOTIONS-FEELINGS			
Shows pleasure in watching others.			
Shows pleasure in repetitive play.			
Shows depression.			
Shows fear: of strangers; of falling down.			
Shows frustration with stimulation overload.			
Shows happiness, delight, joy, humor.			
Shows rage.			
CONTROL OF EMOTIONS-FEELINGS			
Sometimes stops crying when talked to, sung to.			
TEMPERAMENT (List two behaviors which indicate basic style)			
Activity level.			
Regularity.			
Approach or withdrawal as a characteristic response to a new situation.			
Adaptability to change in routine.			
Level of sensory threshold.			
Positive or negative mood.			
Intensity of response.			
Distractibility.			
Persistence and attention span.			
Social Development			
ATTACHMENT			
Shows strong attachment to parent.			

CHILD BEHAVIOR	DATE FIRST OBSERVED	PRACTICING	PROFICIENT
Differentiates response to parent.			
Shows familiarity with one specific caregiver.			
Shows intense pleasure and frustration to person with whom attached.			

SELF

Recognizes self in mirror.

Seeks independence in actions.

Plays self-designed games.

OTHERS

Observes others.

Imitates others.

Recognizes children.

Plays with people.

Seeks parent's and caregiver's attention by movement, sounds, smiles, cries.

Follows parent and caregiver to be in same room.

Resists pressures from others regarding feeding and eating.

Acts shy with some strangers.

Cognitive Development

SENSORIMOTOR STAGE 3

Produces a motor activity, catches interest, and intentionally repeats the activity over and over.

Repeats interesting action.

Develops hand-eye coordination further. Looks for object, reaches for it, and accurately touches it.

Imitates behavior can see or hear.

OBJECT PERMANENCE: STAGE 3

Visually follows object.

Searches visually for short time when object disappears.

Does not search manually.

Sees part of object; looks for whole object.

Language Development

Coos vowel-like sounds for many minutes.

Babbles syllable-like sounds.

Responds to talking by cooing, babbling, smiling.

Imitates sounds.

CHILD BEHAVIOR	DATE FIRST OBSERVED	PRACTICING	PROFICIENT
Initiates sounds.			
Makes vowel sounds.Looks for person speaking.			
Looks when name is called.			
Makes consonant sounds.			
Babbles conversation with others.			
Reflects happiness, unhappiness in sounds made.			
Babbles two- and three-syllable sounds.			
Uses intensity,			
volume,			
pitch,			
rhythm.			

APPROXIMATELY FROM EIGHT TO TWELVE MONTHS OF AGE

CHILD BEHAVIOR	DATE FIRST OBSERVED	PRACTICING	PROFICIENT
Physical Development			
MUSCULAR CONTROL			
Trunk and leg			
Raises self to sitting position.			
Sits alone.			
Stands holding onto furniture or hand.			
Stands without assistance.			
Sits from standing.			
Squats and stands.			
Locomotion			
Crawls.			
Steps forward.			
Crawls up steps.			
Steps sideways.			
Walks with help.			
Climbs on furniture.			
Hand			
Uses thumb and forefinger.			
Uses thumb and two fingers.			
Brings both hands to middle of body.			
Uses finger to poke.			
Carries objects in hands.			
Holds and uses pen and crayon.			
Reaches, touches, strokes object.			
Uses one hand to hold object, one hand to reach and explore.			
Stacks blocks with dominant hand.			
Takes off clothes.			

CHILD BEHAVIOR	DATE FIRST OBSERVED	PRACTICING	PROFICIENT

SLEEPING

    May have trouble sleeping.

    Takes morning nap and afternoon nap.

    Seeks parent or caregiver presence.

EATING

    Holds bottle.

    Holds cup.

    Holds and uses spoon.

    Uses fingers to eat most food.

    Starts establishing food preferences.

    May eat less.

TEETH

    Begins to get teeth.

Emotional Development

TYPES OF EMOTIONS-FEELINGS

    Shows happiness, joy, pleasure.

    Shows anxiety.

    Shows fear.

    Shows anger, frustration.

    May have tantrums.

    Rejects items, situations.

    Develops preferences with toys, people.

    Shows independence—helps with feeding and dressing self.

    Shows affection.

    Begins developing self-esteem.

CONTROL

    Learning to obey "No."

    Sometimes inhibits own behavior.

    Obeys commands: No-No, Stop.

TEMPERAMENT (List two behaviors which indicate basic style)

    Activity level.

    Regularity.

    Approach or withdrawal as a characteristic response to a new situation.

    Adaptability to change in routine.

    Level of sensory threshold.

    Positive or negative mood.

    Intensity of response.

    Distractibility.

    Persistence and attention span.

CHILD BEHAVIOR	DATE FIRST OBSERVED	PRACTICING	PROFICIENT

Social Development

OTHERS

  Initiates interactions with others.

  Responds.

  May fear strangers.

  Keeps parent or caregiver in sight.

  Initiates play.

  Begins to identify with children of own sex.

  Becomes assertive.

  Wants own pleasure; may not consider others.

  Imitates play.

  Is possessive of people.

  Is possessive of materials.

  May become shy, clinging.

  May demand attention.

Cognitive Development

SENSORIMOTOR STAGE 4

  Differentiates goals

    Can focus on reaching and focus on toy.

  Object permanence

    Object permanence established; object exists when it is no longer visible; child seeks toy that rolls behind object.

  Causality

    Understands that others cause actions.

Imitation and play

    Imitates other's actions; uses actions as play.

Language Development

  Babbles.

  Shouts.

  Labels object sounds.

  Uses names: mama, dada.

  Responds to familiar sounds.

  Responds to familiar words.

  Responds to own name.

  Makes sounds which reflect emotions.

  Repeats syllables, words, e.g., bye-bye.

  Makes sounds like conversation.

  Repeats, practices word over and over.

  Connects word with objects: says word and points to object.

APPROXIMATELY TWELVE TO EIGHTEEN MONTHS OF AGE

CHILD BEHAVIOR	DATE FIRST OBSERVED	PRACTICING	PROFICIENT

Physical Development

MUSCULAR CONTROL

Trunk

Shows high energy, is active, moves from one activity to another.

Raises self to standing.

Locomotion

May prefer crawling to walking.

Walks alone.

Climbs up stairs with help.

Climbs down stairs with help.

Climbs over objects.

Hand

Uses thumb against fingers.

Shows hand preference.

Points with finger.

Carries, exchanges objects in hands.

Flings objects.

Throws objects.

Rolls and catches objects.

Eye-hand coordination

Reaches and grasps accurately.

Scribbles.

Helps in dressing, undressing.

SEEING

Watches people, objects, actions.

Bends, looks from different directions.

Visually scans surrounding area.

Visually searches.

SLEEPING

Begins to move from morning and afternoon nap to afternoon nap.

EATING

Eats three meals.

Feeds self; uses cup, spoon, and fingers.

Expresses food likes and dislikes.

May eat less food.

CHILD BEHAVIOR	DATE FIRST OBSERVED	PRACTICING	PROFICIENT

Emotional Development

TYPES OF EMOTIONS-FEELINGS

Expresses emotions in behavior and language.

Recognizes emotions in others.

May fear strangeness.

Shows excitement, delight.

Expresses sense of humor.

Shows affection.

Displays negativism.

May have tantrums.

Uses play to express emotions, resolve conflicts.

Seeks dependency, security with parent and caregiver.

Seeks to expand independence.

CONTROL OF EMOTIONS-FEELINGS

Begins to understand right and wrong.

Reinforces desired behavior.

TEMPERAMENT (List two behaviors which indicate basic style)

Activity level.

Regularity.

Approach or withdrawal as a characteristic response to a new situation.

Adaptability to change in routine.

Level of sensory threshold.

Positive or negative mood.

Intensity of response.

Distractibility.

Persistence and attention span.

Social Development

SELF

Has concept of self.

Is egocentric: understands only own viewpoint.

OTHERS

Seeks presence of parent or caregiver.

Plays games.

Occasionally shares.

Acts differently toward different people.

Uses variety of behaviors to gain attention.

May be shy with some people.

Engages in parallel play.

CHILD BEHAVIOR	DATE FIRST OBSERVED	PRACTICING	PROFICIENT

Cognitive Development

SENSORIMOTOR DEVELOPMENT: STAGE 5

Object permanence

Watches toy hidden and moved.

Looks for it where moved.

Causality

Investigates cause and effect.

Sees self as causal agent.

Explores various ways things happen.

Employs active trial-and-error to solve problems.

Experiments.

Imitation and play

Copies behaviors of others.

Turns play with imitation into rituals.

Language Development

Uses intonation.

Babbles sentences.

Repeats, practices words.

Imitates sounds of other people, objects.

Responds to word and gesture conversation.

Responds to many questions and commands child cannot say.

Uses word approximation for some words.

Uses words in immediate context.

Identifies familiar pictures.

Uses markers.

APPROXIMATELY EIGHTEEN TO TWENTY-FOUR MONTHS OF AGE

CHILD BEHAVIOR	DATE FIRST OBSERVED	PRACTICING	PROFICIENT

Physical Development

MUSCULAR CONTROL

Locomotion

Walks forward.

Walks backward.

Walks sideways.

Runs with stops and starts.

Jumps with both feet.

Kicks object.

Walks up stairs holding railing; walks down stairs holding railing.

CHILD BEHAVIOR	DATE FIRST OBSERVED	PRACTICING	PROFICIENT
Pushes and pulls objects while walking.			
Climbs.			
Pedals cycle.			
Arm			
Throws object at target.			
Hand			
Grasps and releases with developing finger muscles.			
Pulls zippers.			
Helps dress and undress self.			
Scribbles.			
Increases wrist flexibility, turns wrist to turn object.			
Establishing right- or left-handedness.			
Turns book pages.			
Digs with tool.			
Makes individual marks with crayon or pen.			
SLEEPING			
May move from crib to bed or cot.			
EATING			
Controls cup and spoon better.			
May eat anything, then change to picky eating.			
TEETH			
Has most baby teeth.			
Uses toothbrush.			
ELIMINATION			
May show interest in and readiness for toilet training.			
Emotional Development			
TYPES OF EMOTIONS-FEELINGS			
Views internal feelings and external behavior as same.			
Shows one or more emotions at same time.			
Continues to develop feelings about self.			
Changes feelings about self.			
Seeks approval.			
May develop new fears.			
Increases fantasy.			
May increase aggressiveness.			
Seeks security in routines.			

CHILD BEHAVIOR	DATE FIRST OBSERVED	PRACTICING	PROFICIENT
May become shy again.			
Sometimes rejects parent or caregiver.			

CONTROL OF EMOTIONS-FEELINGS

Uses reactions of others as a controller of own behavior.			
May resist change.			
Moves to extremes, from lovable to demanding and stubborn.			

TEMPERAMENT (List two behaviors which indicate basic style)

Activity level.			
Regularity.			
Approach or withdrawal as a characteristic response to a new situation.			
Adaptability to change in routine.			
Level of sensory threshold.			
Positive or negative mood.			
Intensity of response.			
Distractibility.			
Persistence and attention span.			

Social Development

SELF

Is egocentric, sees things from own point of view.			
May change identity of self from day to day.			
Identifies materials as belonging to self.			
Uses I, mine, me, you.			

OTHERS

Demands attention.			
Begins to be aware of others' feelings.			
Believes people have changes in identity.			
Expands social relationships.			
Looks to others for help.			
Imitates tasks of others.			
Wants to help, assists with tasks.			
May do opposite of what is requested.			
Difficulty sharing.			
Engages in parallel play.			

Cognitive Development

SENSORIMOTOR DEVELOPMENT: STAGE 6

Mental trial and error

Tries out ideas mentally, based on past concrete experiences.			

CHILD BEHAVIOR	DATE FIRST OBSERVED	PRACTICING	PROFICIENT
Object permanence			
Sees object disappear, mentally remembers object and figures out where it went.			
Deferred imitation and symbolization			
Imitates past events.			
Engages in symbolic play.			
Resolves conflict.			
Compensates for unsatisfied needs.			
Tries roles.			
Language Development			
Uses language to reflect own meaning; expects others to have same meaning.			
Expands vocabulary rapidly, labeling objects.			
Points to objects and pictures named by others.			
Learns social words—hello, please, thank you.			
Uses language to express needs, desires.			
Uses language to direct others.			
Questions.			
Uses nouns,			
verbs,			
pronouns.			
Is learning prepositions.			
Calls self by name.			
Follows directions of one-step or two-steps.			
Uses two-word sentences; three-word sentences.			
Looks at books.			
Listens to stories and rhymes.			
Scribbles.			

APPROXIMATELY TWENTY-FOUR TO THIRTY MONTHS OF AGE

CHILD BEHAVIOR	DATE FIRST OBSERVED	PRACTICING	PROFICIENT
Physical Development			
MUSCULAR CONTROL			
Movement			
Bends at waist.			
Climbs.			
Jumps.			
Stands on one foot.			

CHILD BEHAVIOR	DATE FIRST OBSERVED	PRACTICING	PROFICIENT
Arm			
Throws.			
Hand			
Touches.			
Twists.			
EATING			
Uses spoon.			
Is learning to use fork.			
Uses fingers.			
TEETH			
Has all twenty baby teeth.			
Brushes teeth.			
ELIMINATION			
Is learning to use toilet.			
Has completed toilet training.			
Emotional Development			
TYPES OF EMOTIONS-FEELINGS			
Self-esteem			
Feels comfortable with self.			
Feels positive self-worth.			
Feels negative self-worth.			
CONTROL OF EMOTIONS-FEELINGS			
Expresses emotions.			
TEMPERAMENT (List two behaviors which indicate basic style)			
Activity level.			
Regularity.			
Approach or withdrawal as a characteristic response to a new situation.			
Adaptability to change in routine.			
Level of sensory threshold.			
Positive or negative mood.			
Intensity of response.			
Distractibility.			
Persistence and attention span.			
Social Development			
SELF			
Realizes own skills.			
OTHERS			
Shows independence.			
Acts to please adult.			

CHILD BEHAVIOR	DATE FIRST OBSERVED	PRACTICING	PROFICIENT
Shows feelings to others.			
Recognizes emotions in others.			
Recognizes the difference between "mine" and "yours."			
Shares.			
Helps others.			
Engages in parallel play.			

Cognitive Development

PREOPERATIONAL STAGE: PRECONCEPTUAL

Nonverbal classification

Makes graphic collections.

Verbal preconcepts

Uses words differently at different times.

Uses words with private meanings.

Labels objects in one class.

Focuses on one attribute.

Verbal reasoning

Reasons from particular to particular.

Quantity

Understands some,

more,

gone,

big.

Number

Understands more.

Space

Understands up,

down,

behind,

under,

over.

Time

Understands now,

soon.

Language Development

Uses demonstrative naming.

Uses attribution.

Uses possession.

Uses action

Uses recurrence.

CHILD BEHAVIOR	DATE FIRST OBSERVED	PRACTICING	PROFICIENT
Uses negation.			
Learns word order.			
Learns prosodic patterning.			
Uses subject–verb.			
Uses verb–object.			
Omits function words.			
Selects and uses books.			
Uses controlled scribbling.			

APPROXIMATELY THIRTY TO THIRTY-SIX MONTHS OF AGE

CHILD BEHAVIOR	DATE FIRST OBSERVED	PRACTICING	PROFICIENT
Physical Development			
MOVEMENT AND COORDINATION			
Walks evenly.			
Runs.			
Jumps in place and forward.			
Dresses and undresses self with assistance.			
Has established handedness.			
SLEEPING			
Assists with preparation of routines.			
ELIMINATION			
Is in process of or has completed toilet training.			
Emotional Development			
TYPES OF EMOTIONS-FEELINGS			
Reacts strongly.			
Acts negatively.			
Learns enthusiastically.			
Is mastering skills.			
CONTROL OF EMOTIONS-FEELINGS			
Is physically aggressive.			
TEMPERAMENT (List two behaviors which indicate basic style)			
Activity level.			
Regularity.			
Approach or withdrawal as a characteristic response to a new situation.			
Adaptability to change in routine.			
Level of sensory threshold.			

CHILD BEHAVIOR	DATE FIRST OBSERVED	PRACTICING	PROFICIENT
Positive or negative mood.			
Intensity of response.			
Distractibility.			
Persistence and attention span.			

Social Development

SELF

Acts possessive.

OTHERS Seeks assistance.

Directs others.

Helps others.

CONTROL OF SELF

Plays cooperatively.

Shares.

Takes turns.

Cognitive Development

PREOPERATIONAL STAGE: PRECONCEPTUAL

Nonverbal classification

Makes graphic collections.

Verbal preconcepts

Uses words differently at different times.

Labels objects in one class.

Verbal reasoning

Thinks one action is like another action.

Reasons from effect to cause.

Quantity

Understands some,

more,

gone,

big.

Number

Understands more.

Space

Understands up,

down,

behind,

under,

over.

Time

Understands now,

soon,

CHILD BEHAVIOR	DATE FIRST OBSERVED	PRACTICING	PROFICIENT
before,			
after.			
Language Development			
INCREASES VOCABULARY			
IMPROVES SYNTAX			
Word order.			
Two- and three-word sentences.			
Longer sentences.			
IMPROVES WORD FORMS			
Plurals.			
Past tense.			
IMPROVES READING SKILLS			
Listens to stories, "reads" pictures, storybooks.			
USES CONTROLLED SCRIBBLING			

Appendix ■B

Developmental Profile and Instructions

INSTRUCTIONS

Copy the Developmental Profile form. Create a profile for each child in care by following these instructions:

1. Write the child's name, date(s) of assessment(s), and date of birth (D.O.B.) on the profile. (Use the Sample Profile in Figure 3-2 as an example.)
2. Calculate Chronological Age (C.A.) by using the following method:

		Year	Month	Day
Assessment	=	1993	2	24
D.O.B.	=	1992	2	21
C.A.	=	1(12 mo)	0	3

3. Place the C.A. in months in the middle shaded C.A. row on the profile and put one-month intervals at each row for children with C.A.s from 1–17 months and two-month intervals for C.A.s from 18 months up (see Figure B-1 for example).
4. Write the child behaviors assessed from the Developmental Prescription (Appendix A) under each major Developmental Area on the Profile (see Sample Profile in Figure B-2).
5. Observe how the child performs on each skill and place an X on the row representing the monthly development for each listed Child Behavior.
6. Connect the Xs to graphically illustrate the child's Developmental Profile.
7. Write notes regarding strengths and weaknesses illustrated by the Profile.

Name: _____
Date: _____

Date of Birth: _____
C.A.: _____

MONTH AGE EXPECT.	AREA I PHYSICAL	AREA II EMOTIONAL	AREA III SOCIAL	AREA IV COGNITIVE	AREA V LEARNING SKILLS	MONTH AGE EXPECT.

C.A.

Notes:

Figure B–1 Blank Developmental Profile

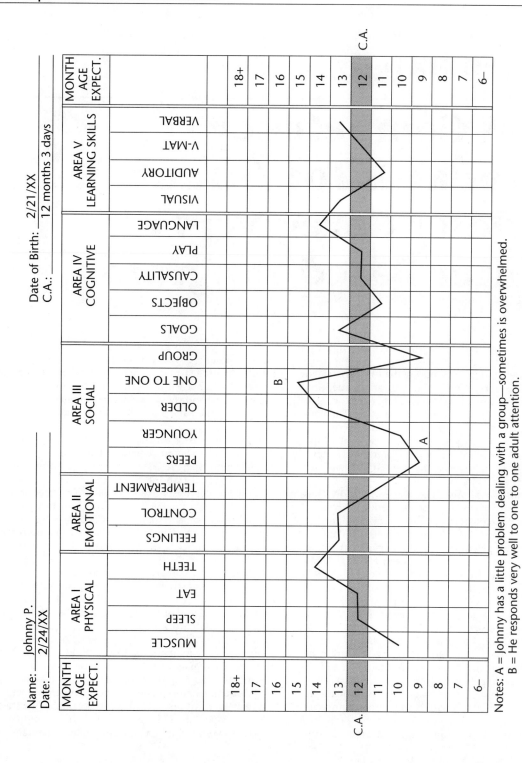

Figure B–2 Sample of completed Developmental Profile

Appendix C

CDA Competency Standards for Infant/Toddler Caregivers in Center-Based Programs

The CDA Competency Standards are the national standards used to evaluate a caregiver's performance with children and families during the CDA assessment process. The Competency Standards are divided into six **competency goals**, which are statements of a general purpose or goal for caregiver behavior. The competency goals are common to all child care settings. The six goals are defined in more detail in 13 **functional areas**, which describe the major tasks or functions that a caregiver must complete in order to carry out the competency goal.

Each functional area is explained by a **developmental context**, which presents a brief overview of child development from birth to 3 years and provides a rationale for the functional area definition and examples of competent caregiver behavior that follow. Three different developmental levels are identified—young infants (birth–8 months), mobile infants (9–17 months), and toddlers (18–36 months). Children develop at different rates, and descriptions of these levels emphasize the unique characteristics and needs of children at each stage of development.

Each functional area is further explained by a list of sample caregiver behaviors. These examples describe behavior that demonstrates that a caregiver is acting in a competent way or exhibiting a skill in a particular functional area. During the assessment process, most Candidates will exhibit other competent behavior, and a competent Candidate might not demonstrate all the examples listed under a functional area. The examples are organized according to developmental stages of children from birth to 3 years, in order to emphasize the importance of the special skills needed to work with young infants, mobile infants, and toddlers. Special bilingual specialization examples are presented for several functional areas.

The samples of caregiver competency included in the standards should serve as a basis for recognizing other, more specific behaviors that are important to the individual Candidate. A competent Candidate might not demonstrate all the examples listed in the following pages. CDA Candidates and individuals conducting or participating in CDA training will be able to think of many different ways to demonstrate skill in the six competency goals and 13 functional areas.

Competent caregivers integrate their work and constantly adapt their skills—always thinking of the development of the whole child. In all functional areas, it is important for competent caregivers to individualize their work with each child while meeting the needs of the group. In every area, too, caregivers must promote multiculturalism, support families with different languages, and meet the needs of children with handicapping conditions and special needs. And, while demonstrating skills and knowledge, competent caregivers must also demonstrate personal qualities, such as flexibility and a positive style of communicating with young children and working with families.

COMPETENCY GOAL I

To establish and maintain a safe, healthy, learning environment

1. FUNCTIONAL AREA: SAFE

Candidate provides a safe environment to prevent and reduce injuries.

Developmental Context

One of the most essential services for children is to ensure their safety and well-being. Indoor and outdoor areas should be free of dangerous conditions and materials. Adults should teach children about safety and comfort children when hurt. Adults should be attentive and have the skills and knowledge to prevent injuries and to handle emergencies, accidents, and injuries appropriately when they occur. In a safe environment, children will learn gradually to protect themselves and look out for others.

Young infants (birth–8 months) must be attended to carefully. A safe and secure environment is essential to their development. Because of infants' vulnerability and relative helplessness, adults must attend to each infant at all times in order to ensure his/her continued safety.

Mobile infants (9–17 months) are changing each day. As their rapidly increasing motor skills lead them into new areas, adults must anticipate new hazards that may arise.

Toddlers (18–36 months) are increasingly curious about their world. They stretch boundaries and test everything in their surroundings. Adults must be attentive to their activities and ensure their safety while giving them simple explanations for safety precautions.

Examples

For example, the competent Candidate working with infants and toddlers:

- Keeps both the inside of the center and the outdoor play areas free of debris, structural hazards, unguarded space heaters, tools, and dangerous substances (e.g., medicine, cleaning products, matches, chipping paint, toxic plants, small objects that could be swallowed, balloons, and plastic bags).
- Ensures that safety equipment (e.g., fire extinguishers and smoke detectors) are in place and operable and knows how to use them.
- Maintains an easily accessible and current list of phone numbers for contacting parents and emergency services, including poison control, fire company, and medical help.
- Uses diagrams, pictures, and words understood by children and adults to post instructions and practice procedures for fires and other emergencies, including safety procedures for children with handicapping conditions.
- Plans and practices monthly fire drills for moving all children in care to safety as quickly as possible.
- Ensures that outdoor play equipment is safe for small children and in good repair.
- Responds immediately and sympathetically to a child's injury or fear of injury and encourages the same response by the children.
- Takes safety precautions in a reassuring manner without overprotecting or making children fearful.
- Anticipates and makes plans to prevent potentially dangerous situations (e.g., children left unattended while sleeping or separated while on a field trip).
- Maintains first aid supplies—gauze, tape, syrup of ipecac, tweezers, scissors, and soap—and knows basic first aid procedures appropriate for young children (e.g., how to handle choking, treating cuts, etc.).
- Uses safe auto and bus travel procedures, including use of appropriate car seats for children.
- Discusses safety information with parents and tells them about resources (e.g., poison control centers) that provide services to families in their own language.
- Makes areas safe for children at different developmental stages; for example, putting safety gates on stairways; covering electrical outlets with safety plugs; inspecting children's equipment (e.g., cribs and car seats) at least weekly; securing, rearranging, or removing furniture that could fall or be pulled over, and securing carpeting and rugs.
- Supervises all children's indoors and outdoors activities.
- Keeps informed about safety standards for toys and equipment and shares this information with parents.
- Adapts the indoor and outdoor environment so that children with handicapping conditions can maximize their independence (e.g., safe use of mechanical aids or equipment).
- Requires parents to authorize in writing all persons allowed to pick children up from the program.

Young Infants

The competent Candidate working with young infants also, for example:

- Locks side rails on cribs in "up" position when children are napping.

- Places infants in a comfortable and safe position for sleeping.
- Stays with infants on changing table or when bathing.

Mobile Infants

The competent Candidate working with mobile infants, for example:

- Holds child's hand when near dangerous areas (e.g., roads, deep water, or steps).
- Knows children's individual differences in their tendency to bite, climb, and escape. Watches or stays close to children to anticipate and respond to these actions.

Toddlers

The competent Candidate working with toddlers also, for example:

- Helps toddlers stop dangerous actions toward themselves and others.
- Explains cause and effect in dangerous situations in simple language, demonstrating as much as possible.
- Teaches safe use of playground equipment.

Bilingual Specialization

In addition, the competent Candidate working towards the bilingual specialization:

- Explains and practices safety procedures (e.g., fire drills) using the language best understood by the children.
- Utilizes cultural values and practices in providing safety education.

2. FUNCTIONAL AREA: HEALTHY

Candidate promotes good health and nutrition and provides an environment that contributes to the prevention of illness.

Developmental Context

Good health involves sound medical and dental practices and good nutrition. Adults should model and encourage good health and nutrition habits with children. Food should be nutritious, prepared carefully, and served in a relaxed atmosphere. Prompt care should be given to children who are or become ill or hurt. Children need a clean environment that is properly lighted, ventilated, and heated or cooled. Indoor and outdoor areas should be free of materials or conditions that endanger children's health. Care of the child's physical needs communicates positive feelings about his/her value and influences the child's developing identity and feelings of self-worth. Parents and caregivers should exchange information about children's physical health frequently.

Young and mobile infants (birth–17 months) need affectionate and competent physical care geared to their individual needs and rhythms. Adults can help infants regulate their eating, sleeping, and other activities gradually, while continuing to balance the infant's and the group's needs.

Toddlers (18–36 months) imitate and learn from the activities of those around them. Good health habits can be established through modeling and encouraging tooth brushing, hand washing, nutritious eating, etc.

Examples

For example, the competent Candidate working with infants and toddlers.

- Learns about good nutrition for children from birth to 3 years old and helps plan age-appropriate, nutritious meals and snacks. While respecting family customs and habits, the caregiver shares nutrition information with parents and encourages them to provide healthy foods when they contribute food to the center.
- Conducts activities in a positive, relaxed, and pleasant atmosphere to reduce tension and stress.
- Washes hands before and after toileting a child, helping child blow nose, and food preparation and eating.
- Attends to each child's physical needs (e.g., toileting, eating, exercising, and napping).
- Provides affection for all children.
- Provides adequate ventilation and lighting, comfortable room temperatures, and good sanitation.
- Makes sure play areas and materials are cleaned daily.
- Establishes procedures for care of sick children; for example, isolating a child with a contagious illness from well children, contacting parents and medical providers, and administering medicine.
- Helps children develop basic health habits.
- Keeps handy current emergency telephone numbers for each child's parent(s), nearest relative, and medical providers.
- Communicates frequently with parents about children's health, nutrition, communicable diseases, and medications and cooperates with parents and health specialists.
- Follows center procedures for maintaining health records, administering medications, first aid, and cooperates with health and nutrition staff.
- Establishes a relaxed mealtime routine that makes eating pleasant for each child.
- Limits sugar, salt, processed foods, unnecessary chemical additives, and artificial coloring and flavoring in meals and snacks and encourages parents to do the same.

- Informs parents about health resources (e.g., physicians or community clinics) that provide services to families in their primary language.
- Recognizes unusual behavior and physical symptoms in children and encourages parents to obtain appropriate treatment.
- Works cooperatively with health professionals and parents to meet the needs of children with handicapping conditions.
- Recognizes symptoms of possible abuse and neglect and is alert to play or behavior that indicates physical or sexual abuse. If physical or sexual abuse is suspected, the competent Candidate seeks out resources for information and support, follows state law in response, responds sensitively to child's and family's needs and cooperates in carrying out treatment plans.
- Recognizes the signs of a health crisis that children with special needs may have and responds appropriately (e.g., seizures).

Infants

The competent Candidate working with **young and mobile infants** also, for example:

- Cleans with sanitizing solution, at least daily, all toys and objects used and "mouthed" by infants.
- Makes provisions for sanitary diaper changing and disposal.
- Washes hands thoroughly before and after each diaper change and before each feeding.
- Supports mothers who wish to continue breast feeding infants.
- Follows a sanitary procedure for preparing, storing, and labeling baby bottles.
- Responds to infant's individual rhythms, while working towards regularity in feeding, sleeping and toileting.
- Manages group so as to be able to concentrate on the individual feeding of infants and to hold infants for bottle feeding.
- Recognizes rashes and skin irritations and works with parents to prevent and treat them.
- Recognizes conditions that cause tooth decay in infants and takes measures to prevent them.
- Works cooperatively with parents and shares information frequently concerning nutrition, weaning, and introducing solid foods, while showing respect for different practices and values.
- Offers children opportunities to gradually feed themselves by providing finger foods and allowing adequate time for pleasurable feeding.
- Does not put children to bed with a bottle unless it contains water.

Toddlers

The competent Candidate working with **toddlers** also, for example:

- Uses role playing, modeling, visual material, and real objects to teach healthy physical, mental, dental, and nutritional practices.
- Plans health care and educational activities that integrate health and nutrition information from the children's cultures with medically accepted health and nutritional practices.
- Has age-appropriate expectations of toddlers' abilities and helps them to develop self-help skills in eating, toileting, washing hands, tooth brushing, etc.
- Works with parents in planning for toilet learning, respects different family practices and expectations, and is sensitive to each child's readiness.
- Understands toddlers' explorations, concerns, and curiosities about their own and others' bodies and responds with information at their level; for example, explaining the physical differences between boys and girls matter-of-factly in simple terms.

Bilingual Specialization

The competent Candidate working towards the **bilingual specialization**, for example:

- Provides written health information for parents (e.g., notices about immunizations) in both languages.
- Utilizes cultural values and practices in providing health and nutrition education.

3. FUNCTIONAL AREA: LEARNING ENVIRONMENT

Candidate uses space, relationships, materials, and routines as resources for constructing an interesting, secure, and enjoyable environment that encourages play, exploration, and learning.

Developmental Context

Children of all ages learn from their own experience and by imitation. Adults can guide and encourage children's learning by ensuring that the environment is emotionally supportive; invites active exploration, play, and movement by children; and supports a broad array of experiences. A reliable routine together with a stimulating choice of materials, activities, and relationships enhances children's learning and development.

Young infants (birth–8 months) begin to learn from their immediate surroundings and daily experiences. The sense of well-being and emotional security conveyed by a loving and skilled caregiver creates a readiness for other experiences. Before infants can creep and crawl, adults should provide a variety of sensory experiences and encourage movement and playfulness.

Mobile infants (9–17 months) are active, independent, and curious. They are increasingly persistent and purposeful in doing things. They need many opportunities to practice new skills and explore the environment within safe boundaries. Adults can share children's delight in themselves, their skills, and discoveries, and gradually add variety to the learning environment.

Toddlers (18–36 months) are developing new language skills, physical control, and awareness of themselves and others each day. They enjoy participating in planned and group activities, but they are not yet ready to sit still or work in a group for a very long time. Adults can support their learning in all areas by maintaining an environment that is dependable but flexible enough to provide opportunities for them to extend their skills, understanding, and judgment in individualized ways.

Examples

For example, the competent Candidate working with infants and toddlers:

- Uses materials, books, and equipment that are stimulating to each child and suitable to individual learning styles, including those of children with handicapping conditions.
- Uses materials that demonstrate acceptance of each child's sex, family, race, language, and culture.
- Provides easily accessible learning materials (e.g., puzzles, books, stacking toys) that children can explore by themselves as well as putting some materials away for special times or for use at later stages of development.
- Organizes space into identifiable areas that encourage appropriate and independent use of materials.
- Balances active and quiet, free and structured, individual and group, indoor and outdoor activities.
- Provides many opportunities for children to develop their senses and ability to concentrate.
- Provides a variety of natural and pleasurable sounds such as music, normal conversation, outdoor sounds, etc.
- Observes individual children and the group frequently and modifies the environment to meet their changing abilities, needs, and interests.
- Varies routines spontaneously to take advantage of unusual opportunities (e.g., goes outside in the snow, invites a visiting grandmother to

share stories or songs with children, lets the children watch workers and machinery on the street, or plays with one child for an extra period of time when additional adults are available to care for group).

- Supports relationships between adults and children, as well as between children in care, as an important aspect of the learning environment.
- Schedules day so there is time for individual attention to each child.
- Encourages children to become involved in activities that extend their attention spans.
- Provides simple and consistent routines for mealtimes, naps, preparing to go out, changing activities, clean up, etc.; supports children's learning through these routines.
- Makes and helps parents make toys and equipment from easily available materials for use in the home and center.
- Adapts the daily schedule to accommodate children with special needs rather than requiring them to fit the schedule.

Young Infants

The competent Candidate working with young infants also, for example:

- Changes an infant's position and location often during the day and responds to the child's developing skills (e.g., sitting up, rolling over, reaching for objects, and making noises).
- Provides a learning environment for nonmobile infants that encourages mouthing, reaching, batting, grasping, babbling, and social interaction.
- Understands and respects the individual eating and sleeping needs of healthy infants.
- Frequently carries the child about in arms, on a hip, or in a sling.
- Takes the infant out of doors to experience various temperatures, light variations, breezes, etc.
- Provides the infant with the sights and sounds of other living things—humans, animals, and plants—including caregiver's own face.
- Recognizes the importance of a consistent relationship between a caregiver and infant and makes caregiver-child interaction the base of the infant's learning environment.

Mobile Infants

The competent Candidate working with mobile infants also, for example:

- Arranges room so that mobile infants have an area for free movement protected from older children.
- Provides space indoors and outside for exploration initiated by the child.

- "Baby-proofs" the environment so that there are many opportunities for child-initiated learning and limit-setting is minimized.
- Understands that intense feelings and rapid changes in mood and energy influence the child's response to the environment and adjusts routines, activities, and materials supportively.

Toddlers

The competent Candidate working with toddlers also, for example:

- Expands the learning environment to include the community when possible; for example, short trips to the local shops, walks around the block, community events.
- Introduces a variety of materials and opportunities for learning based on an understanding of toddlers' developmental level, abilities, and interests; for example, provides water play in an area that can get wet, covers children's clothes with plastic smocks or removes clothing in warm weather, and limits such play to few children so each has plenty of room and free use of utensils.
- Provides a step stool when necessary so that children can use toilet and wash hands independently as soon as possible.

Bilingual Specialization

In addition, the competent Candidate working towards the bilingual specialization, for example:

- Uses objects, music activities, and celebrations that are meaningful to young children to encourage development of both languages and cultures.
- Helps parents identify resources in their homes, families, and community that will support the development of both languages.

COMPETENCY GOAL II

To advance physical and intellectual competence.

4. FUNCTIONAL AREA: PHYSICAL

Candidate provides a variety of equipment, activities, and opportunities to promote the physical development of children.

Developmental Context

Physical development is an essential part of the total development of children. Developing physically includes using large and small muscles, coordinating movements, and using the senses. Large-motor development includes strengthening and coordinating the muscles and nervous system, controlling large motions using the arms, legs, torso, or whole body. Small-motor development involves the ability to control and coordinate small, specialized motions using the eyes, mouth, hands and feet. Adults should provide materials, equipment, and opportunities for indoor and outdoor activities that encourage this development and recognize and respect the wide differences in individual rates of physical development.

Establishes and maintains a routine for use of the second language in daily activities.

Young infants (birth–8 months) begin all learning through physical movement, taste, touch, smell, sight, and sound. By moving their arms, hands, legs, and other body parts, by touching and being touched, infants develop an awareness of their bodies and their ability to move and interact with the environment. By using their mouths to explore, hands to reach and grasp, whole bodies to roll over and sit up, they master the necessary skills needed for developmental stages that follow.

Mobile infants (9–17 months) delight in practicing and achieving new physical skills—crawling, standing, sitting down, cruising, and walking. They interact with their environment in a practical way, using all senses to examine and manipulate objects, and begin to understand cause and effect, space, and distance in this way.

Toddlers (18–36 months) continue to master physical skills at their own individual rates. Their learning and interaction with the environment continue to be active. Although they are gaining greater control and satisfaction through use of their small muscles (e.g., painting, drawing, or working with puzzles), they need opportunities to exercise their large muscles often each day.

Examples

For example, the competent Candidate working with infants and toddlers:

- Arranges and encourages physical activities, knowing how children's physical development affects their cognitive, social, and emotional development.
- Observes and evaluates children's developmental levels in order to provide activities for physical skills and development of the senses at the appropriate level for each child.
- Plans and participates daily in appropriate large-muscle activities (e.g., playing ball, running, jumping, climbing with children both indoors and outdoors).
- Provides a variety of activities from children's culture(s) (e.g., dances, music, fingerplays, and active games).

- Provides opportunities for children to develop their senses by noticing colors, smelling odors, distinguishing sounds, feeling and touching a variety of objects, and tasting different foods.
- Communicates to children and their parents the importance of outdoor play and physical activity for healthy growth and development.
- Plans for and supports children's changing needs for active play, quiet activity, and rest.
- Supports and encourages, but never forces, children who are fearful of physical activity because of illness, accidents, abuse, limited opportunity, or overprotective caregivers and parents.
- Observes and evaluates children's physical development, recognizes signs of possible physical handicaps and developmental delays, refers parents to appropriate services, and follows up on referrals or individual development plans.
- Adapts the program to meet the special needs of children with handicapping conditions, taking into account the importance of physical development to self-concept and social development.
- Avoids overprotecting children with handicaps, supports their independence, includes them in physical activities with other children (making modifications only when necessary), and encourages parents to do the same.

Young Infants
The competent Candidate working with young infants also, for example:
- Gives infants freedom and opportunities to move and explore in a variety of safe spaces (e.g., bare floor, carpet, mattress, grass).
- Maximizes warm and loving physical contact with infants by providing a variety of physical contact from soothing to stimulating, depending on the infant's readiness and need.
- Provides appropriate activities and materials to help infants develop small muscles by grasping, dropping, pulling, pushing, throwing, fingering, and mouthing.

Mobile Infants
The competent Candidate working with mobile infants also, for example:
- Encourages active manipulation of a variety of objects and the use of tools; for example, strings to pull toys, a pail to carry objects, a shovel to scoop sand.
- Shares children's pleasure in and provides them safe opportunities to practice repeatedly creeping, crawling, cruising, walking, climbing, descending stairs, and other physical movements.

- Provides opportunities for the development of eye-hand coordination in ways that are challenging and satisfying for the child; for example, fitting objects into a hole in a box, self-feeding.

Toddlers
The competent Candidate working with toddlers also, for example:
- Increases variety of opportunities for large- and small-muscle activities and sensory development as children are ready (e.g., introducing ride-on toys, play dough, puzzles, listening games, fingerplays, boxes for climbing).
- Cooperates with parents in toilet learning when toddlers appear to be ready.
- Provides extended opportunities for children to repeatedly practice their physical skills.

5. FUNCTIONAL AREA: COGNITIVE

Candidate provides activities and opportunities that encourage curiosity, exploration, and problem solving appropriate to the developmental levels and learning styles of children.

Developmental Context
Exploring and trying to understand the world is natural and necessary for children's cognitive or intellectual development. As children learn and grow, their thinking capacities expand and become more flexible. Adults should support and guide this process by responding to children's interests with new learning opportunities and to their questions, with information and enthusiasm. Cognitive growth also requires healthy development in other areas: consistent physical growth, secure emotional behavior, and positive social interaction.

Young infants (birth–8 months) begin cognitive or intellectual learning through their interactions with caring adults in a secure environment. Some of their early learning includes becoming familiar with distance and space relationships, sounds, similarity and differences among things, and visual perspectives from various positions—front, back, under, and over.

Mobile infants (9–17 months) actively learn through trying things out; using objects as tools; comparing, imitating, looking for lost objects; and naming familiar objects, places, and people. By giving them opportunities to explore space, objects, and people and by sharing children's pleasure in discovery, adults can build children's confidence in their ability to learn and understand.

Toddlers (18–36 months) enter into a new and expansive phase of mental activity. They are beginning to think in words and symbols, remember, and imagine.

Their curiosity leads them to try out materials in many ways, and adults can encourage this natural interest by providing a variety of new materials for experimentation. Adults can create a supportive social environment for learning by showing enthusiasm for children's individual discoveries and by helping them use words to describe and understand their experiences.

Examples

For example, the competent Candidate working with infant and toddlers:

- Observes children's play frequently to assess their cognitive development and readiness for new learning opportunities.
- Uses techniques and activities that stimulate children's curiosity, inventiveness, and problem-solving and communication skills.
- Gives children time and space for extended concentrated play and adjusts routines and schedules for this purpose.
- Provides opportunities for children to try out and begin to understand the relationships between cause and effect and means and ends.
- Understands the importance of play and often joins children's play as a partner and facilitator.
- Uses the center environment, everyday activities, and homemade materials to encourage children's intellectual development.
- Helps children discover ways to solve problems that arise in daily activities.
- Supports children's repetitions of the familiar and introduces new experiences, activities, and materials when children are interested and ready.
- Recognizes differences in individual learning styles and finds ways to work effectively with each child.
- Encourages active learning, rather than emphasizing adult talking and children's passive listening.
- Obtains (or makes) and uses special learning materials and equipment for children whose handicaps affect their ability to learn.
- Provides equipment and materials that children can explore and master by themselves.
- Is alert to the task a child is attempting and provides appropriate support.
- Recognizes learning problems and makes referrals according to center's policy.

Young Infants

The competent Candidate working with young infants also, for example:

- Talks to infants, describing what they feel, hear, touch, and see.
- Encourages manipulation and inspection of a variety of objects.

- Provides opportunities for infants to interact with adults and children and watch interactions of adults and children.
- Encourages infants in imitating others.
- Frequently plays with infants.

Mobile Infants

The competent Candidate working with mobile infants also, for example:

- Talks, sings, plays with, and reads to mobile infants.
- Gives children more space to explore as they become more mobile.
- Gives children many opportunities to figure out cause and effect, how things work.
- Provides many experiences with moving, hiding, and changing objects.

Toddlers

The competent Candidate working with toddlers also, for example:

- Encourages children to ask questions and seek help and responds to them in ways that extend their thinking; for example, "That's a good question; let's see if we can find out."
- Asks questions that have more than one answer, encouraging children to wonder, guess, and talk about their ideas; for example, "What do you think might happen . . . ?" or "How do you feel when . . . ?"
- Encourages children to name objects and talk about their experiences and observations.
- Provides opportunities to organize and group, compare and contrast thoughts, words, objects, and sensations.
- Involves toddlers in projects (e.g., cooking, gardening, and repairing) when possible.
- Reduces distractions and interruptions so that toddlers have opportunities to extend their attention span and work on one activity (e.g., block building or water play) for a long period of time.

Bilingual Specialization

In addition, the competent Candidate working towards the bilingual specialization, for example:

- Provides learning experiences that lead to the understanding of basic concepts in the language most familiar to each child.
- Encourages learning of both languages through everyday experiences and activities.

6. FUNCTIONAL AREA: COMMUNICATION

Candidate actively communicates with children and provides opportunities and support for children to understand, acquire, and use verbal and nonverbal means of communicating thoughts and feelings.

Developmental Context

Communication between people can take many forms, including spoken words or sounds, gestures, eye and body movements, and touch. Children need to understand verbal and nonverbal means of communicating thoughts, feelings, and ideas. Adults can help children develop their communication skills by encouraging communication and providing ample opportunity for children to listen, interact, and express themselves freely with other children and adults.

Young infants (birth–8 months) need adults who are attentive to their nonverbal and pre-verbal communication. Adults can provide better care when they respond sensitively to the individual signals of each infant. Infants' early babblings and cooings are important practice for later word expression. Infants' speech development is facilitated by an encouraging partner who responds to their beginning communications and who talks with them about themselves and their world.

Mobile infants (9–17 months) begin to jabber expressively, name familiar objects and people, and understand many words and phrases. Adults can build on this communication by showing an active interest in children's expressions, interpreting their first attempts at words, repeating and expanding on what they say, talking to them clearly, and telling simple stories.

Toddlers (18–36 months) increase their vocabularies and use of sentences daily. There is a wide range of normal language development during this time; some children are early, and some are late talkers. Adults should communicate actively with all toddlers—modeling good speech, listening to them carefully, and helping them with new words and phrases. Language should be used in a variety of pleasurable ways each day, including songs, stories, directions, comfort, conversations, information, and play.

For example, the competent Candidate working with infants and toddlers:

- Has realistic expectations for each child's understanding and use of speech based on knowledge of language development and the individual child.
- Talks often with individual children and stimulates conversation among children and with adults in the room.
- Provides activities that encourage children to develop listening and comprehension skills.
- Helps children connect word meaning(s) to experiences and real objects.

- Recognizes, understands, and respects local speech patterns and idioms.
- Respects the language of non-English-speaking families, encourages them to communicate freely with their children in the language parents prefer, and helps them find opportunities to learn English.
- Is aware of the caregiver's role as a language model for children and uses affectionate and playful tones, clear speech, and responsive conversation.
- Listens attentively to children, tries to understand what they want to communicate, and helps them to express themselves.
- Shares children's communication/language achievements with parents.
- Uses a variety of songs, stories, books, and games—including those from the children's cultures—for language development.
- Talks with children about special experiences and relationships in their families and home lives.
- Recognizes possible impairments or delays that affect hearing and speech, helps families find resources, cooperates with treatment plans, and finds ways to communicate positively with these children.

Young Infants

The competent Candidate working with young infants also, for example:

- Responds to the infant's cooing sounds and imitates them, encouraging a "conversation" in which the infant can often take the lead.
- Talks to infants about what they can see while giving physical care (e.g., diapering and feeding).
- Talks with parents about the meaning of an infant's beginning communications (e.g., different kinds of crying).
- Responds to infant's body signs and nonverbal cues that signal discomfort, excitement, pleasure, etc., and verbally describes the infant's feeling.
- Sings to infants or uses voice in interesting ways that encourage infants to listen.

Mobile Infants

The competent Candidate working with mobile infants also, for example:

- Responds enthusiastically to an infant's first words.
- Uses gestures to demonstrate the meaning of words to infants.
- Names and talks about infants' feelings, behaviors, activities, clothing, body parts, etc., to help expand their vocabularies.

- Elaborates on children's short phrases to help them express intended meaning.

Toddlers
The competent Candidate working with toddlers also, for example:

- Uses everyday conversations with children to enrich and expand their vocabulary.
- Provides opportunities for children to represent their ideas nonverbally through activities (e.g., painting, music making, and creative movement).
- Helps children learn, understand, and use words to express thoughts, ideas, questions, feelings, and physical needs.
- Writes toddlers' "stories" and labels their drawings, showing the relationship between spoken and printed words.
- Looks at picture books and magazines with children to stimulate talking.
- Listens to taped stories using a variety of voices reflecting gender and culture differences.

Bilingual Specialization
In addition, the competent Candidate working towards a bilingual specialization, for example:

- Demonstrates ability to understand, speak, read, and write in both languages.
- Understands the principles and characteristics of bilingual language development in children and explains these to parents.
- Assesses each child's language abilities and uses activities that are appropriate to the child's level of development in each language.
- Helps children associate word meanings in both languages with familiar objects and experiences.
- Encourages older toddlers who are fluent in either language to help less fluent children.
- Helps parents understand the important of children's learning the home language and culture and their role in providing experiences to meet this goal.
- Helps parents understand the child's attempts at communication in a second language.
- Allows children opportunities to express themselves in the language of their choice.
- Encourages English-speaking children and families to learn a second language.
- Uses lullabies, songs, games, stories, books, and fingerplays from both languages, asking parents for examples from their childhood.
- Makes sure there are consistent language models for both languages used in the program, through selection and use of materials and personnel.

- Takes an active role in labeling children's actions and surroundings in their home language and encourages children to use these words.

7. FUNCTIONAL AREA: CREATIVE
Candidate provides opportunities that stimulate children to play with sound, rhythm, language, materials, space, and ideas in individual ways and to express their creative abilities.

Developmental Context
All children are imaginative and have creative potential. They need opportunities to develop and express these capacities. Creative play serves many purposes for children in their cognitive, social, physical, and emotional development. Adults should support the development of children's creative impulses by respecting creative play and by providing a wide variety of activities and materials that encourage spontaneous expression and expand children's imagination.

Young and mobile infants (birth–17 months) are creative in their unique and individual ways of interacting with the world. Adults can support their creativity by respecting and enjoying the variety of ways very young children express themselves and act on their environment.

Toddlers (18–36 months) are interested in using materials to create their own product—sometimes to destroy and create it again or to move on. For example, they become absorbed in dipping a brush in paint and watching their stroke of color on paper. They use their voices and bodies creatively—swaying, chanting, and singing. They enjoy making up their own words and rhythms as well as learning traditional songs and rhymes. Adults can provide water, sand and other raw materials and opportunities for toddlers' creativity, and can show respect for what they do. Make-believe and pretend appear gradually, and adults can join in imaginative play, while helping toddlers distinguish between what is real and what is not.

Examples
For example, the competent Candidate working with infants and toddlers:

- Recognizes that the process of creating is as important—and sometimes more important—than the product.
- Understands that each child's creative expression is unique and does not encourage uniformity.
- Allows time for spontaneous and extended play within the daily routine.
- Includes a variety of music, art, literature, dance, role playing, celebrations, and other creative activities from the children's culture(s) in program activities.

- Participates in make-believe games with children.
- Models and encourages children's creativity in language; for example, through rhymes, imaginative stories, and nonsense words.
- Provides unstructured materials (e.g., blocks, paint, clay, or musical instruments) that are appropriate for children at different ages.
- Encourages thorough, repeated exploration of creative materials whenever possible; for example, by letting a block structure stand so that building can continue the next day or by letting one child play with soap suds for an extended period of time.
- Models creativity by using homemade materials and found objects.
- Helps parents understand the importance of creative expression in children's development and the need to provide children with opportunities for creative activities (e.g., storytelling, playing make-believe, using art materials).
- Encourages children to try new and different activities.
- Provides for "messy" activities with children (e.g., water and sand play, finger painting, and drawing with markers).

Young and Mobile Infants

The competent Candidate working with young and mobile infants also, for example:

- Recognizes that exploration and discovery by infants through their movements, voice, and expression are creative acts.
- Is alert and responsive to infants' initiatives to play, move, and use materials, gradually introducing new things to be combined and used in ways that infants can invent; for example, pieces of fabric of different colors and textures, rhythm instruments or objects that make different noises, assorted empty food containers.
- Provides a variety of music and rhythm experiences for infants.
- Shares infants' joy in a variety of ways—clapping, smiling, hugging—in order to encourage their spontaneity and creativity.

Toddlers

The competent Candidate working with toddlers also, for example:

- Gradually introduces a variety of art materials, allows toddlers time to explore in their own ways, and shows interest in what they do.
- Provides and rotates a variety of male and female dress-up clothes and other "props," including those from the children's culture(s).

- Plays make-believe with each toddler, following the child's lead and taking care not to overstimulate or frighten the child.
- Keeps informed about cultural resources in the community and uses them with children when possible.

Bilingual Specialization

In addition, the competent Candidate working towards a bilingual specialization, for example:

- Helps children develop creative abilities through activities and discussion in both languages.
- Helps children identify and imitate creative forms found in the art, music, and dance of both cultures.

COMPETENCY GOAL III

To support social and emotional development and provide positive guidance

8. FUNCTIONAL AREA: SELF

Candidate provides physical and emotional security for each child and helps each child to know, accept, and take pride in himself or herself and to develop a sense of independence.

Developmental Context

All children need a physically and emotionally secure environment that supports their developing self-knowledge, self-control, and self-esteem and, at the same time, encourages respect for the feelings and rights of others. Knowing one's self includes knowing about one's body, feelings, and abilities. It also means identifying one's self as a girl or boy and a member of a family and a larger cultural community. Accepting and taking pride in one's self comes from experiencing success and being accepted by others as a unique individual. Self-esteem develops as children master new abilities, experience success as well as failure, and realize their effectiveness in handling increasingly challenging demands in their own ways.

Young infants (birth–8 months), during the first few weeks and months, begin to build a sense of self-confidence and security in an environment where they can trust that an adult will lovingly care for their needs. The adult is someone who is consistently available and feeds the child when hungry; keeps the child warm and comfortable; soothes the child when distressed; and provides interesting things to look at, taste, smell, feel, hear, and touch.

For mobile infants (9–17 months), a loving caregiver is a resource or "home base" who is readily available and provides warm physical comfort and a safe environment to explore and master. This emotional stability is essential for the development of self-confidence as well as language, physical, cognitive, and social growth.

Toddlers (18–36 months) become aware of many things about themselves, including their separateness from others. A sense of self and growing feelings of independence develop at the same time that toddlers realize the importance of parents and other caregivers. The healthy toddler's inner world is filled with conflicting feelings and ideas—independence and dependence, confidence and doubt, fear and power, hostility and love, anger and tenderness, aggression and passivity. The wide range of toddlers' feelings and actions challenge the resourcefulness and knowledge of adults who provide them emotional security.

Examples

For example, the competent Candidate working with infants and toddlers:

- Treats each child as an individual with his or her own strengths and needs and unique characteristics.
- Is sensitive to differing cultural values and expectations concerning independence and expression of feelings.
- Addresses each child by name, talks with each child every day, and encourages each child to call other children and adults by name.
- Has affectionate and appropriate physical contact with each child daily in ways that convey love, affection, and security.
- Helps children through periods of stress, separation, transition, and other crises.
- Offers children, when possible, choices in activities, materials, and foods and respects their choices.
- Encourages and helps children practice skills when eating, getting dressed, using toys and equipment, cleaning up, and helping others.
- Gives one-to-one attention to each child as much as possible.
- Enjoys children and directly expresses the enjoyment to them.
- Delights in each child's success, expresses kindness and support when a child is having trouble, and helps him/her learn from mistakes.
- Helps children recognize, label, and accept their feelings (e.g., joy, affection, anger, jealousy, sadness, and fear) and express feelings in culturally appropriate ways.
- Models the recognition and expression of feelings by naming his/her own feelings while expressing them.

- Provides many opportunities for all children, including those with handicaps, to feel effective, experience success, and gain the positive recognition of others.
- Understands the effect of abuse and neglect on children's self-concept and works sensitively with such children.

Young Infants

The competent Candidate working with young infants also, for example:

- Listens carefully to an infant's cry and makes decisions quickly and appropriately: allows an infant to cry briefly when settling into sleep, comforts an infant who is distressed, or feeds an infant who is hungry.
- Provides appropriate affection using personal attention rather than food or "things."
- Gently and pleasantly provides basic physical care—feeding, bathing, dressing, diapering—respecting the tempo and sensitivities of the baby.
- Holds the infant close, allowing him/her to feel the caregiver's body warmth and heartbeat and to feel comfortable in the adult's arms.
- Creates a personal relationship with each infant and knows the kind of cuddling, stroking, talking, and playing that brings comfort and good feelings to each individual infant.

Mobile Infants

The competent Candidate with mobile infants also, for example:

- Removes the exploring infant from an obstacle that is too frustrating, comforts the child, and provides an alternative activity.
- Recognizes periods when the child has difficulty separating from parents or is fearful of new adults and is supportive of the child.
- Talks to child frequently about his/her family— where they are, when they will come back, and what they do together.
- Communicates, with eyes and voice, attention and interest to an exploring child at a distance from the caregiver.
- Welcomes a child who comes for nurturing with a loving voice, hugging, or stroking.

Toddlers

The competent Candidate working with toddlers also, for example:

- Responds to toddler's intense feelings of love, joy, loneliness, anger, and disappointment with sympathetic attention.
- Provides opportunities for toddlers to learn to help themselves (e.g., taking off jackets or pour-

ing juice) and shares children's pleasure in new skills.

- Helps the toddler understand his/her own feelings and express feelings in acceptable ways.
- Supports child's developing awareness of him/herself as a member of a family and of an ethnic or social group by talking about families (using photographs, mirrors, or other appropriate objects) and by celebrating cultural events with children.
- Uses simple books, pictures, stories, and discussion to help children identify positively with the events and experiences of their lives; for example, single-parent families, extended families, divorce, moving, or birth of siblings.

Bilingual Specialization
In addition, the competent Candidate working towards a bilingual specialization, for example:

- Helps children feel good about themselves as speakers of each language.
- Supports the child's attempt to use a second language.
- Helps each child deal with the stress of separation, using the child's home language and a tone and style compatible with the family's heritage.

9. FUNCTIONAL AREA: SOCIAL

Candidate helps each child feel accepted in the group, helps children learn to communicate and get along with others, and encourages feelings of empathy and mutual respect among children and adults.

Developmental Context
Children need to develop social skills that help them work and play cooperatively and productively with other children and adults. To do this, children need to feel secure about themselves, appreciate other people, and enjoy positive social interaction.

Young infants (birth–8 months) enter the world with a capacity and a need for social contact. Yet each one is unique in styles of interacting and readiness for different kinds of interactions. Infants need both protective and stimulating social interactions with a few consistent, caring adults who get to know them as individuals. The adults' understanding responses to their signals increase infants' participation in social interactions and their ability to "read" the signals of others.

Mobile infants (9–17 months) are curious about others but need assistance and supervision in interacting with other children. They continue to need one or a few consistent adults as their most important social partner(s).

Toddler's (18–36 months) social awareness is much more complex than that of younger children.

Toddlers can begin to understand that others have feelings too—sometimes similar to and sometimes different from their own. They imitate many of the social behaviors of other children and adults. As toddlers become increasingly interested in other children, adults should guide and support their interactions, recognizing that they continue to rely upon familiar adults for emotional stability.

Examples
For example, the competent Candidate working with infants and toddlers:

- Learns about children's stages of social development and helps children and parents deal with such typical issues as separation anxiety, negative behavior, shyness, sexual identity, and making friends.
- Has realistic expectations for young children's social behavior based on their level of development.
- Serves as a social model by building a positive relationship with each child and parent and by maintaining positive relationships with other adults in the center.
- Responds quickly and calmly to prevent children from hurting each other.
- Helps children learn to respect the rights and possessions of others, in light of local expectations regarding sharing.
- Encourages children to ask for, accept, and give help to one another.
- Encourages children to make friends.
- Helps the children become aware of their feelings and those of others by talking about feelings with each child.
- Encourages children to express their feelings and assert their rights in socially acceptable ways.
- Encourages play and relationships among all children across racial, language, ethnic, age, and gender groupings, including children with handicaps.

Young Infants
The competent Candidate working with young infants also, for example:

- Recognizes that infants need a consistent social partner (caregiver) who is dependable, warm, and loving.
- Responds to social gestures and noises of infants and elaborates appropriately, playing responsive social games.
- Takes advantage of opportunities for social play during feeding, bathing, dressing, and other aspects of physical care.
- Makes eye contact often.

Mobile Infants

The competent Candidate working with mobile infants also, for example:

- Structures periods of time for social interaction with other children, remains available to protect, comfort, or facilitate, but does not interfere unless necessary.
- Provides infants with opportunities to observe social interactions among older children and among adults.
- Provides more than one attractive toy to minimize conflicts and waiting.
- Engages in social play with children that supports their developing social skills (e.g., taking turns with a ball, conversing at mealtime, sharing a snack, putting toys away).
- Encourages children to comfort and help each other.

Toddlers

The competent Candidate working with toddlers also, for example:

- Encourages children to interact with each other in playful and caring ways.
- Understands that sharing, taking turns, and playing with others is difficult for toddlers and encourages their attempts to use words to resolve conflicts.
- Encourages cooperation rather than competition.
- Helps toddlers understand that sometimes they must wait for attention because of other children's needs.

Bilingual Specialization

In addition, the competent Candidate working towards a bilingual specialization, for example:

- Recognizes when social roles and expectations for children in their family setting are different from those of the child care program, and helps children behave appropriately in each.
- Recognizes when culture conflicts arise and works jointly with parents to resolve them.

10. FUNCTIONAL AREA: GUIDANCE

Candidate provides a supportive environment in which children can begin to learn and practice appropriate and acceptable behaviors as individuals and as a group.

Developmental Context

Knowing what behavior is appropriate or acceptable in a situation is an important skill. Children develop this understanding when consistent limits and realistic expectations of their behavior are clearly and positively defined. Understanding and following simple rules can help children develop self-control. Children feel more secure when they know what is expected of them and when adult expectations realistically take into account each child's development and needs.

Young infants (birth–8 months) begin to adapt their rhythms of eating and sleeping to the expectations of their social environment through the gentle guidance of sensitive caregivers who meet their needs. The basic trust in adults and the environment that is established at this time directly affects the child's responsiveness to positive guidance later and promotes the development of self-discipline.

Mobile infants (9–17 months) want to do everything but they have little understanding about what is permissible and cannot remember rules. Adults can organize the environment in ways that clearly define limits and minimize conflicts. While respecting the child's experiments with saying "no," they can reinforce positive social interaction (e.g., hugging) and discourage negative behaviors (e.g., biting).

Toddlers (18–36 months) move through recurring phases of extreme dependence and independence as they gain new skills and awareness. They require an understanding caregiver who remains calm and supportive during their struggle to become independent. Adults must be resourceful in recognizing and encouraging self-reliant behavior while setting clear limits.

Examples

For example, the competent Candidate working with infants and toddlers:

- Knows a variety of techniques for positive guidance (e.g., listening, reinforcement, and redirection) and uses each appropriately.
- Relates guidance practices to knowledge of each child's personality and level of development.
- Avoids negative methods (e.g., spanking, threatening, shouting, isolating, or shaming children).
- Establishes guidelines for children's behavior that are simple, reasonable, and consistent to encourage self-control.
- Establishes routines that are consistent and reliable, yet flexible to children's needs.
- Alerts children to changes in activities or routines well in advance and handles transitions from one activity to another with clear directions and patience.
- Is able to modify play when it becomes overstimulating for any of the children, including children with handicapping conditions.
- Builds a trusting relationship with children as a foundation for positive guidance and self-discipline.
- Anticipates confrontations between children and defuses provocative behavior.

- Addresses the problem behavior or situation rather than labeling the child involved.
- Accepts children's sad or angry feelings, provides acceptable outlets for children to express them, and teaches words for feelings.
- Helps parents develop realistic expectations for children's behavior in ways that help avoid disciplinary problems (e.g., discussing how long children can sit still).
- Encourages parents to talk about childrearing, guidance, and self-discipline and refers them to classes, books, and other resources, as appropriate.
- Knows parents' disciplinary methods and expectations and selects those appropriate for use in the center.
- Recognizes that sometimes serious behavior problems are related to developmental or emotional problems and works cooperatively with parents towards solutions.
- Is aware of each child's limitations and abilities, uses guidance techniques accordingly, and explains rules at child's level of understanding.

Young Infants
The competent Candidate working with young infants also, for example:
- Creates an environment of love and trust through warmth and responsive caring.
- Guides infants gradually into regular sleeping and eating patterns while remaining responsive to individual needs.
- Responds to infants' needs for comfort and protection.

Mobile Infants
The competent Candidate working with mobile infants also, for example:
- Provides children with a variety of positive options, focusing on what children can do.
- Uses firm "no" only when necessary to maintain children's safety; moves the child or dangerous object, and gives a simple explanation.
- Has realistic expectations about children's attention spans, interests, social abilities, and physical needs, including those of children with handicapping conditions.
- Redirects children gently while explaining limits.
- Gives children realistic choices and accepts the choices made; for example, "Do you want to read a book with me or play on the climber?" or "Shall we have the apples or bananas for snack today?"

Toddlers
The competent Candidate working with toddlers also, for example:

- Lets toddlers solve some of their own problems.
- Limits inappropriate behavior in ways that show respect and support for the toddler's sense of dignity.
- Avoids power struggles with toddlers who say "no" or refuse to cooperate, by using redirection, distraction, acceptance, or active listening.
- Explains the reasons for limits in simple words, demonstrating whenever possible.
- Uses firm and friendly techniques (e.g., reminding and persuading) when rules are forgotten or disobeyed.
- Uses positive language with children, for example, "walk" rather than "don't run."

Bilingual Specialization
In addition, the competent Candidate working towards a bilingual specialization, for example:
- Uses the language in which each child understands expectations, limits, and guidance.

COMPETENCY GOAL IV

To establish positive and productive relationships with families

11. FUNCTIONAL AREA: FAMILIES

Candidate maintains an open, friendly, and cooperative relationship with each child's family, encourages their involvement in the program, and supports the child's relationship with his or her family.

Developmental Context
Today's families take many different forms. Each family has primary responsibility for its own children, and parents may share this responsibility for their children with others. The parents and the caregiver become partners who communicate respectfully and openly for the mutual benefit of the children, the family, and the caregiver. Caregivers also recognize that parenthood, too, is a developmental process and that they can support parents in their role.

Young infants (birth–8 months) are establishing patterns of sleeping, waking, eating, playing, and social activity. They can be supported in developing some stability in these routines by the sensitive and consistent response of adults. Parents and caregivers can respond more appropriately to the infant's signals when they share details with each other about the baby's day—sleeping, eating, diapering, playing activities, and moods.

Mobile infants (9–17 months) may have difficulty separating from the parents even when the caregiver is a familiar and trusted person. Caregivers and parents need to discuss ways of handling this, recognizing that it may be upsetting both for the adults and the child. Caregivers should recognize the potential for competition between themselves and parents and work to avoid it. Caregivers and parents also need to agree on reasonable and safe limits as children begin to explore and wander.

Toddlers (18–36 months) develop their own special routines and rituals in order to feel more organized and secure. It is essential that parents and caregivers share common understanding of the child's patterns and provide constant, dependable support for the toddler's growth towards self-definition.

Examples

For example, the competent Candidate working with infants and toddlers:

- Recognizes that children's primary caregivers may be single mothers or fathers, both parents, stepparents, grandparents, uncles, aunts, sisters, brothers, foster parents, or guardians.
- Helps parents understand the development of their child and understand the child's point of view.
- Provides opportunities for parents and other family members to share their skills and talents in the program.
- Recognizes that caregivers can support parents in their role.
- Offers parents information about health and social services and other resources in the community.
- Respects each family's cultural background, religious beliefs, and childrearing practices.
- Observes strict confidentiality regarding children and families and makes parents aware of this policy.
- Suggests activities and materials that parents can share with their children at home.
- Encourages parents to talk about important family events and their children's special interests and behavior at home and shares information frequently with parents about the child's experiences in the center.
- Is able to discuss problem behavior with parents in a constructive, supportive manner.
- Supports parents in making arrangements for school or an alternative child care program when necessary.
- Develops attachment towards children without competing with parents.
- Encourages parents to visit the center, participate in activities, and make suggestion for the daily program.

- Respects and tries to understand the parents' views when they differ from the program's goals or policies and attempts to resolve the differences.
- Tells parents about children's achievements and shares their pleasure in new abilities.
- Helps parents with separations from child, recognizing parents' possible concerns about leaving their child.
- Supports children and families under stress, working cooperatively with other professionals, as appropriate.
- Helps parents recognize their feelings and attitudes about handicapping conditions.
- Helps parents identify resources to diagnose and treat children with handicapping conditions.
- Helps parents obtain clear and understandable information about their children's special needs and information about the family's legal right to services.
- Encourages and assists parents to communicate confidently about their children with government and other community agencies.

Young Infants

The competent Candidate working with young infants also, for example:

- Supports parents in becoming involved observers of their infant.
- Exchanges information regularly with parents about the child's life at home and in the center, including routines and changes in care, favorite activities, etc.
- Responds with interest and information to concerns of parents about sleep, waking, feeding, or particulars related to infant's needs and development.
- Shares parents' desire to understand meaning of baby's cries and to respond sensitively.
- Makes suggestions to parents about how to stimulate infants' vision, touch, and hearing at home.

Mobile Infants

The competent Candidate working with mobile infants also, for example:

- Recognizes the recurring stress of separation for child and parents and attempts to ease it for them.
- Helps parents understand child's possible fear of strangers.
- Helps parents to provide safe home environment for mobile infant.
- Talks with parents of mobile infants about the beginning of independence and the child's use of the word "no."

- Decides with parents what limits to set.
- Suggests use of household items to provide a stimulating environment and to encourage the curiosity of mobile infants.

Toddlers
The competent Candidate working with toddlers also, for example:

- Discusses child's rituals and routines with parents.
- Discusses with parents the reasons for toddlers' emotional outbursts and negative behaviors and possible ways of handling them.
- Explains the toddler's pride and interest in imitating adults and learning to use tools to make things.
- Sends home projects made by the children.
- Helps parents find ways to enjoy time with their toddlers and to help toddlers after time in group setting.
- Coordinates toilet learning plans with parents and frequently communicates on child's progress.
- Supports toddler's sense of belonging to his/her family.

Bilingual Specialization
In addition, the competent Candidate working towards a bilingual specialization, for example:

- Regularly communicates, orally and in writing, with parents and children in their preferred language.
- Helps parents understand the program goals for bilingual development.
- Knows parents' views on such issues as the use of the home language within the program, childrearing, and biculturalism and incorporates their views into program planning.
- Regularly communicates with parents about child's bilingual development and helps them find ways to support this within the family.
- Supports families' desires to communicate their language and cultural heritage to their children through cultural practices.

COMPETENCY GOAL V

To ensure a well-run, purposeful program responsive to participant needs

12. FUNCTIONAL AREA: PROGRAM MANAGEMENT

Candidate is a manager who uses all available resources to ensure an effective program operation. The Candidate is a competent organizer, planner, recordkeeper, communicator, and a cooperative co-worker.

Developmental Context
Running an effective program requires a systematic approach. A systematic approach means that the Candidate can determine the needs of her/his operation, families, and children; can make plans based on those needs; and can keep accurate records of needs, plans, and practices. Such a systematic approach should be applied to keeping records of attendance, fees, health status, and home visits. It should include specific plans for meeting the needs of children and their families and coordinating communication among involved adults through written information, meetings with parents and resources persons, and frequent informal discussion.

Examples
For example, the competent Candidate working with infants and toddlers:

- Works with parents to identify the strengths and needs of each child.
- Develops skills in observing and recording information about children and their families in a nonjudgmental manner; uses the information in the planning and implementation of the daily program.
- Maintains up-to-date records concerning the growth, health, behavior, and progress of each child and the group, and shares the information with parents and appropriate center personnel.
- Considers goals and objectives for each child and for the group as a whole and develops realistic plans responsive to the needs of all, including children with handicapping conditions.
- Implements plans for each child by identifying developmentally and culturally appropriate activities and materials for each day.
- Has a clear understanding of her/his responsibilities within the program.
- Discusses issues that affect the program with appropriate staff and follows up on their resolution.
- Works as a member of a team with others in the classroom and the program, including substitutes, parents, and volunteers.
- Supports other staff by offering assistance and supervision when needed.
- Makes or obtains materials and equipment appropriate to the developmental needs of the children.
- Coordinates program plans (including guidance and discipline techniques) with parents, specialists, and program personnel, when appropriate.
- Knows the language resources of each family and uses these in the program.

- Works with appropriate staff to choose substitutes carefully, requiring experience with children of the same ages whenever possible.
- Orients new or substitute caregivers and volunteers to routines and special needs and abilities of each child.
- Implements procedures that help children make a smooth transition from one group to another.
- Knows the social service, health, and education resources of the community and uses them when appropriate.
- Recognizes possible developmental programs, works with parents and specialists to develop plans specific to the needs of each child, and implements recommended treatment by following up on referrals, and working with the family to meet goals for the child.
- Establishes liaison with community services that respond to family violence (e.g., Parents Anonymous, Child Protective Services, and local shelter programs).

Bilingual Specialization

In addition, the competent Candidate working towards a bilingual specialization, for example:

- Uses knowledge of language development and bilingualism to plan for each child and group.
- Recognizes and helps others recognize the needs of children and families who speak a different language and operate in a different cultural context.
- Makes use of available evaluation instruments in the non-English language.
- Takes account of families' concerns about such issues as language usage and culturally different styles of relating.
- Works with appropriate staff in choosing substitutes who meet the language needs of the children and program whenever possible.

COMPETENCY GOAL VI

To maintain a commitment to professionalism

13. FUNCTIONAL AREA: PROFESSIONALISM

Candidate makes decisions based on knowledge of early childhood theories and practices; promotes quality in child care services; and takes advantage of opportunities to improve competence, both for personal and professional growth and for the benefit of children and families.

Developmental Context

Professionals working with young children and their families make decisions based on knowledge of early childhood education and family life and demonstrate a commitment towards quality care for young children. The professional caregiver continues to set new goals and take advantage of training or educational experiences that will help her/him to grow more competent. Recognizing that the way they relate to one another directly affects the quality of child care and sets an example for children, adults in a child care setting work to resolve issues and problems among themselves cooperatively and respectfully. They also work together to educate the community at large about the needs of young children. The child care provider should develop relationships with other child care professionals and establish a network for information and support.

Examples

For example, the competent Candidate working with infants and toddlers:

- Enjoys working with young children in a group setting and demonstrates a positive attitude in her/his role.
- Understands the philosophy of the program and can describe its goals and objectives to others.
- Continues to gain knowledge of physical, cognitive, language, emotional and social development as a basis for planning program goals.
- Keeps all personal information about children and families confidential.
- Continually evaluates own performance to identify needs for professional growth.
- Participates in peer evaluation and is able to accept comments and criticism from colleagues, supervisors, and parents in a constructive way.
- Takes advantage of opportunities for professional and personal development by joining appropriate professional organizations and attending meetings, training courses, and conferences.
- Keeps informed about child care practices, research, legislation, and other developments in early childhood education.
- Seeks information relevant to the needs of the children s/he is serving (e.g., information on infant development, bilingual development, children with handicapping conditions) from professional magazines, community colleges, community services, other caregivers, and community members.
- Recognizes that caregiver fatigue, low morale, and lack of work satisfaction decrease effectiveness, and finds ways to meet her/his own needs and maintain energy and enthusiasm.
- Works cooperatively with other staff members, accepts supervision, and helps promote a positive atmosphere in the center.

- Learns about new laws and regulations affecting center care, children, and families.
- Advocates quality services and rights for children and families.
- Keeps abreast of current regulatory legislative and workforce issues that affect young children and families.
- Works with other professionals and parents to develop effective strategies to communicate to decisionmakers the needs of children and families.
- Develops the ability to state needs for additional resources for individual children or some aspect of the program.
- Recognizes that special skills are necessary for working with children at different ages and developmental stages and seeks appropriate information and training.
- Is aware that some of the normal developmental characteristics of children (e.g., crying, messiness, dependency, willfulness, negative behavior, curiosity about genital differences, etc.) often make adults uncomfortable. The caregiver can acknowledge these feelings in her/himself, coworkers, and parents while minimizing negative reactions toward children.

- Seeks information about sexual abuse and child abuse and neglect, keeps up-to-date on laws and policies concerning reporting and treatment of abuse, and learns effective ways of working with affected children and families.

Bilingual Specialization

In addition, the competent Candidate working towards a bilingual specialization, for example:

- Demonstrates ability to understand, speak, read, and write in both languages and uses these skills in all aspects of the program.
- Increases knowledge about bilingual education by reading, attending workshops, and consulting professionals.
- Maintains and works to increase fluency in her/his second language.
- Consistently provides opportunities for all children to acquire a second language.
- Promotes the effective functioning of the bilingual program by attempting to clarify issues relating to bilingualism and multiculturalism.
- Advocates for children's and families' rights to use and develop their own language and culture.

Appendix **D**

The Celebration
of Life Calendar

The celebration of Life Calendar can be used as a cornerstone for cultural diversity in your curriculum. Please feel free to copy it and fill in special days for children in care, share copies with parents, enlarge it on a copier and hang it on the wall, and /or use it as a basis for activities during the day.

Having each parent fill in their own cultural celebrations is a good way to get families involved because you can ask parents to come in on their celebration days or send in special activities so that all children in care experience various ethnic foods, activities, and customs. Also, if your group is homogeneous, you can use the special days listed at the bottom of each month to help children broaden their experiences of other cultures.

January

1, New Year's Day
7, Nandkusa Festival—Japan
15, Martin Luther King, Jr. National
    Holiday—United States

February

5, Constitution Day—Mexico
11, National Day—Iran
19, Independence Day—Estonia

March

3, Hinamatsuri—Japan
17, St. Patrick's Day—Ireland
22, New Year Day—India

Unscheduled, Purim—Israel
Unscheduled, Taiwan Al-Qudr—Muslim countries

April

Unscheduled, Good Friday—Christian countries
Easter—Christian countries
Festival of Redvan-Baha'i

May

1, National Holiday—Mexico
22, Slavery Abolition Day—French West Indies
25, Independence from Foreign Rule—Africa

June

2, Republic Day—Italy   21, Festival of Lord Gagannath—India
6, Memorial Day—Korea
12, Independence Day—Philippines
18, Evacuation Day—Egypt

July

4, Independence Day—United States
14, Bastille Day—France
17, World Indian Day—Eskimo
26, Independence Day—Liberia

Unscheduled, Tanabuta (Star Festival)—Japan

August

31, Independence Day—India
Unscheduled, Festival of Hungry Ghosts—China

September

3, Independence Day—Chile
8, United Nation's International
　Literacy Day—World
21, World Gratitude Day—World

29, Michaelmas—Greek Orthodox and Roman Catholic
　Celebration
Unscheduled, Rosh Hashanah—Israel

October

17, Black Poetry Day—United States
24, United Nations Day—World
Unscheduled, Grandparents' Day
　—United States

Unscheduled, White Sunday—Samoa
Unscheduled, National Book Day—United States
Unscheduled, United Nations Day for the
　Elderly—World

November

3, Sandwich Day—United States
15, Schichi-Go-San—Japan
17, National Young Readers Day
   —United States

21, World Hello Day—World
Unscheduled, World Community Day—World
Unscheduled, Thanksgiving Day—United States

December

6, Independence Day—Finland
13, Santa Lucia Day—Sweden
25, Christmas—Christian countries
31, New Year's Eve—World

Glossary

3 A's: Attention, Approval, and Affection; the most powerful motivators of people and most effective rewards in behavior shaping.

Active Listening: The skill of listening for deeper messages than the words of a sender. Involves feedback of what the deep message seems to be.

Activity Areas: Spaces designed to accommodate groups of children engaging in certain tasks, e.g., art, muscle, etc.

Adaptability: Ability to change readily, adapt to new circumstances.

Analyzing: To separate (a thing, idea, etc.) into parts to find out its nature. To examine in detail.

Attachment: Term used to describe the dependency behaviors/the amount of responsiveness to being cared for by others.

Attachment Theory: Has identified phases of social attachment including egocentric in infancy.

Auditory Channel: The perceptual skills necessary to accurately input, associate, store, and recall auditory stimuli.

Caregiving: To fuel love or a liking to take charge over; to look out for; to have responsibility.

Causality: Piaget's theory. The realizing of cause and effect: action and reaction. Piaget believed that this develops between 12 and 18 months of life.

C.D.A.: Child Development Associates—An organization given support by the federal government to establish and maintain standards for and certification of child care and child care providers.

Child Care: Caring for all of children's needs—physical, emotional and psychological—according to their development. Interchangeable with *day care* in this book.

Child Care Setting: Home- and center-based group care—family child care, on-site corporate center, etc.

Child or Day Care Center: Category for licensing which allows for child care with a large number of children in a facility designed for large numbers of children.

Choke Tube: Plastic tube used to determine safe sizes of objects for child play.

Chronological Age (C.A.): Actual age from birth to present date.

Cognitive Function: To name, indicate, manipulate, and express desire.

Colleague: A person functioning on a similar skill level with similar goals; a co-worker.

Communication: The complete process in which one person sends a message and another person receives the message, interprets it, and gives feedback on it.

Competency Standards: Six general Goals and Thirteen Functional Areas which are used by the C.D.A. to measure the adequacy of infant and toddler child care.

Curricula: A structural program of study usually developed in steps from simple to more complex tasks.

DCAP; Dependent Care Assistance Program: A federal tax program to help employers provide child care to employees.

Designing: A plan to carry out in a skillful way; a purpose; to intend to set apart for a special purpose.

Development: A step or stage in growth.

Developmental Child Care: Programming that considers the growth and development of each individual in the system, including parents, staff, and children.

Developmental Milestones: Important skills and behaviors exhibited at certain ages by the majority of children (e.g., crawling, walking, talking, etc.)

Developmental Prescription: Task analysis of skills and behaviors exhibited by a majority of children at various chronological ages placed in a hierarchy from simple to complex.

Developmental Profile: Graphic illustration of estimated development (in months) of child in five major areas: (1) Physical, (2) Emotional, (3) Social, (4) Cognitive, and (5) Language Skills.

Distractibility: Loss of attention on one thing because of sensory awareness of other stimuli.

Egocentric: Perceiving the world through one's own point of view; self-centered and self-involved. A normal characteristic at different times during development.

Environment: The conditions, circumstances, and influences surrounding and effecting the development of an organism.

Equipment: Goods used in providing service; the special things needed for some special purpose.

Family Child Care: Category for licensing allowing a small number of children (usually up to 6) with one caregiver in a private home setting.

Flexibility: Able to bend without breaking, not stiff or rigid, adjustable to change, capable of modification.

Gratification: The reward.

Group Family Child Care: Category for licensing which allows for more children than family child care and less than core centers (usually up to 12) in a home setting.

Holistic Child Care: Program that considers all aspects of the child and family.

Human Energy Field (HEF): The human energy field which comes from the Universal Energy Field of which all living things are a part.

Instrumental Function: To request, reject, manipulate, and express desire.

Internal Control: The ability of a child to decide what behavior is appropriate without an adult influencing them by manipulating their environment.

Learning Center: Physical space dedicated to specific learning tasks with equipment, materials, and activities intended to teach specific skills (e.g., music center, listening center, etc.)

Learning Themes: Areas of focus for infant and toddler curriculum (e.g., holiday theme, season theme, etc.)

Logical-Mathematical Knowledge: The use of objects to represent quantity, numbers, space, and time (i.e., block building).

Milestone: A behavior or skill used as a standard for growth and development (e.g., walking is a developmental milestone). (Ch 11)

Model: A person observed by another with the intent to imitate.

Object Permanence: In Piaget's theory of cognitive development, the concept that objects and people continue to exist when out of sight, sound, touch, or smell. Piaget predicated that this concept developed within the first four months of life.

Parent Conference: Formal meeting with parents, usually scheduled ahead of time, in which information regarding a child's performance is shared and discussed.

Positive Propaganda: The telling of a positive story to a person about someone else.

PRANA: The ancient word used to describe the Universal Energy Field (UEF).

Prosocial: Liking to be with others, conforming to the standards, doing what is socially acceptable.

Sensorimotor Stage: Piaget's first stage of cognitive development, which is focused on motor activity.

Strategies: The science of planning; the maneuvering of focus into the most advantageous position before making actual contact. Skill of planning.

Tantrum: Loss of behavioral control and the result of frustration and/or anger. Normal in children learning to express emotion.

Task Analysis: Process of breaking down a task into the specific behaviors and skills necessary in a sequence from simple to complex.

Teaching: To show or help to learn how to do something, give lessons to, to provide someone with knowledge or insight.

Temperament: Basic style of behavior, including regularity, adaptability, sensory thresholds, etc.

Thematic Unit: A plan for presenting information based upon a theme or topic. *Therapeutic Touch:* A way in which one person touching another results in benefit for that person (e.g., healing, helping, etc.).

Unit Plan: A plan for presenting information over a period of weeks or months; a major theme or topic including objectives, materials, activities, and evaluation of learning.

Universal Energy Field (UEF): The energy field of which all life is a part, including the Human Energy Field (HEF) of which all human life is a part.

Unlimited Child: Theory of development that asserts that the maximum potential of each person is available at birth and is either arrested or inhibited in its development by environmental factors.

Visual Channel: The perceptual skills necessary to accurately input, associate, store, and recall visual stimuli.

Index

Acceptance, 109
Accommodation, 30
Action sentences, 378-379
Activities
    children: birth to four months of age, 253-255
    children: eighteen to twenty-four months of age, 344-345
    children: eight to twelve months of age, 302-303
    children: four to eight months of age, 280-282
    children: thirty to thirty-six months, 385-387, 398-399
    children: twenty-four to thirty months, 365-369
Activity level, 105-106
    of children: birth to four months of age, 267
    of children: four to eight months of age, 291
Adaptability to change in routine, 106-107
Adaptation, 30
Affection
    inward expression of, 55-56
    outward expression of, 51
Affective education, 75-77
Age groups, defined, 3
Aka hunters and gatherers, infant care by fathers, 48
Alert time, scheduling, 228-229
American Academy of Pediatrics, 91, 92
    on child specialists preparation, 94-95
    on HIV infection, 197
    immunization schedule, 185
    on SIDS, 198
American Institute of Physics Child Care Centers, 15, 206
Anal stage of development, 32
Antibias curriculum, 208-209
Anxiety, children: four to eight months of age, 290-291
Approach or withdrawal, response to new situation, 106
    children: four to eight months of age, 291-292
Approval
    inward expression of, 54-55
    outward expression of, 50
Approval process, 70-71
Arrival time, scheduling, 225-226
Assimilation, 30
Associated level, learning skills model, 38
Association, in organization of information, 7
Associations, 164-165
At-Risk children. See Special needs children
Attachment
    children: birth to four months of age, 270-271, 405
    children: four to eight months of age, 294-295, 409-410
    fathers and secure attachment, 48
    to the parent and caregiver, 116-119
    secure vs. insecure patterns, 47
    separation anxiety and, 47-48
Attachment-in-the-making phase, 35
Attending technique, 52-53
Attention

inward expression of, 53-54
outward expression of, 50
Attentional skills, 37-38, 37t
Attention span, 108
Attribution, 378
Auditory channels of learning skills, 127t
Autism, 22
Avoidant attachment, 47

Babbling, children: four to eight months of age, 297-299
Baby caregiving, assessment of caregiver behaviors, 87
Back to Sleep Campaign, 197-198
Bandura, Albert, 5
Bathrooms, safety checklist for, 193t
Behavior(s)
    See also Emotional development; Temperament
    caregiver, 203, 204
    infant, 202-203, 203-204
    interrelatedness of interactions with others, 99-100
    interrelatedness of the child's behavior, 99
    limiting steps, 114-115
Behaviorism, 5
Berk, Laura, 49
Bilingual specialization, caregiver competency goals for, 430, 431, 433, 435, 437, 438, 440, 441, 442, 444, 445, 446
Binet, Alfred, 4
Biologically at-risk infants and toddlers, 21
Biting behavior, 78, 115
Blankenhorn, David, 49
Blueprint for Action under the Healthy Child Care America Campaign, 91
Books. See Reading and books
Bowlby, J., 34-35, 40
Brain
    anatomy of, 217-218
    new research on, 218-219
Brain Gym, 217-218
Braun, Terri, 206
Brennan, Barbara, 57
Bronfenbrenner, Urie, 8, 71
    See also Ecological systems theory
Brown, Nancy, 209, 210

Cardiopulmonary resuscitation (CPR), 183
Caregiver Self-Health, 52-53
Caregiver Training (Douville-Watson), 180
Caregiving
    changing of the guard, 67-68
    children's needs and conscious care, 67
    circle of safety, 68
    ruing, 69
    shadowing, 68-69
    your work, 74

Care plans or prescriptions, organizing, 88
"Care Sheets," 83-84
Carolina Curriculum for Infants and Toddlers with Special Needs, 23
Castellanos, Linda, 87
Causality
    children: eight to twelve months of age, 317, 413
    children: twelve to eighteen months of age, 337, 416
CDA Competency Standards, 428-446
    Competency Goal I
        1. functional area: safe, 429-430
        2. functional area: healthy, 430-431
        3. functional area: learning environment, 431-433
    Competency Goal II
        4. functional area: physical, 433-434
        5. functional area: cognitive, 434-435
        6. functional area: communication, 435-437
        7. functional area: creative, 437-438
    Competency Goal III
        8. functional area: self, 438-440
        9. functional area: social, 440-441
        10. functional area: guidance, 441-442
    Competency Goal IV, 11. functional area: families, 442-444
    Competency Goal V, 12. functional area: program management, 444-445
    Competency Goal VI, 13. functional area: professionalism, 445-446
Celebrating Diversity: A Multicultural Resource, 211-213
Celebration of Life Calendar, 209, 211-213, 447-453
Center-based child care settings
    influences on curriculum, 214
    regulations, 159
    staffing, 157
    unique characteristics of, 157-159
Certification, of family child care homes, 156
Changing of the guard, 67-68
Childcare Accountability Programs: CAPS, 111
Child care networks, 162-164
Child care settings
    center-based care
        regulations, 159
        staffing, 157
        unique characteristics of, 157-159
    family-based, 154-156
        regulations, 156
        staffing, 154
        unique characteristics of, 155-156
    program emphases
        developmental, 160
        holistic, 159-160
        quality, 160-161
    program funding, 161-162
    support groups, 162-165
Child Care Specialists
    See also Child Development Associate (CDA)
    acquiring knowledge, 65-66
    assessing the caregiver, 84-87
    behaviors and strategies, 74-82
        affective education, 75-77
        expression of feelings in healthy ways, 77-78
        observing, 78-80
        observing and recording, 80-82

        record keeping, 82-84
    consistent and appropriate behavior, 103-104
    health and awareness, 62-65
    personal characteristics
        caring, 64
        commitment to excellence, 64
        enjoyment of learning, 64-65
        have a positive self-image, 63
        mentally healthy, 63
        open-mindedness, 64
        professionalism, 64
    professional preparation of, 93-95
    relating to infants and toddlers, 65
Child care systems, 162
Child Development Associate (CDA)
    See also CDA Competency Standards
    assessing the caregiver, 84-87
    caregiver competencies, 222
    credential, 94
        program/caregiver goals, 221t
    functional areas, 20, 45
    objectives, relationship to child, parent, and caregiver, 223t
    ten principles of caregiving, 101
    training trend toward, 12-13
Children
    abuse of, 92-93
    assessing, 87-88
    caregiver assessment for, 85
Children: birth to four months of age
    cognitive development, 272-274
    developmental profile, 255-256, 257f
    emotional development, 266-270
    learning skills/language development, 274-277
    materials and activities, 253-255
    physical development, 258-266
    social development, 270-272
Children: eighteen to twenty-four months of age
    cognitive development, 355-357
    developmental profile, 346t, 347
    emotional development, 351-353
    learning skills/language development, 357-361
    materials and activities, 344-345
    physical development, 347-351
    social development, 353-355
Children: eight to twelve months of age
    cognitive development, 315-317
    emotional development, 311-314
    learning skills/language development, 317-319
    materials and activities, 302-303
    physical development, 305-310
    social development, 314-315
Children: four to eight months of age
    cognitive development, 296-297
    developmental profile, 282, 283f
    emotional development, 290-293
    learning skills/language development, 297-299
    materials and activities for, 280-282
    physical development, 284-290
    social development, 293-295
Children: thirty to thirty-six months
    cognitive development, 394-396
    developmental profile, 387-389, 388f

emotional development, 390-392
learning skills/language development, 396-398
materials and activities, 385-387
physical development, 389-390
social development, 392-394
Children: twelve to eighteen months of age
cognitive development, 336-338
developmental profile, 326-327, 326f
emotional development, 331-334
learning skills/language development, 338-340
materials and activities, 323-325
physical development, 327-331
social development, 334-336
the toddler, 323
Children: twenty-four to thirty months
cognitive development, 376-378
developmental profile, 370f, 371
emotional development, 373-375
learning skills/language development, 378-382
materials and activities, 365-369
physical development, 371-373
social development, 375-376
Children's Defense Fund, 92
Choices, teaching child to choose wisely, 113
"Choke tube," 179
Churches, as child care providers, 162
Circle of safety, 68
Classical conditioning, 5, 112
Clear-cut attachment phase, 35
Clifford, Richard, 14
Climbing equipment, safety checklist for, 195t
Clinton, Bill, 13, 206
Clinton, Hillary, 14
Cognitive development, 30-31, 40, 121-125
caregiver competency goals for, 434-435
children: birth to four months of age, 272-274, 406
children: eighteen to twenty-four months of age, 355-357, 418-419
children: eight to twelve months of age, 315-317, 413
children: four to eight months of age, 296-297, 410
children: thirty to thirty-six months, 394-396, 423-424
children: twelve to eighteen months of age, 336-338, 416
children: twenty-four to thirty months, 376-378, 421
cognitive functions, 123-124
cognitive structures, 124
development and learning, 123-124
knowledge, 124-125
stages of, 121-123
preoperational stage, 122-123, 376-378, 395-396
sensorimotor stage, 122, 272-274, 296-297, 317, 356-357
theory of, 5, 30
Cognitive disorders, 21
Cognitive equilibrium/disequilibrium, 30
Cognitive function of language, 358
Cohen, Jonathan, 401
Communication, caregiver competency goals for, 435-437
Communication disorders, 22
Community resources, 90-93
Competency Standards. See CDA Competency Standards
Concepts development, assessment of caregiver behaviors, 86

Conceptualization level, learning skills model, 39
Conscious care. See Caregiving
Cooing, children: birth to four months of age, 276-277, 407
Cooperative Extension Services, 91
Coordination, development of, 122
Coping
coping tasks of infancy, 110-111
defined, 110
Corporate child care advocacy, influences on curriculum, 206
Crawley, Margaret, 12
Creativity, caregiver competency goals for, 437-438
Creche, The, 210
Crying, children: birth to four months of age, 276-277, 407
Cultural diversity
influences on curriculum, 207-213
programs, 15-16
Cultural expectations, influences on curriculum, 206-207
Current perspectives on development and care
current needs and trends, 8-14
current theories and views, 7-8
Curriculum
cross-cultural, 15-16
defined, 3
development of, 219-224
cycle of, 219f
evaluation of, 224
feedback, 224
goals, 221-223, 221t
materials, 223-224
methods, 222
objectives, 222, 223t
purposes and philosophy, 220-221
implementing
daily written plans, 239-245, 244-245t
nutrition for young children, 226-228
routines, 229-238
schedule, 225-226
infant-toddler
definition and scope of, 201-204
purposes for, 204
influences on
the child, 215-216
child care center, 214
child care home, 214
corporate child care advocacy, 206
cultural diversity, 207-213
cultural expectations, 206-207
parents, 205-206
television, 213-214
time, 215
for special needs children, 23, 216-219

Daily activities, 238
Daily written plans, 239-245, 244-245t
daily and weekly, 239, 239t
thematic units, 240-244
unit plans, 239-240
Darwin, Charles, 4, 39
Deferred imitation, 377, 419
Demonstrative naming, 378

Dennison, Gail, 218
Dennison, Paul, 218
Dependent Care Assistance Program (DCAP), 161, 162
Developmental disorders, 21
Developmental prescription, 70, 103, 250
Developmental Profile (Watson), 25-28, 250
    children: birth to four months of age, 255-256, 257f
    children: eight to twelve months of age, 304f, 305
    children: four to eight months of age, 282, 283f
    children: thirty to thirty-six months, 387-389, 388f
    children: twelve to eighteen months of age, 326-327, 326f
    children: twenty-four to thirty months, 370f, 371
    Developmental Learning Skills model, 36-39, 37f
    major development skill areas, 26t
    sample profile, 26, 27f, 28
Developmental program emphasis, 160
Developmental skill areas, 26t, 29-41
    cognitive development, 30-31, 40
    emotional development, 31-34, 40
    infant-toddler curriculum and, 201-204
    learning skill development, 36-39, 40-41
    physical development, 29, 39-40
    social development, 34-35, 40
Development and learning
    areas of
        biting behavior, 115
        coping, 110-111
        discipline, 111-115
        emotional development, 103
        physical development, 101-102
        security and trust, 103-104
        self-esteem, 108-109
        social development, 115-121
        stress, 109-110
        temperament, 104-108
    cognitive development, 121-125
    development and learning, 123-124
    early intervention and special needs children, 127
    knowledge, 124-125
    learning skills development, 126, 127t
    the whole child
        interrelatedness of interactions with others, 99-100
        interrelatedness of the child's behavior, 99
        ten principles of caregiving, 101
Differentiation, development of, 122
Discipline, 111-115
    behavior limiting steps, 114-115
    classical conditioning of the word "no," 112-113
    defined, 111
    diverting attention, 113
    giving choices, 113
    nonverbal steps, 114-115
    phrasing rules as the positive behavior, 113
    rules, 113-114, 114t
    "time-in" concept, 111
Discrimination, in organization of information, 7
Discrimination level, learning skills model, 38
Disinfecting equipment/site areas, 190, 196-197
Disoriented attachment, 47
Distractibility, 107-108
Diverting attention, 113
Douville-Watson, Linda, 9

Early Childhood Educator. *See* Caregiver
Early Head Start, budget, 14
Early intervention
    impact of, 87
    and special needs children, 127
Eating, 231-233, 265-266
    children: eighteen to twenty-four months of age, 350, 417
    children: eight to twelve months of age, 310, 412
    children: four to eight months of age, 286, 289-290, 404, 409
    children: twelve to eighteen months of age, 330-331, 414
    children: twenty-four to thirty months, 373, 420
    scheduling, 226, 227
Ecological systems theory, 8-14, 15
    exosystem, 12-13
    macrosystem, 13-14
    mentor programs, 10-12
    mesosystem, 8, 9-10
    microsystem, 8, 9
Ecumenical Child Care Network, 164
Education of All Handicapped Children Act (1976), 216
Effectiveness of Early Intervention for At-Risk and Handicapped Children, 21-23
Ego Needs (Maslow), 24, 24t
Elimination, 236-238
    children: birth to four months of age, 266, 404
    children: eighteen to twenty-four months of age, 350-351, 417
    children: four to eight months of age, 266, 409
    children: thirty to thirty-six months, 390, 422
    children: twenty-four to thirty months, 373, 420
    scheduling, 228
Emergency care, 93
Emergency preparation, safety checklist for, 193t
Emotional development, 31-34, 40
    children: birth to four months of age, 266-270, 405
    children: eighteen to twenty-four months of age, 351-353, 417-418
    children: eight to twelve months of age, 311-314, 412
    children: four to eight months of age, 290-293, 409
    children: thirty to thirty-six months, 390-392, 422-423
    children: twelve to eighteen months of age, 331-334, 415
    children: twenty-four to thirty months, 373-375, 420
    Erickson psychosocial theory, 32-33
    feelings of children, 33-34, 34f
    Freud theory, 31-32
End of the day, 229
Energy level, of children: birth to four months of age, 268
Environment
    assessment of caregiver behaviors, 87
    caregiver assessment for, 85
    fostering safety and health, 180-198, 191-193t, 194-196t
    materials, 176-180, 177t, 178t
    organizing, 89
    play yard arrangement, 174-176
    quiet zone, 180-181
    room arrangement
        basic equipment for infant/toddlers, 171t

infant/toddler activity areas, 172-173
infant/toddler settings, 168-172
thematic units for, 241
Environmentally at-risk infants and toddlers, 21
Equipment. *See* Materials and equipment
Erickson, Erik, 4, 40, 50, 57
See also Psychosocial theory of child development
Establishing a Positive Learning Environment, 111
Ethnology, 7-8
Ethological theory of attachment (Bowlby), 35
Evolutionary theory of child development, 4
Existential self, 34
Exosystem, 8, 12-13
Experimentation, development of, 122

Face washing, 229
Facilitator, 77
Family(ies)
    caregiver competency goals for, 442-444
    as total caregiver for early childhood, 5-7
Family-based child care settings, 154-156
    influences on curriculum, 214
    regulations, 156
    staffing, 154
    unique characteristics of, 155-156
Family Day Care Advisory Project (1991), 161
Fatherless America, 49
Fathers
    presence of in families, 49
    and secure attachment, 48
Feelings, 33-34, 34f, 76-77
    See also Emotional development
    children: birth to four months of age, 269-270, 405
    children: eighteen to twenty-four months of age, 351-352, 417-418
    children: eight to twelve months of age, 312-313, 412
    children: four to eight months of age, 292-293, 409
    children: thirty to thirty-six months, 392, 422
    children: twelve to eighteen months of age, 333-334, 415
    children: twenty-four to thirty months, 375, 420
    expression of feelings in healthy ways, 77-78
Fingerprinting, of child care providers, 93
Fire prevention and emergency numbers, 187-188
First aid/first aid kits, 186-187
Focal attention, 37, 38
Food activities, 398-399
Food choices, 226-228
Formation of a reciprocal relationship phase, 35
Freud, Sigmund, 4, 31-32, 34, 40
Full Catastrophe Living Using the Wisdom of Your Body and Mind to Face Stress, Pain, and Illness, 46
Functional areas. *See* CDA Competency Standards
Funding for child care programs
    private support, 162
    public tax support, 161

Genital stage of development, 32
Gerber, Magda, 9, 10
Gesell, Arnold, 4
Gnezda, M. Theresa, 14
Goals of child care curriculum, 221-223, 221t

Guidance, caregiver competency goals for, 441-442
Guide, defined, 3
Gullagher, Pamela, 217

Hall, G. Stanley, 4
Hallways/stairs, safety checklist for, 192t
Hand, Gail Stewart, 9
Hands, use of
    children: eighteen to twenty-four months of age, 349-350, 417
    children: eight to twelve months of age, 308-309, 411
    children: four to eight months of age, 408
    children: thirty to thirty-six months, 390
    children: twelve to eighteen months of age, 329-330, 414
    children: twenty-four to thirty months, 373
Hands of Light, 57
Hand washing, 229-230
Hannsford, Carla, 218
Head Start, 161
    mentor programs, 12
Health, caregiver competency goals for, 430-431
Health and Human Services Grants, 14
Health considerations. See Safety and health considerations
Health insurance, numbers of children without, 92
Healthy Kids, 94-95
Healy, Jane, 45, 272, 394
Hearing
    children: birth to four months of age, 259, 264, 404
    children: four to eight months of age, 285-286, 289, 408
Hearing impairments, 22-23
Hierarchy of Human Needs (Maslow), 23-24, 23t
Historical perspectives, 3-7
    past needs and trends, 5-6
    theories of child development, 4-5
Holistic program emphasis, 159-160
Home-based child care. See Family-based child care settings
Home Visitor Certificate Program, 163
Honig, Alice, 73, 110
Human Energy Field, 57
Human immunodeficiency virus (HIV) infection, 197

"Ideal caregiving," 28
"I messages," 55, 57
Imitation and play, 5
    children: eight to twelve months of age, 317
    children: twelve to eighteen months of age, 338
"Infant Assessment: Early Intervention," 87
Information and referral services, 163
Information processing, 5, 7
Inputted, 36
Instrumental function of language, 358
Interactions with others, 116-119
International Playgroups, 209
International Preschool Child Care Facility, 15
International Preschools, 209-210
Intersubjectivity, 31

Jalimek, Mrs., 221-222
James, William, 34, 40

Kabet-Zinn, Jon, 46, 54
Kitchen, safety checklist for, 192-193t
Knowledge
    constructing knowledge, 124
    logico-mathematical knowledge, 125
    physical knowledge, 124-125
    social-arbitrary knowledge, 125
Krieger, Dolores, 57

Lally, Ron, 9, 10
Landon, Elliot, 10
Language development, 338-340
    assessment of caregiver behaviors, 86
    children: birth to four months of age, 274-277, 406-
        407
    children: eighteen to twenty-four months of age, 357-
        361, 419
    children: eight to twelve months of age, 317-319, 413
    children: four to eight months of age, 297-299, 410-
        411
    children: thirty to thirty-six months, 396-398, 424
    children: twelve to eighteen months of age, 338-340
    children: twenty-four to thirty months, 378-382, 421-
        422
    imitation and, 416
Language disorders, 22
Language facilitation, caregiver assessment of, 84-85
Latency stage of development, 32
Learning. See Development and learning
Learning centers, thematic units for, 241
Learning environment, caregiver competency goals for,
    431-433
Learning skills development, 36-39, 40-41, 126, 127t, 338-
    340
    children: birth to four months of age, 274-277
    children: eighteen to twenty-four months of age, 357-
        361
    children: eight to twelve months of age, 317-319
    children: four to eight months of age, 297-299
    children: thirty to thirty-six months, 396-398
    children: twelve to eighteen months of age, 338-340
    children: twenty-four to thirty months, 378-382
    Developmental Learning Skills model, 36-39, 37f
Leipzig, Judy, 73
Levels of processing model, 36
Licensing, of family child care homes, 156
Limits, setting boundaries on behavior, 109
Linto, Gerry, 12
Locke, John, 4
Locomotion
    children: eighteen to twenty-four months of age, 348-
        350, 416-417
    children: eight to twelve months of age, 305-306, 308,
        411
    children: four to eight months of age, 285, 408
    children: thirty to thirty-six months, 422
    children: twelve to eighteen months of age, 328, 329,
        414
Locus of control, 119-121
    external influences, 119
    independence, 120-121
    internal controls, 119-120
Logico-mathematical knowledge, 387

Long-term memory, 36
Lorenz, Konrad, 7-8
Love Medicine and Miracles, 54

Macrosystem, 8, 13-14
Make-believe play, 31
Managing
    materials, 89-90
    people, 90
    space, 89
    time, 89
Manipulation, children: four to eight months of age, 285
Mastery, 69-71
Materials and equipment, 176-180
    age-appropriate, 176-178
        children: birth to four months of age, 253-255
        children: eighteen to twenty-four months of age,
            344-345
        children: eight to twelve months of age, 302-303
        children: four to eight months of age, 280-282
        children: thirty to thirty-six months, 385-387
        children: twelve to eighteen months of age, 323-
            325
        children: twenty-four to thirty months, 365-369
    cost-effective, 179-180
    curriculum development and, 223-224
    guide for analyzing, 178t
    homemade, 180, 181f
    managing, 89-90
    matching goals with materials, 176
    organizing, 89
    safety and health considerations and, 188-190
    thematic units for, 241-242
    types of, 177t
Maturation, defined, 4
McCarton, Cecilia, 216
Meditation, 53-54
Memory level, learning skills model, 38
Mental images, 377
Mental trial and error, children: eighteen to twenty-four
    months of age, 418
Mentor programs, 10-12, 94, 163
Mesosystem, 8, 9-10
Message board, 82
Microsystem, 8, 9
Mobile infants, defined, 3
Modeling, 5
Mood, positive or negative, 107
Mother(s)
    as only proper caregiver, 7
    secure attachment and, 49
Motor handicaps, 21-22
Motor responses, 7
Movements, development of, children: birth to four
    months of age, 259-260
Murphy, Lois Barclay, 110
Muscular control
    children: birth to four months of age, 261-263, 403-
        404
    children: eighteen to twenty-four months of age, 348-
        350, 416-417
    children: eight to twelve months of age, 307-309, 411-
        412

children: four to eight months of age, 287-289, 407-408

children: thirty to thirty-six months, 390

children: twelve to eighteen months of age, 329-330, 414

children: twenty-four to thirty months, 372-373, 419-420

Napping

See Sleeping

Nassau Cleft Palate Center, 217

National Academy of Early Childhood Programs, 160-161

National Association for Family Day Care (NAFDC), 164

Accreditation Program, 160

National Association for the Education of Young Children (NAEYC), 14, 160, 164

National Center for Early Childhood Workforce, 164

National Child Care Association, 165

National Head Start Association, 165

Negative reinforcers, 5

Negative sentences, 379

Negativism, toddlers, 331, 333, 390

Neurnberger, Debbie, 218

Neurnberger, Phil, 53

Neuroscience research findings, 29-30, 39

Newman, Frank, 219

"No," classical conditioning of the word "no," 112-113

"Noble savages," children as, 4

Nonverbal classification, development of, 421, 423

Nonverbal steps, 114-115

Normative approach, 4

Number concepts, development of, 123, 396, 421, 423

Number of children in childcare, 9

Nutrition for young children, 226-228

Object permanence

children: birth to four months of age, 274, 406-407

children: eighteen to twenty-four months of age, 419

children: eight to twelve months of age, 317, 413

children: four to eight months of age, 297, 410

children: twelve to eighteen months of age, 334, 337, 416

Observational learning, 5

Observing, 78-80

how to observe and record, 80-82

what to observe?, 79-80

who to observe?, 78-79

why observe?, 78

Operant conditioning theory, 5

Oral stage of development, 32

Organization, 30

Organizing

care plans or prescriptions, 88

environment, 89

materials, 89

schedule, 88

Original sin, belief in, 3

Others, concept of

children: birth to four months of age, 271-272, 405

children: eighteen to twenty-four months of age, 355, 418

children: eight to twelve months of age, 295, 413

children: four to eight months of age, 295, 410

children: thirty to thirty-six months, 394, 423

children: twelve to eighteen months of age, 335-336, 415

children: twenty-four to thirty months, 376, 420-421

Parents, influences on curriculum, 205-206

Pavlov, Ivan, 5

Pediatrician, as resource, 91

People, managing, 90

Perceptual level, 36

Perceptual screening, 37-38

Persistence, 108

Personal Responsibility and Work Opportunity Reconciliation Act (1996), 13

Phallic stage of development, 32

Philosophy of child care, 220-221

Phonemic features, 36

Physical and intellectual competence, caregiver competency goals for, 433-434

Physical development, 29, 39-40

caregiver assessment for, 85-86

children: birth to four months of age, 258-266, 403-404

children: eighteen to twenty-four months of age, 347-351, 416-419

children: eight to twelve months of age, 305-310, 411-413

children: four to eight months of age, 284-290, 404-411

children: thirty to thirty-six months, 389-390, 422-424

children: twelve to eighteen months of age, 327-331, 414-416

children: twenty-four to thirty months, 371-373, 419-422

Physical Needs (Maslow), 24, 24t

Piagentian tasks, caregiver assessment of, 85

Piaget, Jean, 5, 30, 40

See also Cognitive development

Play

dramatic, 397

imitation and, 5

children: eight to twelve months of age, 317, 413

children: twelve to eighteen months of age, 338, 416

make-believe, 31

as medium for learning and development, 380

sand/water, 176

symbolic, 356, 377

Playground

arrangement of, 174-176

designing areas, 174

safety considerations, 175-176

sharing space, 174-175

safety checklist, 193-196t

Poison Control Center, 93

Positive Perspective, 311

vs. 3A's of child care, 73

Positive reinforcers, 5

Positive self-talk, 70-71

Possession, 378

PRANA, 57

Preattachment phase, 35

Preconceptual stage of development, 376-378, 395-396, 421, 424

Prefocal attention, 37, 38
Preoperational stage of development, 122-123, 376-378, 395-396, 421, 424
Principles of caregiving, 101
Private speech, 30
Professionalism, caregiver competency goals for, 445-446
Program management, caregiver competency goals for, 444-445
Psychoanalytic theory of personality development, 4
Psychosexual stages (Freud), 32
Psychosocial theory of child development (Erickson), 4
    autonomy *vs.* shame and doubt, 32, 57
    basic trust *vs.* mistrust, 32
    children: twelve to eighteen months of age, 327
    ego integrity *vs.* despair, 33
    generativity *vs.* stagnation, 33
    identity *vs.* identity diffusion, 33
    industry *vs.* inferiority, 32-33
    initiative *vs.* guilt, 32
    intimacy *vs.* isolation, 33
Public health nurses, as resource, 92
Purposes of child care, 220

Qualitative categories, assessment of caregiver behaviors, 87
Quality program emphasis, 160-161
Quantity concepts, development of, 123, 396, 421, 423
Quest for Personal Power: Transforming Stress into Strength, 53
Quiet zone, 180-181

Reading and books
    children: eighteen to twenty-four months of age, 359
    children: thirty to thirty-six months, 397, 398, 424
    children: twelve to eighteen months of age, 338-339
    children: twenty-four to thirty months, 380
Reback, Phillip S., 95
Record keeping, 82-84
Recurrence sentences, 379
Reflective self, 34
Reflexes, development of, 122
    children: birth to four months of age, 262, 403
Register, 36
Regularity, 106
Regulations
    center-based care child care settings, 159
    family-based child care settings, 156
Relaxation techniques, 234-236
Reporting sheets, 83-84
Representation, development of, 122
Reproduction of actions, development of, 122
Resistant attachment, 47
Respect, 109
Response, intensity of, 107
Response generator, 36
Responses to stimuli, 5
Riback, Phillip S., 46
Rousseau, Jean-Jacques, 4
Routines
    daily activities, 238
    daily written plans, 239-245
    eating, 231-233
    face washing, 229
    hand washing, 229-230

    purposes for, 229
    sleeping, 233-236
    toileting, 236-238
    toothbrushing, 230
Ruing, 69, 78
Rules, 113-114, 114t
    phrasing rules as the positive behavior, 113

Safety, caregiver competency goals for, 429-430
Safety and health considerations, 179, 180-198
    cardiopulmonary resuscitation (CPR) training, 183
    disinfecting equipment/site areas, 190, 196-197
    fire prevention and emergency numbers, 187-188
    first aid/first aid kits, 186-187
    human immunodeficiency virus (HIV) infection, 197
    immunization schedule, 185
    materials/equipment selection and, 188-190
    parent awareness of, 181-183
    play yard arrangement, 175-176
    policies for, 182-183
    signs and symptoms of possible severe illness, 184-185
    site safety/playground safety checklists, 191-196t
    sudden infant death syndrome and Back to Sleep Campaign, 197-198
    traffic safety, 190
    transportation of children, 186
    universal precautions, 183-184
Safety Needs (Maslow), 24, 24t
Sandboxes, safety checklist for, 196t
Sand play, 176
Scaffolding, 31, 71, 114
Schedule, organizing, 88
Schedules
    elimination and, 228
    flexibility of, 225
    time blocks
        arrival time, 225-226
        eating, 226
        sleeping, 226
Schemes, 30
Scribbling
    See also Writing
    role of in writing development, 318, 359-360, 397-398, 424
Secure attachment, 47
SEED Project on Inclusive Curriculum, 209
Seeing
    children: birth to four months of age, 258, 264, 404
    children: four to eight months of age, 285-286, 289, 408
    children: twelve to eighteen months of age, 330, 414
Seesaws, safety checklist for, 196t
Seigel, Bernie, 54
"Selecting Appropriate Materials for Very Young children," 180
Self, concept of
    children: birth to four months of age, 271, 405
    children: eighteen to twenty-four months of age, 354, 418
    children: four to eight months of age, 295, 410
    children: thirty to thirty-six months, 394, 423
    children: twelve to eighteen months of age, 335, 415
    children: twenty-four to thirty months, 375, 420

Self-Actualization Needs (Maslow), 24-25, 24t
Self-care, 52-53
Self-control, children: thirty to thirty-six months, 393, 394, 423
Self-esteem, 108-109, 356
    caregiver competency goals for, 438-440
Self-health, 52-53
Self-recognition, 34
Semantic features, 36
Sense of agency, 35
Sensorimotor stage of cognitive development, 122
    children: birth to four months of age, 272-274, 406
    children: eighteen to twenty-four months of age, 356-357, 418-419
    children: eight to twelve months of age, 317, 413
    children: four to eight months of age, 296-297, 410
    children: twelve to eighteen months of age, 337-338, 416
Sensory coordination level, learning skills model, 36-37, 37t
Sensory input, 7
Sensory modalities, 36, 39
Sensory threshold, 107
Sentence construction, children: twenty-four to thirty months, 378-380
Separation-individuation, 34
Seriation, development of, 123
Sexual identity stage of development, 32
Shadowing, 68-69
Short-term memory, 36
Site safety checklist, 191-193t
Skills development, assessment of caregiver behaviors, 86
Skinner, B.F., 5
Sleeping, 233-236
    children: eighteen to twenty-four months of age, 350, 417
    children: eight to twelve months of age, 309-310, 412
    children: four to eight months of age, 289, 404, 409
    children: thirty to thirty-six months, 422
    children: twelve to eighteen months of age, 330, 414
    scheduling, 226
Sleep patterns, children: birth to four months of age, 261, 265
Slides, safety checklist for, 195t
Smart Moves: Why Learning is Not All in Your Head, 218
Smart Toys, 180
Smell, development of, children: birth to four months of age, 259
Social-arbitrary knowledge, 387
Social development, 34-35, 40, 115-116
    assessment of caregiver behaviors, 86-87
    caregiver competency goals for, 440-441
    children: birth to four months of age, 270-272, 405-406
    children: eighteen to twenty-four months of age, 353-355, 418
    children: eight to twelve months of age, 314-315, 413
    children: four to eight months of age, 293-295, 409-410
    children: thirty to thirty-six months, 392-394, 423
    children: twelve to eighteen months of age, 334-336, 415
    children: twenty-four to thirty months, 375-376, 420-421

interactions with others, 116-119
    locus of control, 119-121
    self and not self, 115-116
Social-emotional behaviors, caregiver assessment of, 85
Social learning theories, 5
Social Needs (Maslow), 24, 24t
Sociocultural theory, 8, 30-31
Somyak, Bibi Lobo, 12
Space, managing, 89
Space concepts, development of, 123, 396, 421, 423
Special needs children, 20
    with autism, 22
    biologically at-risk infants and toddlers, 21
    categories of, 21-23
    with cognitive disorders, 21
    with communication disorders, 22
    curricula for, 23, 216-219
        Brain Gym, 217-218
        brain research, 218-219
        community support for, 217
        functional ability vs. actual age, 216-217
        public programs for, 216
    with developmental disorders, 21
    early intervention and, 127
    environmentally at-risk infants and toddlers, 21
    with hearing impairments, 22-23
    with language disorders, 22
    with motor handicaps, 21-22
    with visual impairments, 22
Stability, development of, children: birth to four months of age, 260-261
Staffing
    center-based care child care settings, 157
    family-based child care settings, 154
Stages of child development, historical theories of, 4-5
Starting Points, 14
Stimuli, responses to, 5
Store model, 36
Stress, 109-110
Successive approximation, principle of, 114
Sudden infant death syndrome and Back to Sleep Campaign, 197-198
Support groups
    associations, 164-165
    child care networks, 162-164
child care systems, 162
Survival of the fittest, 4
Swings, safety checklist for, 195-196t
Symbiosis, 34

Tabula rasa, 4
Talking. See Language development
Task analysis, 29
Taste, development of, children: birth to four months of age, 259
Teaching, defined, 3
Teeth/teething
    children: eighteen to twenty-four months of age, 350, 417
    children: eight to twelve months of age, 310, 412
    children: four to eight months of age, 286, 290, 409
    children: twenty-four to thirty months, 373, 420
Television, influences on curriculum, 213-214

Temperament, 104-108
    behavior categories of, 105t
        activity level, 105-106
        adaptability to change in routine, 106-107
        approach or withdrawal, response to new situation, 106
        distractibility, 107-108
        intensity of response, 107
        level of sensory threshold, 107
        persistence and attention span, 108
        positive or negative mood, 107
        regularity, 106
    children: birth to four months of age, 267, 270, 405
    children: eighteen to twenty-four months of age, 353, 418
    children: eight to twelve months of age, 311, 313-314, 412
    children: four to eight months of age, 291-292, 293, 409
    children: thirty to thirty-six months, 392, 422-423
    children: twelve to eighteen months of age, 334, 415
    children: twenty-four to thirty months, 375, 420
    defined, 104
Temper tantrums, 331, 333
    children: eighteen to twenty-four months of age, 347
    children: twenty-four to thirty months, 373-374
"Terrible twos," 373-374
Thematic units
    the environment, 241
    learning centers, 241
    materials, 241-242
    objectives, 240-241
    sample thematic unit on riding, 242-244
    strategies, 242
Theories of child development, 4-5, 7-14
    See also specific theories
Therapeutic Touch, 57
Thomas, Caroline Bell, 46
3A's of child care, 46-47
    approval process, 70-71
    combining with Positive Perspective, 72
    inward expression of
        affection, 55-56
        approval, 54-55
        attention, 53-54
    mastery through the attention process, 69-71
    outward expression of, 50-53
        affection, 51
        approval, 50
        attention, 50
    successful use of, 56-58
Time
    influences on curriculum, 215
    managing, 89
Time concepts, development of, 123, 396, 421, 423-424
"Time-in" concept, 111
Tinbergen, Niko, 7-8
Title XX Social Services, 161
Toddler Caregiver Competencies, 221t
Toddlers
    See also Children, eighteen through thirty-six months of age

assessment of caregiver behaviors and, 86-87
caregivers of, 323
defined, 3
Toileting. See Elimination
Toothbrushing, 230
Touch, development of, children: birth to four months of age, 259
Traffic safety, 190
Transactional Theories, 8-14, 15
Transportation of children, safety and health considerations, 186

United Association for the Education of Young People, 210
Unit plans, 239-240, 245t
    thematic units, 240-244, 243f
Unlimited Child, theory of, 20
U.S. Army Child Development Services, mentor programs, 12
U.S. Department of Agriculture (USDA), 90-91

Verbal preconcepts, development of, 421, 423
Verbal reasoning, development of, 123, 396, 421, 423
Verbal responses, 7
Video cassette recorder (VCR), curriculum enhancement and, 214
Visual channels of learning skills, 127t
Visual impairments, 22
Visual perception. See Seeing
Vocabulary
    of children: thirty to thirty-six months, 398, 424
    of children: twenty-four to thirty months, 378
Vygotsky, Lev Semenovich, 8, 15, 30-31, 40

Walking. See Locomotion
Water play, 176
Watson, John, 5, 40-41
    See also Developmental Profile
Webbing, 242, 243f
Welfare Reform Legislature, changes in, 13
Word(s)
    See also Language development
    formation of plurals/past tense, 380, 398, 424
    overregularization/overgeneralization of, 380
    patterns, 379, 398
    syntax, 398, 424
Writing development
    children: eighteen to twenty-four months of age, 318, 359-360
    children: eight to twelve months of age, 318
    children: thirty to thirty-six months, 397-398, 424
    children: twelve to eighteen months of age, 339, 340
    children: twenty-four to thirty months, 380-381

"You messages," 55, 57
Young infants, defined, 3
Your Child's Growing Mind, 45, 272, 394-395

"Zone of proximal development," 31, 101